# Voices from the Wings

# Voices from the Wings

## A Connoisseur's Collection of

# GREAT
# THEATRICAL

### and Showbiz

# ANECDOTES

## NED SHERRIN

BOOKS

First published in Great Britain in 2007 by
JR Books, 10 Greenland Street, London NW1 0ND
www.jrbooks.com

*Ned Sherrin's Theatrical Anecdotes* first published 1991

A catalogue record for this book is available from the British Library.

ISBN 978-1-906217-23-5

1 3 5 7 9 10 8 6 4 2

Typeset by SX Composing DTP, Rayleigh, Essex
Printed in by MPG Books, Bodmin, Cornwall

In memory of Michael Williams KSG
(1935 – 2001)

# Introduction

I don't know where a passion for handing on anecdotes, gossip and *bonmots* comes from. I do vividly remember an early piece of theatrical information which excited me greatly. During the war I lived on a farm in Kingweston, Somerset. The 'big house' had been taken over as headquarters of the Searchlight Brigade for the area. The officer of the Mess worked hard to keep on good terms with the villagers.

Among other delights we were asked to ENSA (Entertainments National Service Association) concerts. On one occasion, half-a-dozen village children were the entire audience for a hard-working but not very proficient company from the nearby town of Wells. The military had wisely decided to give them a miss and they had to suffer the indignity of performing for us. They did so with ill-grace.

On another evening my parents, my brother and I were asked to an officers' mess cocktail party. My mother and father hated cocktail parties and sent my brother and me to represent the family. I must have been ten or eleven, I was a devoted reader of *Picture Post*, drawing all my theatrical knowledge from its glossy photo features.

I remember clutching a glass of lemonade and hearing a conversation between two officers' wives who towered above me. They were discussing the theatre and two matinée idols; 'I hear Ivor Novello has inherited the mantle of Owen Nares,' said one to the other. This was priceless news to me and I cherished it until I realised that there was no one to whom I could pass it on. No one I knew would derive the same pleasure that it had given me. It is the essence of anecdotage to pass on.

Perhaps it will be easier for these stories to find an audience.

I have tried to strike a balance between the 'chestnuts' that cannot be left out lest the reader says, 'I'm surprised he didn't know the one about . . . !' and rarer gems handed down by oral tradition, not yet pickled in print and difficult to authenticate.

Although I have always listened avidly to theatrical anecdotes and devoured published collections, I cannot claim that my research matches the fervour of a French historian of the theatre who set himself the task of finding out what happened, years later, to twenty unclad – supposedly female – bodies who early in the 20th century, took part in a 'living curtain' finale at the Folies Bergere. He discovered that three had been men, of whom one had been murdered, one had become a Jesuit, and a third a stall holder of pornographic books on the banks of the Seine. Six of the girls went into brothels, two married industrialists, two committed suicide, one wrote a bawdy novel; four settled for respectability. Between them the seventeen women had eleven children and 96 abortions.

Not surprisingly there is a fair amount of bawdy and raffishness in these pages. Although the gentrification of the acting profession has proceeded apace, spurred on by Irving's knighthood and subsequent honours, the instincts of the rogue and vagabond can mercifully still occasionally be spotted.

In the 1820s Daniel Teny wrote to Sir Walter Scott: '. . . the conviction and conduct of our national theatres is certainly not such as to give great hopes of improvement either to the character of the art or the exertions of the artists. The want of a combination of the qualities to combine must, I fear, be both acknowledged and lamented. Garrick exhibited them in a most universal, brilliant and dexterous manner; poor John Kemble with a sombre, but not less correct or pure influence. But to whom shall we look now? Elliston has nothing but a blind but dauntless energy of animal spirits . . . Charles Kemble has the refinement but he wants the talent and is biliously indolent and nervous. Kean has the talent but is a thorough-paced blackguard. Alas! for the poor Stage; it is still below all the other Arts in its standing with Society . . .'

I hope that for all the reported lapses in behaviour, the wit, gallantry and attractiveness of the acting profession will shine through.

I confess to a readiness to believe a poetic truth when I have not been able to confirm a particularly winning story. Sometimes I may have identified the wrong protagonist, sometimes the incident may have been the product of wishful thinking or of vivid embellishment in the course of constant retelling.

I have allowed the poetic truth to stand where the real truth may be contradicted.

It occurs to me that I have let myself off rather lightly, so I will attempt to redress the balance by including one anecdote which does me no great credit. An American friend, David Yakir, bumped into the inspired provincial and touring director Toby Robertson in New York and dragged the conversation round to me without disclosing that we knew each other. 'A funny thing about Ned Sherrin,' said Toby. 'Everybody in England thinks he must be well known in America. Everybody in America thinks he must be well known in England. In fact, he isn't well known anywhere.'

# − 𝒶 −

**ABBOTT**, George Francis. When I published a book of theatrical anecdotes in 1991 the great George Abbott was still alive. In fact he was 104. His professional career, started in 1913 – before Lillian Baylis transformed the Old Vic. He was considered too old to be called to arms in the 1914–18 war.

Such was his eminence that he was always known as 'Mister Abbott' – the title of his autobiography. It symbolised the discipline he brought to the Broadway theatre and the authority he exercised over his casts. He early employed the classic senior director's answer to a method actor's plea: 'What's my motivation?' 'Your job'.

Keith Waterhouse and Willis Hall witnessed an example of this when Abbott directed their successful West End comedy *Say Who You Are* for Broadway. At one point in rehearsals he instructed the leading actor, Francis Matthews, to take an ashtray from a chimney piece and bring it downstage to a table. Matthews reasonably pointed out that since neither he nor any other member of the cast was smoking why should he make the move? Quietly and politely Abbott replied, 'Because I ask you to, Mr Matthews.'

Born in 1887 George Abbott went to military academy and became interested in the theatre when he went to Harvard in 1912. There he worked under George Pierce Baker – a vital influence in modern American theatre. Baker was Professor of Dramatic Literature and the creator in 1905 of a course in practical playwrighting, the famous ' '47 Workshop'. Sidney Howard and Eugene O'Neill were other playwrights who studied with him. Abbott continued to act in plays such as *Dulcy* or *Hell-bent Fer Heaven* until 1925. He also had a success with *The Fall Guy*, a play he wrote with James Gleason.

From the mid-twenties he wrote and directed – at first fast-moving melodramas and later even faster-moving farces, *Chicago, Broadway,*

*Twentieth Century* and *Three Men on a Horse* were among them.

He won six Tonys, a Pulitzer Prize, a Kennedy Center Honor and countless other awards. Pace and precision continued to be his trademarks. For his successful collaborations with fledgling writers he became known as 'the apprentice's sorcerer'.

After assisting John Murray Anderson on *Jumbo*, his first musical was Rodgers and Hart's *On Your Toes*. While it played out of town in Boston he gained a reputation as a magical play doctor. He dismissed it, saying that he had simply swept away the accretions added by ill-disciplined actors. Twenty-six years later he was again out of town, this time in Washington, when he hit trouble directing a troubled *A Funny Thing Happened on the Way to the Forum*. He turned to his producer, Hal Prince (one of Abbott's many protégés) and said wryly, 'I don't know what to do. You'd better call in George Abbott.' In fact Prince called in another protégé, Jerome Robbins, who encouraged Stephen Sondheim to write a new opening number, 'A Comedy Tonight', which prepared the audience for the wild Roman farce which was to follow.

When we took the Sondheim compilation, *Side by Side by Sondheim* to New York in 1977, I was narrating the show. 'A Comedy Tonight' was our opening but the sequence included sketches of two other songs which had failed to do the job and an explanation of Robbins' intervention saved the day. On four occasions I got calls from Sondheim saying that 'Mister Abbott' was coming to that performance and would I please excise these parts of the narration which suggested that he had got it wrong. Four times I made the cuts. Four times he didn't turn up.

Burt Shevelove, co-book writer of the show with Larry Gelbart, recalled another rehearsal incident. From the stage the star, Zero Mostel, lamented a fifteen-minute diatribe at the 75-year-old director, who sat stoically in the stalls until Mostel ran out of steam and retreated into the wings. Shevelove went to Abbott to commiserate and apologise. Unmoved, Abbott waved him away, saying simply, 'Oh, he's just an actor.'

A great ladies' man until the end of his life, Abbott had a winter–autumn romance with the actress Maureen Stapleton. She sang his praises so loudly that one of her contemporaries asked, 'Does he have any friends his age?'

In 1987 I was telephoned by *The Times* obituary editor who had just realised that Abbott was 100. They had no obituary on file. I wrote the obit and I was asked to update it when he was 105 because he was directing a revival of his success *Damn Yankees*. He went on to plan another revival of his 1954 hit *The Pyjama Game*. He died aged 107 before he could bring it to the stage. It was good to read my obituary notice in print at last.

**ADLER**, Christopher. Christopher Adler was a charming and talented young lyric writer who died, long before his time, soon after Peter Hall's National Theatre production of *Jean Seberg,* the musical he wrote with Marvin Hamlisch (composer of A *Chorus Line* and *They're Playing Our Song)* and Julian Barry.

When they came to London to audition for the title role they kept hearing about a young singer actress, Stephanie Lawrence. They wanted to see her. The casting people at the National called her agents and were surprised to learn that she did not do auditions. Hamlisch and Adler were amazed – and intrigued. I've never been quite sure why they didn't go to see her in *Evita,* in which she was starring at the time, but this is the story as Christopher told it to me. Finally, after much negotiation, Miss Lawrence agreed to meet them one morning in her Chelsea apartment. They arrived on time around eleven and were given coffee. She descended about an hour later, coughing slightly. She apologised for the condition of her voice but they persuaded her to sing a little of 'Don't Cry For Me, Argentina'. Quite soon she stopped – again blaming the early hour. The songwriters tried once more. Was there something less demanding in her repertoire?

She looked at Marvin Hamlisch seated at the piano. 'Do you know "What I Did For Love"?'

**ADLER**, Stella. A distinguished actress and teacher, Stella Adler's teaching method was Stanislavskian but it led her to major differences with Lee Strasberg and the method as practised at the Actors Studio. When he died in 1982 she spoke to her class in terms which are hard to beat for rival disapproval.

'A man of the theatre died last night,' she intoned, having asked her class to stand for a minute's silence. 'It will take a hundred years before the harm that man has done to the art of acting can be corrected.'

**AGATE**, James. James Agate – critic, wit, spendthrift, homosexual, eccentric, gossip monger, 'a philistine with the equipment of an intellectual', passionate follower of golf, cricket and Hackney ponies, encyclopaedic expert on 19th century French theatre, Balzac and Zola, habitué of opera house, theatre and male brothels – was perhaps the most flamboyant critic the English theatre has known, not excluding Kenneth Tynan. His extravagance and his battles with bankruptcy were legendary. As his biographer, James Harding, puts it: 'He would hire a taxi just to cross the road, and then keep it waiting for him into the early hours of the morning while he played bridge at the Savage and took a masochistic pleasure in the thought of the meter ticking away pound after pound.'

Agate's financial affairs were always in disorder through his extravagance, though in later life the accountant Alfred Chenhalls did something to sort them out. Agate denied that this was possible. He said he was 'mortgaged up to the hilt'.

'My dear fellow,' Chenhalls countered, 'you don't know where the hilt is.' He once suffered the ultimate critic's comeuppance. Having dealt out vigorous criticism over years on the *Manchester Guardian* and the *Sunday Times* – mixed with perceptive praise for certain performers – he was unwise enough to collaborate on an adaptation of *Blessed Are the Rich*, which was staged at the Vaudeville Theatre. It played to a lukewarm house but enemies of Agate had laid a trap, and as the curtain fell they gave the piece such a rousing reception that the critic was persuaded to take a curtain call. The moment he appeared on stage, the mood of the house changed to boos, whistles and calls of 'rubbish' for which he was utterly unprepared.

Seeing Irving and Bernhardt in his native Manchester, he later wrote of Irving 'If anybody thinks Irving was the greatest English actor of modern times and does not say so, he lies. If he does not think so he is mad.' Of Bernhardt in *Pelleas and Melisande*: 'Her acting . . . unveiled for me the ecstasy of the body and the torture of the mind.' After his early attempt at acting, he was discouraged by his father, who happily agreed with his mumbling speculation that he was not much good: 'Not worth a damn and never will be!'

He journeyed to Paris to see Rejane and, finding her walking through her role, sent round a note during the interval and was rewarded by an inspired last act and an imperious bow to his seat during the curtain calls. During the 1914–1918 war he met her in Arles and she told him that 'You taught me a lesson that has lasted all my life. You made me realise that there may be somebody in any theatre at any time to whom you are opening a new door, a new gateway to beauty.'

Agate was largely responsible for the success of *Journey's End*. Seeing it at a Sunday matinée, he demanded to know why the three commercial managers present would not produce it. They said it was 'too good for the general public'. Agate, who had an influential radio spot on Sundays, tore up his prepared talk and raved about the play. When he heard that a manager had now taken an option, he broadcast again – this time he suggested, ironically, that the play should be dropped. The public was not worthy of it. The double bluff worked and *Journey's End* had its deserved success.

Agate's criticism was sounder on players than on plays; but, of course, he was witnessing a period of polite playwriting and he had a blind spot for revue and musical comedy. His other claim to fame was his prodigious output of *Ego* – volumes of gossip and correspondence published as a sort of lively diary and cuttings book. A typical exchange featured the Ivy, the fashionable theatrical restaurant; 'Looked in at the Ivy, which was crowded. Asked Abel if any one was there, meaning theatre-folk. Abel said, "No, sair. Only trash!"'

One scandal in Agate's life involved Beverly Nichols, whose pacifist play, *Avalanche,* was denied a London production because Agate had damned it out of town. In *Country Life,* their critic 'George Warrington' reviewed it favourably. Nichols discovered that George Warrington was one of Agate's pseudonyms and threatened to give the police details of Agate's involvement with guardsmen and other rough trade. He also sent him a review copy of his book *Cry Havoc,* with a recommendation that Agate would be wise to praise it.

When Agate's chauffeur was stopped by a police motorcyclist for speeding, the critic was surprised to see the policeman break into a smile and plant a smacking kiss on his driver's mouth. 'On your way,' he added, 'and don't get caught again.'

'Do you know him?' Agate asked.

'I can't remember his name, sir,' said the chauffeur, 'but we was in the Guards together.'

In another titbit from *Ego,* Agate recorded that Sir Seymour Hicks once attended a production in Athens of a play called *The Sister of the Mother of Karolos.* It was some way in that he realised the play was *Charley's Aunt* – in Greek. Ivor Novello said he was 'entranced' by *Ego* but that he thought Grossmith's *Diary of a Nobody* was better. Mrs Patrick Campbell had the last dismissive word. 'I did so enjoy your book. Everything that everybody writes in it is so good.'

Picking up an acquaintance with Mrs Patrick Campbell on a visit to America, where the critic John Mason Brown said she was staying in a cheap hotel, Agate had commented, 'She is committing the wittiest form of hari-kari.' She was still enthusiastically spreading vitriol. A famous prima donna 'looks like I do in a spoon'; an American actress has 'such a beautiful voice you won't understand a word she says . . . such a nice woman. If you knew her you'd even admire her acting.'

Among younger players he admired Edith Evans, Wolfit and Gielgud, but had an uneasy relationship with Olivier, who claimed once to have hit him in the stalls of a darkened theatre. Of his many protégés, Ken Tynan was one of the last whom he 'discovered' when he addressed Tynan's Birmingham school. Encountering a twenty-year-old 'Don' Sinden in Brighton, he was asked if he had spoken to Irving.

'Certainly not,' he snapped. '*Greatness* is not to be spoken to – I don't know how you can sit there speaking to *me* like that!'

When Agate worked on the *Sunday Times* he engaged the young Alan Dent as his secretary. Later Dent was to say of him, 'Of course, Jimmy will die naturally – in his sleep at a first night.'

Towards the end of his career he was nearly sacked by Lord Kemsley after a scandal in a male brothel near Gray's Inn Road. Kemsley wanted to promote Harold Hobson – 'Hobson's all right. Hobson has a daughter. Let's have Hobson' – but he was eventually dissuaded.

Agate died suddenly in 1947, having recently insisted on reading the generous obituary Jock Dent had written of him. Discreditably, though he had always encouraged Dent to believe that he would succeed him, Agate wrote a letter to Sydney Carroll, a powerful advisor to Lord Kemsley, stating that he wanted to be succeeded by Harold Hobson. James Harding ascribed this to his fear 'that Hobson had it in his power to ruin him and that his friendship must be secured at all costs. This misjudgement of an honourable and Christian soul resulted in the cruel betrayal of his long-suffering secretary, colleague and friend.'

**ALDA**, Alan. Alan Alda has a career more firmly based in the theatre than most actors. He was virtually born in a trunk. As a child he watched his father from the wings, mothered by strippers as Robert Alda played the burlesque circuit before creating the role of Sky Masterson in *Guys and Dolls* in 1950. Then he went on to a seven-year contract with Warner Brothers.

In his memoir *Never Have Your Dog Stuffed*, Alan Alda describes a traumatic experience in childhood when his much-loved dog died. Seeing how upset he was, his father took it to be stuffed. When it was returned it looked so mean they had to leave it outside on the porch when, dead as it was, it still managed to frighten away delivery people.

More relevant to the long career in the television series *M\*A\*S\*H*, which really made his name, Alan Alda was taken ill and sent to a small Chilean hospital in agony. The young doctor told him his options. 'You can be operated on here or you could fly to Santiago where the hospitals are much bigger. But the airport is totally fogged up. If you wait for the fog to lift it may be too late.' The doctor then explained the problem. 'The blood supply to some of your small intestine has been choked off and it's dying. I have to go in and resect the bad part and then sew the good part together.'

'Oh' said Alda. 'You're going to do an end-to-end anastomosis.'

The doctor was surprised. 'How did you know that?'

'I did many of them in *M\*A\*S\*H*.' said Alda. He survived.

**ALEXANDER**, Sir George (George Alexander Gibb Samson). George Alexander, a handsome actor-manager, graduated to his own theatre, the St James's, after an apprenticeship with the Bancrofts, Hare and especially with Irving at the Lyceum. Something of a matinée idol, Irving's famous rehearsal note to him was: 'Now, Alexander, not quite so much Piccadilly.' As an actor-manager Alexander's unique contribution to the theatre was to commission contemporary playwrights – Wilde, Pinero, A.E.W. Mason, Henry Arthur Jones, Henry James, Anthony Hope and Stephen Phillips. He paid Wilde an advance of £100 for *Lady Windermere's Fan* and on delivery offered £1000 to buy it outright. Wilde's reply was, 'I have so much confidence in your excellent judgement, my dear Aleck, that I cannot but refuse your generous offer.' As a result Wilde cleared £7000.

His second and less happy association with Wilde was his production of *The Importance of Being Earnest* (originally called *Lady Lancing)* at the climax of Wilde's feud with Lord Queensberry. On Wilde's arrest, Alexander obliterated his name from the playbills and on his bankruptcy purchased the rights to this play and to *Lady Windermere's Fan* for a paltry sum. He is said subsequently to have cut Wilde in the south of France but to have made amends later by seeking him out in Paris, and by paying a royalty to Wilde's family and leaving the rights to Wilde's son after his death.

He was exasperated by Mrs Patrick Campbell in *The Second Mrs Tanqueray,* and even more in *The Masqueraders* by Henry Arthur Jones.

She complained that one night, at a moment when the script called for him to look into her face and call her beautiful, he looked at her as though he could wring her neck. She burst out laughing. After the performance the stage manager came to her dressing room. By now she and Alexander were only speaking on stage. Alexander's compliments were delivered with a request please not to laugh at him on stage. She replied, 'My compliments to Mr Alexander, and please tell him I never laugh at him until I get home.'

Alexander's production of *Guy Domville* was traumatic for Henry James, unable to face sitting through the programme. After a smooth first act, the second was dismal and the third did not recapture the audience. James arrived at the theatre as the curtain fell. A lacklustre reception was converted into disaster when a few cries of 'author' caused Alexander to beckon James on stage. A storm of disapproval burst on James, who had to stand and face 'the sound of public scorn'. Finally 'the novelist turned suddenly and fled'.

Alexander played mainly in London but on one occasion, on tour, gathered up a cat which had strayed onto the stage and handed it off to a stage manager through a fireplace alight with red tinsel flames. An irate cat lover in the gallery hurled her ginger-beer bottle at him in disapproval of his imagined cruelty.

An interest in LCC politics and the strain of diabetes took their toll on Alexander's later years. He died of consumption in 1918. John Gielgud remembered his widow as a survivor on Church Parade in Hyde Park, 'heavily made up, with black patches on her cheek and chin like an eighteenth-century marquise, and very fantastically overdressed and hatted'. His mother confided, 'She is dressed by the famous couturiers Reville and Rossiter and they say she is given her clothes by them for nothing because she is such a good advertisement.' In 1945, when Gielgud produced the famous revival of *Lady Windermere's Fan* at the Haymarket, 53 years after her husband's first production, she was carried in and out of the theatre on opening night, 'wrapping her purple velvet cloak around her as if she were a doll about to be packed into a box for Christmas'.

**ALLEN**, Kelsey. Kelsey Allen was a Broadway critic who attended a disastrous production *of Macbeth*. He found himself sitting next to a well-known ticket speculator called McBride.

'When the hapless cast arrived at the line "Lay on, Macduff," Allen capped Shakespeare's line, whispering, "Lay off, McBride."'

**ALLEN**, Maude. Maude Allen was notorious on the music halls in the early years of the 20th century for her *Salome* seven-veils dance. An MP accused her of lesbianism in an article daringly entitled, 'The Cult of the Clitoris'. Miss Allen sued him for libel. A backwoods peer, Lord Albemarle, visiting his club during the much-publicised lawsuit was heard remarking vaguely, 'I've never heard of this Greek chap Clitoris they're all talking about.'

**ALLEN**, Tony. Tony Allen, a comedian who started in the earliest years of the Edinburgh Festival Fringe, produced one of the most devastating replies to an improvising comic. The visiting American, Larry Amoros, had a routine of joshing the audience with shafts of wit of the order of 'Who's that you're with and how much did you pay for her?' One night Allen sat himself at the end of the front row where Amoros habitually finished his routine. When Amoros came to him he asked, 'And what do you do?' Allen's reply was, 'I'm a comedian. What do you do?'

**'ALWAYS'**. One of Irving Berlin's most popular songs had an odd genesis. The composer's musical secretary in 1913, Arthur Johnston, had a girlfriend called Mona. Overhearing her boyfriend and his boss discussing the money a song could make, she asked Berlin why he didn't write one about her sometime. He replied that there was no time like the present, hummed a tune which Johnston noted on a napkin and came up with 'I'll be loving you, Mona.' In 1925, with Mona long forgotten, Berlin needed a song for the Marx Brothers' vehicle, *The Cocoanuts.* No one could remember who Mona was, certainly not the lad-about-town Johnston, so Berlin changed 'Mona' to 'Always' and finished the song. Then he lost confidence in *The Cocoanuts* as a vehicle to launch the song and withdrew it. A year later, when he married Ellen Mackay, Berlin dedicated 'Always', to his wife. The royalties flowed in profusion; at one count they had received $300,000.

A parody of the song in the thirties (authorship unknown) satirised Lorenz Hart's facility with comic rhyme by suggesting how he would have written the chorus:

> . . . In saloons and drab hallways
> I'll be loving you always.
> Our love will be as grand
> As Paul Whiteman's Band

And will weigh as much as Paul weighs.
See how I dispense
Rhymes which are immense.
But do they make sense?
Not always.

**AMECHE**, Don. Don Ameche starred with Claudette Colbert in *Midnight* in 1939. He played one of the better pranks in the tiresome history of practical jokery on his co-star. He paid the most decrepit, ancient extra on the set to knock on her dressing-room door. When she opened it he asked for her autograph saying, 'Miss Colbert, I've adored you ever since I was a little boy.'

Sadly, her reaction is not recorded.

When I was producing the first Marty Feldman movie *Every Home Should Have One*, shooting was nearly brought to a standstill when an extra persuaded a girl to go up to Marty's clever but insecure American co-star Shelly Herman (famous for his album of very funny phone calls) and ask for his autograph. She claimed she had always loved his *Driving Instructor* record – the huge hit by his rival Bob Newhart. He duly exploded.

**ANDERSON**, Dame Judith. Jean Barrere was stage manager when the Australian actress played her notable Medea in John Gielgud's production. According to Barrere, one of Dame Judith's great problems was to achieve the emotional pitch she needed to enter screaming, 'Death! Death!' However, on one occasion she had ready-made inspiration.

No love was lost between Dame Judith and Florence Reed, who was also in the play. Dame Judith asked Barrere to deliver a note to Miss Reed verbatim:

'Tell that old bitch she is not to move a muscle, not a muscle, during my soliloquy. Now tell her that exactly.'

The stage manager did as he was told, to which Miss Reed replied, 'Tell Judith to go fuck herself!' He did not see the star until she was about to go on. She demanded to know what Miss Reed's reply had been. Finally, Barrere conceded: 'Tell Judith to go fuck herself!'

That night the Dame found it unusually easy to enter screaming, 'Death! Death!' with conviction.

Dame Judith played twice at the Old Vic. In 1960 she was Atkadina with Tom Courtenay, making his professional stage debut as Konstantin in *The Seagull.*

However, she had played Lady Macbeth there in November 1937, transferring the following month to the New Theatre. I do not know at which theatre Queen Mary paid a visit but she certainly received Dame Judith after the performance saying, 'I did so sympathise with you trying to make that dinner party go with a swing.'

**ANDREWS**, Eamonn. The ultra-conservative Irish broadcaster should really be excluded from a book of showbiz anecdotes. When one journalist was writing a profile of him, he found that he was short of amusing stories so he telephoned one of the researchers on *This Is Your Life,* the television programme Andrews hosted for many years.

'Can you give me a nice anecdote about Eamonn?' he enquired.

'Oh,' said the researcher, dubiously. 'I don't think Eamonn would want to be involved in anything as risque as an anecdote.'

**ANDREWS**, Harry. The late splendid Harry Andrews, whose career embraced solid and sensitive appearances in classic and modern plays and films, always behind a rugged exterior, had often had trouble with remembering lines. Especially, and understandably, these occasions increased towards the end of his life. However, in his prime at the Old Vic, he hated himself when he dried. George Baker tells me that on one occasion at the theatre in The Cut, he stopped spectacularly, stomped off-stage, consulted 'the book' and was so annoyed with himself that before going back on to complete the scene, he threw an inanimate object violently into a corner of the wings.

When he came offstage, having completed the scene, he was all contrition. He apologised gently to the revered stage manager, Julia Jones, and added, 'I'm terribly sorry, Julia; and I think I threw something into a corner, I don't know what.'

'That's all right, Harry,' she said, 'it was only me.'

**ANYTHING GOES**. The mongrel birth *of Anything Goes,* the classic, thirties' escapist musical, is an extraordinary story. Two Broadway producers, Vinton Freedley and Alex Aarons (their joint first names were preserved on the marquee of the Alvin Theater) had presented many hits, often by the Gershwins. They split after the flop of the Gershwin show, *Pardon My English*: both lost a great deal of money.

Freedley sailed for Europe, keen to sign Cole Porter for a new musical. He had a vague idea of setting it on a pleasure steamer which is wrecked. He wanted Wodehouse and Bolton to write the book. Porter was excited, went to work and produced several songs. Wodehouse and Bolton had not picked up their pens. Freedley was exasperated. Then the USS *Mono Castle*, a cruise ship, went down off the coast of New Jersey with 134 lives lost. A pleasure steamer was no longer a possible premise for a frothy musical.

Wodehouse and Bolton were now otherwise engaged, so Freedley took his Porter score to Howard Lindsay, who agreed to direct and come up with some sort of story. All he asked was a collaborator. A friend of Porter's had recourse to her ouija board (literally) and produced the name of Russell Crouse. A cast had been assembled but on the first day of rehearsals only the first half of the plot had been sketched in. Lindsay ad-libbed Act Two and after the euphoria with which it was received no one could remember it. (It was the pre-tape recorder era.) They remembered enough by the time the show reached Boston and when it opened in New York it was a confident hit, 'the greatest Gala since the Depression began', with Porter even more composed than usual, turning around airily in the interval to his huge party of guests and calling out, 'Good, isn't it?'

**APRIL**, Elsie. Elsie April was Noel Coward's musical right hand. She notated, harmonised and sophisticated his music and, having perfect pitch, listened to his singers and musicians with sharp concern. She called it 'Soling and Healing'. When Coward asked her why she never wrote anything herself she said, 'Well, dear, I don't seem to have the time.'

James Harding, in his biography of Cochran, suggests that Coward took the theme of 'I'll See You Again' from a moment when April was 'doodling at her piano and hit on a pleasing motif that went from B flat, down to F again and on to E flat, ending up after a few bars on A flat'. In a footnote, Harding suggests that Coward himself said the tune came to him when he was stuck in a New York traffic jam; though in fact this is the source Coward gives for 'I'll Follow My Secret Heart', the principal waltz in *Conversation Piece*.

**ARCHER**, Jeffrey. Prolific novelist, consummate self-publicist, past politician and future playwright. His first play, *Beyond Reasonable Doubt*, produced a fine burst of spleen from the Irish author Hugh Leonard, who called it 'the most insultingly juvenile play I've seen in a long time'. Asked if Archer had a future as a popular playwright he said: 'He doesn't even have a past.' But his sharpest skewer followed Archer's revelation that he had written the play on a Friday. 'What I would like to know,' said Leonard, 'is what time on Friday.'

In an unusual twist to play construction, when Archer sent his play to Frank Finlay, the actor suggested that Act Two should be played before Act One. The author agreed and the play was produced in this shape. It is difficult to think of any other drama with which this would be possible.

**ASHCROFT**, Dame Peggy. Peggy Ashcroft and Edith Evans played in Gielgud's famous production of *Romeo* for the Oxford University Drama Society (OUDS). The company also included Christopher Hassall as Romeo, William Devlin as Tybalt, George Devine (president of the OUDS) as Mercutio, Hugh Hunt as Friar Laurence and Terence Rattigan, who echoed his single 'put up your pipes' line when he wrote *Harlequinade,* based on a touring production of the play. Gielgud made his first-night speech the occasion of one of his earliest recorded Gielgoodies: he referred to Evans and Ashcroft as 'the like of whom I hope I shall never meet again'.

I was always fascinated by Dame Peggy Ashcroft's passion for cricket. Unwisely, I once boasted that I'd seen Arthur Wellard hit five sixes in one over, off Frank Woolley at Wells in 1938.

'That's nothing,' she said, 'I saw Sobers hit *six* sixes in one over in the West Indies.' (Cricket buffs will know that he had also done it in Britain against Glamorgan.)

Perhaps the most endearing memory of Dame Peggy belongs to the distinguished radio producer, John Tydeman, who produced the first version of Tom Stoppard's play *Indian Ink* on Radio 4. It was with some dismay that Tydeman and Stoppard realised that the Dame was expecting both aspects of her character – her elderly self and her very young self – in important flashbacks. Dame Peggy had a famously 'young' voice. Tom volunteered to disillusion her. Lovely though the voice was it was no longer 'young young'. She wept and stormed and said, 'I only accepted the part because of that scene.' Then she pulled herself together and said, 'Oh well, it was worth a try,' and beautifully got on with it.

**ASHE**, Rosemary. Rosemary Ashe, opera singer, musical star and devoted wearer of pink, is a diligent reader of *PCR* (Production and Casting Report), the actor's news sheet, where she found an extraordinary announcement of future plans by the National Theatre. It was to present a new play by Paul Godfrey, *Once in a While the Odd Thing Happens.* 'It tells the story of Benjamin Britten and his relationship with Sir Peter Grimes.'

**ASTAIRE**, Fred. The greatest stage and screen dancer was not immediately welcomed to Hollywood. His 1933 screen test for RKO produced the famous report: 'Can't act. Slightly bald. Also dances.' It continued: 'Enormous ears and bad chin-line' but conceded that 'his charm is tremendous'.

Astaire's first reaction to being teamed with Ginger Rogers was 'I did not go into pictures with the thought of becoming part of a team.'

In their first film together, the staging of 'Cheek to Cheek' was nearly ruined by Rogers's feathered costume. As they danced, the ostrich feathers repeatedly got up Astaire's nose, inducing sneezing fits. He berated first his leading lady and then her mother, Lola, who moved protectively into the argument. Eventually the fatal feathers were securely moored and the song scene was shot, but Astaire and his choreographer, Hermes Pan, ran up a parody of the number to let off steam:

> Feathers – I hate feathers –
> And I hate them so that I can hardly speak
> With those chicken feathers dancing
> Cheek to cheek.

An odd sidelight on Astaire's working relationship with Hermes Pan, who looked remarkably like him, was that they frequently rehearsed together, giving the effect of a mirror dance until Rogers arrived to rehearse and Pan bowed out to supervise the routine.

**ATKINS**, Eileen. A fine actress (and, with Jean Marsh co-creator of the television series *Upstairs, Downstairs* and *The House of Elliot*) who plays down her attractiveness, replied when asked if she had much trouble with the press: 'I never have any. They think I am a social worker.'

She has revealed, on the side, a talent for tap-dancing, learnt as a child; a formidable understanding of the work of Virginia Woolf; and an ability as a witty raconteur. She tells two stories against herself.

Back in the 1960s, when women were burning their bras, she went shopping in Harrods. On her way she passed some scaffolding on which

workmen did what workmen usually do when young women pass –
whistle or shout compliments or catcalls. Since Eileen is what Russ Meyer
describes as, 'insufficiently cantilevered', she got catcalls along the lines of
''Ardly worth 'er burning 'er bra, was it?'

Furious at the insult she dived into Harrods buying everything she had
on her list and many things that were not. Her anger smouldered until
she left the shop and then in a burst of fury strode across to the
scaffolding and yelled, 'I suppose you've all got small cocks but I don't go
around shouting about it!' With that she turned her back on the puzzled
workmen and marched away. It was not until she rounded the next
corner that she realised she had come out of a quite different door than
the one through which she went in and confronted a different group of
men.

Acting on Broadway she paid an afternoon visit to see the film *Nicholas
and Alexandra*. She went with a friend. Early on in the film her first
husband Julian Glover appeared as a Russian Orthodox Archimandrite,
Eileen nudged her friend and said – 'Oh! he was my first husband!' Quite
soon another old lover appeared and again she confided the information.
Finally Michael Bryant came on the screen as Lenin. Once again she
turned to her friend and whispered, 'Him, too', only to hear an
incredulous American friend behind her say, 'Now she's thinks she
fucked Lenin!'

Any career which stretches from tap-dancing as a juvenile in working
men's clubs to touring your own one-woman show as Virginia Woolf is
remarkable. Appearing as Virginia in Los Angeles she got a call from
Paramount studios to play a CIA agent in a movie. There were two
conditions. She must have a perfect American accent and she must be
able to get out of her show. She thought for a moment and said 'No' on
both counts. On the latter she added, 'Besides it's a one-woman show.'
The brash reply came without hesitation. 'Close it.'

Dame Eileen's mother always regretted that she 'never did a play with
a few laughs in it – a nice play I can tell the neighbours about.' After her
great success in T.S. Eliot's *The Cocktail Party* and her character's
macabre fate, she went home one Sunday reckoning that the notices of
her triumph might have penetrated the family circle. 'Once I'd admired
the new lino, been up to the allotment and through everybody's illnesses,
I finally said, "Did you read any of the reviews?" "Oh, yes," Mother said.
"You weren't the *Daily Mirror*'s idea of a martyr."'

Dame Eileen has strong views on accents. Recently she said, 'It's a

damn shame we have this immediate thing of ticking off in the mind how
people sound. On the other hand, how many people want to be operated
on by a surgeon who talks broad cockney?'

In 2006 she was filming (aged 72) with the young Irish star Colin
Farrell. She hit the headlines describing his romantic siege throughout a
long night – a challenge she managed to resist.

**ATKINS**, Robert. A splendid bravura actor and director, who started
with Beerbohm Tree and Benson and whose career was devoted to
Shakespeare, he was particularly known in his latter years for his
productions in the Open Air Theatre in Regent's Park, which he co-
founded with Sydney Carroll.

He was a legend for his frank language to actors and actresses. Perhaps
his most notorious rebuke was addressed to a young woman who failed
to come in on her cue during the read-through. Seeing her a picture of
unhappiness, her head down in her lap, he barked: 'It's no good looking
up your entrance, dear. You've missed it!'

Atkins once had occasion to give a stiffening note to a young actor who
had nothing to do throughout a Shakespeare play but hold his spear,
which he did, as Dulcie Gray puts it, 'with drooping elegance'.

'I don't like your conception,' Atkins told him. 'It's unsoldierly,
inaccurate and arouses the greatest suspicions, old man.'

One of Michael Bentine's apprentice jobs was playing Demetrius
opposite the much taller Helen Cherry. Atkins advised him to get some
lifts, only to bellow, when Bentine made his tottering, uncertain entrance:
'You're supposed to come from Athens, my boy, not bloody Pisa!'

With the wind in the right direction it was an open question whether
you could hear Atkins or the lions more clearly across Regent's Park. To
another youth who failed horribly to satisfy him in rehearsal he intoned,
'Scenery by God. The words by the greatest poet the world has ever
known. A director – not bad, and then . . . *You* come on.' To yet another
he offered: 'I asked you to be light, mercurial and swift – so why are you
heavy, lugubrious and dull?'

Donald Sinden ascribes a story to him which is sometimes attributed
to Bernard Miles during the building of the Mermaid. Sinden places it on
the docks in Bristol. Atkins was walking with Ralph Truman when a four-
masted schooner hove into view. Atkins grew expansive. 'Look at her,
that beautiful barque has sailed the seven seas bringing us tea from
Ceylon, jewels from India, silks from China, spices from Samarkand and

there she lies about to depart at our behest.' He boomed to a sailor: 'Sailor! Whither sailest thou?'

The sailor hardly looked up. 'Fuck off, you silly old bugger.' Atkins got another rebuff when he was leading the company at Stratford and was not asked, as was traditionally the custom, to read the lesson in Holy Trinity Church on the Sunday nearest Shakespeare's birthday. He demanded an explanation of the parson: 'Give me one cogent reason why I should not read the fucking lesson?' The parson protested lamely that someone else had been asked earlier. 'Well,' snapped Atkins, 'you can stuff yer church and you can stuff yer steeple! Except, of course, the bells, which I understand are the most melodious in Warwickshire.'

He could be brusque about performances he witnessed. Of John Neville's Hamlet at the Old Vic he said, 'A little more sex and a little less sanctity and he'd make a very passable Laertes.' Not too far away from his friendly advice to Peter O'Toole when they were both at Bristol: 'Take the crucifix out of your mouth and put some cock in it.'

When he and O'Toole were in Joseph O'Connor's *Othello* at the Bristol Old Vic, he asked O'Toole at the first rehearsal what he was playing. O'Toole said he was giving his Lodovico. 'Ah! The cunt who forgets the letter.' And sure enough on the first night O'Toole forgot to bring it on.

When Atkins and Vivian van Damm were both awarded OBEs – Atkins for keeping the King's Theatre, Hammersmith open during the war, van Damm for doing the same thing for the non-stop nudes at the Windmill – Atkins congratulated him and added, 'A different form of our art – but not a different courage.'

Ian Atkins, his son, reports that in his eightieth year he had a heart attack and was confined to a hospital ward, but he kept up his Shakespearean vocal exercises. Lying behind screens was another old man who protested to the matron that he couldn't stand the noise. Atkins soon loomed up in front of his bed, saying, 'I hear you don't like Shakespeare. I *also* hear you are about to meet him.'

He had been a great prop of the early Old Vic and with a new production of *Father Andrews, The Hope of the World* about to go into production, Lilian Baylis asked him who would play the Virgin Mary.

'I haven't decided yet.'

'This time,' said the formidably religious Miss Baylis, 'I *will* have a virgin.'

Atkins thought he had gone too far when he asked eagerly, 'When shall we hold the auditions?' But she collapsed in laughter.

**ATKINSON**, Rowan. I like this story so much that I have not dared to check its authenticity. Atkinson had been filming one of his credit card commercials in Florida. When shooting was over he flew back in first class, of course. Also in first class was a particularly objectionable drunk who kept calling for more drinks during the in-flight entertainment – which happened to be an episode of Atkinson's *Mr Bean* series. The drunk laughed uproariously until the lights came up and he looked around the cabin for the first time. Catching sight of Rowan he was so bemused and shocked that he had a heart attack and died.

**AUBER**, Daniel François Esprit. The talented French opera composer sometimes reviewed the work of other composers. Confronted by one which was brimming with precocity, he commented, 'He will go far when he has had less experience.'

**AUBERT**, Jeanne. A French twenties' and thirties' musical comedy star who played in England and America, she was once cast in London in the Ethel Merman role in *Anything Goes*. The ribald rhyme which ran around the town was:

> If Jeanne Aubert can fill the Palace
> I say without malice
> Well, God knows
> Anything Goes!

In New York she had appeared in Rodgers and Hart's *America's Sweetheart* in 1931, attracting this comment from Dorothy Parker: 'And there is, besides, Jeanne Aubert, whose husband, if you can believe the papers, recently pled, through the French courts, that he be allowed to restrain his wife from appearing on the stage. Professional or not, the man is a dramatic critic.'

**AYCKBOURNE**, Sir Alan. Perhaps the most performed British playwright of his generation, Alan Ayckbourne started his career as an actor in Wolfit's companies and, on one occasion in a regional company playing in Pinter's *The Birthday Party*. It was not long after the play's disastrous first night at the Lyric, Hammersmith and Pinter attended a rehearsal. Ayckbourne ventured to ask him about the character he was playing to which the playwright responded, 'Mind your own fucking business. Concentrate on what's on the page.'

This response is not Pinter's reply to a correspondent who asked him if the characters in *The Birthday Party* were supposed to be normal because 'you will appreciate that without the answer to my questions I cannot fully understand your play.'

Pinter's response was, 'Where do you come from? Are you supposed to be normal? You will appreciate that without answers to my questions I cannot fully understand your letter.'

To get back to Alan Ayckbourne. He and his fellow playwright Alan Plater were both represented by the formidable Margaret Ramsay – a great agent but occasionally disorganised in her office. At the end of one month, the two Alans received their royalty statements with cheques enclosed. Alan Ayckbourne, who was just starting his writing career was pleasantly surprised to see that his cheque was for a far larger sum than usual. As he prepared to celebrate the phone rang. It was Alan Plater who was already established as a high-earning television dramatist. 'Alan,' he said, 'I'm afraid Peggy has sent me your cheque.' Ayckbourne looked at his statement and saw that this was indeed the truth. They agreed to swap the letters and cheques. As Ayckbourne was putting the phone down he heard Plater say, 'I'm so sorry, Alan.'

**AYRTON**, Randle. Randle Ayrton was an authoritarian stage manager who became an actor much later – towards middle age. He preferred not to play in London and made his base Stratford-upon-Avon. Lear was perhaps his most famous role. In the great tradition of handing on famous props, in the year of his retirement he strode into Donald Wolfit's dressing room.

'Well, Don,' he said, 'I hear you're going to don the purple.'

Wolfit asked what he meant.

'That's what we used to call going into management in the good old days. Well, bloody good luck to you, my boy, and here's my Lear whip for you as a keepsake to use as Petruchio. It belonged to Oscar Asche as well, so take care of it.'

# — $\mathcal{B}$ —

**BACALL**, Lauren. Advice for widows: 'Don't sell the house and don't sleep with Frank Sinatra.'

**BADDELEY**, Hermione ('Totie'). The great revue rivalry of the forties was between Baddeley and Gingold – the two Hermiones. No revue stage could easily hold both and soon they had their own vehicles, though they did come together for a revival of Noel Coward's *Fallen Angels* – a commercial hit in spite of the author's dismay at their antics in Plymouth: 'Gingold at moments showed that she could be funny. Baddeley was disgusting. Afterwards I told them exactly what I thought . . . after this fragrant little evening I returned to London.'

In the sixties the BBC brought them together for a television revival of their most famous sketches. Everyone expected fireworks. I visited the studios. The two old girls were far too tired trying to remember their lines and their business to spar, but over in the corner of the studio was the edifying spectacle of their two tiny young agents arguing billing, hammer and tongs.

I last saw Totie in Daphne's Restaurant, a guest of her nephew, Julian Tennant; also at the table was Sir Robin Day. It was a wonderful occasion of cross purposes. Sir Robin thought she had been a music hall star and kept trying to get her to join him in choruses of 'Any Old Iron' – part of his favourite repertoire. She was determined to talk earnestly of politics with him – a subject on which she knew nothing and had less interest.

On tour with Totie, Dulcie Gray was privy to an extraordinary romantic encounter. Totie was travelling with her current husband, one 'Dozie' Willis, late of the Indian Army. At lunch in Oxford at The Welsh Pony where they were staying, she picked up a young man at the bar and took him upstairs. Just as they had undressed and were getting into bed the door opened and the husband entered. The young man was delighted.

'Dozie Willis, by all that's holy!' he yelped.

'Good God! Haven't seen you since Waziristan!' said Dozie, and adultery was replaced by reminiscences of the North West Frontier, much to Totie's annoyance.

**BAKER STORY, THE.** One of the classic (and most cruel) theatre tales – ascribed variously to John Barrymore and to both the great Jewish actors Tomashevsky and Adler (the first the ancestor of Michael Tilson Thomas, the popular conductor, the latter of Luther and Stella Adler) – might, in a less polite age, have jostled with 'Wait till you see Buckingham' as a possible title for this book.

The great actor entertains a poor young woman in his dressing room before the show. After they have had sex, she asks for money. He hands her two tickets for the evening performance.

She pleads with him, 'Money, money for bread, bread for my children!' 'Madam,' he says, dismissing her, 'you want bread, go fuck a baker.'

**BALL,** Lucille. In her early days in Hollywood, Lucille Ball was under contract to Harry Cohn at Columbia Pictures. It had not been a happy association and near the end of her term Cohn still owed her $85,000. To avoid paying her he sent her a script he knew she must refuse. Seeing through his ploy, she accepted enthusiastically, aware that if she turned the film down she would be in breach of contract and would lose the money he owed her. Cohn was forced to make the picture and pay her the money. Meanwhile, Cecil B. DeMille wanted her for a major picture which she was keen to accept. Halfway through the Columbia film she realised that she was pregnant. In these circumstances Cohn could dismiss her for natural causes. She couldn't tell Cohn and she couldn't tell DeMille in case it got back to Cohn.

However, having completed the Columbia movie and collected her cash she and her husband, Desi Arnaz, called on DeMille to make a clean breast of it and apologise. When DeMille realised that there was no chance that she could make his film he was determined to be magnanimous. 'You're the only woman I know who's ever screwed Desi Arnaz, Harry Cohn, Paramount Pictures and Cecil B. DeMille all at the same time!'

**BANBURY,** (Frederick Harold) Frith. As I write, the veteran director Frith Banbury is 94 years old. Banbury greatly helped to reveal and nurture the writing talents of Wynyard Browne, N.C. Hunter, Rodney Ackland, John Whiting and Robert Bolt (*The Flowering Cherry, A Man for All Seasons*).

It was a very different era from ours today. After Wynyard Browne's first play, *Dark Summer* in 1947, Banbury's mother was satisfied that at 35 her boy (after years as an actor in everything from revue to Shakespeare) had settled in his career. She gave him £10,000. Immediately, he paid Browne £1000 – one half non-returnable, the other in advance of royalties on his next four plays.

In 1995 Charles Duff wrote a book, *The Lost Summer: the Heyday of the West End Theatre*, which, while not quite a biography of Banbury, revolves around his work. Another of his achievements was sensitively to restore middle-aged Rattigan with *The Deep Blue Sea*. In the book he disposes of the rumour that a gay version of the play ever existed.

Duff is very funny about Banbury's reaction to being memorialised. 'From a non-committed, "Well I won't stop you," "it" suddenly became far too over-excited. I was bombarded with suggestions: who to see; what to focus on, even what opinions to hold . . . I took to switching on my answerphone to monitor all calls. Then after one Banbury message – the longest I have ever received from anyone – I disconnected the phone. Then the letters started . . .'

The Banbury story is crammed with anecdotes. The demands of Dame Edith Evans and Dame Sybil Thorndike during the run of N.C. Hunter's *Waters of the Moon* are recorded elsewhere in this book. However, the designer also came under fire. The producer, Binkie Beaumont, removed a snowman from the set because it upset Dame Edith. The designer was reduced to tears. 'The Dame's tears', came the steely response, 'Are more important than the designer's tears. Get rid of it.'

On Gladys Cooper's entrance on the first night of Browne's *The Holly and the Ivy* the notoriously casual actress forgot to take out a Polo mint she was sucking. With her first line she spat it across the stage past a bemused Paul Scofield. At the dress rehearsal Banbury observed her sitting in the stalls fascinated by Act One. Not being in it, she had not bothered to read it.

Best, perhaps, is the gentle N.C. Hunter's widow. She turned to spiritualism after her husband's death. In the grave his determination appeared to stiffen. During a revival of *Waters of the Moon* in 1977, the management asked Mrs Hunter to accept a smaller author's royalty to keep down the costs. She consulted her dead spouse. Norman said, 'No.'

**BANCROFT**, Sir Squire and Lady (Marie Wilton). Lady Bancroft's life began with anecdote. After a night of crying, her impoverished touring actor parents found her body a mass of finger and thumb pinch-marks. A passing gypsy woman prophesied a life full of good fortune for her, something Lady Bancroft continued to believe in religiously.

As a child she had supported her parents and acted with Macready – she played boys in burlesque and was idolised by Dickens. Tired of playing young lads, she was saved from this fate by her brother-in-law, who gave her £1000 to reclaim a discredited theatre off the Tottenham Court Road as actor-manager. Known as 'the Dusthole' but officially the Queens, she renamed it the Prince of Wales and was successful from the start. Another anecdote attends its re-opening. Her mother, nervous for her success, took a coach drive round rural Willesden. Just as she was praying to know the outcome of the venture, she passed a signpost which read 'Mary's Place, Fortune's Gate.'

Marie Wilton met Squire Bancroft on tour in burlesque in Liverpool and soon after engaged him for her new company. Together they promoted the plays of T.W. Robertson: neat, realistic plays with neat, explanatory titles: *Society, Ours, Caste, Play, School, MP.* They were pioneers in practicable scenery, following the example of Madame Vestris, with the box set, real door handles, real carpets and actual furniture – all revolutionary concepts at the time. 'Cup and saucer comedy' became as popular a label in the 1870s as 'kitchen sink drama' in the 1960s.

In the decoration of their theatre, in providing shorter evenings with a single play, in sending out touring companies, providing actresses' wardrobes and introducing matinées, the Bancrofts were also pioneers. They disapproved the 'benefit system' of rewarding actors who were ill paid, preferring to pay a living wage in the first place and to deliver pay packets to actors' dressing rooms rather than have them queue with cleaners, dressers and stagehands.

When they produced *The School for Scandal* they combed the British Museum for ideas on authentic props, engaged a real black boy as the page, who lived in their house for the run, and introduced a dance at Lady Sneerwell's reception which became such a feature of later productions that when Marie Lohr, who had played Lady Teazle for Tree at Her Majesty's, saw Gielgud's production with Ralph Richardson at the Haymarket many, many years later, she could not understand 'why they have cut the ball scene'.

They prepared their *Merchant* by visiting Venice and returned with so much authenticity that they blamed the failure of the production on being ahead of their time: 'It all looked so unlike a theatre and so much more like old Italian pictures than anything that had previously been shown upon the stage.' A more probable reason for the failure was Charles Coghlan's Shylock. According to his Portia, Ellen Terry: 'Coghlan's Shylock was not even bad. It was nothing.'

After Robertson's death, they found it harder to obtain new plays. One of their great successes was *Diplomacy*, adapted from *Dora* by Sardou and often revived by Gerald du Maurier and Gladys Cooper. But they continued to break new ground. When their friend and former colleague, John Hare, bought the St James Theatre and went into partnership with the formidable Kendals, Bancroft invaded the Haymarket, which he had long coveted, and made an immediate offer to buy the lease with an extension. He succeeded and expensively redecorated the theatre, abolishing 'the pit' at the back of the stalls. This was greeted by riots on the first night and cries of 'Where's the pit?' The answer was, in the gallery – the sole remaining cheap seats.

During the course of their Haymarket tenure they launched Lillie Langtry at a charity matinée in *She Stoops to Conquer* and subsequently in her professional debut in a revival of Robertson's *Ours*. They had reckoned that it would take ten years to make their fortune at the Haymarket. They cracked it in four and retired in 1885. Marie Wilton was 46, her husband two years younger. They both lived until their eighties, making only occasional appearances for other managements but invariably present on first nights as dignified members of the audience.

When Sir Squire appeared with Irving at the Lyceum in a play called *The Dead Heart,* Irving said after one performance, 'What a big name you might have made for yourself had you never come across those Robertson plays! What a pity, for your own sake: for no actor can be remembered long who does not appear in classical drama.' Bancroft was content with his innovations and his fortune and a memory of that play with Irving. In the course of it they had to fight a duel. Both were short-sighted. In rehearsal Irving wore pince-nez and Bancroft an eyeglass: 'It was a grim business in the sombre, moonlit room, and certainly gave the impression that one of the two combatants would not leave the room alive.'

John Gielgud records that after Lady Bancroft's death, the old boy moved into Albany: 'From there he would walk each morning to his bank, where he would demand a slip with the amount of his current balance, which he would diligently examine before proceeding to lunch at the Garrick Club.' Another foible was a fascination with death – and visits to his friends' sickbeds, carrying a large bunch of black muscat grapes. One visit to a cremation – something of an innovation – stirred him: 'A most impressive occasion,' he reported, 'and afterwards the relatives were kind enough to ask me to go behind.'

**BARONOVA**, Irina. Baronova, one of Diaghilev's legendary baby ballerinas, eloped with her first husband, Jerry Sevastianov, while touring America with Colonel de Basil's company. Sevastianov was one of de Basil's managers. Still a 'baby' with de Basil, she fretted under her parents' strict discipline. As the company moved from Cleveland to Cincinnati, de Basil arranged for her to speed ahead with her beau straight from her performance. By the time parents and company caught up with the lovers in Cincinnati, the marriage was a *fait accompli.* Baronova insists that she was so naive on her wedding night that she kept her husband waiting while she put her hair in curlers. Later she married Cecil Tennant, the agent, and after his death remarried Sevastianov. She is Victoria Tennant's mother and became mother-in-law to Steve Martin for a time.

**BARRYMORE**, Ethel. Ethel Barrymore's long and distinguished career began in New York when she was fifteen, under the management of her grandmother, Mrs John Drew. When she was 19 she appeared in London with Irving. She went on to score successes in New York in *Captain Jinks of the Horse Marines, A Doll's House, Trelawney of the Wells, The Lady of the Camellias, Romeo And Juliet, The Second Mrs Tanqueray, Hamlet* and *The Merchant of Venice.* In tune with the times, she played Barrie's one-acter *The Twelve-Pound Look* in vaudeville, including an appearance at the London Palladium. *Whiteoaks* and *The Corn Is Green* were notable later successes.

One of the plays of her middle period was an adaptation of Edna Ferber's *Our Mrs Chesney.* Ferber left a vivid memoir of the star's nervousness in preparing for a first night in Atlantic City in a *A Peculiar Treasure*: 'Miss Barrymore spent the rest of the day buying hats and vomiting. She couldn't sit still. She couldn't digest anything . . . she bought hats and hats and hats, none of which she ever wore afterwards.' The nausea was repeated when the show opened in New York at the Lyceum Theater in 1915.

A story, probably apocryphal, has a young actress wangling an invitation to a dinner party *chez* Barrymore, then she neither turned up nor apologised. However, some days later she did run into the great lady. 'I believe I was invited to your house for dinner last week,' was her lame opening. 'And did you come?' was Barrymore's response.

Ms Barrymore also had the last word in one famous exchange with noisy latecomers who chattered rudely from a stage box when she was playing a scene with the elderly and slightly deaf actor, Charles Cherry. Eventually she advanced on the misbehavers and said, 'Excuse me, I can hear every word you are saying, but Mr Cherry is slightly hard of hearing. I wonder if you would speak up for him?'

Towards the end of her career, Ethel Barrymore had an embarrassing run-in with the tax man. According to Helen Hayes, some agents from the Internal Revenue Service called on her to remind her that she had paid no taxes for several years and was many thousands of dollars in arrears. They pointed out that if she did not pay, the interest and additional penalties would make the total rise astronomically. Finally she dismissed them with a grand, exhausted gesture: 'Gentlemen, I have worked all my life and I am very tired.' By some miracle Washington decided she was 'a national treasure', and passed a special law exempting Ms Barrymore from paying income tax 'past, present and future'.

Her career took an immediate turn for the better and she passed into the period of Hollywood stardom, winning an Oscar for Best Supporting Actress in *None But the Lonely Heart*. She continued to be a highly paid movie character actress 'without having to pay a cent to Uncle Sam'.

**BARRYMORE**, John. Greatest of all the Barrymores as a Shakespearean actor, lover, drinker and character, John Barrymore's professional career began in 1903. Originally a light comedian and matinée idol, he was 40 when he astonished New York with his Hamlet, which he brought to London with equal success three years later in 1925. His performance was meticulous and scholarly, enhanced by his romantic profile and beautifully clear and unexaggerated speaking of the verse – in complete contrast to his rumbustious subsequent career.

Following his triumphant tours as Hamlet, Barrymore was often invited to lecture on Shakespeare. To one earnest inquiry as to whether Romeo and Juliet as teenagers had 'enjoyed a full physical relationship', he famously replied, 'They certainly did in the Chicago company.' He had short shrift from a group of girls who in one production bore Ophelia's bier to the graveside. He impatiently told them that they were playing virgins.

'Mr Barrymore,' the leader replied, 'we are extras, not character actresses.'

Trouble sometimes threatened from the audience. When Jane Cowl – a big star at the time – attended a matinée, she compounded the distraction her mere presence provided by chatting to her companions throughout the performance. Barrymore uncharacteristically concealed his annoyance until his curtain call when he elected to make a speech. Bowing deeply in her direction, he said, 'I'd like to take this opportunity to thank Miss Cowl for the privilege of co-starring with her this afternoon.'

He was quicker to anger during an earlier performance as Fedor in *The Living Corpse,* a version of Tolstoy's *Redemption,* in 1918. Infuriated by frequent outbreaks of bronchial barking, he sent out for fish during the interval. As the second act began and the first volley of coughs rang out, he whipped a large sea bass from under his overcoat and hurled it into the audience saying. 'Busy yourselves with that, you damned walruses!'

After a fourteen-year absence from the stage – mainly spent in films – he returned unsuccessfully to Broadway in *My Dear Children* by Catherine Turney and Jenny Horivin, a play said to be in some ways autobiographical of its star. George Jean Nathan, reviewing Barrymore's overstated clowning, wrote, 'I always said that I'd like Barrymore's acting till the cows came home. Well, ladies and gentlemen, last night the cows came home.'

One of the most quoted Barrymore stories has echoes of a famous line about Junius Brutus Booth's addiction to drink – Booth is said to have stumbled in the wings into the arms of an anxious theatre manager, and asked: 'Where's the stage?' Well adrift from the script in one of his last, disastrous stage appearances, Barrymore staggered to the wings and hissed, 'What's the line? What's the line?'

The answer was unhelpful.

'What's the play?'

A more shocking Barrymore story was once told by Anne Fleming. Barrymore was sitting with Errol Flynn. His daughter, Diana, passed by. Barrymore asked, 'Ever fucked her?' Flynn had, but as the girl was 16 he thought it wise to deny it. 'Don't miss it,' advised Barrymore. 'She's terrific!'

**BARRYMORE**, Maurice (Herbert Blythe). The father of Ethel, John and Lionel was born in England and took his stage name from a playbill at the Haymarket. He first went to New York in 1875. A handsome leading man, he married the actress Georgina Drew in 1876. On her death, Maurice was said to be found weeping, surrounded by her obituaries, moaning, 'It's a cruel loss, I shall never get over it. But I must say they've given the old girl some damn fine notices!'

He wrote *Nadjesda* for Modjeska in 1886 and later charged Sardou with stealing the plot for *Tosca*. On the other hand, Maurice Barrymore was so often accused of plagiarising French plays that when reporters asked him how his five-year-old son John was doing he replied, 'Fine. He is in fact the only thing I ever owned that the newspapers have not accused me of taking from the French.'

He had a sharp tongue for other performers. Berated by a friend for not seeing E.M. Sothern's Hamlet, he answered: 'I never encourage vice.' Quizzed about a flop in which he appeared with a Madame Beere, an actress whose dignified name belied her coarse humour, he sought to blame the disaster on the size of the theatre, designed for opera: 'In that house,' he concluded, 'one can be obscene but not heard.'

Barrymore's death – or rather his funeral – called out the acting profession and, naturally, his two sons. There was a hitch as the coffin was lowered, and it had to be brought up and lowered again. Before it went down for a second time Lionel whispered to John: 'How like Father – a curtain call.'

**BART**, Lionel. In the late fifties and early sixties, Lionel Bart justified his position as the white hope of the British musical with successes like *Fings Ain't What They Used To Be* and *Lock Up Your Daughters*. Later ventures – *Blitz* and *Maggie May* – were less successful. Of *Blitz*, Noel Coward said that it was 'as long as the real thing and twice as noisy'. A subsequent work, *Quasimodo*, based on *The Hunchback of Notre Dame*, has not so far reached the stage. At one point Bart was in Hollywood discussing the show with a film producer (who was interested in financing it) in a bungalow at the Beverly Hills Hotel. In mid-conference he asked Lionel who his ideal set designer would be. Lionel said someone like Brueghel or Doré. The producer turned to his secretary.

'Check if those guys are available,' he said.

**BASTEDO**, Alexandra. Alexandra Bastedo had a unique opportunity to study the romantic techniques of Warren Beatty and Steve McQueen at first hand. McQueen's opening line was, 'I asked you here as a woman, Alexandra.' Beatty gets the award for persistence. At the time of his overtures, Alexandra and her flatmate were working on the same film. Both met Beatty when he visited the set. Soon afterwards he telephoned Alexandra, well after midnight, to ask her out. She said it was too late, she was filming in the morning. Three hours later the phone rang again. It was Beatty again, who had worked through his book to 'S', the initial of the flatmate.

**BAYLIS**, Lilian Mary. Lilian Baylis first assisted her aunt, Emma Cons, to run the old Victoria Theatre – later known as the Old Vic – and took over control on Ms Cons' death in 1912. She was an immensely strong-willed, single-minded and religious woman who devoted her life to opening and running popular homes for drama (especially Shakespeare), for opera and for dance – at the Old Vic and at Sadlers Wells, where her companies evolved eventually into the English National Opera and the Royal Ballet.

The Vic was a rough and ready house as Baylis abandoned music hall and invested in Shakespeare: sawdust covered the floors, and coffee and cocoa rather than beer or spirits were served in the bars. Wooden benches were smothered in red oil-cloth. Cooking smells filled the house from both ends: in the refreshment rooms at the back of the pit, patrons could buy a steak for fourpence and in her box Miss Baylis was likely to be frying her lunch or dinner. Mice and rats infested the house – on one occasion the critic William Archer found a rat chewing at his boot in mid-performance.

During World War One many men's parts were played by women – notably by Sybil Thorndike and Winifred Oughton. Baylis's first *Hamlet* opened with less than two pounds in receipts. Dame Sybil has recalled a performance which started with 'about five people in the pit and three boys and an orange in the gallery'. About twenty had arrived by the end.

Dame Sybil gave Richard Findlater a glimpse of the Baylis priorities when she was playing *Richard II* and an air raid threatened her journey to the theatre. She was stopped by a policeman.

"'I can't help the raid," I cried, clinging to his brass buttons. "The curtain's up at the Old Vic, and I shan't be on for my entrance."

"'Old Vic, is it?" he said. "Oh, I know Miss Baylis. Yes, you're right," and a lull coming in the bomb sounds, he gave me a push into Waterloo Road with a "Now run for your life, and if you're killed, don't blame me

– blame Her." I got to the pit door – first door I reached – and found Lilian in a fume and fret.

' "Why on earth weren't you in before this?"

' "A raid," I said. "Everything underground at Waterloo – everything impossible."

' "Raid," she snorted. "What's a raid when my curtain's up?"'

On one occasion when an air raid interrupted a rehearsal and bombs were dropping nearby, the ill-paid cast sensibly dived for cover.

'I'm ashamed of you all,' Baylis shouted. 'If you have to be killed, at least die at your job.'

**BEATON**, Cecil Walter Hardy. A designer and photographer, Beaton was also, very occasionally, an actor and a playwright. He appeared as Cecil Graham in the New York production of *Lady Windermere's Fan*, for which he designed scenery and costumes; Donald Wolfit starred in his play *The Gainsborough Girls*, which never came to London.

Beaton's attention to detail was notorious. When H.M. Tennent presented Coward's *Quadrille* with the Lunts, Hugh Beaumont's right hand, Lily Taylor, scoured London for the materials he described. He rejected them all. Beaumont sent her further afield – as far as India, looking for rare silks and other exotic cloths. On her return she placed them before Beaton. He examined them silently and when he had finished looked up and said simply, 'Lily Taylor, you're just not trying.'

**BEECHAM**, Sir Thomas. At the beginning of the eighties, Caryl Brahms and I wrote a play about Sir Thomas Beecham – the Disraeli, Wilde, Shaw or Mencken of music, so often and so widely is he quoted. In his mouth innumerable quips have been placed by re-tellers anxious to clothe a suspect story with more authority and the promise of laughter. We were lucky enough to get Timothy West, who harboured a keenness to conduct, to play the part.

As we talked to Sir Thomas's old colleagues and adversaries the familiar jokes were dusted down and as the show went into rehearsal more were offered by post and telephone. Neville Cardus has even confessed to making up and circulating one Beecham story and Beecham accused him of fabricating one about a singer in his opera company which turned out to be true in character but not in fact. The singer confided in the great man about his son. 'He'll be leaving Oxford next year. I've spent a lot of money on him and he doesn't know what sort of a job to take up.'

Beecham stroked his chin. 'Aren't you going to make a singer of him?'

'Oh no, Sir Thomas.'

'Why?'

'Well, he hasn't got a voice, not really.'

'Ah,' said Sir Thomas in dulcet tones. 'Ah, I see – a family failing.'

That joins the brood of 'offspring' foisted on Beecham, like 'Try anything once except incest and folk dancing,' which we used shamelessly in our play, but which can be traced back to Sir Arnold Bax's *Farewell My Youth*, published in 1943.

We also used another story with a doubtful provenance. It has Beecham in Fortnum and Masons accosted by a stately woman fan and struggling to identify her and not admitting that he cannot. He tried all the routine questions: 'How's your husband?' 'He's very well.' 'How are your children?' 'Oh, they're very well,' and so on until, getting nowhere, he enquired, 'And how's your brother?' To which she replied, 'Still king.' It is probably only a matter of time before Beecham is awarded W.S. Gilbert's reply to a musically illiterate woman who asked if Bach was still composing – 'No, madam, decomposing,' came the answer.

Cardus in his *Memoir* (1961) was elegant and perceptive on Beecham's humour. 'He was a comedian. Or, as this is a term which the English associate with red-nosed buffoonery, I had better describe him as an artist in comedy. But he was not a wit in the epigrammatic way of Oscar Wilde . . . Sir Thomas indulged not so much in wit as in waggery.'

Beecham's was a Lancastrian family, 'enriched by the manufacture of pills'. One of his earliest excursions into studied humour was a commission from his father to produce a version of a Christmas carol which would promote the family product. Young Thomas came up with:

> Hark! the herald angels sing!
> Beecham's pills are just the thing.
> Two for a woman, one for a child . . .
> Peace on earth and mercy mild.

'These sentiments,' he explained later, 'especially the ellipsis, seemed to me admirably to express the rapture which is occasioned by a good effortless release.'

'A musicologist,' Beecham enjoyed saying, 'is a person who can read music but can't hear it.'

Beecham's contempt was directed towards the inferior, the unadventurous, the pretentious and the foreign. 'Why do we in England engage at our concerts so many third-rate continental conductors when we have so many second-rate ones of our own?' He knew his own worth, of course: 'I am not the greatest conductor in this country. On the other hand, I'm better than any damned foreigner.' As far as English music is concerned, Beecham was determined to make it better: 'British music is in a state of perpetual promise. It might almost be said to be one long promissory note.' He knew his public, too: 'The English may not like music but they absolutely love the noise it makes.' He had two golden rules for an orchestra: 'Start together and finish together. The public doesn't give a damn what goes on in between.'

Cardus once caught Beecham being cavalier with the last act of *Siegfried* at Covent Garden in the thirties. The first two acts were a dream. 'In the third act Beecham went berserk.' The conductor answered Cardus's criticism forthrightly: 'You critics are inhumane. I chanced to look at my watch, laid on my desk before me, and we were still not half-way through Act III. It was getting on for eleven o'clock. In the audience were many poor souls who had to go home to such remote habitations as Putney, Streatham and Swiss Cottage. And the public houses would close at eleven, and my orchestra, slaving away since six o'clock, were thirsty. So I just let Wagner rip!'

Beecham believed that 'Nearly all the questionable works of the great musical geniuses have been prompted by religion. Wagner's *Parsifal*, the Requiem of Brahms, and Elgar's *Gerontius*, described by my friend George Moore as holy water in a German beer barrel. Each is, I think, my most potent aversion. Too much counterpoint. Protestant counterpoint. What dreadful crimes have been committed in the name of religion.'

Beecham was the ace when it came to explosions between singers, players and other conductors. To one player Beecham said silkily, 'We cannot expect you to be with us all the time, but perhaps you could be good enough to keep in touch now and again.' To another, 'Cor anglais, kindly give me some indication of your presence at four bars after the letter G.' When an oboist called on to give an A came up with a wide vibrato, he looked around the orchestra and said simply, 'Take your pick.' With Jean Pouquet, the violinist, he appeared with an orchestra so overawed that their opening rehearsal bars were disastrous. Beecham persevered and they got better. 'Don't look now,' he said, leaning towards Pouquet, 'but I believe we're being followed.' Again: 'Gentlemen in the clarinet department, how can you resist such an impassioned appeal from the second violins? Give them an answer, I beg you.'

Perhaps the cruellest Beecham anecdote features the player who arrived late for rehearsal. Beecham asked his name. 'Ball, sir.'

'I beg your pardon?'

'Ball, Sir Thomas.'

'Ah, Ball! How very singular!'

Or is it beaten by the comment to an inadequate cellist? 'Madam, you have between your legs an instrument capable of giving pleasure to thousands and all you can do is scratch it.' His attitude to women in the orchestra was unequivocal. 'If they are attractive it will upset my players and if they are not they will upset me.'

Beecham's grapeshot splattered singers and orchestras impartially. He stopped a rehearsal of *La Bohème* ebecause the tenor was inaudible. The man was lying on the bed upon which Mimi was also dying. Beecham yelled, 'Mr Nash, I can't hear you. Sing up!'

'How do you expect me to sing my best in this position, Sir Thomas?' said Nash.

'In that position, my dear fellow,' replied Beecham, 'I have given some of my best performances.'

Diaghilev's Russian dancers had no language in which to protest when Beecham upped the tempo on their first London appearance. 'I made the little buggers hop,' he smiled.

'How would you like it, tonight, madam?' he enquired tetchily of a soprano. 'Too fast or too slow?' An Australian soprano had trouble with the score of the *Messiah*, but pleaded that she would be all right for the performance. She said that she had been working hard on the score for months, taking it to bed with her every night. 'In that case,' he reassured her, 'I'm sure we shall have an immaculate conception.'

However, from the hero of Dame Ethel Smyth's maritime opera *The Wreckers*, which he rehearsed for its first performance in 1909, Beecham had to cope with some of his own medicine. The tenor stopped, 'What's the matter, Mr Coates?' asked Sir Thomas.

'I was just wondering . . .' said Coates. 'Is this the place where I'm supposed to be drowned by the waves or the orchestra?'

Conductors have composers, singers and players as targets: but most especially they have each other. Take Beecham on Von Karajan: 'a sort of musical Malcolm Sargent.'

On Toscanini: 'a glorified Italian bandmaster' and 'Much is made of the fact that he conducts without a score – Toscanini is so short-sighted that he would not be able to use a score . . . but though it is generally known that Toscanini is blind, nobody apparently is aware that he is also tone-deaf!'

On Sir John Barbirolli: 'He has done splendid work with the Hallé since they brought him back from New York . . . a good, strong, north of England orchestra, masculine and vigorous . . . Barbirolli has transformed it into the finest chamber orchestra in the country.'

On Sir Adrian Boult: 'He came to see me this morning – positively reeking of Horlicks.'

Malcolm Sargent: 'Malcolm is an extremely accomplished musician and an incredibly accomplished conductor. I appointed him my deputy . . . take my advice, if ever you appoint a deputy, appoint one whom you can trust technically, but his calibre must be such that the public will always be glad to see *you* back again.' On hearing that Mr Sargent had become Sir Malcolm, Beecham retorted, 'I didn't know he'd been knighted. I knew he'd been doctored.' When Sargent, whose nickname was Flash Harry, had been in Tokyo, Beecham said: 'Malcolm in Tokyo? What was he doing?' 'Conducting,' came the reply. 'Ah, I see. A flash in Japan.' On that same Japanese tour, a news report claimed that a gun had gone off in the audience one night when Sir Malcolm was conducting. 'I had no idea the Japanese were so musical,' Sir Thomas mused.

Edgard Varèse, the composer, made a distinction between European and American conductors: 'In Europe when a rich woman has an affair with a conductor she has a baby. In America she endows an orchestra for him.' Beecham was more sweeping: 'All the arts in America are a gigantic racket run by unscrupulous men for unhealthy women.'

Beecham also kicked around the reputations of composers. On Vaughan Williams: 'I very much like some of Vaughan Williams, for example his *Fantasia on a Theme of Thomas Tallis*. Unfortunately, in his compositions published subsequently he omitted to take the precaution of including a theme of *Thomas Tallis*.' After conducting Vaughan Williams's *Pastoral Symphony* for the BBC he leaned over to the celeste player and said briskly, 'A city life for me.'

On a symphony by Bruckner in which the composer fails to organise and develop an idea: 'in the first movement I took note of a dozen pregnancies and half-a-dozen miscarriages.' On a symphony which Elgar declined to allow him to cut, 'Elgar's A-flat symphony is a large work . . . the musical equivalent of St Pancras Station, Neo-Gothic, don't you know!'

He was sharp with Beethoven. 'The best of Beethoven's music, excepting the first four of his piano concertos, and the third, fourth and sixth of his symphonies is second-rate measured by the values set up by Mozart.' Of the third movement of Beethoven's Seventh Symphony: 'What can you do with it? It's like a lot of yaks jumping about.'

Mozart alone escaped Beecham's sallies. (Poor Stockhausen! 'Have you conducted Stockhausen, Sir Thomas?' 'No, but I've stepped in a lot.') Mozart was the only composer he would never 'misconduct'. 'The only thing that is really important, in playing, in conducting – yes, even in misconducting – is this. Whatever you do, do it with conviction.'

Beecham also had it in for harpsichords. 'The harpsichord sounds like two skeletons copulating on an iron roof – in a thunderstorm.'

In the course of a diligent research for our Beecham play I asked Leonard Bernstein if he had any suitable stories. 'Not really,' he told me. 'We had a dressing room together once at the Met. We were sharing a ballet programme. He was extremely kind to me – but that's not really what you want, is it?'

Beecham's second wife was the pianist Betty Humby. After she had rehearsed a piece in the Fairfield Halls in Croydon, Beecham saw two stage hands arrive to move the piano offstage. 'Don't bother,' he told them. 'After that performance it will probably slink off.'

Lady Beecham died while they were touring in South America. On his return he met an old friend who had not heard the news. He enquired, 'How's Betty?'

'On tour,' said Sir Thomas, 'with Vaughan Williams.'

At lunch to celebrate his 70th birthday, telegrams were read out. Each was received with loud applause, especially those from the great surviving composers who included Strauss, Sibelius and Stravinsky. Maintaining his reputation for waggery Beecham waited until the final round had died down and then asked hopefully, 'Nothing from Mozart?'

**BEERBOHM**, Sir (Henry) Max(imilian). A writer, critic, dramatist and caricaturist, Max Beerbohm was also a sly wit. In 1909 he attended George Meredith's memorial service in Westminster Abbey. As he left, a girl mistook him for J.M. Barrie and asked for an autograph.

'A devil rose up in me,' he recalled, 'and I did not resist. I wrote, "Aye, lassie, it's a sad day for us all the noo, JMB."'

**BEHN**, Mrs Aphra. Mrs Behn was a playwright and novelist who claimed to be the first woman in England to earn her living by her pen. Born in the West Indies, the scene of her first novel *Oroonoko,* she packed into a full life marriage to a Dutch captain, spying in the Netherlands, imprisonment for debt, and fifteen plays which matched those of her male contemporaries in coarseness. During her spying career, one of her many affairs was with John Hoyle, variously described as 'an Atheist, a sodomite professed, a corrupter of youth and a blasphemy of Christ'.

**BENCHLEY**, Robert. Robert Benchley's careers were many but not terribly various. Critic, Algonquin wit, revue actor, screenwriter and performer, most of all he was quotable, and like so many other quotable souls, if a quote lacked the credentials of a father or mother it was often fostered onto Benchley. When he shared an office with Dorothy Parker he said, 'One cubic foot less of space and it would have constituted adultery.'

A favourite Benchley anecdote recalls a first night on Broadway and the critic of the *New Yorker* bored to distraction. On the empty stage a telephone rings. Heading for the exit, Benchley mouths, 'I think that's for me.' He had a running battle with *Abie's Irish Rose.* In a summary re-review early on he wrote: 'In another two or three years, we'll have this play driven out of town.' Later this changed to: 'We understand that a performance of this play in modern dress is now underway.' The simple quote 'Hebrews 13:8', if followed up, revealed 'Jesus Christ, the same yesterday and today and forever.'

Benchley's limited patience produced a scatter-shot of dismissives: 'People laugh at this every night, which explains why democracy can never be a success.' 'Just about as low as good clean fun can get.' 'The kind of comedy you eat peanuts at.' 'Don't ask.' 'And that, my dears, is how I came to marry your grandfather.'

Faced in New York by a 'pidgin'-speaking character, Nubi, a gypsy waif in a melodrama *The Squall,* Benchley pounced on her line, 'Nubi good girl. Nubi stay?' and answered it with his brief notice: 'Benchley bad boy. Benchley go.' However, the play managed an eight-month run, thanks to the producer, Richard Maney, who advertised regularly in the *New York Times* that *The Squall* was 'the play that made a street walker out of Robert Benchley'.

One of Benchley's most famous comments has had a new lease of life lately. I was talking to his grandson, Peter Benchley, who engagingly calls his block-busting bestseller *Jaws* 'the fish book', about the remark attributed to his grandfather: 'Get me out of this wet raincoat and into a dry martini.' Peter Benchley testified that Robert did not say it: it was put about by a PR man. Benchley Sr felt he was able to manage his own witticisms and resented that impostor.

However, Peter Benchley offered: 'You know the Coolidge story?' This has the President dead, Benchley Sr reporting the news to Dorothy Parker and Parker saying, 'How did they know?'

Peter Benchley was driving with his grandmother long after her husband's death. By now, though still a very proper old lady, she drifted in and out of senility. Suddenly she sat up in her seat at the back of the car and lucidly insisted that received versions of that particular story were incomplete. By her account, Benchley arrived with the news and announced: 'Coolidge is dead.' Mrs Parker asked, 'How did they know?' and Benchley capped it with the missing quip: 'He had an erection.'

As a postscript, Alistair Cooke wrote to *The Listener,* claiming that everyone knows that the original remark was made by H.L. Mencken in Baltimore – a claim which Peter Benchley refutes. The jest is also claimed by some for Wilson Mizner. I suppose they could all have said it.

When Benchley moved to Hollywood he found new targets.

'Would you get me a taxi?' he asked a uniformed man outside the Brown Derby restaurant. The man protested indignantly that he was a Rear Admiral in the United States Navy.

'All right,' said Benchley. 'Get us a battleship.'

**BENJAMIN**, Louis. Louis Benjamin worked for most of his life inside the Moss Empires/Stoll Moss group, starting in the mail room and ending up, at his retirement, in charge. He always showed a charming inclination to create his own Goldwyn-esque legends.

A colleague visited an out-of-town production of a play they were considering for the Globe Theatre in Shaftesbury Avenue.

'What's it like?' asked Benjamin.

'Oh, another black comedy,' was the bored response.

'Do all the actors *have* to be black?'

Later he enthused to Jack Tinker about his plans for a new all-British musical, *Windy City:* 'The first all-British musical ever.'

Tinker pointed out that it was based on the Hecht-McArthur

American play, *The Front Page,* that the director at that stage was the American, Burt Shevelove, that book and lyrics were by the American, Dick Vosburgh. Shown Carl Toms's first white cardboard model for the set, Louis's response was plaintive, 'Does it have to be white?'

When I met him at the first night of a particularly maladroit tribute to the great lyric writer, E.Y. Harburg, which nearly destroyed Harburg's reputation in this country, he said proudly, 'When I put up the money I thought it was Romberg.'

On the phone to a BBC executive over one of the many Royal Variety Performances which he staged, he complained that he was worried. The BBC man countered that it was no good asking for more money – the BBC were already paying top whack.

'No, it's not that. I've booked Joe Loss.'

BBC man: 'Good idea. He's 70, he's been in the business fifty years.'

Louis: 'I know, but he wants to bring his own band.'

**BENNETT**, (Enoch) Arnold. Arnold Bennett's copious journal contains a wealth of theatrical gossip. Here are three entries.

*January, 1908:*
I called and saw Vedrenne at the Queen's Theatre yesterday afternoon. Seemed a decent sort of chap, more sincere than the run of them; also he kept his appointment to the minute. He said that in the theatre he thought that 'the author was everything'. I of course agreed. Said he had been paying G.B. Shaw £4000 a year for four years past. And that he took £1000 in Dublin in a week with a Shaw play.

*Milestones,* written with Edward Knoblock, was perhaps the most durable of Bennett's plays:

*June, 1914:*
Edgar Selwyn told us about Alf Woods, once a cheap-theatre manager, thence out of that by cinema, and now one of the chief New York producers. It was he who said that after 1st Act of *Milestones,* 'Who is this guy Bennett?'; after the second, 'No, you couldn't give it me!' and after the third, 'He's got me. It'll never stop running in New York.' He says he *smells* a good or bad play. Showing MS of an accepted play to Edgar, he said, 'Smell that. Smell it. Doesn't it smell good?' Once, when listening to an idea for a play,

he sniffed all the time, sniff, sniff, sniff, and at the end said 'No, that don't seem to me to smell very good.'

*June, 1919:*
Basil Dean said that they rehearsed Shaw's *Pygmalion* for nine weeks at His Majesty's and that in the middle Mrs Pat Campbell went away for two weeks on her honeymoon. When she returned she merely said by way of explanation, 'George [her new husband] is a golden man.' There was some trouble about her rendering. When she had altered it, she said to Shaw, 'Is that better?' Shaw said, 'No, it isn't. I don't want any of your flamboyant creatures, I want a simple human ordinary creation such as I have drawn.' He was getting shirty. Mrs P.C. was taken aback. She replied, however, 'You are a terrible man, Mr Shaw. One day you'll eat a beefsteak and then God help all women.' It is said that Shaw blushed.

**BENSON**, Sir Frank. The Benson legend is compounded of his unique distinction in being knighted backstage during a performance; his long and arduous touring record; and, above all, his passion for cricket. He was an all-round athlete and, so report is handed down, would advertise for an actor 'to play the Ghost in *Hamlet* and keep wicket' or 'Fast bowler to play Laertes'. The Bensons would pick up extras to fill out their companies as they toured. In Scotland they had ordered fairies in advance. Confronted by a group of large women at the stage door – obviously mothers or chaperones – Lady Benson told them to go home and come back later for their kids. The manager swiftly disillusioned her. 'Those are the fairies,' he told her.

The Bensons were great crusaders for Shakespeare with their countrywide tours and their support of Stratford-upon-Avon. With his own athleticism and vitality, Benson often drove his company hard. On one occasion he rehearsed *Macbeth* for seven hours with no meal breaks. When he reached the cry, 'They have tied me to a stake!' William Morrison, a supporting actor, muttered, 'I wish they'd tie me to one!'

**BENTHALL**, Michael. During his long reign over the Old Vic Company, Michael Benthall once had cause to complain that their crowd scenes lacked animation, urging them to mutter something more imaginative than a mere repetition of 'Rhubarb, rhubarb!'

A few days later he had to call the company together again. 'I know I asked you to avoid muttering "Rhubarb!" and say something realistic, but I don't want a repetition of Thursday night when I heard a plebeian leave the Forum crying, "Taxi!"'

There was an echo of this on Tony Richardson's film set for *Tom Jones* when he asked the crowd for more realism as they stoned Diane Cilento's slut. At the rushes, a voice could clearly be heard yelling, 'Piss off, you eighteenth-century cunt!'

**BERLIN**, Irving. Asked to define Irving Berlin's place in American music, Jerome Kern insisted that he had no 'place' in American music – 'Irving Berlin *is* American music.'

Berlin started life in Siberia as Israel Baline. As a boy on the Lower East Side of Manhattan, in extreme poverty, he scratched a living leading a blind singer round the streets of the Bowery, working as a singing waiter and promoting new songs at Tony Pastor's music hall by leading the choruses from the circle. Soon he was writing his own songs. He achieved his new surname when a printer's error revised it for him; Irving he invented for himself. He had always resisted the idea of taking music lessons. As he told Victor Herbert, 'In that time I could have written a few songs.' When he had blossomed with success and 'Alexander's Ragtime Band', George M. Cohan greeted him at the Friar's Club with a speech which would be several stations out of order these days – 'Irving Berlin is a Jewboy who named himself after an English actor and a German city.'

Of his two marriages, the first was idyllic but brief. Dorothy Goetz died of typhoid on their honeymoon in Cuba. He had met her when she and another girl fought to sing one of his songs. Her rival got the song. Dorothy got Irving. His therapy for grief was to write a hit, 'When I Lost You'. When he courted his second wife, the daughter of Clarence Mackay, head of the American Post and Telegraph Company, who disapproved of the match, Berlin had her serenaded from the stage of his Music Box Theater with his 'singing telegrams' – 'Remember' and 'Always'. On their marriage he presented her with the royalties of 'Always'.

She was automatically dropped from the Society *Register* – 'Irving Berlin has no place in Society.' When their only son died, Society said it was God's revenge on Ellen Berlin for marrying a Jew. The Berlins were never fully reconciled with Mackay, even though after his father-in-law's disastrous crash in the Depression, Berlin bailed him out with a million dollars. Years after Mackay's death, Berlin opened a bottle from Mackay's wine cellar to share with a friend.

'My father-in-law,' he remarked, 'would turn over in his grave if he knew that two Jews were drinking his wine.'

He went to that grave pursued by the *canard* that he had a little black boy tucked away in a back room who composed his best tunes. When we opened *Side by Side by Sondheim* at his Music Box Theater (by then Berlin was 89), both Stephen Sondheim and Hal Prince pleaded with me *not* to improvise a joke on those lines on the first night, when many of his family were in the audience.

He was an inveterate plugger of his own songs, and not above sneaking one of them into a Rodgers and Hart show for Belle Baker without telling them and then basking in the spotlight which Ziegfeld swung on him on the first night. The song was 'Blue Skies'. The estrangement between the writers lasted for years. When Rudy Vallee was separated from his wife, Berlin rang him up and warbled 'Say It Isn't So' at him. Vallee poured it over the airwaves.

Reworking flops was another trait. The tune of 'Easter Parade' started life as 'Smile And Show your Dimple' and a fortune was spent launching it. When it failed, Irving popped it back in his trunk of songs and waited. His alternative national anthem, 'God Bless America', started its closet life in 1918 when the composer felt the patriotic song had been overworked. He saved it for two decades until Kate Smith needed just such a number. He gave the royalties to the Girl Guides of America.

In both World Wars Berlin supplied songs and troop shows and took them to the armies in Europe. In London, in World War Two, he supplied a cringe-making 'My British Buddy' and managed to meet Winston Churchill. This classic misunderstanding is authenticated by his biographer, Laurence Bergreen. Isaiah Berlin was supplying Number 10 with interesting information from Washington. Churchill asked to see him at a time when Irving Berlin was in London, lines got crossed and Irving Berlin was summoned. After a couple of questions about American opinion, to which he replied with loyal Republican enthusiasm, Berlin sensed that he was out of his depth and clammed up. Churchill, taking this as another example of a civil servant with infinite ability to express himself on paper and no conversation, ignored him for the rest of the meal.

Perhaps Berlin's greatest musical achievement was to compose the score for *Annie Get Your Gun* and hoist himself high into the ranks of the post-war adult musical as exemplified by *Oklahoma!*. He inherited that song-writing chore when Jerome Kern suffered a fatal heart attack in New York – and displaced Dorothy Fields as the potential lyricist. At first doubtful of his ability to write in the hill-billy idiom, he was suddenly unstoppable. 'There's No Business Like Show Business' was nearly lost when he played it to his producers, Rodgers and Hammerstein, and thought Hammerstein did not like it. Fortunately the next time he played the score without it, Hammerstein asked what had happened to it.

A friend rashly described the show as 'old-fashioned'. 'Yes,' said Berlin, 'a good old-fashioned smash.'

When the show was revived twenty years later, Ethel Merman greeted Berlin (78): 'Irving, you look great. What are you doing for sex?'

Berlin replied, 'Ethel, if you can get it up, I can get it in!'

He was a private, driven little man who guarded his privacy and his copyrights jealously. Towards the end of his life he took up painting. A grandchild, asked at school what her grandfather did replied, 'Oh, he paints flowers.' He became a recluse, frustrating attempts to mount projects involving his songs. In a famous and foul-mouthed phone call to James T. Maker, who, with Alec Wilder, was compiling *American Popular Song*, he attempted to scare them off publishing their chapter on him which they had courteously allowed him to read: Wilder became a 'fucking longhair' because he preferred some of Berlin's other songs to 'Always'. Elected with Richard Rodgers to the Songwriters' Hall of Fame in 1969, he blew his top three years later when other composers were admitted.

'You've just destroyed the Songwriters' Hall of Fame. By opening it up to everybody you have destroyed its exclusivity. I will no longer support this group.'

As his 100th birthday approached there was no let-up in his control of his copyrights. He refused Steven Spielberg's attempt to negotiate with him to use 'Always' in a film. Spielberg, thinking he wanted more money, offered more – and more. Berlin said 'No' again, finally explaining that he was keeping the song for use in one of his own projects. The American Society of Composers, Authors and Publishers had sought to celebrate his 99th birthday with a full page ad. in the *New York Times*. When he heard of the scheme, Berlin had been furious. 'Do you know how much an ad. in the *Times* costs? I pay you to administer my money, not to squander it.' A few months later Morton Gould, then president of the ASCAP board, called Berlin to ask permission to stage a vast charity tribute for his centenary at Carnegie Hall.

'What's your hurry?' he was asked. He hadn't finished teasing. As the day approached, he warned ASCAP, 'You know, I might screw up all your plans. I might die before my hundredth birthday.'

Later in life his habit of working through the night had made sleeping difficult and he had constant recourse to sedatives. Meeting a colleague one day when he was in his seventies, Berlin was asked if he had slept well.

'Yes,' he said grudgingly, 'but I dreamt I was awake.'

Towards the end of his spectacularly successful career he had a Broadway flop *Mr President*. Two songwriters met on the sidewalk outside the theatre.

'Are you in there?' asked one. 'At the Irving show?'

'Yes,' said the other.

'How is it?' said the first.

'It's even worse than I hoped.'


**BERNARD**, Jeffrey. Apart from working with Joan Littlewood as an actor, and as a stage hand at the Royal Opera House and the Old Vic, as well as at many West End theatres – including the Apollo, which was home for the play Keith Waterhouse wrote about him – Jeffrey had other theatrical connections. He was once discussing in The Salisbury the break-up of the marriage of an actress he knew. A friend asked him who the husband was suing – Jeffrey's reply was brief and to the point: '*Spotlight.*' By a curious irony – since part of the play deals with Jeffrey's occasional impotence – one piece of scenery was labelled to enable the set constructors to identify it. The notice read: 'Jeff Bernard. Centre leg. Extra stiffening.'

During the first run of *Jeffrey Bernard Is Unwell*, the eponymous hero took to visiting the stalls bar presided over by 'Mrs Mac', an enchanting bar person whom he had often met in the course of lunch-time race meetings. Once the play had started Jeffrey would settle down to his large vodka and soda and quite often drop off to sleep. At the interval, punters would point him out as a tourist attraction. One night the regular front of house manager was away and a temporary replacement routinely checked the bar before the interval to make sure that all was well. Confronted by a strange, frail figure apparently incapable over his glass, he reacted strongly: 'Get that drunk out of here!' he shouted.

'You can't do that,' Mrs Mac countered. 'That's Jeffrey Bernard.'

'Don't try to fool me,' snapped the manager. 'Jeffrey Bernard's up on the fucking stage!'

When the play was revived triumphantly with Peter O'Toole at the Shaftesbury Theatre, Jeffrey produced a column in the *Sunday Mirror* four weeks before the opening. It described the excitement with which he had attended a preview, the full house, the gales of laughter, the welcome and the vodka and soda he had received from O'Toole after the performance. Meeting him in the Groucho Club two days later, Keith Waterhouse asked him what he thought he was up to. Jeffrey repeated his joy at his visit to the Shaftesbury. Waterhouse pointed out that previews would not start for four weeks.

'Christ!' said Jeff. 'D'you mean I dreamt it?' And he had. And written it up. No so much 'Bottom's dream' as 'Bottoms-up dream'.

**BERNHARDT**, Sarah (Marie Henriette). Sarah Bernhardt's spectacular career needed an early kick-start. She was languishing in some obscurity at the Comédie-Française until the annual ceremony of homage to Molière, when actors measured their popularity by the applause which greeted them as they laid palm fronds around Molière's statue. Sarah was accompanied by her younger sister, Regina, who, in her excitement, stepped on the train of a middle-aged actress. Already nervous, the woman lashed out at Regina and slammed her against a pillar, cutting her face. Incensed, Bernhardt slapped the senior woman's cheek. The actress fainted, the Comédie company was outraged, the spectators fascinated – and Bernhardt, although not yet a success, was certainly not an obscure failure.

Apart from her beauty, her *voix d'or* and her great acting ability, her great instinct was for publicity. Her house was a menagerie of animals, she dined off a skull autographed by Victor Hugo – who added verses to his signature – and she travelled with her coffin on her tours and placed it in her bedroom. When her young sister was dying of TB, she slept in it, giving her bed to Regina.

In the course of her many world tours, Bernhardt played in Turin with the Italian company at the Teatro Carignano. As usual, she largely ignored the local actors, but the actress whom she displaced from her dressing room watched her with particular closeness. Bernhardt was now 37, the girl was only 23. She was Eleanora Duse.

During the siege of Paris (Franco-Prussian War, 1870), when Bernhardt was leasing the Odeon, she converted it into a military hospital, supervising the nursing and encouraging the soldiers. One wounded young lieutenant particularly pleased her and she autographed her photograph for him. They remained in touch and when she went to hospital during World War One for her leg amputation, he visited her. By now he was Commander-in-Chief of the Allied Forces. He was Marshal Foch.

She had been playing in Sardou's *Tosca* before the operation and shortly afterwards received a cable from the Pan American Exposition, which was being held in San Francisco. The director offered her a hundred thousand dollars to exhibit her leg. Her reply was succinct: 'Which leg?' Bernhardt was constantly on the look-out for more comfortable and more efficient artificial limbs. There was in England a very fine firm of engineers who made bits for very large bridges and also exquisite artificial limbs – later they made Douglas Bader's legs. Long before that they had made one for Sarah, which is still in their museum. It was a very fine leg and the actress was delighted – till they sent her the bill. Then she was livid.

'Think of the *réclame*,' she insisted. The manufacturer wrote to the old lady and said that if she didn't pay she would have to send it back – so she sent it.

No two witnesses seem to have agreed about Bernhardt in decline. Perhaps the most vivid difference of opinion is between mother and son – Pamela Tennant and Stephen. Pamela, who had seen Bernhardt in her prime – before her return after the amputation and Cocteau's cry of '*C'est elle!*' greeted the traditional three knocks on the stage – was dismayed to see her at 69 in a wheelchair. Her verdict in 1922: 'An old woman, with a cracked voice ... obscene, struggling in a bath chair, screeching at a world that had forgotten her.'

Her son's view?

'A star-dusted festival, a legend of incomparable romance.'

**BERNSTEIN**, Leonard. Bernstein, a charismatic old cove, loved to dominate a dinner table. After the first night of *Company* (Sondheim's most important Broadway score as a composer so far), his table lavished compliments on the brilliant score. Finally it was Bernstein's turn to testify. He found exactly the right scalpel to twist: 'Another Gilbert!' he enthused.

On another occasion André Previn was among the company. Previn is also an accomplished conversationalist and at one point the table was oriented in his direction. To redress the balance, Bernstein said loudly, 'André, this will interest you ...' He then explained that he had just been auditioning assistant conductors and explained his method – which was to give the candidates a classic piece of their own choice, then a classic piece of his choice and then 'a piece of which no one has ever heard . . . I gave them your *Comedy Overture.*'

Bernstein used to say that all good songwriters were Jewish or gay and he had an advantage – he was both.

**BETJEMAN**, Sir John. The late Poet Laureate's acting exploits are not widely known but he was a member of the OUDS in the twenties and in May 1926 was nearly expelled 'Under Rule 47', whatever that was, though he was allowed to play in *A Midsummer Night's Dream*. A *Cherwell* pen-portrait of Betjeman as an OUDS member records: 'He is the club naughty boy. He could be a poet if he took the trouble.'

*BEYOND THE FRINGE.* The show that changed the face of revue – or rather obliterated it – started life at the Edinburgh Festival when John Bassett, the director's assistant, brought together Alan Bennett and Dudley Moore from Oxford and Jonathan Miller and Peter Cook from Cambridge. After success in Edinburgh they were eventually brought to the Fortune Theatre by William Donaldson, heir to a shipping fortune and subsequently 'Henry Root', and by the late Anna Deere Wiman, daughter of the more famous Broadway impresario, Dwight Deere Wiman.

Somewhere along the way they needed more cash or more clout to achieve a West End theatre and it was arranged that the quartet should audition for Donald Albery, who controlled five West End theatres. Unknown to the quartet, Albery had a false leg and a pronounced limp. He was a tough businessman and the sick West End joke was that the only way to get out of an Albery contract was to offer to race him to the end of the street. At this time the running order of *Beyond the Fringe* included the famous one-legged man sketch – a bad taste audition scene featuring Dudley Moore and an apparently limbless Peter Cook, which did not appear in the show as finally presented in the West End.

The first time they auditioned for Albery, the sketch was in Act One. At the end of the first half Albery had to go elsewhere, and they arranged to audition Act Two later in the week. In the meantime, they re-arranged the running order and the one-legged man featured again. Albery did *not* involve himself in the show and it was only much later that the team heard of his disability.

**BIGGINS**, Chistopher. Faced as an actor/ASM in his early days at the Salisbury Playhouse with the job of pulling back a curtain to reveal a lavish set featuring an alcove equipped for cocktails, Christopher Biggins's opening line, as written, was 'Would you like a drink?'

Unfortunately, as he pulled the curtain ropes from the corner, they swept everything – glasses, bottles, cocktail cabinet – crashing to the floor. Biggins made his entrance with a new speech. 'Well, I was going to offer you a drink.'

At a charity polo occasion at the Guards Polo Club at Windsor the commentator was at pains to explain the finer points of the sport to newcomers. Helpfully he announced, 'In polo we change ends after a score.'

From the stands the theatrically trained voice of Christopher Biggins boomed out, 'Just like in life, dear.'

**BLOOMINGDALE**, Alfred. The store-owning millionaire became a theatrical angel for a short time in his early days. One of his least successful productions was a musical, *Allah Be Praised*. It had failed in Boston, Philadelphia and Wilmington when George S. Kaufman was called in to look at it. 'If I were you I'd close the show and keep the store open late at nights.' The end of Bloomingdale's life was tarnished by the revelation that he enjoyed an extra-marital relationship with a hooker, who beat him. Coral Browne, seeing his wife enter a chic Hollywood restaurant, muttered darkly, 'Oh look, there's Betsy Bloomingdale – thin as a whip.'

**BLUES BROTHERS, THE**. One morning, when she was still in power, Mrs Thatcher appeared on morning television on the same programme as two actors who were about to go out on tour in *The Blues Brothers*. Sarah Greene interviewed the Prime Minister and then said in a 'neat' link, 'And now from one True Blue to another True Blue – *The Blues Brothers*' – who launched into their song.

Maggie (thinking they must be a young Tory band) refused to be hustled away to her car and insisted on crossing to the boys after their number and asking, 'Tell me which Association are you from?' They had not a clue what she meant and stood open-mouthed. One roadie had the sense to say, 'Oh, from all over . . .' and she pottered away so rejoicing happily, 'keep up the good work!'

**BOGDANOVICH**, Peter. The ex-movie critic and momentary directorial *wunderkind* of Hollywood – *The Last Picture Show, Paper Moon, What's Up, Doc?* – Peter Bogdanovich inspired one of Billy Wilder's most acid comments before he hit the doldrums. 'It isn't true that Hollywood is a bitter place, divided by hatred, greed and jealousy,' Wilder said. 'All it takes to bring the community together is a flop by Peter Bogdanovich.'

**BOLT**, Robert. In his autobiography *Just Williams*, Kenneth Williams quoted Robert Bolt on his tendency to embroider an anecdote. A friend later reproved Williams: 'That isn't how it happened and you know it, Kenneth. The man was slightly unsteady and the woman's blouse had come awry, but the way you tell it she was doing a striptease and he was dead drunk.'

Bolt came to Williams's rescue.

'It does sound better as Kenneth describes it.'

The critic was not satisfied: 'It's not true, he's a liar.'

Bolt's answer goes to the heart of anecdotage. 'Yes,' he said, 'but a liar in search of the truth.'

**BOOTH**, John Wilkes. Legends surrounded John Wilkes Booth after he assassinated Lincoln in Ford's Theater, Washington. ('Apart from that, Mrs Lincoln, how did you enjoy the play?') He was shot and buried under the floor of the old Capitol Prison, but like Elvis Presley in modern times, Booth was frequently 'sighted' in the South. The theory was that he had escaped – old colleagues, including a comedian, Jefferson, testified that they had seen him. Ironically, a few months before Lincoln's death, Booth's elder brother Edwin had pulled a young man to safety on a crowded Jersey City railway platform, when the crush pushed him into the path of an approaching train. The boy was Lincoln's son, Robert.

'That was narrow escape, Mr Booth,' he said in thanks.

**BOOTH**, Junius Brutus. Booth was the father of John Wilkes, Lincoln's assassin, and of Edwin, who left a vivid account of his father's approach to his roles.

'Whatever the part he had to personate, he was from the time of its rehearsal until he slept at night imbued with its very essence. If *Othello* was billed for the evening he would, perhaps, wear a crescent pin on his breast that day; or, disregarding the fact that Shakespeare's Moor was a Christian, he would mumble maxims of the Koran.

'Once, when he was about to perform *Othello* in Baltimore, a band of Arabs visited that city to exhibit their acrobatic feats and jugglery. To my mother's great disgust, but to the infinite delight of her children, my father entertained the unsavoury sons of "Araby the blest" in the parlour.

'As a linguist he was proficient, and among his many tongues he acquired some use of Arabic, in which he conversed with his guests, or rather with their spokesman, Budh, whose name suggested consanguinity; "For," said he, "Booth and Budh are from the same root." If Shylock was to be his part at night, he was a Jew all day; and if in Baltimore at the time, he would pass hours with a learned Israelite who lived nearby, discussing Hebrew history in the vernacular and insisting that, although he was of Welsh descent, that nation is of Hebraic origin: a belief for which there is some foundation . . .'

**BOOTH LUCE**, Clare. When Clare Booth Luce's play *The Woman* was produced in London in 1939, she obtained an introduction to George Bernard Shaw, whom she rated the major inspiration of her writing career. Gushingly she confessed to him, 'Oh, Mr Shaw, if it weren't for you I wouldn't be here.'

'Let me see,' Shaw nodded. 'What was your dear mother's name?'

Ms Luce is perhaps most famous for standing back to let Dorothy Parker pass with the remark, 'Age before beauty' and eliciting the response, 'Pearls before swine' as Ms Parker swept through.

**BOUCICAULT**, Dion. Boucicault, a sensationally prolific nineteenth-century playwright, surprised himself by praising Shakespeare. As Boucicault put it, 'Surely great men may admire each other.'

**BOULAYE**, Patti. A charming soprano in *The Black Mikado* at the Cambridge Theatre, Patricia Ebigiwei changed her name to Patti Boulaye on the advice of her manager, a fan of Evelyn ('Boo') Laye. At one point in her pop career, she was interviewed on the ill-fated Birmingham *Pebble Mill* late-night chat show. After she had mimed her song round the studio, she settled down to talk to the interviewer, whose first, entirely straight-faced question was: 'Where do you people get your sense of rhythm?'

**BOW**, Clara. The sensational early Hollywood star was probably most famous as the 'it' girl, and flamboyantly sexy. Dorothy Parker was not impressed by the label: 'It . . . well,' she wrote, 'she had *those*.'

Bow just about made the transition to sound but had lost her following. She began to regard the microphone as her enemy and during one shot grabbed it and assaulted it. She had notorious affairs with, among others, Gilbert Roland and Gary Cooper. Of the latter she said, to explain their break-up: 'Poor Gary, the biggest cock in Hollywood an' no ass t' push it with.' She died in September 1965 watching *The Virginian*, a Western starring Cooper and directed by another of her old lovers, Victor Fleming.

**BRADLEY**, A.C. The Shakespeare critic and commentator, especially known for his Shakespearean tragedy notices, was mocked by Guy Boas in 1926:

> I dreamt last night that Shakespeare's Ghost
> Sat for a Civil Service post;
> The English paper for the year
> Had several questions on *King Lear*
> Which Shakespeare answered very badly
> Because he hadn't read his Bradley.

**BRAITHWAITE**, Dame Lilian. Richard Huggett, Hugh Beaumont's biographer, quotes Lilian Braithwaite, a great exponent of the sharp tongue, describing the lanky Tyrone Guthrie and the neat, petite Binkie Beaumont hastening down Regent Street: 'It was like watching a Pekinese rushing to pee against a mobile lamp-post.' On hearing that a producer was giving cufflinks to the men of a cast and earrings to the women as first-night presents, she sniffed, 'And one of each for the others?'

A friend of Ivor Novello's, she took another friend to see an early matinée of one of his musicals. During the second act the orchestra struck up a particularly romantic tune for the 'big ballad'. Recognising its source, the friend tut-tutted, 'Naughty Ivor! That's an old Welsh hymn.'

'More than can be said for its author, dear,' was Braithwaite's dark reply.

Another Braithwaite exchange capped a condescending compliment from James Agate, doyen of critics, who told her she was the second-best actress in London.

'I shall cherish that,' she replied, 'coming from the second-best dramatic critic.'

Dulcie Gray, after noting her asperity and her sharp eyes, supplies a graceful footnote to Braithwaite's long career. Novello had brought Sonia Dresdel across the Ivy to her table and introduced her with, 'My dear, would you like to meet Sonia Dresdel?' Braithwaite replied, 'No, thank you, dear' and went on with her luncheon. On another occasion, Novello gave her and Fay Compton diamond brooches and she thought Fay's was bigger than hers. Finding them together, she said sweetly to Compton, 'Fay darling, what a lovely brooch Ivor has given you. Can you *see* mine?'

After these two shafts Dulcie explains that later on, when Dame Lilian was playing a small role in the film *A Man About the House* as well as sustaining a heavy once-nightly in *Arsenic and Old Lace,* the film company did not provide Braithwaite with a named chair. Dulcie, the star, had her own name taken off her chair and Braithwaite's name substituted. No mention was made of the gesture, but after filming was completed a huge bouquet of flowers arrived with the message, 'I saw what you did, my dear. With love from an autumn actress to a spring one. Lilian.'

**BRANAGH**, Kenneth. Kenneth Branagh, who has done so much to bring back the actor/manager and to challenge the pre-eminence of the director, has a favourite note from a director which sets a high standard for pretension.

'It was in a rather famous play. There were thirty of us walking around the stage "feeling the space" and he said, "What would be wonderful, when the king and queen come on, is if you could embody the concept of kingship and in a strange way absent yourself from yourself and give yourself a nationhood."

'And so I said: "You'd like us to bow?"

' "Yes."

'You try absenting yourself from yourself. That was when I thought, "Oh God, one of us is pulling somebody's leg here."'

**BRANDSTRUP**, Ludwig. I sold poor Mr Brandstrup short in a previous collection of anecdotes. This is the first opportunity I have had to right the wrong. A Danish correspondent, Hansgeill Rasmussen, gave me the following story:

'Christian Gottschalk was a Danish actor working in Copenhagen at the beginning of the German occupation in World War II. He came on stage to face an audience of German officers, entering with his right arm raised straight up in the air. The young Germans jumped up and lifted their arms in a "Heil Hitler" salute. Gottschalk faced them for a few seconds and then said, "The snow was *that* high outside my front door this morning."'

Mr Rasmussen later wrote to me enclosing a copy of the Copenhagen newspaper *Berlinske Tidende*, dated 10 April, 1940. He had got the name wrong – the witty and courageous Dane was, in fact, not Christian Gottschalk but Ludwig Brandstrup.

Apologies all round.

**BRIGHT**, R. Goulding. Although a successful literary agent, Goulding Bright's place in the history of theatrical anecdote is probably secured by an act of provocation. On the first night of George Bernard Shaw's *Arms and the Man*, the author took a curtain call and was generally received with cheers. However, Goulding Bright, under a misapprehension, thought the florid Balkan soldiers had been a satire on the British Army and from the gallery sent a solitary but very audible hiss.

Shaw picked it up, bowed to him and said, 'I quite agree with you, sir, but what can two do against so many?'

**BRINDLEY**, Madge. The late Burt Shevelove, co-author of *A Funny Thing Happened on the Way to the Forum*, rang me once to ask if I could think of an old actress who could play a small role as an unappealing vagrant in a television film of *The Canterville Ghost*. I suggested the splendid Madge Brindley, wonderful grouchy in aspect but enchanting in conversation, a lady whose greatest success was with Paul Scofield in Rodney Ackland's *Dead Secret*. Burt rang off gratefully. Some weeks later he called again. He could not trace her. He had called *Spotlight* and Equity. They all knew the name but had no record of her. I offered to trace Madge for him – she was usually available. As I said 'Madge', he said 'Who?' I replied, 'Madge Brindley.'

'Was that the name you gave me?' I said that it was. 'That explains it,' he said. 'We've been looking for Myra Hindley.' Neither Burt, *Spotlight* nor Equity had recognised the name of the Moors murderer into which he had scrambled Madge's name. Madge got the part.

She had been a nurse during World War Two and one of the first into Belsen. She appeared regularly on *That Was The Week That Was* in the sixties in small roles and David Frost took to calling her Dame Madge until she pointed out that her local tradespeople were becoming importunate for their bills now that they believed she was a Dame and could afford to pay. Malcolm Muggeridge appeared on a subsequent show and asked if he might be introduced – he, too, was convinced that the honour was real.

The director, Lionel Harris, told a touching tale of Madge. She had come to him after one rehearsal and asked to speak to him on a matter of some importance. She had asked an actor back to her lodgings. She had given him brown Windsor soup, a chop and trifle.

'Yes, Madge,' he said, anxious to know what had happened. 'And then?'

'That's what I wanted to ask you about,' she said.

'Yes, Madge?' He was excited by the unlikely prospect of romance.

'It was very embarrassing.'

'Yes, Madge, but what happened?'

'You don't mind if I ask you?'

'No, Madge, tell me, what happened?'

'I charged him seven and sixpence. Do you think that was too much?'

**BRITTEN**, Sir Benjamin. The edited letters and diaries of Benjamin Britten and the biography by Humphrey Carpenter have revealed most of what there is to be told about the composer and his relationship with Peter Pears and with young boys (blameless).

Reviewing the letters, John Amis remembered once asking Britten why, after the opera *Paul Bunyan*, produced during his self-imposed exile in North America from May 1939 to March 1942, he had never asked Auden for another full-length libretto. Britten answered, 'Well, you see, Johnny, when writing an opera the composer *must* wear his trousers. But with Auden one never could.' Amis guffawed at this and was rewarded by one of Britten's characteristic dismissals: he 'was out in the cold for a year.'

David Hemmings was Britten's famous first boy soprano as Miles in *The Turn of the Screw*, and much admired by Britten and Pears. As they walked on the shingle at Aldeburgh one day the two men asked young Hemmings what he wanted to be when he grew up. 'A doctor,' he said.

'Why', they asked, with visions of an angelic child who wanted to devote his life to the selfless service of others.

Hemmings soon disillusioned them. 'So I can see all those women naked,' he said.

Britten and Pears attracted light versifiers. Michael Flanders sent them sky-high in a revue song in *Airs on a Shoe String*. Their fans were dismissed as 'The Doggy, Doggy Few'; *Gloriana* became *Orgy and Bess*, and the Sweep's cry in *Let's Make an Opera*, 'Don't send him up again!', was neatly transposed to the composer and his favourite singer. All the culprits were out in the cold for ever.

So, probably, was the clerihew contributor to *Punch* who observed:

> There's no need for Peter Pears
> To give himself airs.
> He has them written
> By Benjamin Britten.

**BROADWAY**. The Broadway, curling eccentrically from Yonkers to the lowest tip of the island of Manhattan, was given a suitably lurid definition by one of its most sentimental psalmists, Walter Winchell:

'Broadway, for most of its denizens, is a place to make a living and to get ahead in life by the methods best suited to the talents God gave them. So to the lovely and aspiring hoofer, the fannie-falling comedian, the ukulele player with the special technique and the singer with something peculiar about his voice, trooping the one-night stands in the Southern swamps and Western prairies, Broadway is the Big Apple, the Main Stein, the goal of all ambition, the pot of gold at the end of a drab and somewhat colorless rainbow. To those who have struggled their way to Broadway and have played for a brief while before its glittering lights and to Broadway's applause – and have lost, or slipped out of, popular favor – it is a tragedy of hope.

'It is a place where actresses and chorus girls, good actors and ham actors, talented people and untalented people, are out of work for long stretches at a time, where poverty stalks in tarnished tinsel, and where competition is perhaps crueller and more cut-throat in its methods than in any other place in the world.'

**BROOKFIELD**, Charles. Charles Brookfield was a Victorian actor, a companiable club man and a raconteur who charmingly invented an appropriate conclusion for his obituary: 'Never a great actor, he was invaluable in small parts. But, after all it is at his club that he will be most missed.'

**BROOKS**, Mel. Interviewer: What do you think of critics?

Brooks: They're very noisy at night. You can't sleep in the country because of them.

Interviewer: No, I said critics, not crickets.

Brooks: Oh, critics! What good are they? They can't make music with their hind legs.

**BROWNE**, Coral. Behind her classic beauty, her famously acerbic wit and her acting skill, Coral Browne was a woman of infinite loyalty and kindness which she worked hard to conceal.

She was born in Melbourne in 1913 and arrived in England in 1934, having had considerable success at home in commercial plays since her debut at seventeen and some encouragement from Sybil Thorndike, who saw her during an Australian tour. By the time the 21-year-old reached England, Sybil had uncharacteristically forgotten the encounter and Coral's first English engagement was as understudy to Nora Swinburne, who had to warn her to restrict her forthright vocabulary when she invited her to stay with her parents.

Coral's reputations as actress, beauty and shocking wit ran together through her long career. She referred to an early admirer, Firth Shepherd, a successful impresario, as 'Firth is my Shepherd, I shall not want . . . he maketh me to lie down . . .'

She could cast a jaundiced eye on a boring player – 'like acting with half a hundredweight of condemned veal' or a busy one – 'like watching a rat up a rope'. She went to Russia with an RSC *King Lear* and asked the management if there was not a role for her husband, Philip Pearmain, then still an actor.

'Nothing suitable', she was told. She demanded a script and, riffling through it, found the page she was looking for.

'There you are,' she said triumphantly. 'The perfect part: "A camp near Dover."'

I once entertained a young visitor from South Africa who had been sent to me with a letter of introduction. I was innocently giving him dinner and a few pointers about the London scene, when Coral and Jill Melford came into the restaurant. As we left, we went across to say good evening. The young man was extremely handsome and after presenting him there was an awkward pause as they looked him up and down. To fill the the gap I explained, 'He's just arrived from South Africa this morning.'

'Oh, I see,' said Coral briskly. 'Got the trip wires out at Waterloo Station again, have we?'

Between marriages, Coral arrived at the Old Vic one day for rehearsals of *A Midsummer Night's Dream* with a new company. She spotted an attractive member of the troupe, not known as a ladies' man, made enquiries and was told she was unlikely to score. Fired by the challenge, she bet a pound that she could bring it off and her informant was somewhat disappointed to see her leave rehearsals with the young man. Next morning he rushed across to find if he had won his wager. Coral was straightforward.

'I owe you seven and six,' she said. She showed the same frankness when commenting on a spring and winter romance between Jill Bennett and Sir Godfrey Tearle: 'I could never understand what he saw in her,' she drawled, 'until I saw her eating corn on the cob at the Caprice.'

One of her most famous screen appearances was as herself in Alan Bennett's screenplay, *An Englishman Abroad,* in which the RSC took *Hamlet* to Moscow, as a result of which she met Guy Burgess. The television film was a huge success and everybody who worked on it was thrilled with the awards it got in England. When it was shown in America, the reaction was equally enthusiastic. Coral attended a Hollywood party at which an indifferent writer came up to congratulate her: 'I loved your performance,' he cooed, 'and I thought Alan was superb . . . and John's direction was just exquisite . . . the only thing that worried me just a little, just a little, was the quality of the writing.'

'The quality of the writing?' she exploded. 'You couldn't write fuck in the dust on a Venetian blind!'

She was infectiously scathing when the Queen of Spain visited her after a performance of *The Right Honourable Gentleman* at the Haymarket, insisting that *she* had had to provide for the reception a bar full of drink, and that her co-stars, whom she adored, had supplied no more than a lemon in Anna Massey's case and a half a bottle of tonic water in Anthony Quayle's – '. . . and the next night he came in to ask if there was any left'. I sent her a half of tonic and a lemon on first nights for some years after that.

She had a classic row with Tony Walton about a red costume in Anouilh's *The Rehearsal;* and when, confronted by the scenery as she walked the stage on arriving in Brighton to commence the pre-London tour, she surveyed a dinky French castle on the backdrop she muttered, 'Château? Shithouse!' There was, of course, a vulnerable, nervous side under the brash, assured exterior. When she appeared (live) as a guest on *TW3,* she copied her first line onto her immaculately manicured finger-nails and then her hand shook so violently that she could not read it.

Her autumnal romance with Vincent Price was aided and abetted by Diana Rigg, who also starred in *Theatre of Blood,* the film on which they met. When they ordered a bed at Harrods, the assistant told them it would take three months to deliver. Coral fixed him with a basilisk stare and demanded: 'Just look at us. D'you think we've got that long?'

Her acting was sometimes inhibited by the careful presentation of a façade through which she seemed reluctant to break – perhaps inhibited by the polite London theatre scene to which she first arrived. But she was a memorable Gertrude – Judi Dench, playing the part years later, found it hard to rid her mind of Coral's cadences; and Coral probably regretted publicly prophesying that in Lady Macbeth's letter scene, the diminutive Judi would make it 'the postcard scene'. She was certainly proved wrong.

She kept innumerable glossy commercial vehicles afloat in the forties and fifties and, particularly in later life, found a new theatrical bravery – a robust Emilia; a funny, lovelorn Helena; a tremendous, raw Mrs Warren; and the infinitely touching Mrs Hargreaves (Alice's original) in the film *Dreamchild.*

*Alice in Wonderland* is a far cry from her battle with another taxi-hailer. As she settled into her seat, her rival for it remonstrated with the driver. The driver was on Coral's side: 'I think,' he said, 'the lady hailed me first.'

'Which lady?' asked the man.

'This fuckin' lady,' announced Coral, as they drove off.

Her devotion to Vincent and his to her were special. I remember her receiving for him, an immaculate, dressing room wife, as he played his successful Oscar Wilde one-man show in New York; and I last saw them together, more frail, but touchingly supporting each other, at a BAFTA Hollywood garden party a few years later. Coral Browne stories will live on. In time, some will be ascribed to other actresses, but *I* shall remember the *onlie begetter* with love.

She was sometimes shocked by her own sharpness. She seemed embarrassed when told that a remark about Anna Massey's near-absence of chin had got back to its subject. And she asked me to cut one story from some pages I sent her for the first editon of this book because she thought there might be legal action. However, now that the showbiz journalist and *Hollywood Reporter* mainstay, Radie Harris, has joined the Great Green Room in the sky it can be told.

Ms Harris had two great claims to fame. She had only one leg and she claimed to have passed one night of passion with Clark Gable. In later life she was often surrounded by a court of young sycophants to such an extent that Coral, entering a party to find Radie so attended said sharply, 'Oh, look, there's Radie Harris with all New York at her foot.'

Another one that got away is Coral's appearance in Robert Aldridge's film of *The Killing of Sister George*. In a steamy scene she was scripted to go down on Childie, the girl played by Susannah York. Aldridge, fearing that the actress might baulk, called her into his office to ask if there were any objections. If so, would she please voice them now. He did not want any embarrassing trouble on the set. Coral's reply was unequivocal; 'I'll eat through the mattress if you don't say cut.'

**BROWNE**, Irene. Towards the end of Irene Browne's long career she appeared as the Duchess of Berwick in Noel Coward's musical *After the Ball*, adapted from Wilde's *Lady Windermere's Fan*. It was an unhappy production. One cause of Ms Browne's particular unhappiness was her lack of critical attention on the pre-London tour, which was in sharp contrast to that lavished on an enchanting and ethereal young singer-dancer, Patricia Cree. She saw her chance of revenge one night in Bristol when Miss Cree was late and kept the stage waiting. When they came off-stage she bore down on her in such a fury that Vanessa Lee, one of the two leading ladies, intervened. 'Don't hit her, Irene,' she pleaded, 'she's as thin as a match.' 'Precisely,' was the reply. 'She should be struck and thrown away!'

**BRYANT**, Michael. One of Michael Bryant's biggest successes in a distinguished career – in recent years, most of them at the National Theatre – was as Badger in Alan Bennett's version of *The Wind in the Willows*. However, he was reluctant to throw himself into the choreographer's classes, which were designed to endow the animal characters with animal movements. Eventually, she thought she had made a breakthrough when Bryant asked if he could take home some videotapes of badgers in the wild which she had mentioned. Returning the tapes the next morning, he thanked her and said, 'I've watched those tapes and, you know, it's an extraordinary thing – all badgers seem to move like Michael Bryant.'

**BULL**, Peter. Peter Bull, accomplished raconteur and essayist as well as actor, played Pozzo in Peter Hall's original English production in the 1950s of *Waiting for Godot*. His mother, Lady Bull, attended a matinée with her elderly lady companion. Going round afterwards, she found it hard to pay a compliment. Finally she was reduced to 'Gladys thought the brass-work in the stalls was beautifully polished.'

Perhaps Bull's finest acting hour was as Pozzo. He has recorded the anger of some early audiences, who punctuated the play with cries of 'Rubbish!' 'It's a disgrace!' 'Disgusting!' and, on one regrettable occasion, when a fight broke out, 'Balls!' One exchange between the tramps, Hugh Burden and Peter Woodthorpe, ran: 'I'm happy' to which the other replied, 'I am happy too,' which provoked, 'Well, I'm bloody well not!' from a man in Row F, who then addressed the audience: 'And nor are you. You've been hoaxed like me.'

Hugh Burden averted the seemingly inevitable brawl by saying quietly, in a lull, 'I think it's Godot,' restoring the house to good humour and giving the front of house staff a chance to remove the angry offender.

In another *Waiting for Godot* incident, Bull had to go on acting after overhearing the dismaying comment from a woman in a front row stalls seat: 'I do wish the fat one would go away.'

**Burton**, Richard. John Osborne had an endearing Burton story. Someone suggested that Burton be invited to head a Welsh National Theatre Company. A leading figure in the principality asked what his qualifications were and it was explained that he had played Henry V at Stratford and a Hamlet at the Old Vic which had been applauded by Winston Churchill. The reply was discouraging.

'Yes, but what has he done in Wales?'

Directing the young Burton in *The Lady's Not for Burning,* John Gielgud said, 'I never had to tell him anything at all, except not to yawn so much when he wanted his lunch.' Gielgud had seen Burton's first Hamlet when the actor was suffering from a cold, and muttered: 'I'll come back when you're better . . . in health, I mean, of course!'

**Byron**, H.T. Byron, a Victorian dramatist, once spent a flea-infested night in theatrical lodgings. In the morning he paid his bill and complained vigorously as he left. The landlady protested that she had never had any complaints before – 'There isn't a single flea in the house.' 'No, you're quite right,' Byron said. 'They're all married with large families.' (The comic Fred Leslie sometimes shares the credit for this response.)

# — 𝒞 —

**CAMPBELL** (née Tanner), Mrs Patrick (Beatrice Stella). Mrs Campbell was a rogue artist, a woman of legend and of legendary performances and legendary insults. Her first celebrated appearance was in Sheridan Knowles' *The Hunchback* in 1890, but Dame May Whitty, an exact contemporary, recorded the earlier sensation Mrs Pat – 'an odd name' – caused at the Adelphi in a disastrous melodrama, *The Trumpet Call* when, on the first night, her skirt fell off. She gathered it up with great self-possession and played the rest of the scene as if nothing amiss had occurred. She went on to create two leading Pinero roles, *The Second Mrs Tanqueray* and *The Notorious Mrs Ebbsmith*. She was Forbes Robertson's Juliet, Magda in Sudermann's *Heimat* and played Melisande in French to Bernhardt's Pelleas at the Coronet in Notting Hill Gate – playing a teasing trick on Sarah by putting a real fish into her hand in a critical scene. Bernhardt adored her.

Sir John Martin Harvey has reported her appearance in a Lyceum *Hamlet*, where her Ophelia was not well received. An old member of Irving's staff, proud of his distant connection with her, would always call her 'my cousin' but after the débâcle he modified it: 'She's only my *second* cousin, you know.' Henry Arthur Jones, the playwright who did not always manage his 'H's, once read her a play – as was the custom – to be met with the verdict, 'It's very long, Mr Jones, even without the aitches!' When she was nearly fifty, Shaw wrote *Pygmalion* for her.

She was a gold mine of put-downs. Asked why Tallulah Bankhead was such a success in London, she said, 'She's always skating on thin ice – and the British public wants to be there when it breaks.' She is supposed to have said, about Oscar Wilde's sad predicament – 'What do I care as long as they don't do it in the street and frighten the horses?' Opening a present sent by a fan, she found it was a hideous vase. She read the inscription on the base: 'Made in Czechoslovakia'. Casting it to the floor, she intoned, 'Smashed in Belgravia!'

She famously referred to marriage as the deep calm of the double bed after the 'hurly-burly of the *chaise-longue*' and she was probably the originator of a phrase which has been endlessly plagiarised, often by her. As it goes, Lillian Braithwaite was playing in Ivor Novello's *Party* a role undeniably based on Mrs Pat. Mrs Pat was about to visit the provinces. When they met, Mrs Pat 'throaty and over-articulated' (according to Emlyn Williams) said, 'Lillian, darling, I hear you are a perfect *tour de force* playing me! And here am I, forced to tour!' She is reported as saying it so often that this may easily not be the first time. Hermione Gingold's revue writers recycled it for Gingold in one of her Ambassador revues in the forties: 'Olivier is a *tour de force* and Wolfit is forced to tour.'

John Gielgud both acted with her and attempted to direct her, in *Strange Orchestra*. She affected not to understand the play: 'Who are these people? . . . Where do they live . . . Does Gladys Cooper know them?' but when Gielgud rehearsed one of Hugh Williams's scenes and suggested that he cut a certain line, she boomed out (at a moment when the company thought she was asleep): 'You know, his whole character is in that line. I wouldn't cut it if I was you.' Gielgud adds, 'Of course, she was perfectly right.'

In her autobiography, Helen Hayes quotes the remark which sabotaged Mrs Campbell's hopes of a Hollywood career. After an enthusiastic reception by the powerful studio head Irving Thalberg and his wife, Norma Shearer, she was invited to their home for a screening of one of Ms Shearer's films. When it was over, Mrs Pat addressed Thalberg: 'Your wife is charming. Such a dainty creature, she. Such tiny hands, a tiny waist, and tiny, tiny eyes.' Thalberg withdrew his patronage.

In London, on Broadway and in Hollywood she was described as a sinking ship firing on her rescuers. Towards the very end of her life, she called on the young author Patrick Campbell (not Lord Glenavy), mounting several flights of stairs to his West London flat to insist that she was losing work because her offers were being addressed to him by mistake.

As she grew older she became ruder, dismissing an American actress who was playing Gertrude for sitting in the bedroom scene with Hamlet: 'Bourgeois,' she told her. Emlyn Williams for his success in translating *Prenez Garde à la Peinture* from the French by René Fauchois into a huge success as *The Late Christopher Bean* for Edith Evans: 'Oh, you poor dear,' she declaimed, 'a *translation?*' According to Williams's account, 'She made it sound like a dirty book.' She turned the knife even more sharply:

'I've got a *spiffing* idea. Why not write a play out of your *very own head*, for a penniless old harridan who can still act? . . . Goodbye, you naughty *cribber*, goodbye.'

Dismissing one rival she said, 'Such a clever actress. Pity she does her hair with Bovril!'

Another of her Hollywood indiscretions was provoked by the well-known actor, Joseph Shildkraut, who, when he first saw her had not heard of her formidable reputation. He asked around about her. Apprised of his researches, Mrs Pat was annoyed. She bided her time until they were introduced. She pretended not to know him and asked his name. It was his turn to be annoyed. 'Joseph Shildkraut,' he snapped. 'Oh, well,' she said. 'You could always change it.'

Mrs Pat's most foolhardy gesture was probably her confession when she carried her dog away from a taxi after it had made a mess on the back seat. The cabbie berated the dog.

'He didn't do it,' lied Mrs Campbell majestically. 'I did.'

**CANTOR**, Arthur. Arthur Cantor, a successful New York publicist, became one of 'Binkie' Beaumont's bankers at H.M. Tennent and then, for a time, controlling producer at the firm. His reputation as an economically conservative administrator was confirmed when he presented Alec McCowan and Emlyn Williams in one-man shows in New York. On the Sunday between the closure of McCowan's run and opening Williams's, the frugal Cantor threw a 'joint cast party'. When he sent McCowan on tour with a stage manager, he suggested that since McCowan got on so well with his colleague he might prefer to fly with him in the economy section rather than be isolated in first class. McCowan thought it would be a better idea to promote the companionable stage manager.

**CANTZEN**, Conrad. Conrad Cantzen's final distinction was not his performances, dignified and professional as they were, but his will. He left $266,890 to the Actors' Fund with the stipulation that any unemployed actor could, by application to the fund, be given a certificate exchangeable for footwear at an established shoe store in Manhattan.

'Cantzen had died with $11.85 in his pockets and had for years worn threadbare but carefully preserved clothes which betrayed his poverty. There was no explanation as to how he came to leave eighteen savings accounts with balances close to $100,000 and $127,000 in corporate stocks.' According to the Actors' Fund biography: 'It was simply there, the sum total of all the meals he had not eaten, the drinks he had denied himself, the rooms he had not occupied on the road, preferring to spend the night in railroad stations, bus terminals or even parks.'

Cantzen's will stated simply: 'Many times I have been on my uppers and the thinner the inner soles of my shoes were, the less courage I had to face a manager in looking for a job.'

**CARILLO**, Frank G. Frank Carillo stands as a footnote to theatrical history, typical of the surviving actor-laddies of the early years of the twentieth century – 'bred in the old drama days' and for some time a member of Fred Terry's company. According to Ronald Harwood, 'short and square, [Carillo] intoned rather than talked, in a deep, trembling voice ideally suited to melodrama and he used it with equal fortissimo both on and off the stage . . . Carillo was like a caricature of an "actor-laddie", except that he was never well off enough to afford an astrakhan collar.' Wolfit cited him as one of the few actors he had ever heard actually use the word 'laddie'. He was voluble and exuberant, with a kind of old-fashioned charm and good manners that he reserved for pretty women; the most lavish term of endearment he could bestow on a man was 'bloody villain!' He had a fund of theatrical stories that always seemed to begin: 'On the Saturday night, in Rochester, when we played as I remember, alas, to only £19 14s. 3d. etc.'

His passions and prejudices were both typical of the profession and of the period. The passions were theatre and cricket, the prejudices a lengthier list. They included homosexuals, 'gentlemen of the Hebrew fraternity' and ugly actresses, who served no useful purpose 'except to play landladies and prison wardresses, and God knows why *they* should be unattractive'. Africans, black or white, were all 'Scotch-arsed Zulus'. Sir John Martin Harvey, whose Laertes he had been, was 'a four-foot ponce'. He dismissed a well-known modern actor's Shylock as 'The finest portrait of a Jewish lesbian I have ever witnessed, but by Christ, laddie, not quite what the Bard of Avon intended, was it?'

**CARPENTER**, Maud. The late Maud Carpenter was famous as the manageress of the Liverpool Playhouse, first under William Armstrong; then during World War Two and just afterwards, when the Playhouse became the Liverpool Old Vic; and finally under John Fernald and his successors. She was a lady of great character and forthrightness, as was her contemporary Lilian Baylis. She lacked Miss Baylis's love of Shakespeare and the classics and was further hampered by an imperfect grasp of the English language: at the end of the first night of a production of Ibsen's *A Doll's House,* in which the part of Nora had been played by Lally Bowers, Maud appeared in her dressing room, announcing herself with the words, 'Lally, I knew I'd seen this play before somewhere when I 'eard that door bang at the end.'

One night, during a performance of *King Lear,* with Abraham Sofaer in the leading role, Maud paused briefly in the wings on her way from her front of house duties to her office back-stage, surveyed the goings-on on the stage with evident distaste, then whispered to one of the actors awaiting his entrance: 'That's what I call 'is Mad Scene.' Then, after a brief pause for further reflection, she added: 'In the old Armstrong days, we joost did extracts – it was quite enough.' In her later years, Maud was once asked by Cyril Luckham if the 'bricks' she was so famous for dropping were intentional or not.

'Oh, my goodness no, Cyril,' she replied. 'I'm a proper old Mrs Molotov.'

**CARROLL**, Sydney. An Australian actor and occasional drama critic, Carroll was co-founder with Robert Atkins of the Regent's Park Open Air Theatre. Taking a call in the (then) vast auditorium with his assembled company, he briefly acknowledged the new turf and then, looking up, intoned, 'Ladies and gentlemen, I want you to know that every sod on this stage comes from Richmond.'

**CASSON**, Sir Lewis. Lewis Casson on 'PQ': 'Edith's got PQ, Sybil hasn't PQ.'

No one (Michael Meyer tells us in his autobiography, *Not Prince Hamlet)* knew what PQ meant. At last someone asked and Lewis replied, 'Peasant quality.'

**CASTING**. The late John Murphy was a casting director for Granada Television. He drank frequently at Gerry's Club off Shaftesbury Avenue. Indeed, on one occasion he drank so successfully that he fell asleep in the lavatory and found himself locked in for the night. The event gave Keith Waterhouse the idea for the predicament of Jeffrey Bernard in *Jeffrey Bernard is Unwell,* but in Murphy's case, he phoned Gerald Campion, who was on the premises, to let him out within minutes. On another occasion Murphy was drinking in Gerry's when he spotted an actor and went across to congratulate him.

'You were very good at the National,' he enthused.

'I'm sorry, Mr Murphy, I've never worked at the National.'

'I know I've seen you somewhere. Maybe it was the RSC?'

'I've never been with the RSC either, Mr Murphy.'

'I know I've seen you somewhere. Where have you been working?'

'To tell you the truth, Mr Murphy, I haven't had a job for years. I've been working on the bacon counter in the Food Hall at Harrods.'

'That's where I saw you! You were fantastic!'

My friend Desmond O'Donovan was once casting for a Wole Soyinka play at the Royal Court. He interviewed the clever West Indian actor Calvin Lockhart, who was later to have a successful career in films. Desmond expounded on the theatre's keenness to work with black actors. A black Hamlet, Peer Gynt, Uncle Vanya, why not?

'Where do you come from?' he asked Calvin.

'The West Indies.'

'Oh, what a pity. This is an African play.'

**CECIL**, Jonathan. Jonathan Cecil, a busy actor with a special gift for silly-ass comedy, is the son of Sir David Cecil. While he was a child in Oxford he appeared as a fairy in a New College production of *A Midsummer Night's Dream*. Interviewed by an enterprising *Oxford Mail* reporter, he was asked what he wanted to be when he grew up.

'An aesthete, like Daddy,' was the reply.

There is, perhaps, an echo of the young Stephen Tennant's answer when his father asked him what he intended to be in later life. 'A great beauty, sir.'

**CHANEL**, Coco. Alan J. Lerner and André Previn misconceived the idea of making a musical out of the life of the great French dress designer Coco Chanel. She was delighted with the casting. She was to be played by Hepburn. She thought Audrey. They thought Kate. Although the show failed, there had been a great deal of romance in her life. Of the many men to whom she was mistress, the Duke of Westminster was the most famous between the wars. During World War Two she had an affair with a senior German officer. When hostilities ceased she was accused of collaborating. She answered the charge fiercely, 'My heart is French; but my cunt is international.'

**CHAPLIN**, Sir Charles. One of Chaplin's more bizarre adventures happened because of his untidy love-life. He was staying at a New York hotel and feared the interruption of a process server with a writ. He rushed out of the hotel and hailed the first passing taxi, telling the cabbie to drive him round and round Central Park. After some hours, the driver complained that he had a home and family to go to and asked what it was all about. Chaplin revealed his identity and his predicament, whereupon the driver took him up to the Bronx and put him into a bed with his sleeping son. When Chaplin woke, the boy had gone to school and the cabbie to work. The startled wife offered a cup of coffee, which Chaplin rejected. He then left to find a crowd of kids outside yelling, 'Charlie! Charlie!' He did not escape the writ.

The final years of Chaplin's life were passed in aged vagueness, but in his last film, *The Countess from Hong Kong*, he directed not only Marlon Brando and Sophia Loren but also the fine English light comedian and *farceur*, Patrick Cargill. Cargill had no happy memories of the experience. Chaplin acted out his entire scene for him in front of the crew, raising great gusts of laughter with his hilarious inventions. Then he told Cargill to play the scene for the cameras, and repeatedly stopped and criticised him for not garnering the laughs as he had done. It says much for Cargill's impeccable comic technique that his performance is funny in the final cut.

**CHARKE**, Mrs Charlotte. Mrs Charke was the daughter of Colley Cibber and one of the most eccentric actresses of her day. Her husband's violent behaviour drove her onto the stage, where she loved to play male roles, including a notable Macheath at the Haymarket in 1745. She has recently acquired a responsible biographer but the legend that clings to her is that she once dressed as a highwayman in real life and held up her famous father at pistol-point.

**CHARLESON**, Ian. Ian Charleson was a talented actor best remembered for his role in the film *Chariots of Fire* and his brave Hamlet at the National Theatre which he played until he was within days of his death from AIDS. At his moving memorial service at St James's, Piccadilly, Richard Griffiths touched a wonderful joking chord, recalling two of Ian's favourite anecdotes.

There was the American fan who waited for him at the stage door at Stratford and asked him about his Ariel transformation costume in *The*

*Tempest.* It had a five-foot-wide collar in which Ian's head nestled like a pearl in a vast oyster shell. 'Was that supposed to represent a sea nymph?' the fan enquired.

'Yes,' he said.

'Well,' she came back, 'you didn't cut it.'

And there was the famous under-rehearsed Stratford *Shrew:* 'Everybody knew their lines but nobody knew when to say them.' After half a technical and no dress rehearsal, the actors had the statutory two hours' break before the first night. Ian and Anthony Higgins made their way separately to Stratford Church and found themselves looking up at the famous bust of Shakespeare. Higgins heard Ian muttering: 'Oh, William, forgive us, for we know not what we do.'

As Griffiths said at the service in St James's: 'Remember him.'

**CHAT**, Barri. Barri Chat, a *travestie* artist *par excellence,* was immortalised by Peter Nichols in *Privates on Parade* and by Kenneth Williams who served with him during World War Two (and with Nichols, Stanley Baxter and John Schlesinger, in a concert party in the Far East) in his autobiography, *Just Williams.*

He describes Chat's enthusiastic exit line to service audiences:

'He took bows with great panache, smiling archly and calling out, "Thank you, lads! Thank you. See you at the stage door. There's more round the back!"' And the invitation seldom went unheeded. Kenneth also quotes Chat on his attitude to make-up. At the end of a show, when most actors take their make-up off, Chat was putting another lot on – deep bronze matt under his upswept blond hair.

'I never shave, dear, never. Pull all the hairs out with tweezers in a magnifying mirror, and rub in cream. Face like a baby's bum, dear. You'd never *guess* my age. We must keep the illusion. Let's face it, lovies, it's life, it's the theatre!'

As a senior entertainer during the war, he travelled as Captain Chat. On waking in the top bunk of a troopship cabin, he dismayed a peppery colonel by showering him with powder as he applied his make-up. The colonel rushed from the cabin, complaining, 'There's a woman in my cabin.' The NCO escorting the concert party was summoned by the ship's captain.

'Are you aware of the morning rituals?'

'Professional players often practise their make-up at seven in the morning. These players are perfectionists.'

'But he's a captain.'

'Rank means nothing to artists. They live in another world.'

The colonel was allocated another cabin and Captain Chat occupied his alone . . . 'We thespians need the privacy, dear. Let's face it, the mask must be maintained. It's life, lovies, it's the theatre.'

**CHRISTIE**, Julie. Julie Christie's sensational screen debut in *Billy Liar* was nearly upstaged by an earlier theatre experience. For a long time during the stages of preparation, she was part of the master plan for *Beyond the Fringe,* in which it was intended that she should cross the stage silently at certain strategic moments. Sadly, this came to nothing. She had had some previous revue experience at the Birmingham Rep., where she sang an unaccompanied blues. According to the local paper review that she submitted for Diana Rigg's book of critical insults: 'Julie Christie should never, ever, be allowed to sing unaccompanied on stage again.'

**CIBBER**, Colley. Colley Cibber has come down to us as a despised re-writer of Shakespeare, particularly of *Richard III,* to which he added the famous line: 'Off with his head – so much for Buckingham!'

In his day, he was much ridiculed as an actor: under the name of Master Colley he pleaded for small parts at Drury Lane. His incompetence ruined a scene he played with Betterton, who demanded he be forfeited.

Donnes, the prompter, who would have to impose the fine, protested, 'Why, sir, he has no salary.'

'No?' Betterton was unimpressed. 'Why, sir, put him down ten shillings a week and forfeit him five shillings!'

**CLAIRE**, Ina. Ina Claire, who died in the 1990s, in her nineties, had been a Ziegfeld girl, a distinguished stage high-comedienne and a stylish supporting actress in movies. When she married John Gilbert at the height of his fame, an unwary film reporter asked her how it felt to be married to a great star. 'I don't know,' she told him, 'You'd better ask Mr Gilbert.'

**CLARK**, Petula. Petula Clark wrote the score for her own musical *Someone Like You* at the Strand Theatre in 1990. The show closed quickly after an uneasy first night. At one point near the denouement, Miss Clark confronted her no-good husband in front of a gaggle of American civil war soldiers. Exasperated, she picked up a rifle and pointed it at him. There was a stir among the troops. The husband squared up and said brazenly, 'Don't worry, she won't shoot.'

A sneaky whisper from the gallery punctured the moment: 'She mi-ight!'

CLIMIE, David. David Climie, the witty revue and comedy writer, was one of the principal contributors to the revue *Intimacy at 8.30* in the fifties. One of the stars was the Scandinavian actress Aud Johansen. Climie waited for days until he thought she was looking unhappy. Then he was able to go to her dressing room and ask, 'Aud, dear, what can the matter be?'

Climie claims to have invented the phrase 'A legend in his own lunchtime' and to have lavished it on the mercurial BBC comedy innovator, Dennis Main Wilson.

To Gary Glitter, entering the BBC club in four-inch heels with a seven-inch bouffant hair-do and a multi-sequined suit of lights, he said, 'Really, you must try to overcome this crippling shyness.'

Another of Climie's word games is culinary. He recalled that in the sixties, avocados were called alligator pears because of their tough skins. By the same analogy, he points out that an over-baked cake should be called a Crocodile Dundee.

CLOONEY, George. When George Clooney appeared in his first play he was visited by his uncle José Ferrer, married at the time to Rosemary Clooney. George had 'acted up the proverbial scenery'. He asked Uncle Joe what he thought. The advice he got was, 'Be very careful, my boy, when you chew up the scenery – you never know where it's been.'

CLUNES, Martin. Before Martin Clunes sprang to stardom with Neil Morrissey in *Men Behaving Badly*, he was busily employed as a jobbing actor. One of his roles was in *The Admirable Crichton*, Rex Harrison's last appearance at the Haymarket Theatre. Rex was playing Lord Loam and hating it. He was ill, virtually blind and very unsure of his lines. He also farted a great deal on stage. Martin particularly cherished one exit towards the end of the first act when Rex was steered off stage by Margaret Courtney, playing his wife. They were going in to dine. When another member asked, in accordance with the script, what was for dinner, Rex enunciated clearly, loudly and bitterly, 'A turkey in three acts.'

**CLURMAN**, Harold. In a mood of Stanislavskian earnestness, Harold Clurman was directing Luther Adler, who, using heavy-method jargon, suddenly said, 'Harold, I just don't know what my "action" is supposed to be.'

'It should be perfectly clear, Luther,' said Clurman. 'You want to fuck the girl.'

Adler considered the information. 'Ah, now I understand.'

**COCHRAN**, Sir Charles Blake. C.B. Cochran or 'Cocky' was the greatest English showman, a word he did not despise: 'Many times I have said with absolute sincerity that I would rather see a good juggler than a bad Hamlet, a good clown than a bad King Lear.'

However, this did not stop him presenting the odd indifferent Hamlet – like Alexander Moissi, who played it in German at the Globe in 1930. According to John Gielgud: 'He appeared permanently sorry for himself, crying into his handkerchief in the nunnery scene and finally stabbing the king in the back . . . he was wearing a costume which combined Peter Pan with the Middle Ages and it did not suit him very well.'

Cochran's range was wider than bad Hamlets and good jugglers, though: it embraced any spectacle – circus, drama, rodeo, freak show, boxing match, musical, operetta, foreign importation and, especially, any revue.

Born in Brighton, he apprenticed himself to the great American actor, Richard Mansfield, and weaned himself from an ambition to be a comic. His first boyhood love for the stage had been born of a visit to the Theatre Royal, Brighton where the owner, Mrs H. Nye Chart, presented an annual pantomime. A big, well-upholstered woman, she always took a bow at the end of the show which, on Cochran's first visit, was *Sinbad the Sailor*. According to the theatre historian, James Harding, 'She always wore a low-cut dress and always bowed very deeply.' One evening a stagehand lurched on from 'The Single Gulp', the small bar which used to stand by the wings on the o.p. side of the stage. He made his appearance 'when her bow was at its deepest, and impiously grasped what she so generously revealed. 'Now,' he shouted, staggering back into the wings, a lifetime's ambition achieved, 'Sack me!'

Cochran's early familiarity with the Parisian theatre enabled him to obtain American rights for Mansfield to *Cyrano de Bergerac,* in which Coquelin was making a huge success. Tradition has it that Coquelin played the first act with a huge nose and made it smaller as the play proceeded. No one noticed the diminution when he reached the autumnal, romantic last act. Later (1919) Cochran produced the play himself in England with Robert Lorraine – an artistic success which lost him £8000.

Twice he presented the massive Reinhardt Volmoller, *The Miracle.* On the first occasion, Ernst Stern converted the huge main hall at Olympia into something very like Cologne Cathedral and Cochran commissioned a score from Englebert Humperdinck. The audition of the Russian ballerina, Natalia Trechanova, dismayed the Humperdinck household where it was held – especially Frau Humperdinck. Trailing clouds of perfume and changing immediately into a gauzy costume which left little to the imagination, the ballerina ran the gauntlet of the puritanical Frau Humperdinck, who frowned and clucked and banished her young son from the room. At Trechanova's high kicks, pictures fell from walls, which shook as ornaments tinkled anxiously. She got the part. After she had gone, Frau Humperdinck set to, exorcising her aura from the cottage, whisking in fresh air and changing the sheets of the bed on which she had dropped her street clothes.

When the spectacular production opened, its first-night triumph was not sustained by audiences, in spite of a series of the publicity coups of which Cochran was a master. In 1932, after *The Miracle* had toured Europe and America, he revived it at the Lyceum with Tilly Losch and, as the Madonna, Lady Diana Cooper, the society beauty and inspiration not only of Burlington Bertie ('I've just had a banana with Lady Diana'), but of Evelyn Waugh's Julia Stitch and of Nancy Mitford's Ambassador's widow. Once again, the opening was a sensation and the run a disappointment.

When he tackled revue, Cochran's early rival was André Chariot, a great discoverer of new talent – the popular *canard* was 'Chariot giveth, Cochran taketh away.'

Alice Delysia, the French star, was his first revue leading lady; Tilly Losch, Hermione Baddeley, Evelyn Laye, Yvonne Printemps and Gertrude Lawrence were to follow in his shows. His inspired invention was Mr Cochran's Young Ladies, who sometimes graduated to stardom, sometimes to the peerage and often, temporarily, into Cochran's own arms.

Evelyn Cochran learned to live with his infidelities; in later years she cheered herself up with a court of young girls and with shots of brandy. When a doctor advised her to substitute an apple for each shot, she doubted if she could manage fifteen apples a night. She became an expert at judging how far an affair had gone: 'I know you haven't slept with my husband, because you don't call him Cocky.' And she could aim a lethal shot at her husband or his girlfriend if she felt the liaison had gone on too long. After a Manchester première she inquired of one girl, 'And how is our husband this morning, dear?' In the middle of Cochran's infatuation with Tilly Losch, she pointed to a dirty green baize cloth covering a roulette table and snapped: 'Yes, Cocky, just like your little friend's knickers.'

One leading lady who frightened Cochran off was Mae West, whom he visited backstage in New York after seeing her performance in her own play, *Diamond Lil.* He asked her if she had a new play in the works. She said, 'Sure, I'm writing one.' He asked her what it was about. She said it was 'about this guy. He's a cock-sucker and . . .' Cochran was shocked, 'made his excuses and left'. When he told his protégé, Noel Coward, the story, Coward said, 'I have never heard a plot begin with so much promise.'

Two leading ladies who did provide him with complications were Jessie Matthews and Evelyn Laye. Matthews was co-respondent in the divorce case when Evelyn Laye divorced Sonnie Hale and Cochran was later best man when Matthews married Hale. He then presented her in *Evergreen* . . . Viewing this as betrayal by a man who had been her friend and mentor, Laye refused to appear in *Bitter Sweet* at Her Majesty's Theatre. Peggy Ann Wood had a success in the role of Sari Linden and Laye, regretting her action, was awarded the part on Broadway, where she had a triumph. She took over in London on her return.

Bankruptcy was always just around the corner for Cochran and he was declared bankrupt on two occasions. The second and more sensational hearing was in 1925: his liabilities were a hundred thousand pounds, his assets two thousand. Within two months he applied for his discharge, and when the Registrar granted it there followed the unique spectacle of all his creditors joining in a chorus of 'For He's A Jolly Good Fellow'.

Although his death in January 1951 was macabre – he had plunged into a too-hot bath to relieve his arthritis and did not survive the scalding – he had had an earlier and more amusing brush with death during World War Two. A Turkish newspaper listed his merits as 'a Christian gentleman, a promoter of fox-hunting and bull-fighting and an expert in *les jolies rues*' and went on to regret: 'It is now a full year since we have mourned the death of the grand Charles B. Cochran, and yet his place is still unfilled.'

Cochran wrote to ask the source of the story. The editor replied, 'Dear and Honoured Sir, Before this information we can furnish you with, we would ask you politely to inform us wherein lies your interest in this matter.'

**COHAN**, George M. Cohan stories run a gamut from selfish exploitation through shameless egotism to unsurpassed generosity. The dynamic composer of 'Yankee Doodle Dandy', 'Mary Is A Grand Old Name' and 'Give My Regards To Broadway' was fanatical in his opposition to the early stirrings of American Actors' Equity, advertising: 'Before I do business with Actors' Equity I will lose every dollar I have, even if I have to run an elevator to earn my living.' Equity responded with a front-window sign: WANTED – ELEVATOR OPERATOR. GEORGE M. COHAN PREFERRED. When the strike was won, Equity charitably opened its doors to Cohan and, when he refused to join, made him a life member.

Cohan's gracelessness extended to his work with Rodgers and Hart. Of their Hollywood collaboration on the movie *The Phantom President*, he said, 'If given a choice I'd rather go to jail than Hollywood.' Nevertheless, on their return to New York, Sam Harris persuaded the song-writing team to provide more material for Cohan in *I'd Rather Be Right* (1937). Summoned to hear the score, he listened deadpan – and at the end of the presentation strolled out of the theatre saying, 'Don't take any wooden nickels, kids.'

Cohan refused to write Jewish characters into his own plays, arguing, 'I don't understand them.' However, arriving at an hotel which practised some religious restrictions on its guests, he was refused a room. He rounded on the manager. 'Because my name is Cohan, you thought I was Jewish and I thought you were American. We are both wrong!'

Cohan's generosity is attested to in more than one anecdote. One old Broadway hang-out was John the Barber's. When the proprietor was in hock for a substantial sum, Cohan and a bunch of cronies bailed him out for $1500 for a new shop and said they would take it out in custom – giving him half-tips in the future to give him the feeling that he was repaying the debt. Similarly, in 1909, Rectors, a famous restaurant, suffered first fame and then notoriety from Paul Potter's play, *The Girl From Rectors*. By implication it made the hotel in which it was located risqué, naughty, everything associated with Parisian vice and no longer respectable. Cohan took a five-room suite in Rectors on a year's lease, although he already had a similar arrangement with the Hotel Knickerbocker, and his ebullient presence assured the return of the most cautious customer.

Cohan was also generous in hand-outs, in bringing his golden touch as a re-write man to many sketch artists and in handing up-and-coming performers songs and sketches from his prolific pen. On a visit to London, he stayed at the Savoy and took the entire staff of waiters and bus boys out for a night on the town. Devoted service was thereafter assured. In contrast, when facing an actor in a rage, he turned and snapped, 'Remind me never to hire that man again – unless we absolutely need him.'

**Cohn**, Al. Al Cohn, saxophone player and arranger, had a sharper line in repartee than many jazz men. He defined a gentleman as someone who knows how to play an accordion and doesn't. When a bum tapped him for money at a bus station he hesitated: 'Hey, how do I know you won't spend this on food?' When a colleague complained that his drummer's tempos varied – slowing down with stick, hurrying with brushes – he offered, 'Tell him to play with one of each.' Asked on a tour of Europe if he'd tried Elephant Beer, he said, 'No. I drink to forget.' And to another barman's 'What'll you have?' the answer was 'One too many.'

Finishing an album featuring 24 mandolin players he was asked where it was possible to find so many. 'Well,' he said, 'all day today you couldn't get a haircut in Jersey City.'

**Cohn**, Harry. The Columbia Pictures tycoon, Harry Cohn, was one of the most ruthless and certainly the most vulgar of Hollywood moguls. He started life as a song plugger and always had a good instinct for what the public wanted. His dictum on critics is often paraphrased, 'Screw the critics. They're like eunuchs. They can tell you how to do it: but they can't do it themselves.'

His 'infallible' test for the popular appeal of a film was 'If my fanny squirms, it's bad. If my fanny doesn't squirm, it's good.' Herman Mankiewicz's comment was succinct: 'Imagine – the whole world wired to Harry Cohn's backside!'

His dictatorial attitude to Columbia employees was expressed simply: 'I am the King here. Whoever eats my bread sings my song.' He explained his ruthless drive by a reference to his boyhood suffering. He behaved the way he did, 'So *my* sons won't have to sleep with their grandmother.'

Cohn interfered at every stage of production. Of one writer he demanded 'a speech that every person in the audience will recognise immediately'.

'You mean like Hamlet's soliloquy?' the writer suggested.'

'No! No! I mean something like "To be or not to be".'

When Cohn got wind of a story called the *Iliad* by an author called Homer he scented commercial possibilities and urgently demanded a treatment. Having read it he was not so sure. 'There are an awful lot of Greeks in it.'

Another of Cohn's Goldwynesque slips was to demand changes in a biblical script where the words 'no, sire' and 'yes, sire' appeared. 'I may not be a college man,' he bellowed, 'but I know goddam well that in biblical times people did not go around saying, "Yes, siree" and "No siree".'

Clifford Odets, one of the writers harangued, said quietly, 'We'll fix it, Harry.'

Cohn was a vivid phrase-maker and inspired a few. Hedda Hopper said of him, 'You had to stand on line to hate him' and Elia Kazan remarked, 'He liked to be the biggest bug in the manure pile.'

Bud Schulberg called him 'The meanest man I know. An unreconstructed dinosaur.' Of Cohn's brother Jack, Harry Kurnitz said, 'He's sometimes known as Harry Cohn without charm.'

Cohn had a fair idea of his own popularity, 'If I wasn't head of a studio who would talk to me?' 'I don't have ulcers, I give them.' He took unlimited advantage of his position as studio head for sexual favours, saying, 'It's better than being a pimp.'

Cohn's end inspired one of the great catty Hollywood remarks – generously attributed to a number of other sources on different but similar occasions. At his funeral someone asked Red Skelton why there were such enormous crowds of people attending. Skelton said, 'Give the public what they want, they'll all show up.' (Some credit the comment to Samuel Goldwyn speaking of Louis B. Meyer.)

**COLBERT**, Claudette. Once when Victor Spinetti was in New York, meeting Leland Heyward, the producer, at the Plaza to discuss a possible role, Colbert entered the room. She had met Spinetti once in Paris but came across and was very effusive, insisting that he call her next day. When he did she said, 'Oh Victor, I hope you didn't mind me doing that, only in this town that sort of thing puts your money up.'

**COLE**, Nat King. Nat King Cole was an admired jazz pianist before he became a world star as a singer. In the thirties, however, he found that it was convenient to break up the monotony of an instrumental by the Cole trio with a few vocals. He noticed that the customers usually wanted more. Quite early on a customer requested a song he didn't know. He offered 'Sweet Lorraine' instead and it netted the trio fifteen cents – a nickel apiece. The big spender requested another tune. Again Cole didn't know it. He asked if there was anything else the man would like. 'Yeah,' he said. 'I'd like my fifteen cents back.'

When Nat King Cole moved into a white suburb in Los Angeles, neighbours petitioned against undesirables. Cole found out when the petition was being passed around and asked if he could sign it. He wasn't keen on undesirables either.

**COLE**, Stephanie. Stephanie Cole, a fine actress and a considerable comedienne (*Waiting For God*), got a job in the West End almost immediately after leaving the Bristol Old Vic school. She was employed as an ASM for a play starring Edward Judd at the Comedy Theatre.

At the end of one performance, her idol came through the pass door and said, 'Could you lead me to the Number One dressing room?' This she did but as she approached the door her mind went blank. She heard herself asking, 'What name shall I say?'

Gently he said, 'John Gielgud.'

'Yes, I know,' she said in final confusion as she knocked on the door.

Years later she was herself starring at The Comedy in Kay Mellor's *A Passionate Woman* when Kenneth Griffiths knocked on the door and offered his congratulations.

'Oh, I'm so pleased to meet you,' she enthused. Then she caught sight of Peter O'Toole immediately behind Griffiths. Some panic propelled her into saying, 'And I'm even *more* pleased to meet you!'

She spent the rest of their visit trying to apologise.

**COLLIER**, Constance. Constance Collier's career spanned many years and ended in drama coaching in America. Earlier in her career, in 1895 to be exact, she had starred with Wilson Barrett in his successful play, *The Sign of the Cross,* as the beautiful Christian girl who would end up in the lions' den with the actor-manager as the Roman grandee she had converted to Christianity. Before facing this ordeal, she presented the star with a newborn lamb. Barrett was too mean to buy new lambs and, as the run stretched, the lamb grew into a sizable sheep. Finally Miss Collier buckled under its weight in full view of the audience, earning an unexpected ovation and forcing Barrett to engage a new lamb.

Miss Collier was animal accident-prone. During the West End run of *Serena Blandish,* she had to make an entrance with two greyhounds on a single leash. Mistaking the door for a trap, the greyhounds raced across the stage and through a fireplace opposite. Miss Collier, who couldn't let go, kept her head and ducked just in time to avoid losing it.

**COLLIER**, William. The American playwright and actor opened his play *The Patriot* on 30 December. From 2 January the next year he advertised it as 'Second Year in New York.'

**COLMAN**, Ronald. When he became an enormous movie star, Ronald Colman could look back with equanimity on an early engagement in the West End. In 1916 he had a small part in *The Misleading Lady,* a Broadway comedy starring Gladys Cooper, Malcolm Cherry and Weedon Grossmith. One evening he overheard Miss Cooper in the wings muttering, 'Such a handsome young man. But why does he have to be such a terrible actor? So very clumsy – and those feet!'

**COMYNS CARR**, J.J. Comyns Carr was a Victorian playwright whom Henry Irving commissioned to write a play for him, suggesting King Arthur as a subject. When he finished it, he had to read it to the actor and Ellen Terry – an ordeal similar to those endured by Henry Arthur Jones at Mrs Patrick Campbell's hand and Frederick Lonsdale at Gerald du Maurier's, which are described elsewhere. The theatrical pair arrived, along with Irving's dog, Fussy, who settled on the great man's lap as Comyns Carr began to read. Always nervous at a reading, he ploughed on, never taking his eyes off the page until, half-way through, he became aware of stentorian snoring. Comyns Carr put up with this for a while then 'exasperated beyond endurance, I closed the book with an abrupt announcement that I felt useless to go on.'

Irving was amazed. 'What do you mean?' Comyns Carr accused him of being asleep. Suddenly, all three realised that the snoring had not stopped, and Ellen Terry pointed to the dog, happily sleeping on Irving's knees.

Irving produced the play and Burne Jones designed the Lyceum production, but it was not much to Ms Terry's taste. Her copy is littered with angry notes: 'First entrance *dreadful!*'; '*Not* good'; 'O Lord! When Joe is *not* inspired, he is hidebound and shy. The whole of this page, for instance, is useless.'

On the evidence, Fussy was an inspired critic, whose instinctive verdict should have been acted upon.

Caryl Brahms, Arthur Schwartz and I once played an entire score of a musical to Sir Harry Secombe, who brought along a music publisher friend, Johnny Franz. The session took place in Arthur's drawing room after lunch, which, in Franz's case, had obviously been a good one. He snored loudly throughout, in spite of the occasional subtle hint from Sir Harry, who always referred to it shamefacedly whenever we met. Indeed, his widow reminded me at his memorial service.

**CONDON**, Eddie. In Bill Crow's fascinating anthology of *Jazz Anecdotes* (OUP), many of the tales are of spectacular instrumental feats, hirings and firings and a distressing number of pranks, put-ons and practical jokes. An exception is the chapter on Eddie Condon, who, in addition to playing banjo and guitar, organised record dates, produced jazz concerts, and kept a saloon. More important, he had a caustic tongue and ready opinions.

When asked what he thought of jazz as an art form he said dismissively, 'Canning peaches is an art form.' To a woman with extravagant headwear: 'Is that a hat or a threat you're wearing?'

When the French jazz critic Hugues Panassie gave him a generally favourable notice he commented, 'I don't see why we need a Frenchman to come over here and tell us how to play American music. I wouldn't think of going to France and telling him how to jump on a grape.'

At a party where an Eddy Duchin record was spinning on the gramophone, a fellow guest said, 'Don't you adore Eddy Duchin, Mr Condon? He really makes the piano talk, doesn't he?' Condon replied, 'He certainly does. And what the piano says is, "Please take your clumsy hands off me."'

After working for Red Nichols he commented, 'Red thought he played like Bix [Beiderbeck], but the similarity stopped the minute he opened his horn case.'

His first 'Eddie Condon's' Club was on West 3rd Street. He had special names for employees – the men's room attendant, for instance, was 'Flush Gordon' and his club policy was 'We don't throw anybody in, and we don't throw anybody out.'

He was not a fan of way-out music. When a waiter dropped a tray of plates and cutlery at West 3rd Street he looked up from his drink and muttered, 'None of that progressive jazz in here.'

Asked the capacity of his club at its launch Condon replied, 'Oh, about 200 cases.' His recommended hangover cure was 'Take the juice of two quarts of whisky.' Invited by a friend to dine at a Middle Eastern restaurant he declined politely, saying, 'The aftertaste of foreign food spoils the clean, pure flavour of gin for hours.'

He drank a great deal but held it well, adding this note to one of his record albums: 'A Mr Dewar from somewhere in the British Isles was also in the studio at the time, very welcome indeed, although exhausted at the end of the ceremony.' When his wife compiled a warning list of musicians they knew who had died of liver complaints, he glanced at it and handed it back with the words, 'There's a drummer missing.' Hearing that English hotel guests could order alcohol at any hour of the day or night he announced, 'I'm taking out papers.'

When seriously ill and given a blood transfusion he said, 'This must be Fats Waller's blood. I'm getting high.' The disease was acute pancreatitis. He could take food neither orally nor intravenously. The doctor suggested the only alternative which he felt was undignified. The doctor tried to persuade him that it would be like having drink. At this he capitulated, turning over and saying, 'See what the boys in the back room will have.'

Faced by a fake electric fire in a friend's suite at the Warwick Hotel in New York he suggested, 'It's cold in there. Could you please throw another bulb on the fire.'

**COOGAN**, Jackie. Jackie Coogan was the biggest child star of his day, especially after Chaplin's first feature film *The Kid* in 1920. On reaching his majority he found that his parents had squandered most of his hard-earned money. A 'Coogan Act' to protect child stars was the one good result.

Coogan's hardest money came from crying, which he found hard to do on cue. In Oliver Twist he could not summon up a tear for the line 'My mother is dead, sir.' Frank Lloyd, the director told him to imagine his own mother was dead. That didn't help. Finally Coogan himself had an idea: 'Sir,' he asked, 'would it be all right if I imagined my dog is dead?'

And that was before he knew what his mother was doing with his money.

**COOKE**, George Frederick. Cooke once played Othello to an unappreciative Liverpool audience. As they hissed, he turned on them and yelled in fury, 'So ye hiss George Frederick Cooke, do ye? Let me tell you that every stone of your damned city was cemented by the blood of a negro!'

Cooke drank himself to death in New York. Kean had the body disinterred and reburied in an elaborate monument. He took one of Cooke's toe-bones back to England as a relic and required the Drury Lane company, who had come out to greet him, to honour the bone in turn. He preserved the bone for many years in reverence until, unknown to him, his wife in a fit of temper threw it out of the window into a well. Kean mourned its disappearance, saying to her, 'Mary, your son has lost his fortune. In possessing Cooke's toe bone he was worth £10,000. Now he is a beggar.'

**COOPER**, Dame Gladys. A legend for her picture-postcard beauty in youth and the fascinating map of lines into which her face later wrinkled under Californian sun, Gladys Cooper was most famous in the theatre for her business-like approach. She was her own manager for years in the twenties at the Playhouse but had the most casual attitude to her lines, to the extreme annoyance of playwrights in whose work she appeared later in her career. In 1951 she played in Coward's *Relative Values* in London.

'It's ridiculous, Noel expects me to be word-perfect at the very first run-through.'

Coward complained, 'It's not the first run-through I worry about. It's the first night.' She was more or less there by the time the play arrived in London but not so securely there that she couldn't scramble a line about 'going into the study' into 'going into the university'.

An author's moans were unlikely to upset her. One of her early Broadway plays, *Call It a Day,* was directed by Tyrone Guthrie: 'Even at the dress rehearsal she still carried the book and did not seem to know the words at all. We played in the Morosco Theatre, which is very small and has no orchestra pit and no footlights. A man in the front row of the stalls imprudently placed his derby hat right on the stage. Gladys, making her first entrance, when most are half-paralysed with fright, saw the hat, advanced upon it, spouting her part a mile a minute and, dead accurate, gave the hat a tremendous kick and sent it flying over the heads of the audience into the nethermost darkness of the pit. There was a laugh, and a round of applause, and Madam proceeded with the business as cool as a cucumber.'

Paul Scofield observed a similar talent for staying calm when they opened together in Wynyard Brown's *A Question of Fact* in 1953. Pamela Brown, also in the cast, had already seen the casual approach. Cooper's part started in Act Two. At the dress rehearsal, she approached Brown at the first interval, saying, 'That was lovely, dear. I'd always wondered what the first act was about. Perhaps I should have read it.'

Scofield's reminiscence is of the first night: 'She made her entrance still sucking a Polo mint she'd forgotten to take out of her mouth, so that on her first night it shot out across the stage and she didn't bat an eyelid.'

I 'directed' her in 1970 in a television special, a life of Dickens, whose centenary it was that year. It had a star-studded cast of high-powered cameos and she played a scene as Jenny Agutter's mother: Jenny was playing Ellen Ternan, Dickens's last young mistress. Gladys had about five lines. There were two days of rehearsal. She spent them phoning British Airways about some jewellery which she (or they) had lost on a transatlantic flight.

On the studio day, she retained two of her lines for the first run but was down to one line and four prompts on the dress rehearsal. At the end of the dress, she appeared in tight close-up in front of the camera, her head enveloped in a scarf and said, 'Tell the boy I'm going to the Ritz for dinner with my agent. I'll be back in good time.'

The next we heard was a call to the gallery, which the production secretary took. 'This is Gladys Cooper. I'm at the Ritz. I'm getting into a taxi. I find I have no money. Please have some to pay the cabbie when I arrive.' During her scene she surprised me by getting her first two lines right the first time but needing separate takes for the other three.

Her iron determination must have come in useful at the first night of *The Crystal Heart,* a disastrous camp American musical which opened at the Saville Theatre in 1957. There had already been trouble when it opened in Scotland and a tray of real glass cocktail glasses was dropped on stage just before a ballet for barefoot sailors. Just after Dilys Laye's line, 'What a lovely afternoon!' had been greeted by a voice in the gallery with 'Not a very lovely evening,' Gladys Cooper was required to preface a song about a bluebird with the lines, 'The bird! The bird!' and was promptly given it. She responded at the curtain call with an extra-imperious low curtsey.

Gladys Cooper had one of those nightmare transatlantic flights with a compulsive talker – one version has her trying to study her script at the time, but that doesn't sound too like Dame Gladys. The man kept defining himself in order to get her interest. He listed his credentials all over America, his mid-Western lumber mills, the fantastic jewellery he had bestowed upon his wife, the money he would leave to his children, ending triumphantly: 'And I started out with absolutely nothing – I am a self-made man.' Finally Dame Gladys, her patience (never her strong suit) exhausted, turned and faced her persecutor. 'Which all goes to prove the dangers of unskilled labour.'

She had a very strict attitude to fans. When she starred at the Playhouse in *Enter Kiki* with Ivor Novello, their different attitudes inspired different reactions from their admirers. Novello's film celebrity encouraged his followers to yell 'Hello, Ivor!' at him. His leading lady received the more respectful, 'Good evening, Miss Cooper!' Sheridan Morley characterised his grandmother's reserved attitude to fans as stemming from her irritable puzzlement that 'they hadn't got homes to go to or something better to do with their lives than hang around stage doors'. When her son-in-law, Robert Morley, took tea with one of his most fervent admirers, a Newcastle lady, Gwen Taylor, who had been sending presents to the Cooper/Morley clan for years, her response was cutting. 'You've ruined that woman. She was a perfectly good fan. Now she'll want to be an acquaintance.'

**COOPER**, Jackie. Like his predecessor, Jackie Coogan, Jackie Cooper, child star of the thirties, had trouble crying on cue. Filming *Skippy* for his uncle Norman Taurog in 1931 he had three crying scenes. For the first Taurog raged and ranted at the dry-eyed kid to no effect – only when he brought another child in an identical costume to the side of the set did Cooper, thinking he was going to be sacked, burst into tears.

In the next crying scene, he was with a dog he adored and he was so happy that once again he could not cry. Eventually, Taurog took the dog away out of sight and ordered a shot to be fired. He told Cooper that he had killed the dog and again got the desired effect. Then the dog was restored to the child.

That left the third crying scene and the same subterfuge would not work again. However, Cooper's mother was on set. She did something that no one had thought to do before. She took her son to one side, quietly explained the scene to him and pointed out how devastated Skippy would be at the death of his beloved dog. He started to weep and continued to do so copiously through the scene. No doubt these torrential tears contributed to his Oscar nomination.

A couple in New York took their son to see Cooper in *Sooky*, the quick follow-up sequel to *Skippy*. The boy adored it. He voted it even better than *Skippy* – especially the happier ending. 'But it doesn't end happier,' his mother argued. 'Doesn't Sooky's mother die?' 'Oh, sure,' said her son, 'but in *Skippy* the dog died.'

**COURTENAY**, Margaret. Margaret Courtenay has a secure position as a character actress in modern and classical roles – she was superb, passionate Magnani-like Nurse in a Bristol Old Vic *Romeo* long ago. She is also the repository and distributor of theatre gossip *par exellence*. Once, when she played Lady Bracknell, she had to leave the company to fulfil a previous engagement. A few weeks later she met an actor who had been to see her replacement.

'What was she like?' she asked and before he could answer added, 'I must warn you she's one of my very best friends. I love her. How was she?'

'Well, she was rather good, actually.'

'Impossible!'

**COWARD**, Sir Noel Pierce. From the time of his first celebrity with *The Vortex*, when he was photographed in every conceivable way – 'with my dear old mother . . . without my dear old mother . . . sitting up in bed looking like a heavily doped Chinese illusionist' – Noel Coward was always quotable, even if some of the shafts of wit owed more to his exquisite timing and impeccably dry delivery than to a special sparkle of their own. He was the master of the clipped one-word reply, especially to the over-deferential reporters of pre-war days:

'Mr Coward, have you anything to say to *The Star?*' – 'Twinkle!' 'To *The Sun?*' – 'Shine!' 'To *The Times?*' – 'Change!' 'Mr Coward, can you say something for Australia?' – 'Kangaroo.' 'What are your views on marriage?' – 'Rather garbled.' 'On Hollywood?' – 'I'm not so keen on Hollywood. I'd rather have a nice cup of cocoa.'

From Hannen Swaffer, an old journalistic warhorse: 'Mr Coward, I always say you act better than you write.' – 'How odd. I'm always saying the same about you.' On being told that his accountant had blown his brains out: 'I'm amazed. I had no idea he was such a good shot.'

When Laurence Olivier was made a Master of Letters to add to his other honours, Coward was unimpressed: 'Four letters, no doubt,' he mused. His doctor, Patrick Woodcock, once confessed that he was beginning to suffer occasional lapses of memory – 'lacunae' he called them, rather grandly. Ever afterwards Coward always greeted him the same way; 'Ah! Here comes the Lily of Lacunae.'

Like most notable wits, Coward often suffered the attribution of remarks not of his making. The most notorious was supposedly uttered during the Queen's Coronation, when he is said to have watched the procession with a group who spotted the enormous Queen of Tonga in an open coach, with the tiny Emperor Haile Selassie of Abyssinia. 'Who's that with the Queen of Tonga?' asked one of the party. 'Her lunch,' Coward is said to have replied. He always denied it, not least, he said, because she was a personal friend and she would have been very upset. Others have pointed the finger at Emlyn Williams.

Soon after I first published the story in 1991 I got a letter from the invaluable John Moffat. He wrote that he and Hugh Manning had been playing in Shaw's play *The Applecart* at the Haymarket Theatre at the time of the Coronation. Coward starred as King Magnus.

'. . . A small group of the company (including Hugh Manning and me) had watched the procession from the front of the Haymarket. Later, an hour or so before the performance, Hugh and I were chatting to Noel just inside the stage-door. Noel had watched the procession on television and was impressed and pleased that we had waited all night on the cold pavement. Queen Salote had been the star of the parade in her open carriage waving and beaming with joy in the light, sunlit drizzle. She was a magnificent sight . . . and we are speaking of Star Quality. One of us . . . I can't now be sure whether it was Hugh or me . . . asked Noel, "who was that little man sitting beside her?" Noel (and I can point out the exact spot where he was standing . . . indeed have several times done so during my subsequent appearances at the Haymarket) raised his forefinger and said, "I think . . ." (and here came that little pause for better effect) ". . . it was her lunch." Those were the exact words.

'John Humphrey may also have been present – my memory doesn't serve me well enough – but it was Hugh and I who were initially responsible for the spreading worldwide of the remark and it has constantly come back to me in vastly inaccurate variations.

'Some years later I told Isabel Deane that Coward had said it to me, "Oh, yes, yes, yes!" replied that delightfully ascerbic lady, "Hugh Manning always claims he said it to him." "He did," I said triumphantly. "He said it to both of us."'

A few months later I was talking to Graham Payn, Coward's long time companion. I told him of the trouble I'd had with authenticating the witticism.

'Oh, no!' he said, 'It wasn't Noel who said it first. It was Noel who asked the question. It was David Niven who said, "Her lunch."'

By that reading Coward was not above appropriating Niven's crack by the time he got to the theatre. Flash forward many years and I was doing an after-dinner talk for the Duke of Edinburgh's Award Scheme – a fund raiser. I told the Queen Salote story and caught sight of the Duke gesticulating to me from the top table. I decided not to interrupt the flow but to ask him what was the matter afterwards. When I tackled him he was still chuckling. 'A few years after the Coronation,' he said 'I took *Britannia* round the world. We pulled up off Malaya and I had all the Sultans on board for dinner. It was a very jolly evening. As it was going so well, I thought I'd risk it, I rapped the table and said, "Now come on – who was her lunch?" They all hooted with laughter and pointed at the little Sultan of Kelantan. He said, "Me! Me! I was her lunch."'

Which may not solve the identity of the originator for all time, but gives some idea of how the story raced round the world.

Keen readers will have noticed that the identity of the 'co-stars' was changed from Haillie Selassie to His Highness Ibrahim, Sultan of Kelantan. It was indeed he. A contemporary photograph shows Salote in her coach waving happily. He sits opposite in all the full splendour of Malay Court Dress with silk Baju and ceremonial headdress.

When it began to rain he asked to have the hood raised. This was vetoed by Salote – so he got colder and colder despite having invested in a pair of longjohns at Austin Reed, having been told it would be chilly in the Abbey. He complained sharply that, 'it was alright for the Queen, she was dressed from head to foot in tree-bark.'

Then there is Coward's response to one of his godsons – Richard Olivier – at a time when the Oliviers were living in the Royal Crescent at Brighton, not far from St Dunstan's, a home for the blind. 'Uncle Noel' was strolling on the front with his young godson when the pair came upon two small dogs vigorously mating in front of them.

'What are those two dogs doing, Uncle Noel?' the boy asked.

'The front one,' said Coward instantly, 'is blind and the other one is pushing her all the way to St Dunstan's.'

Clifton Webb, the ex-dancer/revue star and finally character actor, features in a Coward incident – apart from being a major player in a disastrously social Long Island weekend intended as a rest, which Coward remembered in a short story and a barely-produced play.

Late in Webb's life (he was already over 70) his mother, Mabel, died. He was distraught. Coward was privately unsympathetic. 'Well over ninety and gaga ... it must be tough to be orphaned at seventy-two.' However, he called Webb long-distance to give his condolences, to be met with floods of tears. 'Clifton, if you don't stop crying, I shall reverse the charges.'

Actresses who hadn't done their homework were a frequent target – he himself liked to come to first rehearsal word-perfect.

'Will you call me, Noel?' said one. 'I certainly will – many things.'

'I knew my lines backwards last night.' 'That's the way you're saying them this morning.'

'If you go on like that, Noel, I shall throw something.' 'Why not start with my cues?'

'Why did she become an actress?' 'She didn't.'

John Osborne has recalled a sad little occasion when he was called to Nottingham to see the Royal Court Company trying out Coward's translation of Feydeau's *Look After Lulu (Occupe toi d'Amélie)*. Tony Richardson, who was directing, said, 'You've got to come up. Noel's determined to be witty. All the time.' The signature of Coward's immediately recognisable dialogue was blurring the message of Feydeau's impeccable clockwork farcical construction. However, when they had dinner, it was another subject which Coward wanted to tackle. 'His second or third question was, "How queer are you?" A baffled depression came over me. I felt that both of us deserved better than this. "How queer are you?" The fatuous game was afoot and I played it feebly. "Oh, about thirty per cent." "Really," he rapped back, "I'm ninety-five."'

Osborne was happier with Coward's earlier dictum that 'Work is so much more fun than fun.'

As he grew older, Coward claimed – now an oft-repeated line – that the first thing he did each day was to turn to the obituaries in *The Times*, check to see if he was still alive, and then proceed to enjoy his day.

In 1955 Philip Hoare published the definitive biography of Coward. He reveals a much grander family tree than that to which Coward admitted. It includes Admirals in the early part of the nineteenth century. And he goes into more details of his sexual activity. There were significant early meetings with Robby Ross, Siegfried Sassoon, Scott Moncrieff and Edmund Gosse, a parson who patted him on the knee in a railway carriage and gave him sixpence, and the liaison with Prince George, Duke of Kent. After the Duke's death in a plane crash his cousin the Marquess of Carisbrook told Coward cattily 'You know, of course, Noel, that you can now never be the Dowager Duke of Kent.'

Hoare sets out the limits of Coward's sexual predelictions. 'A revulsion against penetrative sex remained with Coward all his life.' This has the ring of truth. I once entertained a guardsman in the early sixties. 'Have you heard of a bloke called Noel Coward?' he asked. I had. The guardsman had visited him the week before. 'Nice old boy,' was his verdict. 'Only likes the schoolboy stuff.'

There is a sad vignette of Coward towards the end of his life, sitting in the William IV, a gay pub in Hampstead, wearing a little Tyrolean hat. Spotting a nineteen-year-old youth, he said, 'Of course, you know who I am?' 'I hadn't the foggiest,' the boy later confessed. He said, 'I'm the man who wrote *Bittersweet*,' which didn't mean anything to him either.

Another piece of Coward legend came my way recently. It may be apocryphal but it has the ring and speed of a genuine Coward retort. A compulsive American approached him in the lift in the Hassler Hotel in Rome. He said, 'I bet you can't guess my raunchiest sexual fantasy.' Coward replied, 'No, but I'm sure you're going to tell me.'

'My raunchiest sexual fantasy is Gina Lollobrigida going down on me slowly murmuring her name, "Gina Loll-lo-bri-gee-da,"' he said rolling the vowels luxuriously in his mouth.

'Thank God,' said Coward crisply sharpening the consonants, 'it wasn't Anna Magnani.'

Philip Hoare records a rare occasion when Coward – a very young Coward – came off second-best. On meeting Lytton Strachey he said, 'I met you a few years ago.' He received the cool reply, 'Rather a nice interval, don't you think?'

**CRAIG**, Edith. The painter P. D'Arcy Hart remembers being rehearsed – and hounded – by this daughter of Ellen Terry and William Godwin when she rehearsed the undergraduate company of which he was a member. For one production the company was stiffened by a touring professional.

One day, before rehearsal, when Edith Craig had not arrived, he was alone on stage, a few of us around the auditorium. Suddenly he adopted a stance in the nineteenth-century style and declaimed:

'Aha, methinks the girl is late.

To while away the time, I'll masturbate.'

**CRAWFORD**, Cheryl. The Broadway producer with a string of prestigious hits to her credit was at one time pursuing a project with Truman Capote. Capote was pursuing a holiday with friends at the house of a no-nonsense aunt when Ms Crawford rang and enquired, in her uniquely deep voice, if she could speak to Mr Capote.

'No,' said the aunt. 'He's out.'

'Tell him I called.'

'What name?'

'Miss Crawford.'

'Go along with you! I know you boys and your silly games!'

**CRAWFORD**, Dan. Dan Crawford was a much loved American who introduced the idea of the pub-dinner-theatre to Britain in 1970 and battled to keep it going at the King's Head in Islington until his death in 2005. His widow still flies the flag.

The food was appalling, the programmes eclectic and the currency in the bar was reckoned in 'old money'. Crawford was a driven, genuine eccentric who wore 'thrift shop tweed clothes even on his rare holidays on sweltering Spanish beaches.' Tom Stoppard described him as 'Raving Sane' and Benedict Nightingale once called the state of the King's Head when he took it over as 'so derelict even the winos ignored it.' Steven Berkoff, who owed opportunities to Crawford, admired his conversion of 'a dingy pub into a dingy fringe theatre' and remembered 'the spine wrenching seats' and the food: 'if you survived the pre-show dinner even the play seemed good.'

When I directed Dick Vosburgh and Denis King's musical *A Saint She Ain't* at the venue, business, especially for the meal, was so brisk that one night the chef threw a wobbly and ran. Dan's solution was to do a deal with the café next door and shuttle servings of food out of the café along Upper Street and back through the bar to the theatre. Plates of soup were seriously augmented by rain water on an inclement night.

With a dazzling, adventurous programme, but with precious little subsidy, Dan rightly beat the drum for cash and held out buckets to patrons. Maureen Lipman said that when she thought of him as an impresario 'the names of Lilian Baylis, Sir Donald Wolfit and Max Bialystock sprang to mind in no particular order.' He battled a long illness and after his Memorial Service she reflected on his ever-present collecting cans. 'Every time I saw that famous bucket I wondered when Dan was going to kick it.'

**CRAWFORD**, Michael. Michael Crawford is an incredibly hard-working perfectionist. The price he sometimes pays is attacks of self-absorption. The American playwright Bernard Slade wrote the Broadway hit *Some Time Next Year* with which Michael had one of his less successful outings when it played at The Prince of Wales Theatre, London. On one occasion when they met Crawford kept referring to himself in the third person. 'Michael would do this.' 'Michael wouldn't do that.' Finally Slade enquired, 'Who's Michael?' Michael looked amazed. 'Me!' he said.

I first saw Michael being very funny in Neil Simon's first West End hit *Come Blow Your Horn* (also at the Prince of Wales). He was supporting Bob Monkhouse, David Kossoff, Libby Morris and Nyree Dawn Porter. Soon after he was a memorable Feste in a production of *Twelfth Night* by Colin Graham at Lincoln's Inn. I commissioned a series of scripts for him for the late night satirical programme *Not So Much a Programme, More a Way of Life*. Journalists Peter Lewis and Peter Dobereiner invented a character, Byren, a sort of anglicised Holden Caulfield for him. It was a perfect vehicle for Michael. He performed only on Sunday night. He was alone on the screen in a medium close-up. The scripts were funny. The character was immediately appealing, especially to a young audience. We only had one disagreement.

After a script arrived which was not up to scratch I warned Michael that he might not be appearing that week. He was furious. I had some re-writes done but the monologue still didn't work. My decision had to be final. Michael's reaction was explosive – how could he let down his fans?

Dust eventually settled. The next week's script was excellent and in later years Michael used to tell the story of how he learnt the lesson early that the script must be right.

**CRITICAL BATTERINGS**. I am not a great fan of the critical one-liner delivered more for effect than for enlightenment: a trademark of the Algonquin school of criticism, it draws attention to the critic rather than the performance. However, in the interest of completeness, here are some of the most famous. Others are included under individual actors' entries and Robert Benchley earns his own section for virtually inventing the form. For a definitive collection, buy Diana Rigg's *No Turn Unstoned*.

Jane Alexander in *Goodbye Fidel* (Douglas Watt – the *New York Daily News*). '. . . She's about as Latin as a New England boiled dinner.'

Tallulah Bankhead in *Antony and Cleopatra* (John Mason Brown). 'Tallulah Bankhead barged down the Nile last night as Cleopatra and sank.'

Richard Briers in *Hamlet* (W.A. Darlington – the *Daily Telegraph*). 'Richard Briers last night played Hamlet like a demented typewriter.' 'Not a great Hamlet,' was Briers's reply, 'but I was about the fastest.'

Reviewing some Broadway comedy, Heywood Broun told his readers, 'The play opened at 8.40 sharp and closed at 10.40 dull.'

Creston Clark, an American actor touring as King Lear, was reviewed by the *Denver Post.* Their critic, Eugene Field, wrote: 'Mr Clark played the King all evening under constant fear that someone else was about to play the ace.'

Glenda Jackson's Gudrun in *Women in Love* caused Jack de Manio to comment more sharply than usual that she had 'a face to launch a thousand dredgers'.

Stanley Kauffman, covering the American Conservatory Theater's production of *The Taming of the Shrew,* decided that, 'If a director doesn't want to do *The Shrew,* this is a pretty good way of not doing it.'

Dinsdale Landen played Florizel in *The Winter's Tale* at Stratford, directed by Peter Wood, but not to Bernard Levin's approval: 'Last night Mr Landen as Florizel managed to destroy the magic of Bohemia in a minute, nay seconds.'

The late John Penrose, who was an actor *(Kind Hearts and Coronets)* before he became an agent with Millicent Martin among his clients, was a member of the Peter Bull/Robert Morley repertory company at Perranporth before World War Two. Of one of his performances the critic of the *West Cornwall Advertiser* wrote: 'Mr John Penrose gave a sharp twist to both his parts.'

Maureen Stapleton was reviewed by George Jean Nathan in George Tabori's *The Emperor's New Clothes*: 'Miss Stapleton played the part as though she had not yet signed the contract with the producer.'

**CROSBY**, Bing. Legend has it that Bing Crosby was dining one night at Lindy's, Damon Runyon's legendary hang-out in New York, when a gaping out-of-towner approached the table and asked Crosby if he remembered him. Crosby shrugged. The out-of-towner reminded him that he had employed him for some Elk-ish organisation nearly twenty years before. They had dined together afterwards and Crosby had spoken of his certainty that one day he would be a big star. Politely, Crosby pretended that he did remember.

'So tell me, Bing. What happened?'

**CROUSE**, Russell. Russell Crouse's contribution to *Anything Goes,* along with Howard Lindsay's, is chronicled elsewhere. However, during the run of *Life With Father* some five years earlier, he perpetrated one of the worst puns. A small part actor playing a doctor fell ill, and Crouse volunteered to understudy. Not only did he make his entrance too soon and have to go off and return, but next day when asked why he had essayed the role at all, he said, 'I just wanted to see if there was a doctor in the Crouse.'

Lindsay and Crouse had another long run with their adaptation of Joseph Kesselring's *Bodies in Our Cellar,* which they turned into something funny – *Arsenic and Old Lace* (the only time I actually laughed at it was in Robin Phillips's production at London, Ontario, starring William Hutt and John Neville). Lindsay and Crouse were conscientious playwright/producers and devotedly attended even touring productions, taking notes and keeping actors up to scratch. On one such expedition in Pittsburgh, Crouse was still grim-faced and taking notes when the lights went up at the interval. A woman in the audience strode up to them.

'What's the matter with you?' she accused. 'You haven't laughed once tonight. You're one of the reasons Pittsburgh doesn't get more good productions.'

**CUKOR**, George. George Cukor, literate, witty, sophisticated, was a stage director who, in the early days of Hollywood made the change to movies – albeit more adept with actors than with cameras.

When he directed Garbo in *Camille* she was surprised to see the same actor appear for no logical reason in several different scenes.

'Who is he?' Garbo asked, 'What part is he playing?'

'That man is Rex Evans,' Cukor replied, 'and he is playing the part of a friend who needs a job.' Similarly a friend asked Cukor why the camera lingered curiously long on a handsome young man in a sword fight in *Romeo and Juliet.* There didn't seem to be any good reason, said the friend.

'Oh yes,' Cukor teased him. 'There was a *very* good reason.'

Clark Gable had Cukor taken off *Gone with the Wind* apparently because Gable had one drunken sexual encounter with a gay friend of Cukor's (Bill Haines) and feared Hollywood whispers, 'George is directing one of Billy's old tricks.'

He was third choice for *My Fair Lady* after Jerome Robbins and Vincente Minelli. After much battering by Cukor's powerful agent,

'Swiftly' Lazae, the mogul, Jack Warner, found himself on a plane sitting next to Cukor. Warner asked, 'How'd you like to direct *My Fair Lady*?'

Cukor said, 'Very much.' He added, 'And you're making a very good choice.'

Greta Garbo became a confidant of Cukor's who arranged a meeting between her and Ivor Novello who was visiting Hollywood in the thirties. The introduction had to be cloaked in secrecy. Garbo was not to be called Garbo. The fiction was that her name was Harriet Brown. Novello stayed with the invention and referred to her as Miss Brown. They met two or three times at Cukor's house. Finally Novello said, 'Miss Brown, now that we know each other so well, do you think I might call you Harriet?'

Cukor directed Jack Lemmon early in his career. The actor was disconcerted by the number of times the director said 'Less'. After a day or so of 'Less' he protested politely , 'Mr Cukor, if you keep it up I won't be acting at all.' To which Cukor replied, 'You're beginning to get it, boy!'

**CURRIE**, Finlay. Finlay Currie, a marvellously craggy and, as he grew older, increasingly patriarchal Scottish actor, is a popular yardstick for theatrical days of long, long ago . . . 'It was back in the time when Finlay Currie used to get the girl.'

**CURTIZ**, Michael. David Niven has immortalised the odd adventures with the English language which are part of the legend of Hollywood movie director, Michael Curtiz, in the title of his book *Bring on the Empty Horses*. This was a command by Curtiz while filming *The Charge of the Light Brigade*.

However, Niven was not in *Casablanca* where another monumental misunderstanding occurred. Curtiz was yelling on set for 'a poodle, a black poodle!' which he needed urgently for a street scene. Anything for local colour the prop man thought, hitherto unaware that black poodles were characteristic of wartime North Africa. Curtiz was insistent. The prop man was in luck. He tracked a black poodle down and had it on the set within an hour. 'It is a nice dog,' said Curtiz, 'but I don't want a poodle.' The prop man insisted it was a poodle, he volunteered its pedigree.

Curtiz went mad. 'I want a poodle in the street. A poodle of water! Not a goddam dog!'

Curtiz won an Oscar for *Casablanca* in 1943 and delivered the most incomprehensible speech ever. 'So many times I have speech read, but no dice. Always the bridesmaid never a mother.' On another notable occasion he said, 'The next time I send a dumb sonofabitch to do something, I go myself.'

**DALLAS**, Ian. Ian Dallas, an introspective wit and enthusiast, wrote some theatre and television dramas in the fifties and sixties, never quite mooring his conversational wit to the page – though he did describe an ultra modern interior in one aside: 'Between these two-four-six-eight walls.'

He also gave Kenneth Tynan a brilliant comment on the unfortunate first night of Orson Welles's *Moby Dick*. It was not so long after Olivier's *Hamlet,* publicised as 'the tragedy of a man who could not make up his mind'. In *Moby Dick,* Welles exercised his penchant for wearing a false nose. On the first night it fell off and Dallas hissed to Tynan, 'The tragedy of a man who could not make up his nose!', a comment which found its way unacknowledged into the notice.

**DALY**, Augustin. The nineteenth-century American playwright and impressario famously presented Ada Rehan in Shakespeare in London, incurring Shaw's admiration for the actress and his scorn for what Daly's productions did to the plays.

An early actress in his company was Clara Morris, to whom, in spite of her success, he declined to give a rise. Rumour ran rife that she was going to accept a better offer from Wallack, a rival manager. Daly arrived at his theatre one day to find a letter on the rack for Miss Morris from the Wallack Company. He told the stage door keeper to conceal it until he had talked to her. When she arrived, he conceded the salary she was asking for and she signed a contract for some $20 a week more. When she collected her mail she found the Wallack offer for double the money Daly was now paying her – too late!

**DANCE OF DEATH, THE**. Michael Meyer, the translator of Strindberg's *The Dance of Death* for the National Theatre production, went back stage to congratulate Olivier on his performance.

'Olivier deprecated it. "It wasn't difficult. There isn't a line I haven't said to one of my three wives."'

**DANE**, Clemence (Winifred Ashton). Novelist, (*Broome Stages* – a story of a theatrical dynasty) and playwright (*A Bill of Divorcement*, *Moonlight is Silver* (a vehicle for Gertrude Lawrence and Douglas Fairbanks) and *Cousin Muriel* (a vehicle for Edith Evans). She was at the centre of a theatrical coterie in the thirties and forties. Also a painter and sculptor, she held court in her little house in Tavistock Street, Covent Garden, entertaining a circle of poets, authors, playwrights, musicians and film producers. Large, with no pretensions to beauty, she had charm and enormous vitality. She was famous for her innocently, unintentional outrageous remarks.

'Oh the joy of waking up and seeing a row of tits outside your window.'

'My favourite meal is crabs, roast cock and dick on toast.'

Staying in the country with the impresario Hugh 'Binkie' Beaumont, she descended one morning to an open-air breakfast served in sunshine, under a blue sky, on an immaculate lawn. Sitting around the table were Beaumont, John Perry, John Gielgud, Noel Coward, Terence Rattigan and Cecil Beaton. 'Oh, it's too lovely!' she enthused. 'It's just like fairyland!'

James Cairncross passed on two stories, one from Joyce Carey:

'At a dinner party the conversation turned to small London gardens, and in particular to the rockeries and statuary that various people placed there. The usual providential silence having fallen, Miss Dane's voice was heard to ring out with, "Mine's an enormous erection, covered in everlasting pea."'

The other source was the director Lionel Harris:

'Toward the end of their careers, Miss Dane wrote a play for Sybil Thorndike and Lewis Casson. The beginning of the third act proving recalcitrant she invited Lionel to come to her country cottage for the weekend, while she struggled with it.

'On the second morning of his stay he was summoned to her bedroom before breakfast. She was sitting up in bed, triumphant, "I've got it!" she cried, "Just listen to this. The curtain rises on Martin, alone at his typewriter. He types a few words, then stops, tears out a piece of paper, crumples it up and throws it into the wastepaper basket. This process is repeated (perhaps twice). MARTIN: Oh, dear, oh dear, there was a time when I seemed to be able to toss anything off . . . "'

In his biography of Noel Coward, *A Talent to Amuse*, Sheridan Morley suggests that Coward initially intended *Blithe Spirit*'s Madame Arcati to be a small part for Clemence Dane. She had expressed a wish to act. Once he had started to write the role it took over and it was given to Margaret Rutherford who had been playing Mrs Danvers in *Rebecca* with Owen Nares.

**DARE**, Zena. Zena Dare, whose last graceful excursion was in *My Fair Lady* at Drury Lane, had often toured in popular musicals in her youth. Southport was a date where she usually played to full houses but visiting the town in a straight play, she found the theatre virtually empty. An autograph hunter asked her to sign his book at the stage door.

'You don't seem to like straight plays in Southport,' she said pointedly.

'Oh no,' was the honest reply. 'We simply dread them.'

**DAVIES**, Marion. Marion Davies was a Ziegfeld girl who became the mistress of the obsessed newspaper tycoon, William Randolph Hearst, who was determined to turn her into a major movie star. Had he allowed her to develop her considerable talent for light comedy, he might have succeeded, but he preferred to put her in heavy period extravaganzas like *Dorothy Vernon of Haddon Hall*, in which she was awkward and embarrassing. As a result, both she and Hearst were easy targets for Orson Welles in *Citizen Kane*.

Dorothy Parker wrote of her, 'She has two expressions. Joy and indigestion.'

The Los Angeles rumour mill suggested that she had an illegitimate child by Hearst but no sighting was ever reported. One of her endearing traits was to stutter when excited. She arrived late at one Hollywood party escorted by Truman Capote.

'H..h..hello, everybody,' she greeted the gathering. 'I want you to m-m-meet m-m-my illegitimate son by C.C. Calvin C.C. Coolidge.'

Hearst could never marry Davies because his wife, a Catholic, would not divorce him. When he financed the airship Graf Zeppelin, his plan was that on its first transcontinental crossing Mrs Millicent Hearst would crack a bottle of champagne on it in New York, and Marion Davies would greet it on its arrival in Los Angeles. Ms Davies then heard that Mrs Hearst was trying to fly to the coast in order to anticipate the Zeppelin's arrival. She telephoned Hearst and demanded quaintly, 'Wh..wh..who gets the Graf Zeppelin? Me or the other p..p..party?' She got it.

**DAVIS**, Bette. Bette Davis developed a demanding reputation early in her career. Vincent Sherman who directed her and Miriam Hopkins in *Old Acquaintance* in 1930 said, 'I didn't direct them, I refereed.'

During her contract time at Warners she was nicknamed 'the Fifth Warner Brother'. Rehearsing a scene as Elizabeth I in *The Private Lives of Elizabeth and Essex*, in which she had to rebuke Errol Flynn as the Earl of Essex, she struck him a resounding blow. When Flynn protested she said, 'I'm awfully sorry. I don't know how to do it any other way. That's the kind of actress I am. I stress *actress*.' To his surprise when they shot the scene she pulled her punch. He was grateful; but a few days later, when a playful slap on the back was called for he administered a resounding whack. She looked at him in a fury. He said lightly, 'I am awfully sorry, I don't know how to do it any other way.' She never spoke to him again off the set. Perhaps it was the fact that she had always wanted Laurence Olivier to play Essex . . . ?

More sympathetically, when she toured America reading Carl Sandburg poems with her then husband, Gary Merrill, they played one small town where two elderly sisters, lifelong Davis fans, were transported with delight. When one had a heart attack she was carried out of the theatre. The other refused to go with her and stood up, demanding that the actors carry on. At the end Davis asked her up on the stage, 'I adored the performance,' she said. 'And my sister would have too if she hadn't died two hours ago.'

I met Ms Davis for the second time when she was on her 1987 visit to London. She was plugging her book *This 'N' That*, having recently survived a mastectomy, a stroke and a broken hip. She signed books at Hatchards, attracting a crowd of 3,000. Hatchards had to call the police to control the throng – having previously said that it would not be necessary, 'We've had Prince Andrew here.'

I wanted to check my favourite Bette Davis story and see if it was true. As I heard it some years ago, when she was playing in New York in Tennessee Williams' play *A Night of the Iguana*, two gay fans entered their apartment block and stepped into the elevator at the same time as their screen idol. Their delight doubled when they got out on the same floor and found that she was their new neighbour, renting the flat across the hall. Plucking up courage they asked her to dinner. She accepted for Friday, 7.30 prompt.

Right on time and immaculate as ever, she arrived, they dined and talked until eleven when she said she must go to bed. As she left she returned their invitation for the next Friday at the same time. Their joy was unconfined. She went to great trouble to match their splendid meal and at eleven indicated once again that it was bed time. Then, according to my story, as they reached the door, she said, with the utmost finality, 'Well, now we've done that!'

I suggested that this was a wonderful balance between old Yankee politeness and the determination of a strong woman not to encumber her life with hangers on. Miss Davis could not recall any such incident. It could not have happened. Wasn't it funny how stories like that sprang up?

Subsequently I asked Robbie Lantz who had been her agent at the time about the dinner parties and the accuracy of the story. 'Oh yes,' he said. 'I remember the block and the boys.'

She is also credited – but so are several others – of commenting on a passing starlet, 'There goes the good time had by all.'

**DAVIS**, Sammy Jnr. Sammy Davis Jnr was always keen to add Stephen Sondheim's 'I'm Still Here' to his repertoire. Sondheim, having written the song for a female survivor, declined to change the lyric. Davis came round to see me backstage after *Side by Side by Sondheim* in New York and asked me to intercede – 'If Stephen won't change the words, I'll get Sammy Cahn to do it . . . tell him I can make it as big as "Mr Bojangles".' I delivered the message. Once again Sondheim passed.

**DEAN**, Basil. Basil Dean dominated the West End as a much-feared director in the twenties and thirties and later ran ENSA during World War Two. (I once watched a show at RADA with him and he spotted the unsmiling director Jack Minster across the circle. 'What's Minster doing here?' he asked. 'Leading the laughter,' I said, which drew a smile.)

In the late thirties he directed Priestley's *Johnson Over Jordan*. Allan Davis, who was his stage manager, reports that this prestigious production starred Ralph Richardson and Edna Best and featured a score by Benjamin Britten.

'I well remember the slim, young (25), blond, curly-haired, casually-dressed composer sitting at the grand piano backstage – not at all Basil Dean's type. Dean's *gallère* was excessively normal or so he thought.' Britten wrote 'very modern discordant music for the decadent second-act nightclub scene'. (I wonder if anyone has thought of reviving it?)

**DE LAURENTIIS**, Dino. De Laurentiis had a habit of scattering scripts to several actors simultaneously in the rush to get a new movie project moving. On one occasion, Laurence Harvey, Peter Finch and Peter O'Toole compared notes and realised that they were all being offered the same role. Ganging up, they arrived together at De Laurentiis's suite and chorused, 'We don't think we're right for the part.'

**DELYSIA**, Alice (Lapize). A delightful French actress and singer who was C.B. Cochran's first revue leading lady, she had been married to the Anglo-French music hall star, born in Soho, Harvey Wagson (Victor Philippe Pot), who was immensely jealous of her. When Cochran, having heard her sing, asked why she did not go on the stage, her husband snapped. 'She would drive everyone out of the theatre.'

She did appear in Paris and New York in small and chorus roles before Cochran engaged her for *Odds and Ends* in 1914. She played regularly for him, including an engagement at The London Palladium in *On with the Dance* when, with Hermione Baddeley, she introduced 'Poor Little Rich Girl'. When Noel Coward later suggested that Gertrude Lawrence should introduce it in New York, she yelled, in idiomatic English, 'Noel is a sheet and aboogair!'

**DENNIS**, Nigel. Nigel Dennis was a thoughtful novelist, critic and playwright. On one occasion I invited him to lunch at the BBC television studios in Lime Grove where visitors were entertained in a suite of oak-panelled rooms. I was trying to persuade him to write for *Not So Much a Programme More a Way of Life* or *TW3*. When he was late I began to worry. When he finally arrived the explanation for the delay was farcical.

He had arrived at the studios and been shown to a room where a man whose face was familiar greeted him ebulliently, clasping him by the arm and enthusing that Peter was coming and so was Orson and it was going to be a great programme! Dennis was puzzled until a very old withered man was brought to the room and announced as 'Mr Ernest Milton'. The happy host turned on Dennis as an impostor. Huw Wheldon (for it was he) had mistaken him for the old Shakespearean actor, a famous Hamlet in his time and called on that particular occasion to celebrate the National's *Hamlet* with Peter O'Toole, its star, and Orson Welles. Dennis finally arrived at my table in a state of puzzled shock. We never did get him to write a sketch.

**DIETZ**, Howard. Howard Dietz, witty and elegant lyric writer and inventive publicist for MGM, was on the wrong end of an exchange with Greta Garbo. 'How would you like to come out for dinner on Monday?' he asked the star. She replied, 'How do I know I'm going to be hungry on Monday?'

But usually it was Dietz who got the better of a battle of wits. In the seventies, depleted by illness, he insisted on introducing a programme which celebrated his work in Maurice Levine's *Lyrics and Lyricists* series at the YMHA on 92nd Street. He opened: 'I don't like composers who think, it gets in the way of their plagiarism.' He went on to quote his collaborator, Arthur Schwartz, who was asked to write two songs a week for the long-running *The Gibson Family:* 'Won't it take a lot out of you, Arthur?' he asked.

'Yes,' said Schwartz, 'but it'll take a lot more out of Bach, Beethoven and Brahms.'

Dietz's career had a variety of false starts. He tried a very small advertising firm and was asked if he had read Dr Johnson's *Rasselas:* 'I want men who have some truck with culture,' said his potential employer. Dietz surveyed the empty shoe box of an office. 'You don't seem to have many men,' he pointed out. He got the job and Goodman, his employer, decided to break into theatrical production. Dietz wooed an author on his behalf. 'But I've never written a play,' protested the author.

'Neither has Mr Goodman,' Dietz countered. 'You both start without the handicap of knowledge.'

In the theatre, Dietz's great collaborator was Arthur Schwartz who, as a young lawyer, wrote to Dietz on his law firm's printed paper suggesting that they work together. Dietz was evasive and pointed out that as he had started with an established composer, so Schwartz should find a similarly secure lyric writer. It was left to a pair of producers to bring them together for *The Little Show* with Fred Allen, Clifton Webb and Libby Holman.

The story of the show's most durable song, 'I Guess I'll Have to Change My Plan', is interesting. It started life as a summer camp tune, which Schwartz composed for lyrics by Lorenz Hart – 'I Love To Lie Awake In Bed'. When Dietz provided his new lyrics to give Clifton Webb (described by Alexander Woollcott as the 'general futility man') a white tie and tails number, it had only a moderate success. However, the song had a vogue in England thanks to a cabaret act, de Lys and Clarke: they referred to it as 'The Blue Pyjama Song' – there was one reference to blue pyjamas. When they returned to New York, they performed it at the Place Pigalle. Dietz and Schwartz caught the act. Disingenuously, Schwartz asked who had written the song with which they were having such a success.

'I don't know,' said de Lys, 'it dropped in from nowhere. Someone like Noel Coward?'

'It's the best song someone like Noel Coward ever wrote,' said Schwartz, modestly. Soon his publisher asked him if he had heard this new song sensation.

'Dietz and I wrote it,' he was told. 'You published it three years later and I want to congratulate you on the effortless way you go about making a song hit.'

Together Dietz and Schwartz wrote some 500 songs: 'After about five hundred lyrics you get to know the composer,' Dietz has written. 'If you can stand it that long, you must like him.'

Dietz moved towards the movies. Samuel Goldwyn was a client of the advertising firm for which he worked and Dietz designed his trademark, deriving Leo the Lion from the symbol of Columbia University and adding '*Ars Gratia Artis*' as a bonus. He remembered Goldwyn agreeing that his secretary could destroy files from ten years back – 'But keep copies,' he added. Dietz was a shrewd enough publicist to tell the world about Shaw's famous brush-off: 'I am afraid we will not get together, Mr Goldwyn. You are interested in art and I am interested in business.'

Dietz, along with Herman Mankiewicz, laid claim to the famous thirties' line when New York hostesses were discovering wine snobbery. Dietz (or possibly Mankiewicz, a more famous drunk) fled a society dinner table and returned, having been sick. 'Don't worry,' he told his hostess. 'The white wine came up with the fish.'

At MGM he was reproved for his erratic timekeeping: 'You come in late,' said his chief. 'But I go home early,' Dietz replied, reasonably.

A beleaguered Dietz later coined the phrase, 'A day away from Tallulah is like a month in the country.'

As MGM's chief publicist, Dietz was responsible for the promotion of *Gone With the Wind* and masterminded the opening in Atlanta. One woman rang Clark Gable's hotel, asking to be told his room number. When Dietz refused to authorise its disclosure, she changed her tack and booked the room the moment Gable left with the injunction: 'Don't change the sheets.'

Dietz clashed with Ethel Merman when she was cast as Sadie

Thompson in a musical version of *Rain* which Dietz wrote with Vernon Duke. Merman did not like Dietz's lyrics and her husband was keen to rewrite them. According to Duke, 'Dietz's words were chic and she wanted them 'sock'. In rehearsal Merman would get to a song and say 'Number over', rather than deliver the original lyrics. Her agent attempted to mediate. He examined the Dietz lyrics, then those by her husband, Robert Levitt, and he pointed out to Dietz how much better were Levitt's versions. Only then did Dietz tell him that he had switched portfolios and the agent had given the nod to Dietz's original words. Merman left after a week and was replaced by June Havoc.

Dietz and Schwartz resumed their collaboration after World War Two but without the same success, except for the movie *The Band Wagon*. Their last show was *Jennie*, a vehicle for Mary Martin. Again lyric writer and leading lady clashed. Miss Martin suspected lewdness in the lyrics of a charming song, 'When I Leave the World Behind'. The offending lines were: 'Before I go to meet my Maker/I want to use the salt left in the shaker'!

Dietz's last years were beset by Parkinson's disease and by heart attacks, which he resisted with wit and bravery.

**DONALDSON**, William. Sometime theatrical producer, self-professed ex-brothel keeper, occasional columnist, Willie Donaldson was one of the producers of *Beyond the Fringe* and also of J.P. Donleavy's *Fairy Tales of New York*. According to Donaldson, during the run of the latter he became one of the select band who have tried to sue *Private Eye* for libel and failed. They had suggested that he was illegally buying tickets for the play in an attempt to boost receipts above the figure at which the theatre's owner, Sir Donald Albery, could give him notice. He consulted Lord Goodman, who asked if this was true and on being told it was, showed him the door.

Donaldson had, by his own account, been giving an employee £2000 to distribute among the barrow boys of Berwick Market with instructions to go to the theatre and buy front stalls for the play. The queue of unlikely fruiterers at the box office tipped off Sir Donald, who posted his formidable son, Ian, in the foyer to put a stop to it. Soon after his arrival a genuine party of 30 vicars arrived to book for that night's performance. 'Ian, thinking they were actors hired by me, sprang at them shouting, "Bugger off!", tearing at their dog collars and pulling their beards.'

Shortly afterwards Sir Donald arrived in the foyer at the same time as Donleavy turned up to buy some seats for a friend. Albery accused

Donleavy of conspiracy, and Donleavy, 'with a king punch from nowhere, put him on his arse in the foyer of his own theatre'.

**DRAKE**, Betsy. The American actress, once married to Cary Grant, was on board Onassis's yacht when she was told that the bar stool on which she sat was covered with the skin of a whale's penis. She jumped off shouting, 'Oh, my God! Moby's dick!'

**DRAKE**, Fabia. Towards the end of her life, Fabia Drake cornered the theatrical market in imperious dowagers, achieving in *Passage to India* and *A Room with a View* a popular celebrity greater than she had enjoyed in her long and distinguished career as actress and teacher. Her last engagement was in *The Forsyte Saga* for BBC radio. She recorded her last scene after a particularly heavy, suety lunch, went home and died peacefully in her sleep. The next day the cast recorded her funeral (in the play) before the news of her death was broken to them.

**DRAPER**, Ruth. The definitive American monologuist with an infinite capacity to people a stage she occupied alone was also the possessor of a sharp tongue. When her niece, Joyce Grenfell, came round after a performance to congratulate her with a hug and a compliment – 'I don't know how anyone dares to mention my name with yours' – Draper replied, 'They don't.'

She did not always win these exchanges. On meeting the great English comedienne, Irene Vanbrugh, wearing brilliant white kid gloves – was she jealous or an early conservationist? – Draper said rudely: 'Skin of a beast!'

'Why, what do you wear?' asked Ms Vanbrugh.

'Silk, of course,' Ms Draper sniffed.

'Entrails of a worm,' muttered Ms Vanbrugh.

**DRESDEL**, Sonia. Sonia Dresdel was a powerful but unfashionable actress referred to in H. M. Tennent circles as 'Sonia Dreadful'. Her romance with the agent Herbert Van Thal when she was at the Oxford Playhouse was always said to have ended when she 'kicked him in the Woodstock Road'. She inspired one of Kenneth Tynan's strictest reviews:

'What catches one's eye is Sonia Dresdel's performance [in *Doctor Jo* by Joan Morgan at the Aldwych] as the marauding sister, replete with gargantuan *Oeillades* and a fund of reminiscences ranging from the joys of the garden ('I love it, every green blade of grass') to the problems of fighting the tsetse fly. This is a character study worthy of Joan Crawford; an antiseptic, overdressed, malarial virgin who acquired, in one of my more frivolous nightmares, the name of Boofy Schwatzer. A definite curiosity value attaches to Miss Dresdel's attempts to convey benevolence and self-sacrifice. Her affectionate scenes with a young nephew are especially sinister, it being apparent that, given the smallest textual encouragement, Miss Dresdel could and would bite her little friend's arm off at the elbow. It is to the Eumenide's, and not the humanities, that this intimidating actress should confine herself.'

I hope she was one of those who did not read her notices.

**DRESSERS**. James Cairncross remembers that 'During the long run of *Salad Days,* Joe Grieg and myself were dressed by a wonderful old character called Jim Barney. In his youth he had been employed by one of the Railway Companies as a Delivery Man. In those days it was horses and he often used to say that there were few joys to compare with bowling along behind a team of four, blind drunk and singing. By the time he came into our lives he was slightly deaf and suffering from rheumatism; so we used to discourage him from making unnecessary journeys up and down the stairs at the behest of the wardrobe mistress, herself a monument to slapdash inefficiency. One day, as Jim was poring over his *Evening Standard,* we heard her call his name, to which he paid no attention.

'Jim,' we said, 'she's calling for you.'

'Oh, is she?' he answered, looked up briefly from his paper and shouted, 'Comin', darlin'!' Then, as he resumed his reading, he muttered under his breath, 'Piss up 'er leg and play wid the steam!'

Irving once asked his dresser, Walker Collinson, what he thought was his best part. After much thought he said, 'Macbeth.'

Irving was pleased. 'But,' he said, 'it is generally conceded to be Hamlet.'

'Oh, no, sir,' said Collinson. 'Macbeth. You sweat twice as much in that.'

**DRINKWATER**, John. Although Drinkwater, who had been an actor and general manager at the Birmingham Rep, had some success as a playwright – notably with his *Abraham Lincoln* – he came up against an implacable James Agate with one of his English heroes. 'John Drinkwater's *Cromwell* is as dull as the Cromwell Road and very nearly as long.'

**DRUGGER**, Abel (character in Ben Johnson's *The Alchemist*). I could not decide if this story belonged to Garrick, Kean or the Widow Garrick – so Mr Drugger gets the credit. Garrick had made this role in *The Alchemist* his own for his generation. Kean decided to brave it and after the performance received the briefest letter from Garrick's widow.

'Dear Sir, You cannot play Abel Drugger, Yours, Eva Garrick.'

Kean's reply matched her brevity (and honesty): 'Dear Madam, I know it, Yours, Edmund Kean.'

**DRYING**. Drying is the actor's nightmare – particularly on first nights. A fine actor, Paul Greenwood, did it most spectacularly in modern times in a recent revival of John Dighton's *The Happiest Days of Your Life* at the Barbican, when he was barely able to remember a line. The spectre has not, I think, visited him since.

Fay Compton, haunted perhaps by the spirit of Dame Edith (who was still alive at the time), dried on 'The handbag!' line in *The Importance of Being Earnest* during an Old Vic first night. She was prompted from the stalls by, I think, the director (not of that production) Peter Wood.

Frank Thornton, a considerable comedian but not an experienced Savoyard, mangled the First Lord's patter song in a *Pinafore* at the Queen Elizabeth Hall and said hopefully to the producer afterwards, 'I don't think anyone noticed, do you?'

Drying in Shakespeare is supposed to be particularly problematical, but experienced Shakespeareans can usually manufacture instant blank verse with a Shakespearean-colour in an emergency. Members of the cast of Olivier's *Othello* quote some spectacular improvisations.

**DU MAURIER**, Sir Gerald Hubert Edward. Every age has its breakthrough, its 'naturalistic' actor, a trailblazer who revolutionises acting technique. Du Maurier, great-grandson of a French conman, Robert Mathurin Busson, who thrived on his arrival in England as a supposed aristocrat fleeing the French Revolution, was the son of George du Maurier, *Punch* illustrator and the author *of Trilby*.

After an abortive start in a shipping office, he played with Hare, Forbes-Robertson and Beerbohm Tree – in the latter case particularly as

Dodor in *Trilby*. He was much engaged – including once to Ethel Barrymore and, after his marriage, to Muriel Beaumont – much involved with other women, known to his children as 'the stable' when they made bets on the 'runners'. None of these affairs interfered with his marriage – or with the greater part of his career.

*Peter Pan*, where he doubled as Hook and Mr Darling, *Raffles*, *Brewster's Millions*, *What Every Woman Knows*, all benefited from du Maurier's elegance and casual, throwaway style which killed off the melodramatic manner that had preceded it, banished fustian and inspired a gentle acting revolution. 'Ham' was the more easily identifiable after his success. His joint management of Wyndham's provided years of comfortable success during which he introduced Tallulah Bankhead to London. He did not generally produce demanding material but John Gielgud remembered his first-night performance as Dearth in *Dear Brutus* in 1917: when he played it himself some twenty-odd years later, 'I could not touch him in the part.'

Ironically du Maurier's career ended with a story of ill-luck. After a run of failures he needed a success. Frederick Lonsdale brought his new play, *The Last of Mrs Cheney*, to him. After they had dined well, they moved to du Maurier's study, where Lonsdale settled down to read him the piece. Some way into Act One, Lonsdale looked up from the page to find du Maurier asleep. He left in a fury, not mollified by Lady du Maurier's protests that Sir Gerald was not well. Lonsdale gave the play to Gladys Cooper and du Maurier had to ask to be in her production, which ran for 514 performances. The run was at the St James's. Together with the death of his business partner, Frank Curzon, his nap cost him the tenancy of Wyndhams. Tax and brandy hastened the end of his career, but bit parts in films and his earlier successes left his widow properly provided for.

**DURANTE**, Jimmy. Jimmy Durante's name is always associated with his billing row with Ethel Merman when they co-starred in *Red Hot and Blue*, a Cole Porter show. Before the compromise of combining their names in a sort of St Andrew's Cross above the title, Merman's agent had argued that 'the lady's name always comes first'. Durante's reply was, 'Oh, yeah? How about Mister and Missus?'

Durante was an acknowledged expert ad-libber on stage. Appearing in *Jumbo* in 1936, Tuffy, the elephant, misbehaved, Durante's comment was 'Hey, Tuffy, no ad-libbing!' Five years before he had co-starred in *The New Yorkers* with a donkey which threw him and invaded the auditorium. Durante improvised a monologue along the lines, 'Folks, dat animal is sore. De management didn't pay him dis week. Dat's why he's quittin'. Listen, kid, don't walk out on me now. I'll pay you myself if you come back. I'll feed yuh. I'll do anyt'ing you want – but please come back. De show must go on.'

John Barrymore is said to have come back-stage to compliment Durante: 'You know, Jimmy,' he said, 'some day you ought to play Hamlet.'

'Ta hell wit' dem small towns,' Durante responded. 'Noo York's the only place for me.'

An encounter with the Queen of Spain fostered another legend.

'Queen, it's a plesha, I tell ya, it's a plesha.'

'You're very amusing,' the monarch replied.

'Likewise, Queen, likewise.'

Clifton Fadiman recorded an exchange with Durante on his radio programme *Information Please*. The question was, 'Can you touch your scapula with your patella?'

The response: 'I hope your programme ain't gettin' off colour.'

# — *E* —

**EADIE**, Dennis. Dennis Eadie was rehearsing a play by J.M. Barrie. 'Eadie,' Sir James is reputed to have said, 'I want you to indicate by your expression that you have a younger brother who was born in Shropshire.'

**EDDISON**, Robert. I first saw Robert Eddison, a fine, elegant actor and a wonderful verse speaker, at the Bristol Old Vic in the forties when he was Edmund to Devlin's Lear and what the Bristol evening paper described as 'a princely Hamlet'. However, the Hamlet remains in my schoolboy memory for less princely reasons. To begin with, there was a moment when the queen, played by Catherine Lacey, popped a breast, a rare treat for a row of fifth-formers. Then came Hamlet's line 'a motive and a cue for passion'. Now it so happened that at school we had been improving our sex education by passing around a bodice-ripper called *Cue for Passion* – one of those paperbacks which always falls open at the same page. As Eddison delivered the line, our entire, irreverent row collapsed in unsuppressed giggles. I have often wondered if Robert tried vainly to capture the laugh again on subsequent nights.

On one occasion Edith Evans dined with Edison. He had prepared a trifle: 'The custard had curdled slightly, for which I apologised – her eye glinted as she said, "I adore making custard . . . it's the element of *danger!*"'

**ELLIS**, Mary. The delightful nonagenarian soprano and dramatic actress who starred in many pre-war musical spectacles and lived to pass 100. She was perhaps ill-advised to play in Noel Coward's *After the Ball* in the fifties and Coward was ill-advised to compose a score to which justice could only have been done by her younger voice. The result was cruelly lampooned in a Watergate revue . . .

> Sweet voice that used to be
> Still cracking on top C.

Cruelly, but famously, Coward said: 'She couldn't get a laugh if she pulled a kipper out of her cunt.'

**ENSA**. The Entertainments National Service Association. The war-time organisation headed by Basil Dean was usually dismissed as Every Night Something Awful. Noel Coward, however, defined it differently with a line from the fairies' chorus in Rutland Boughton's *The Immortal Hour*: 'They laugh and are glad and are terrible.'

**ERICSON**, Don. My friend the late Don Ericson, variously editor of *Esquire* magazine, *The Dial* and an editor on the colour supplement of the *New York Times*, told me my favourite story of audience optimism.

Once a year his mother came to New York from Kansas City. She always wanted to see whatever was the latest hit and this particular season the prize candidate was *Jennie* by Dietz and Schwartz. It looked bullet-proof. Thinly disguised, it told the story of the great Laurette Taylor. The role would be played by Mary Martin, fresh from enormous hits for Rodgers and Hammerstein.

Don booked tickets well ahead and relaxed. Then he started to hear rumours of trouble in rehearsal. He wondered. Then there were problems on the road and reports of disaster flooded back to New York. The advance bookings for the show were so large that he reckoned it would still be on when his mother came to town, but would a disaster ruin her visit? The word from previews and then the appalling notices confirmed his worst fears. Should he book an alternative? He decided not: she'd asked for *Jennie* and *Jennie* she must get.

Mother arrived in New York and in due course they set off for the theatre. The mezzanine (or circle to the British) and the orchestra were half-empty, the show was lack-lustre and an air of failure hung over the house. Don sat despondent until the final curtain. As they left the theatre his mother turned to him with a smile of pure pleasure.

'Well,' she said proudly, 'we never saw a real flop before!'

**ERTE**. The exotic designer had a curious preference when it came to payment. He had designed costumes and scenery for George Black at the Palladium for *Crazy Gang* shows in the thirties and when Black's sons

George and Alfred employed him in Blackpool for an Opera House revue after World War Two, they asked Alec Shanks, who always executed his designs, what his fee should be. Shanks's answer was 'Oh, buy him something in gold . . . he prefers that to money.' Erte arrived with a bag full of gold – payment from other sources – and added the Blacks' contribution to the rest.

**EVANS**, Clifford. The Welsh actor and director was touring New Zealand with a production of Shaw's *St Joan* with his wife, Hermione Hannen, in the title role. To make one journey from town to town, it was necessary to shorten the play to catch the train, so they cabled Shaw for permission to drop the epilogue. The reply was prompt. 'Permission to cut epilogue granted, provided cast perform it on train.' Loyally, they did.

**EVANS**, Dame Edith Mary. There was always a great deal more to Dame Edith than 'A handbag?' Anecdotes – perhaps apocryphal – cling to her memory. The best known concerns her visit to Fortnum and Mason, across the road from her chambers in Albany, during World War Two. She bought a pineapple and was charged the, to her, exorbitant sum of nineteen shillings and six pence. 'Keep the change,' she is supposed to have said imperiously. 'I trod on a grape on the way in.'

Born to parents of modest means in Pimlico, she exchanged the life of a milliner for that of actress after she had some success in amateur theatricals. A protégée of William Poel, she played Cressida for him in 1912 and then found a secure niche in the West End under the Vedrenne-Eadie management: 'God was so good to me. He never let me go on tour.' He continued the good work when Ellen Terry asked her to join her in a music hall excerpt from *The Merry Wives of Windsor*. She also enquired what wages Miss Evans would require. 'I've never had more than five pounds, Miss Terry.'

'I'll give you fifteen and take it off the man.' Later she played Nerissa with Terry in similar circumstances.

She soon attracted the attention of Shaw and created the role of Lady Utterword in *Heartbreak House*, but she was not properly accepted as a classical actress, as opposed to a critics' favourite and a West End standby, until she was invited to the Old Vic by Lilian Baylis. Six years earlier she had been rejected – in spite of Sybil Thorndike's sponsorship. Miss Baylis complained, 'How dare you send me such an ugly woman,' but later regretted it and admitted, 'I ought to have engaged her then but she didn't look the leading type.'

Evans played in New York off and on from 1931 but never with the same commercial success that she enjoyed in London. She had a typically idiosyncratic view of the town: 'It's a city in which you can do what you want. If you want to drink milk, you may. If you want to stay up late, you may.' Few visitors can have demanded less of the Big Apple.

In the thirties, her great successes included Millamant, *Robert's Wife* and her Rosalind opposite Michael Redgrave's Orlando, during which their onstage romance blossomed briefly and improbably into a real-life involvement. After her appearance as Lady Bracknell, she always had trouble avoiding dragon type-casting. One of her less successful attempts was in Rodney Ackland's adaptation of *Crime and Punishment* in 1946; she played opposite Gielgud. Maria Britneva (Lady St Just) has vividly described her irritation when Dame Edith persistently coughed during one of Sir John's major speeches. One night, when her irritation on Gielgud's behalf got the better of her, she stuffed a cushion over Dame Edith's face which ended the coughing. She received a mild reproof from the impresario, Hugh Beaumont.

One of Evans's most quoted remarks was reported by Frith Banbury, who directed her in N.C. Hunter's *Waters of the Moon* in 1951. She was dressed in splendid style by Balmain. Dame Sybil, who played opposite her, was representing an impoverished gentlewoman. When Binkie Beaumont suggested that as the run was such a long one, Dame Edith's expensive gowns should be replaced by new ones, she was delighted and added, after a moment's thought, 'Sybil must have a new cardigan.'

Towards the end of her life she made more appearances in films and on television. By then, her endearing eccentricities were being collected enthusiastically. When a young actor wished her luck before a transmission she replied, 'With some of us it isn't luck.' And at the Riverside Studios a stage hand who said helpfully, 'This way, dear' was rewarded with a happily muttered, 'Dear? They'll be calling me "Edie" next.'

When she filmed *The Whisperers* for Bryan Forbes, she co-starred with Eric Portman. She tackled Forbes confidentially just before shooting began to ask if the script could indicate that she had married beneath herself. The next day Portman succeeded in a similar ploy to indicate that his character had married an older woman. On location in Manchester she reported that a passer-by had approached her to say, 'Which one of you two is Eric Portman?' She also demonstrated her limited knowledge of young children. Nanette Newman (Mrs Forbes) had a scene to play with a black baby in her arms. She reassured Dame Edith, 'Don't worry, Edith dear, if he starts to squawk during the scene I'll just plough on.'

The Dame replied, 'No, that won't happen. *All* babies sleep after lunch.' When the child screamed and thrust a soggy rusk into her face she was dumbfounded. 'That child,' she said, 'is an exception.'

In a subsequent film, *The Madwoman of Chaillot,* she helped Forbes out at the last moment. Replacing Irene Papas, she had to travel to Monte Carlo. French airlines were on strike, so she flew to Milan and then proceeded by car. She arrived fresh and immaculate. 'Such a nice pilot, he flew very low so that we could get a good view of the coastline.' Making her first entrance into the impressive cellar set which took up two sound stages, she answered the call for 'action' by enquiring of Nanette Newman, who was escorting her as a maid, 'Is this a real cellar, or did dear little Bryan build it?'

'Bryan built it,' said his wife, 'and I think he's waiting for us.'

'Well, I'm ready, so let's get on with it.' With that she made her entrance, said her lines and hit her mark.

'Cut,' said the director as she turned to him and remarked, 'It's very dark down here. I hope they can see me.'

One of her greatest stage roles in her later years was Mrs St Maugham in Enid Bagnold's *The Chalk Garden.* Initially she rejected the role (as did Margaret Rutherford) and the play was first staged in New York with Gladys Cooper. When H.M. Tennent finally brought it to London, she scored a success but during the run became badly constipated. Being a Christian Scientist, she refused treatment and was finally unable to play. Binkie Beaumont, her manager, fearful for his investment, pleaded, cajoled and threatened until she refused to see him. Finally his partner, John Perry, gained access to her chambers in Albany where she was writhing in agony – though she was not so distressed that she could not play the age-old game of confusing two rivals' names.

'Binkie is being so cruel,' she lamented. 'He is threatening to replace me with Gertrude Cooper.' Gladys Cooper did in fact take over the role for some weeks until she recovered.

Dame Edith was not greatly concerned with her surroundings. When she had her set of rooms in Albany re-done, the decorator found a Sickert portrait of the actress behind the wardrobe in her bedroom – a picture, incidentally, which Binkie Beaumont had been trying to buy for years to decorate the Globe foyer. The decorator re-designed Dame Edith's drawing room round the picture and when he unveiled the results to his client he expressed surprise that the painting had languished for years in obscurity. Dame Edith was not surprised. 'I suppose I put it there because there was a hook.'

I collected her for lunch in Albany one day. Her rooms were on the first floor. As we started to come down the stairs, the door of the chambers below opened and an elderly man emerged escorting Sir Kenneth Clark's wife. She looked up and smiled. Blank incomprehension was written across Dame Edith's face. Lady Clark decided to be helpful. 'It's Lady Clark,' she said. Edith swung round to me imperiously. 'Why is she telling me that?' she demanded, going on to lie, 'I know perfectly well who she is!'

She provided Gielgud with one of his notorious 'Gielgoodies' when his production of *Twelfth Night*, with Vivien Leigh and Laurence Olivier, flopped at Stratford after a barrage of criticism led by Ken Tynan, who called Vivien Leigh's Viola, 'dazzlingly monotonous'. Gielgud was in despair. 'Good heavens,' he said, 'after this no one will ever work with me again – except Edith at a pinch.'

To a questioner who asked her if she understood everything she was saying in Shakespeare, she confessed that she did not. He asked what she did in the circumstances. The question was not to her taste. 'I face front and think dirty,' she snapped. Engaged by Peter Hall to play Volumnia to Laurence Olivier's *Coriolanus* at Stratford-upon-Avon, she played a charming practical joke on the company, inserting an incomprehensible word into the Shakespearean text. No one liked to correct her until the situation became serious and the opening loomed. Finally Peter Hall asked her in which folio or quarto she had found it.

'I made it up,' she said, wickedly. 'I thought it might become as famous as "A handbag?"' On another occasion at Stratford, when she was playing the Countess of Roussillon in *All's Well That Ends Well*, she listened to Guthrie explaining a difficult scene to a younger actress. Eventually the girl understood.

'Oh,' she said, 'you mean camp it up!'

Dame Edith jumped in.

'Tony, what does "camp" mean?'

'Don't be silly, Edith. You invented it.'

Victor Spinetti once escorted Mary Martin, who was staying with him in Brighton, mourning the death of her late husband Richard Halliday, to

Dame Edith Evans's one-woman show at the Theatre Royal. When they went round afterwards, Dame Edith welcomed them at the dressing-room door.

Miss Martin burst out, 'Oh Edith, since I last saw you I've lost my dear husband!'

'I lost mine a long time ago. I can't even remember his name. Come in,' was the businesslike reply which stemmed the tears.

She always took an active interest in Equity, the actors' union. In one of the clashes in 1975 led by the Redgrave faction of the Workers' Revolutionary Party, she surveyed her colleagues from a box. The front rows were filled with members of the WRP. 'Who are those people?' she boomed. 'I thought this was an *actors'* meeting?'

However, as Patrick Garland perceptively told Bryan Forbes, 'She had no sense of "class", only of rank.' When she played Betsy Trotwood opposite Robin Phillips's David Copperfield in a movie, she had a long speech to deliver while holding a cat in a basket. Although it had been sedated, the drug wore off in mid-speech and the cat tried to struggle free. Without a pause she pushed it back in, muttering, 'Don't be such an ambitious pussy. You're not in *Dick Whittington*.'

Phillips directed her in her last stage acting performance in *Dear Antoine* at Chichester. She was having trouble with her lines and in the run-up to the opening, he had to dance attendance all day and light the production overnight. On the first occasion he worked till five in the morning, slept until nine and returned to the theatre to find that the new computer had wiped his plot. He had to relight three times and was exhausted by the first preview. He pushed her on and at the end, when all had gone well, went round to congratulate her but, exhausted by three days and nights without sleep, he burst into tears in her dressing room.

'What a shame,' she said, sympathetically. 'I'd prepared such a nice speech of thanks, now I can't deliver it.'

In his biography of Dame Edith, *Ned's Girl,* Bryan Forbes gives an infinitely touching account of her last months and of the documentary film he made with her. She watched it with fascination and, like so many actresses, distanced herself from the woman on the screen: 'Did you like her?' she asked a young projectionist. 'She's quite funny, isn't she? The way she moves her hands! I've never seen her before, you know. Not like that. Not being herself.'

**EYRE**, Sir Richard. Richard Eyre, one of the most popular and successful directors of the National Theatre and increasingly a busy film-maker published his beautifully written memoir *Utopia and Other Places* in 1993. It is delightful to think of this great 'Man of the Theatre' making his stage debut at Hornchurch as Mountjoy, the French herald in *Henry V*. On his first entrance on the cue, 'You know him by his habit,' he was faced with an English army all standing downstage with their backs to the audience, miming 'his habit' as violent masturbation. What a way to start! The only way to go was up.

# — F —

**FAULKNER**, William. During one of his screenwriting periods in Hollywood, William Faulkner was introduced to Clark Gable.

'So, you're a writer, Mr Faulkner.'

'Yes, Mr Gable. What do you do?'

**FAY**, Frank. Monologuist, famous drunk act, composer, lyricist, director, sketch writer, and sometime husband of Barbara Stanwyck, Fay's immortality is assured by his inspired creation of Elwood P. Dowd in *Harvey* in 1944. During the run of *Harvey*, a member of the cast who wanted to suck up to him went with him to Mass every morning. When the show came to the end of its run, the actor stopped going to Mass.

'Look at the bastard,' said Fay, pointing him out in a bar some time later. 'A run-of-the-play Catholic.'

As a producer in the twenties he had taken over a revue in which he starred, *Harry Delmar's Revels*. When he refused to pay writers, Billy Rose sued him and was awarded $1100. Fay paid it in 110,000 pennies. In 1950 he was back producing a flop revue, *If You Please*. When it closed in San Francisco the day after Thanksgiving he was heard to mutter, 'Looks like the turkey came a day late.'

Making a comeback on the nightclub circuit, Fay was heckled by Milton Berle at the Copacabana. Sensing Fay's confusion and a potential kill, Berle crowed, 'This is really going to a battle of wits tonight.'

Fay saw his chance. 'Well, if you insist, Milt,' he said, 'but it's against my principles to fight an unarmed man.'

**FIELDING**, Fenella. To Kenneth Williams, encouraged to move close to her for a tight two-shot in a period carriage in the spoof horror movie, *Carry on Screaming*: 'Why is your bum so hard? Do you leave it out at nights?'

**FIELDS**, Dorothy. Dorothy Fields, the most successful woman lyric writer, was the daughter of Lew Fields of Webber and Fields, a famous vaudeville double act, and the sister of Herbert Fields, a prolific book writer. Although theatrical stories were a commonplace at the Fields' dinner table, other performers were rarely invited home and Mrs Fields counselled her offspring, 'You children must be extra polite to strangers because your father's an actor.'

Dorothy's early attempt to break into showbusiness as an actress for a producer friend of her father was frustrated when he telephoned to say, 'Your daughter's here. Come and fetch her.' When she showed an inclination to write lyrics, Lew Fields was firm. 'Ladies don't write lyrics.' Falling into the family routine (Webber and Fields had pioneered the 'Who was that lady?' exchange), she countered, 'I'm no lady, I'm your daughter.'

Her first songs were written with J. Fred Coots. He introduced her to Jimmy McHugh, who set some of her lyrics himself and bought other tunes from Fats Waller for $50 down. Realising later what he had signed away, Waller refused to let his son play, 'I Can't Give You Anything But Love, Baby' and smashed his fist through a French window one Sunday morning when 'On The Sunny Side Of The Street' was played on the radio.

The genesis of the title line of 'I Can't Give You Anything But Love, Baby' is disputed. Dorothy said she heard a boy outside Tiffany's say, 'I can't give you anything but love, Lindy,' and she changed 'Lindy' to 'Baby' to make it universal. Bert Lahr, who originally sang the song with Patsy Kelly, ascribes it to Lew Brown, of Brown, de Sylva and Henderson, who, he says, gave it to Fields and McHugh.

Dorothy Fields became known as Mills Music's $50-a-night girl for running up instant topical songs. She tried to top 'Varsity Drag' with 'Collegiana'. . . 'every pedagogue goes to bed agog, doing Collegiana'. It must have been about then that Cole Porter gave her a rhyming dictionary, saying, 'You've got to stop this nonsense. Why knock yourself out trying to find the right words.'

When she wrote for a revue at the Cotton Club the whole family turned out, only to be embarrassed when a foul-mouthed female comic interpolated: 'Three of the dirtiest songs you ever heard in your life'. Lew Fields demanded and got a public announcement that his daughter had not written the words.

Her later work was mainly with Jerome Kern, Sigmund Romberg and

Arthur Schwartz. Irving Berlin's biographer reports that after Harold
Arlen was widowed, she wished to marry Arlen but he preferred to stay
faithful to the memory of his wife. He sought Irving Berlin's advice,
which was succinct.

'Tell Dorothy to go fuck herself.'

**FINNEY**, Albert. During Albert Finney's first season at Chichester the
University of Sussex made him an honorary Doctor of Letters. When he
telephoned his father, a bookmaker in Salford, to give him the news,
Finney Senior's only comment was: 'Doctor of Letters? You haven't even
written us a bloody postcard in three months.'

**FIRST NIGHTS**. How many times has Arnold Bennett's journal entry
for 26 February 1924 been echoed as embarrassed friends leave a first
night?

'First night *of Kate* (or Love will find out the way – Good God!) at
Kingsway last night. It fell flat in the audience. The applause exclusively
friendly applause. The thing was killed by a perfectly rotten book. The
plot was unfollowable and the words terribly dull. No one that I saw in
the audience thought other than that the thing was a frost . . . We drove
homewards, Dorothy and I, and say again and again that the thing is
hopeless. And in scores of cabs and autos radiating from the theatre to all
points of the compass people are saying the same thing. But the artists
and the aged authors of the book are trying (not successfully) to convince
themselves that the night is success. This is a 1st night sample of many 1st
nights.'

Barry Sullivan, the nineteenth-century Irish tragedian, came to
*Richard III*'s 'A horse! A horse! My kingdom for a horse!' when a
barracker added, 'And wouldn't a jackass do as well for you?'

'Sure,' Sullivan shot back. 'Come around to the stage door at once.'

All this, of course, pales before the riots of earlier centuries. In 1721 a
fracas between a drunken earl and the manager John Rich spread to the
streets. John Phillip Kemble provoked six nights of rioting in 1809 by
raising pit prices from 3s 6d to 4s. The war of words which characterised
the change of relations between Edwin Forrest, the American tragedian,
and William Macready, who had started as friends and ended as mortal
enemies, provoked showers of rotten eggs and nuts from Forrest's
supporters when Macready played Macbeth in Philadelphia in 1848, and
culminated in the Astor Place Riots in 1849. The Astor Place Opera House

itself was crowded with Macready's supporters on 10 May of that year but the streets outside were crowded with his enemies. The militia were called out – two dozen rioters were killed and over three dozen wounded.

Ireland and the Abbey provided a fair ration of 20th century riots, most notably in 1926 with Sean O'Casey's *The Plough and the Stars.* It took four nights of the run for passions to rise – as they had years before to greet J.M. Synge's *Playboy of the Western World.* W.B. Yeats, having called the police, harangued the audience for O'Casey's play. 'You have disgraced yourselves again, you are rocking the cradle of a new masterpiece.'

Laurette Taylor's return to London at the Garrick in 1920 in *One Night in Rome* (not a very strong vehicle) produced another explosion and a splendid barrage of counter-comments from the senior establishment of the English theatre. The outrage was inspired by a disappointed Australian who thought his girlfriend should have played Miss Taylor's part.

The response was unexpected. Cochran from the stage announced, 'I have brought this great artist three thousand miles to appear in this play. I shall ring down the curtain and give another first night at a later date.'

From his box Seymour Hicks thundered: 'This is not England!' Robert Lorraine intoned, 'Who has done this foul thing?' And amid the increasing pandemonium Gerald du Maurier proposed, 'We will none of us play tomorrow. We will close the theatre as a protest.'

It didn't help the play to run.

In 1921 Coward wrote a play, *Sirocco,* which was produced with Frances Doble as wife and Novello as lover. On the first night, the audience grew restless and in the third act did not conceal their displeasure. Mrs Coward, who was growing deaf, enquired of her son, 'Is it a failure, dear?'

Basil Dean, the director, who had followed his habit of leaving the theatre during the performance, returned to hear the uproar and, interpreting it as wild enthusiasm, kept merrily raising and dropping the curtain. Coward rushed around to stop him and decided to join his stars in their humiliation. This increased the tumult. A voice called for Frances Doble, who walked forward with Coward, who was greeted by a yell of 'Hide behind a woman, would you?' Frances Doble had only one speech on her mind and delivered it.

'Ladies and gentlemen, this is the happiest moment of my life . . .'

The boos and catcalls of the gallery are nearly a thing of the past, though they were still a feature of the fifties and early sixties. The last great tumult was at the Palace Theatre, when most of the second act of John Osborne's *The World of Paul Slickey* was howled into confusion.

Janet Hamilton Smith, an operatic soprano who had had a great success earlier in her career in the Grieg musical *Song of Norway,* had less easy material in the Osborne, playing opposite Harry Welchman, who had years before been a charismatic Red Shadow in *The Desert Song.* Osborne and Christopher Whelan, who wrote the score for *The World of Paul Slickey,* gave her a nostalgic lyric which rhymed the words 'Horses and carriages' with 'Claridges'. It may be possible to sing 'Claridges' – but not when you exit on that word on a climactic high soprano note. (Try it.)

The first night was a disaster. The booing started in Act Two during a Welchman scene and grew louder until the curtain. In a fiery show of displeasure, Adrienne Corrie, who had changed sex in the course of the play, took off her top hat, and letting her red hair cascade round her shoulders, replied to the baying gallery with a bold two-finger gesture.

As Osborne told Herbert Kretzmer at the time, 'Writing lyrics is like writing bad poetry. It's not easy.'

One of Coral Browne's most famous asides was delivered to her escort – and, incidentally, to the entire stalls of the Old Vic – on the first night of Peter Brook's production of Seneca's *Oedipus* starring John Gielgud. (This was also the production during which, at a late rehearsal, Gielgud and the rest of the cast were asked to improvise the most terrifying thing they could imagine. When Gielgud's turn came he stepped forward and said simply. 'We open on Tuesday.') On the first night the curtain rose on a simple setting dominated by a massive phallus. Coral's comment cut through the shocked silence: 'No one we know!' Nearly as good as Robert Helpmann's comment at the first night of *Oh! Calcutta!*: 'The trouble with nude dancing is that not everything stops with the music.'

**FISKE**, Minnie Maddern (Marie Augusta Davey). Mrs Fiske was an immensely celebrated American actress who appeared with her parents – using her mother's name 'Maddern' – at the age of three. She retired when she married Harrison Fiske but returned to the stage as soon as he had written a play for her – *Hester Crewe.*

This formidable actress/manager pioneered Ibsen in America, scoring successes as Hedda and as Mrs Alving and investing her performances with an advanced naturalism for her day – speed of delivery and turning her back on her audience were trademarks of her technique. She was said to have directed a young cousin, Emily Stevens, in *Hedda* with the instruction, 'Now, Emily! In this great emotional scene, I wish your face to depict every emotion that a woman can feel – love, hope, joy, panic [each word shot out like the lash of a whip] – and be *sure* that you turn your back to the audience!'

On another occasion she locked Emily out in the cold while she recreated a scene between Hedda and Lovborg. Emily plucked up the courage to point out that this scene was not in Ibsen's play, but Mrs Fiske had her answer: 'Ibsen shows us only the last hours. To portray them I must know everything that has gone before . . . I must know all that Hedda ever was. When I do, the role will play itself.' (I hope that as a result she was as savagely funny as Joan Greenwood – the best Hedda I was privileged to see.) Emily Stevens was privy to another of Mrs Fiske's sharper moments. They were together standing in the wings while another well-known American actress, Blanche Yurka, rehearsed a scene. Mrs Fiske did not approve. 'Emily, my dear,' she hissed – not too discreetly – 'Act if you must, but never Yurk!'

George Arliss, who played Brack to Mrs Fiske's Hedda, suggested in *Up the Years from Bloomsbury* that she was a princess among unselfish performers: 'She was so interested in getting the best out of everybody else that she seemed to regard herself as a negligible quantity in the play. I remember saying to her, "Are you going to speak all that with your back to the audience?"

'"Yes", she said, "I want them to see your face."

'"But," I remonstrated, "it's a very long speech for you to deliver in that position."

'"Yes, I know," she sighed. "It's such a long speech, I want to get through it as quickly as I can."'

She did make magic for theatre-goers: Alexander Woolcott was a devoted admirer. Some admired her silences – Mary Gardner, the great opera star, said of one performance, 'Ah, to be able to do *nothing* like that!' but Franklin Pierce Adams pointed up the eccentricity of some of her inflections in a favourite piece of verse:

> Some words she runs togetherso
> Some others are distinctly stated
> Somecometoofast and s o m e  t o o  s l o w
> And some are syncopated.
> And yet no voice – I am sincere –
> Exists that I prefer to hear.

**FORBES-ROBERTSON**, Jean. Jean Forbes-Robertson was a powerful, troubled actress, the daughter of Sir Johnston Forbes-Robertson. She was particularly noted for her Peter Pan and her Hedda, which she later toured and turned up to play as a guest star in various repertory companies. John Moffat, who played Tesman opposite her at the Oxford Playhouse, ran into her on the Saturday before the matinée performance. She slammed down two heavy cases with which she travelled and swore. 'My bloody father!'

'What did he do?' asked Moffat.

'He invented bloody matinées!'

**FORBES-ROBERTSON**, Sir Johnston. An actor of great beauty, intellect and education and a reluctant manager, he was brought up in the comfortable, artistic, upper-middle-class family of the art critic of the *Sunday Times*.

He trained as a painter and slipped into acting on an invitation from W.G. Wills, Irving's 'house-dramatist', and played with Calvert in Manhattan, where he met Samuel Phelps in a production of *Henry IV Part II*. Phelps doubled the King and Shallow, Forbes-Robertson was Prince Hal.

At the first rehearsal Phelps admonished him, 'Young man, you know nothing about this part: come to my dressing room tonight at seven o'clock,' instituting a life-long bond between them. Forbes-Robertson enjoyed, as many actors do, the acting lineage with which this provided him: 'Phelps had been Macready's favourite actor. Macready had played with Mrs Siddons and she had played with Garrick. I may boast a good histrionic pedigree. There is a good old school and a bad old school and the former is the best for any time.'

After playing with the Bancrofts and Modjeska, he joined Irving at the Lyceum as Claudio and later toured America with Mary Anderson, a great beauty and one of a line of actresses to whom he proved susceptible. He fell into management when Irving toured America and leased him the Lyceum, where he presented *Romeo and Juliet* with Mrs Patrick Campbell. The season was only a moderate success but the next year, 1897, backed by Horatio Bottomley, he had a triumph as Hamlet with Mrs Pat as Ophelia. She tormented Forbes-Robertson, who was desperately in love with her and, at a performance attended by Ellen Terry, changed her wig from blonde to black in mid-performance, saying that she wanted to see which Miss Terry preferred. After a four-year partnership he went abroad to recuperate and on his return engaged and later married Gertrude Elliot, the American actress who speedily mended his broken heart.

Caesar, after Hamlet his greatest role, nearly cost him his life in Liverpool. During a rehearsal, a carpenter dropped a heavy hammer from the grid, narrowly missing him. In the middle of one of his speeches, he hesitated momentarily, looked up and said politely, 'Please don't do that again' and resumed.

He toured old plays with an occasional new play in his repertoire – and the lines for these he could never master. On record are 'She's killed me twice and now she's daggered me!' instead of 'She's made two attempts on my life and now she's stabbed me.' And instead of 'That woman has unnerved me' – 'Now, by God, she has unsexed me!'

As his repertoire was not exclusively classical he once had occasion to complain to another manager, Clayton, that he had trouble finding the right words for his rejection letters. Clayton replied with a line usually ascribed to Beerbohm Tree and perhaps shared by them: 'I solved it yesterday,' he said. 'I wrote to a man who had sent me an abominable play and said, "My dear Sir, I have read your play. Oh, my very dear, Sir! Yours truly, John Clayton."' Forbes-Robertson told the tale round the town to laughter until he tried it on his secretary, who did not laugh.

'You don't seem to find that funny,' said the employer.

'No, I don't,' said the employee. 'It was to me Mr Clayton wrote that letter!'

Not every play he received was a disappointment. He gave first performances to *The Devil's Disciple, Caesar and Cleopatra,* which Shaw wrote for him ('It is in the great tradition of *Hamlet* and *Macbeth*' – GBS), James's *The High Bid, The Light That Failed,* and his staple money-maker, *The Passing of the Third Floor Back.*

A feature of *The Light That Failed,* Constance Fletcher's adaptation of Kipling's tear-jerker, was a rough-haired terrier belonging to C. Aubrey Smith, called Binkie. The dog behaved beautifully except on one occasion: his growls were later explained by the fact that he had spotted latecomers arriving in the stalls; they swelled to barks when the man rose to remove his overcoat. Forbes-Robertson was supposed to be asleep through this but on hearing the dog's motivation from his owner, thoroughly approved.

The James play, written for Ellen Terry, created some controversy when James was convinced she had no interest in producing it. He re-wrote it as a short story, *Covering End.* Forbes-Robertson admired it and asked James to dramatise it. James despatched *The High Bid* which Forbes-Robertson produced in 1908, only to receive a telegram from Ellen Terry: 'You have my play!'

At 60 he announced a long farewell tour, was knighted and then retired without regret for 23 years. He had written: 'Never at any time have I gone on the stage without longing for the moment when the curtain would come down on the last act.'

**FORREST**, Edwin. Forrest had the distinction of being the first great tragedian to be born in America. It did not make him an easy man to work with. Although he was a bully, he could relent. In Richmond, Virginia a small part actor was ruining his few lines in *Richelieu*. Instruction was useless and finally Forrest abused the panic-stricken actor, who protested, 'Look here, Mr Forrest, if I could read it that way I wouldn't be getting six dollars a week.' Forrest was chastened.

'You are right,' he said. 'I ought not to expect much for that sum.' At the end of the run he sent him a cheque for $40 with a note suggesting that he act up to the money.

He met his match in a Philadelphia manager, William Wood, a grim man not given to praise. Reminiscing before a company which included Forrest, he told the group that the finest debut he had ever seen was when a young man from Philadelphia had appeared as Norval in *Douglas* ('My name is Norval, on the Grampian hills I tend my flock . . .'). Forrest rose and bowed 'with comic gravity', adding: 'Mr Wood, I was that young gentleman.' Embarrassed at being caught paying a compliment to an actor's face, he hit back: 'Well, sir, you have never done so well since.'

Nor did Forrest win in an exchange with a lion tamer whose act followed him on a bill in New York. Forrest boasted that he was unafraid. Driesbach, the lion tamer, invited him home to supper and tricked him into a cage where he was locked in with a lion. Forrest continued to deny that he was afraid until the tamer's instructions to the lion produced genuinely alarming symptoms. Forrest admitted at last that he was afraid and vowed to break every bone in Driesbach's body when he got out. This was a mistake. Driesbach exacted a promise of safety and a champagne supper before the tragedian was freed.

Complimented by an actor on the way he played Lear, Forrest was horrified. '*Play* Lear! I play Hamlet, Othello, Macbeth; but by heaven, sir, I *am* Lear!'

**FRANGCON-DAVIES**, Dame Gwen. An exquisite actress who was Gielgud's first Juliet in the 1920s, in the fifties she played his mother in *The Potting Shed* and his daughter in *King Lear.*

In her nineties, asked for her views on death, she replied, 'I am always a bit afraid of trying something for the first time.' (Compare that with Edmund Gwenn on his deathbed: 'Edmund,' said one of the about to be bereaved, 'is it hard dying?' 'Yes,' he said, 'but not as hard as comedy!')

There is another story, probably apocryphal, that when she heard that Edith Evans's memorial service was to be held at St Paul's, she was dismayed – assuming her informant meant the cathedral rather than St Paul's, Covent Garden.

'She'll never fill it,' was her reported comment.

**FRAYN**, Michael. Michael Frayn has happened upon a highly original and generous way of trying out his new plays – with varying degrees of success. On 10 September 1977, the Prince of Wales was guest of honour at a vast gala which Martin Tickner arranged at Drury Lane: all the proceeds went to the Queen's Jubilee Appeal and the Combined Theatrical Charities Fund. Distinguished playwrights were asked to contribute original sketches which had some connection, however distant, with a royal occasion. Frayn's entry in the programme reads: 'A special Jubilee Touring Production of *Guess Who, Darling!* The adaptors of this typically Ooh la la French farce into English from Georges Feydeau's *Faut pas arroser les fleurs avec ça, ma petite!* say they chose it for the Jubilee year because it was first performed in Paris in 1865, just three years after Queen Victoria's Silver Jubilee and exactly 112 years ago this November.'

Directed by Eric Thompson, it starred Edward Fox, Polly Adams, Dinsdale Landen, Patricia Routledge and Dennis Quilley. It was a huge success. Next morning the impresario Michael Codron rang Tickner and said he'd heard how funny it was. Did Tickner think it would make a play? 'Certainly not!' was the reply. Codron and Frayn disagreed. Removed from its period trappings, the sketch became the second act of Frayn's phenomenally successful farce, *Noises Off.*

A decade later, encouraged by this example, Frayn wrote a sketch for another charity gala in which Robin Bailey appeared. The child of the union on this occasion was *Look Look,* which opened with Stephen Fry and Margaret Courtenay at the Aldwych in April 1990. Unfortunately the play was a massive disappointment and closed very quickly. The saving grace of the disaster was the generosity with which author, impresario, director and stars all blamed themselves and not each other.

**FROHMAN**, Charles. Charles Frohman began his career as an impresario managing tours of America, often in hair-raising Wild West situations. He ended it by going down on the *Lusitania* when she was torpedoed in 1915.

His most famous association was with J.M. Barrie, who brought him *Peter Pan*. Frohman was enchanted by it but Barrie, considering it too risky a project, insisted on giving Frohman *Alice Sit-by-the-Fire* as an insurance. It played fairly successfully for a season while *Peter Pan* went on to become immortal.

# — $\mathcal{G}$ —

**GARRICK**, David. A case can be made for regarding Garrick as the first superstar. He advanced the actor's art and stature and, though small, had enormous stage presence. One of his most famous roles was Abel Drugger in *The Alchemist*. His unprepossessing characterisation twice betrays the naive response of some of his audience. When a fellow townsman of Lichfield, his birthplace, came to London, he brought with him a letter from Garrick's brother, Peter. Seeing Garrick's performance advertised, he paid to see the play but was so disgusted by 'the mean appearance and mercenary conduct' of the character, which he identified with the actor, that he refused to deliver the letter. Similarly, a woman who pleaded that Garrick would consider a well-born, well-off young girl who had fallen in love with his romantic characters, had to explain that now she had seen him play Abel Drugger any romance was out of the question.

Garrick's own reputation for meanness is born out by Henry Fielding, who tipped Garrick's servant a penny and then explained to his master that if he had given more he was sure he would have pocketed it; and by Samuel Foote, who said he felt safe placing Garrick's bust above a drawer which held his money because the bust had no hands.

His affair with the actress Peg Woffington seems to have been shared with numerous members of the aristocracy. One night, when they were in bed together, the current nobleman arrived unannounced and Garrick, though he managed to scramble out with his clothes, left his wig on the floor. The suspicious lover railed at Woffington until she finally persuaded him that she was rehearsing for 'a breeches part'. Sir Harry Wildair in Farquhar's *The Constant Couple* was one of her roles, so the deceived lord was forced to accept her lie and apologise.

Garrick could be severely critical of other performers. In Otway's *Venice Preserved*, he played Jaffier with great effect, but when confronted in rehearsal with a new Belvidera found her so matter-of-fact in her delivery of the heartrending line, 'Would you kill my father, Jaffier?' that he whispered in the same manner, 'Can you chop cabbage?'

His career lasted some 30 years until he retired in 1776. However, between 1763 and 1767 he gave his London audiences a chance to miss him and travelled on the Continent. There he met Lekain, a French actor and favourite of Voltaire's, who, like Garrick in England, brought a more simple, less ranting approach to his stagecraft. Finding themselves together one day in the Champs-Elysées, they pretended to be drunk, creating a good deal of amusement for passers-by. When he decided they had had enough, Lekain turned to Garrick and said, 'Well, my friend, do I perform it well?' To which Garrick replied critically – with a keen eye for detail – 'Very well. You are drunk all over, except for your left leg.'

It is reassuring to know that things could go wrong even with so moving a performance as Garrick's Lear. In Nahum Tate's version, which omits the Fool and marries Cordelia to Edgar at the end, Garrick was still unbearably moving in the last act. However, one hot May night the audience was astonished, as he bent over Cordelia, to see first Lear, then Cordelia and finally Kent 'corpsing' and running off the stage. In the front row a fat Whitechapel butcher was sitting with his mastiff on his lap. As the heat of the evening became too much, he had taken off his wig and rested it on the dog's head. The sight of the bewigged dog, staring earnestly over the edge of the stage at the action, had proved too much for the players.

**GAY LORD QUEX, THE**. H.M. Tennent revived Pinero's play directed by John Gielgud and starring Judi Dench at the New Theatre. Rehearsals were held in the crypt of St James's, Piccadilly. According to Dame Judi, one day was lost when just after work had started an unknown man rushed out of the men's loo carrying a pair of trousers. Soon afterwards, another man appeared in hot pursuit, wearing no trousers. Cast and director laughed so much that they all had to be sent home to try again next day.

**GELBART**, Larry. The witty co-author of *A Funny Thing Happened on the Way to the Forum*, book writer of *City of Angels* and script architect of the television series *M*A*S*H*, Larry Gelbart and his collaborator, Burt Shevelove, came to London for rehearsals and the opening of A *Funny Thing*. The time was the sixties, the heyday of a public breast-feeding craze. On their first night they dined with Tony Walton, the designer and co-producer of the musical, and his wife, Julie Andrews. She skipped pudding and produced her baby to feed. The next night they visited another of their producers, Richard Pilbrow, whose wife repeated the process with her baby. The next morning Larry called Burt at their hotel and said, 'Burt, are we booked in for any good breast feedings tonight?'

Gelbart also worked on the screenplay of *Tootsie* starring Dustin Hoffman, and advised colleagues never to work with stars who are shorter than their Oscars. His scathing commentaries on Hollywood continue: he recently dismissed the Japanese takeover of the movie colony in one memorable phrase – 'It's merely a question of crossing the tees and slanting the eyes.'

**GERSHWIN**, Ira (Israel). A sensitive and elegant lyric writer, Ira Gershwin was fated to be referred to as an afterthought – 'George and his lovely sister Ira' and, in Richard Stilgoe's more knowing version, as the Irish Gershwin, 'George's aunt I. R. A. Gershwin – a pioneer of the rhythm method.'

Unlike his father Morris, a Russian immigrant, Ira revelled in his new American language. To Morris 'Fascinating Rhythm' was forever 'Fashion on de River'. 'Embraceable You' from *Girl Crazy* became 'my song' on account of the words, 'Come to Poppa, come to Poppa, do.' Sometimes his gaffes worked to his advantage. Stopped by a traffic cop, he protested: 'You can't arrest me, officer, I'm the father of Judge Goishwin.' The officer did not recognise the perversion of 'George' to 'Judge'. His verdict on the 'Rhapsody in Blue', which George wrote and Ira named, was, 'Of course it's a good piece. Doesn't it take fifteen minutes to play?'

Ira's career as a lyric writer, specialising in easy, graceful use of contemporary slang expressions, owed a lot to his younger brother's precocity. He had played with light verse but then modestly, under a pseudonym – Arthur Francis, after his other two siblings – he became George's sole lyricist, abandoning the pen name in 1924. His early lyrics were not particularly distinguished, as titles like 'If You Only Knew What I Thought of You, You'd Think a Lot More of Me' and 'You May Throw All the Rice You Desire, But Please, Friends, Throw No Shoes' go to show.

For years experts held that Ira never forgave himself for writing 'The Man I Love' in such a way that it could never become a male vocalist's song. The Gershwins might would have had got away with 'Some day she'll come along, the gal I love . . .' but they would have been on thin ice with 'And she'll be big and strong, the gal I love . . .' and would have had to admit defeat with 'She'll build a little home, from which I'll never roam . . .' – at least until the final victory of feminism. However, Michael Feinstein's subsequent discovery in the Gershwin archive of a fully worked-out man's version gives the lie to this. Somehow it just never got sung.

Perhaps the brothers' quickest creation was the infectious 'Do Do Do' in *Oh, Kay!*, reversing their usual painstaking and, in Ira's case, slow process. Just as they started work on the song, the future Mrs Ira Gershwin telephoned to announce her intention of coming to dinner. It took her less than half an hour to make the journey from 8th Street to West 103rd. When she arrived, they played it to her.

Ira Gershwin's legacy, besides his stylish and amiable lyrics, is his book *Lyrics on Several Occasions*, an analysis of his craft and a disclaimer of poetic aspirations: 'Since most of the lyrics in this lodgment were arrived at by fitting words mosaically to music already composed, any resemblance to actual poetry, living or dead, is highly improbable.'

**GHOSTS**. Theatrical ghosts are the stock-in-trade of any self-respecting ancient house. Mrs Siddons has a claim on the Bristol Old Vic. The Theatre Royal, Drury Lane boasts a Man in Grey, a spectre whose appearances are confined to successful runs. He inhabits the upper parts of the house, has been reported stalking in eighteenth-century costumes – tricorn hat, ruffled shirt, boots, sword and riding cloak – and disappears through solid walls. When the theatre was reconstructed, a skeleton with a dagger in its ribs was found bricked-up and popular theory has it that this is the origin of the ghost, killed in a duel. Although a distinguished team of ghostbusters failed to find him in an investigation concluded in 1938, the next year the entire cast of *The Dancing Years*, assembled for a photo call, claimed that they saw him cross the upper circle.

The Theatre Royal, York, claims a Grey Lady with a white headdress, who confines her appearances to the rehearsal period. Back in London, the Haymarket was managed for nearly 50 years by John Buckstone (1802–1879) and his ghostly appearances, viewed by Dame Margaret Rutherford and by Donald Sinden, are thought to be a benign omen.

William Terriss's death at the hands of an unhinged actor, Richard Arthur Price, occurred at the stage door of the Adelphi Theatre on 16 December 1897: Price stabbed him with a kitchen knife as he was on his way to star in *Secret Service*. Terriss's ghost is said to stray as far as Covent Garden underground station. Beerbohm Tree's ghost apparently prefers the theatre of which he was so proud – Her Majesty's – roaming from his attic apartments down to his personal box. Arthur Bourchier, who ran the Garrick from 1900 to 1915, is reported in the back-stage area and on a mysterious staircase.

Backing onto the Garrick is the Duke of York's, where Violet Melnotte, manager from 1923 to 1928, is seen in black walking through the circle; a fire door which has now been removed is still said to clang mysteriously at ten each night.

In her autobiography, Dulcie Gray tells a story of extraordinary coincidence. She had once discussed the afterlife with Peter Bull, who had been unusually earnest in persuading her to believe in it. When she demurred, he said seriously, 'You must believe. I'll tell you what. When I die, I'll haunt you and then you'll have to believe.' Dulcie told this story to Googie Withers in the lounge of an hotel in Stockholm, where they were on tour, and had read in an English paper of 'Bully's' death. When they arrived at Dulcie's dressing room that night they were confronted by an enormous teddy bear facing them on the sofa – 'Bully' had, of course, been famous for his collection of teddy bears, including Aloysius from the television production of *Brideshead Revisited*. Both actresses were shocked. No explanation was ever provided and the bear had vanished when they arrived for the show next day.

Perhaps the theatre most stuffed with ghostly lengends is the Theatre Royal, Bath. Beautifully restored in 1982 by Jeremy Fry and Carl Toms, it has a noble history of playing and of haunting. In the 17th and 18th centuries, small theatres flourished in the town but in 1750 a more ambitious building went up in Orchard Street, where Mrs Siddons started her career, not altogether happily. As she told her journal, 'I had the mortification of being obliged to impersonate many subordinate characters in comedy, the first roles being in the possession of another lady.' So successful was the Orchard Street theatre that in 1805 an even bigger one went up in Beaufort Square, on the site of Beau Nash's old house; part of the original home still stands on one side of the theatre as a restaurant, Popjoys, named after Nash's last mistress. On the other side is another surviving section, now the theatre pub, The Garrick's Head.

For all the splendours of the refurbishment, it is the profusion of theatre phantoms at Bath which fascinate. Bath is not content with your average Grey Lady. They have one of those, of course – she has been seen in Popjoys and The Garrick's Head, but her favourite stomping ground is the top left-hand box facing the stage and the corridor behind it. Sometimes she appears solid, sometimes as a wispy, smoky figure, always with the smell of jasmine. Her witnesses include a touring ASM; a dog so terrified that he could never again be persuaded to walk where she had walked; and a five-year-old girl who engaged her in conversation while her father, who worked for the theatre, was having a lunch-time drink in The Garrick's Head. She likened the jasmine smell to 'bath salts'.

Then there is the Phantom Doorman, another 18th century figure who haunts the foyer. No story attaches to this ghost, whereas the Grey Lady is reputed to be a suicide. The Doorman's speciality is to appear only to visiting actors – he has never been seen by a member of the theatre staff.

The third and most recent ghost is an elderly cleaner who worked at the theatre for years. No one has *seen* her, but she spoke sharply to a stage technician a few days after her death. Often, when staff arrive in the morning, her patch is damp as if recently mopped and bar lists are knocked over as they habitually were when she dusted them. Moreover, her death was predicted by the theatre's most intriguing phenomenon – The Butterfly. Three dead butterflies were found three days before her death.

When I was a boy the annual Maddox pantomimes were famous at the Theatre Royal. In 1948 the spectacular effect which Reg Maddox had arranged was a Butterfly Ballet. The girls were to be dressed as tortoiseshell butterflies and a large butterfly set piece was built. One day, as the ballet rehearsal began, a dead butterfly was found on the stage. Within hours Reg Maddox died and his son Frank, who took over, abandoned the Butterfly Ballet.

The set piece was put on one side but then, in mid-winter, a live butterfly appeared and things looked up. The scenic butterfly was hoisted into the flies where it hangs today, undusted except by outsider contractors and untouched by the staff unless they explain very carefully to it what they are doing. The theatre legend is that a live appearance at pantomime time, when all good butterflies are hibernating, is a good omen, but that a dead butterfly presages death. Leslie Crowther, playing Wishee Washee in *Aladdin* in the 1979–80 season, remembered one fluttering onto his shoulders and perching there. It was a triumphant season. On the other hand, during a run *of Red Riding Hood,* a dead butterfly was found outside Dressing Room 6. Two hours later the actor who dressed there was dead. Another dead butterfly heralded the suicide by hanging of a conjuror during the run of the 1952 pantomime.

More recently, a stage hand bet a large sum on a seven-horse accumulator at Bath Races. First, he asked the butterfly's blessing. Six horses came up – and then he lost all on the seventh. Back at the theatre, he cursed the butterfly. When the stage crew moved out the heavy set, a massive moulding broke his neck.

Most strange was an incident on a cold February morning in 1981. An abandoned property box was discovered and the curious crew wondered what lay beneath the long unopened lid. They prised it open – and released a cloud of tortoiseshell butterflies, who vanished through the loading bay into the theatre. The only other object inside the box was a dusty photograph of Reg Maddox. Written on the back was *Follies 1932*. Forty-nine years is a long hibernation. The favoured explanation is that Reg Maddox returns to his theatre and uses the butterflies to bless or warn.

*Phantom Performances* by M.L. Cadey, the theatre historian and fireman, is between editions. The next may include a footnote. On the first night of *Jeffrey Bernard Is Unwell* in Bath, Peter O'Toole came to a speech about tortoiseshell hair brushes. As if on cue, down from the flies fluttered a tortoiseshell butterfly. I had not warned O'Toole about the legend and feared he might swat the creature as it was beguiling (distracting) the audience. Fortunately he likes butterflies and smiled on its hoverings. I don't claim a ghostly visitation, but it was a damn sight more encouraging than a dead insect and it certainly seemed to know what it was prophesying.

**GIELGUD**, Sir (Arthur) John. Too rich a harvest of stories attends on Sir John to make selection easy. What follows is a mixture of anecdote and Sir John's famous dropped bricks – Gielgoodies.

Two actors, one of them Sir John, are sitting on a film set, waiting for their call. Sir John is reading. The other actor, doing his *Times* crossword, looks up. 'Is there a character in Shakespeare called the Earl of Westmoreland?'

Sir John, who does not even look up: 'Yes, but it's a very poor part.'

'The nearest John's ever got to politics is the plot of Julius Caesar,' says Richard Clowes. Gielgud met Clement Attlee and his daughter at Stratford when Attlee was Prime Minister. At dinner after a performance, he sat next to the daughter 'and the conversation turned on where we lived. "I have a very convenient home in Westminster," I remarked. "So easy to walk to the theatre. And where do you live?"

'Miss Attlee looked distinctly surprised and replied curtly, "Number 10 Downing Street."'

Asked by Emlyn and Molly Williams to be godfather to their son, he said: 'Not really my part, my dears, but I'll have a shot at it.'

Guinness was lunching with Gielgud in York when a waitress asked him to sign the table cloth. Gielgud said, 'I'm sure she doesn't know me from Adam. She'll be terribly disappointed if I sign my own name. I shall sign Jack Buchanan.' He did and the waitress was ecstatic.

He was also modest about his movement – 'I do have a good figure but I'm inclined to walk badly. The critics were quite right' – and about what he could suitably wear. Alexander Walker overheard him telling his tailor that his new white trousers were too tight. The tailor reassured him, 'Tight as you like, Sir John, you're going south.'

Modesty almost precludes jealousy, but not quite. Discussing *Othello* with Peggy Ashcroft, he said, 'I don't really know what jealousy is. Oh yes, I do! When Larry had a success as Hamlet, I wept.'

Gielgud had a unique experience in being prepared for his 1940 *Lear* by Granville-Barker: 'One day, after an early reading, he said to me, "Well, you've got two lines right. Of course, you're an Ash and this part demands an Oak, but we'll see what can be done."'

Charles Sturridge directed Gielgud in *Brideshead Revisited* for television and after one scene, 'I went over to Gielgud and started to talk in a rather rapid-fire way about some of the ideas I had about how the scene should go. I was really rather nervous. He looked me up and down after my frantic five-minute speech, and after a pause, said, "Oh, so you want me to be funnier?" Which is exactly what I'd meant but hadn't dared to say.'

Dirk Bogarde recorded Gielgud's distress when his French crew on Alain Resnais' *Providence* insisted on calling him Sirjohn. 'It's so frightfully inhibiting. Couldn't you ask them and Alain just to call me John?' Bogarde knew the French would think it disrespectful but agreed to try: 'It'll be almost impossible. But if you find it irritating . . .'

'Well, you see,' Gielgud said, 'I've always been very lucky in having very unsycophantic friends around me who say, "Oh! Stick a crown on his head and shove him on." It's so much more relaxing.'

Bogarde persuaded them but, he said, behind his back he was still 'Sirjohn'. Towards the end of the picture, crew and cast decided to give Resnais a present, a tape recorder. They all wanted the first voice on the first virgin tape to be Gielgud's – they knew how passionate Resnais was about his voice and wanted him to record, 'This is John Gielgud wishing you a happy birthday, Alain, on behalf of the troupe and the actors of *Providence.*' Gielgud was resolute in his refusal, insisting that Bogarde was the star and that he should do it. The 'troupe' were dismayed. Bogarde made one final effort. 'I knelt beside John's chair in my most supplicatory manner, and spoke to him in a low voice. For the troupe had inched nearer anxiously . . . I was desperate.

' "John, please. You probably have one of the most beautiful English speaking voices in the world . . . "

'He looked up over the top of his glasses. "*The!*" he said sharply. And spoke the message.'

Even a modest man can be tetchy about his critics. He said of Tynan, 'It's wonderful when it isn't you' and about a specific notice, 'Tynan said I only had two gestures, the left hand up, the right hand down. What did he want me to do, bring out my prick?'

Gielgud was notorious for first, middle and last changes of mind right up to the last moment. 'Even if the stage doorman tells me he doesn't like the colour of my shoes, I'll worry about it. And if someone says before a play, "I don't think you should wear brown shoes, I think you should wear black," and someone else says, "I don't think you should wear black shoes, I think you should wear brown," I would probably go on wearing one of each colour.'

For his *Macbeth* he commissioned a score from William Walton and added a very complicated effects score – wind, rain, thunder, bells, doors – and kept changing his mind and adding or taking away effects. In the end there were 140 separate effects cues. Kitty Black records that after the last matinée he went to the stage manager and asked her to add one more wind cue to the plot. She was dismayed. 'But, Mr Gielgud, there's only one more performance.'

'Yes, I know, but I would like to hear it just once.'

When he directed Olivier in *Twelfth Night* at Stratford, Olivier records, 'He still had the disconcerting habit of changing moves at every single rehearsal . . . after almost four weeks and with the opening night looming closer, I began to be nervous that the occasion would be a shambles . . . at the rate our *Twelfth Night* was going, our first night would have been more like a game of Blind Man's Buff than anything else.' Olivier asked for Gielgud's absence for a couple of days, 'until we knew the moves well enough to do a run-through without a stop . . . at the end of two days he did not find that he had to alter that much, and he recognised that I had respected his production and, as I had promised, not made a single change in it.'

Gielgud's memory of the production is an interesting comparison.

'Somehow the production did not work, I don't know why. *Twelfth Night* must be one of the most difficult plays to direct, though it is one of my favourites . . . at Stratford I know the actors were not very happy with my production, partly because of the scenery, which was too far up-stage. I thought Vivien Leigh was enchanting – though the critics did not care for her very much – but she was torn between what I was trying to make her do and what Olivier thought she should do, while Olivier was playing Malvolio in his own particular, rather extravagant way. He was extremely moving at the end, but he played the earlier scenes like a Jewish hairdresser, with a lisp and an extraordinary accent, and he insisted on falling backwards off the bench in the garden scene, though I begged him not to do so.'

Honours even, perhaps.

Peter Ustinov had only one play mounted by Binkie Beaumont; it was directed by Gielgud, of whom he was in awe. It was *Halfway Up a Tree,* starring Robert Morley and Ambrosine Philpotts. During a try-out at Oxford and the London opening, he was reluctant to insist on a stronger, harder performance from Ms Philpotts, although he felt she was unbalancing the play. Finally he plucked up his courage and asked Sir John if he could make her more unpleasant.

'Oh God!' said his director. 'I knew I should have made her wear that hat.'

There was no indecision about his verdict on Ingrid Bergman – not delivered to her face: 'Poor Ingrid – speaks five languages and can't act in any of them.'

Perhaps the most endearing thing about Gielgud was his dropping of bricks. According to Harold Hobson, he was the man 'who has brought the art of the impishly desired involuntary gaffe to its highest peak of perfection'. Sir John himself confessed to having 'dropped enough bricks to build a new Wall of China'. The prototype brick is the one early in his career as guest of an older playwright, very famous but notoriously boring. Some accounts place the luncheon table at the Garrick, others at the Ivy. A man passed the table.

'Thank God he didn't stop,' said Gielgud. 'He's a bigger bore than Eddie Knoblock.' His host was Eddie Knoblock.

That incident took place in the twenties. Fifty years later a friend of mine was lunching in The Ivy. At the next table sat the imposing Charles Gray, (famous to a lay public for his cat-stroking villain in a Bond film). Gieigud appeared at the entrance and was shown roughly in their direction. Suddenly he spotted Charles Gray and veered towards his table. Just as he reached it he reared like a nervous horse and zig-zagged away again. Stopping again he turned and came back to Gray and said, 'I'm terribly sorry. I thought for a moment you were that terrible actor Charles Gray. Oh my God! So you are! I do apologise.' With that he sped on again to his intended table.

This formula was repeated with variations which cast aspersions on the skill, suitability or tiresomeness of various actresses with unique names like Athene or Margalo – followed, of course, by anxious, wildy improvised disclaimers like 'not you, Margalo – Margalo . . . Hanhanahan.'

Most people who recall Sir John's gaffes take pains to point out, like Alec Guinness, that 'They spring spontaneously from the heart, without a glimmer of malice.'

Peter Sallis reported a brick to Clive Fisher, who has compiled a whole book of Gielgud stories. Leaving RADA, Sallis had an H.M. Tennent contract and was lined up for Sir John's inspection for a production of *Richard II*. Asked what he would like to play, he opted for the gardener.

' "That's cast," said Gielgud. Then he turned to his colleagues. "He might be Green, he might be Green!"

'He then turned back to me and explained kindly, "We've got two men playing Bushy and Bagot, very beautiful. You might make a good contrast!"'

Rehearsing John Mills in the violently athletic *Charley's Aunt*, Gielgud was deep in the stalls at the Haymarket as Mills ran and ran round the Oxford set at the end of act one. Having finished, pouring sweat, to dead silence, Mills advanced on to the footlights and said, 'Johnny, are you there?'

'Yes, I am.'

'What did you think of it?'

'Interminable, my dear fellow, absolutely interminable.'

A man who called on him to congratulate him after a performance was puzzled when Sir John said, 'How pleased I am to meet you. I used to know your son, we were at school together.'

'I have no son,' the man replied, 'I was at school with you.'

Many people claim to have heard his most famous operatic brick at a dress rehearsal of a Mozart opera at Covent Garden. Sir John acknowledged that it is one of his most famous, but places it in his production of *The Trojans*. Something went wrong on stage and he was heard rushing through the stalls yelling: 'Stop, stop, stop! Do stop that dreadful music.'

When he was casting *The Laughing Woman*, a play about a sculptor and his mistress, he moaned to Emlyn Williams, 'Bronnie is insisting on Stephen Haggard for the part. He's splendid but much too well bred. It calls for an actor who would convey somebody savage, uncouth – Emlyn, you should be playing it.'

Not quite a brick, but produced straight from the top of his head, was his reply when he met a fellow actor in the wings. The actor was surprised – Sir John was supposed to be on the other side of the stage. Worried, he said, 'Sir John, what are you doing over here?'

'I'm hiding from Alan Badel, he will keep giving me notes.'

Joss Ackland supplied a basketful of Gielgoodies. When he appeared in Julian Mitchell's *Haifa Life*, Mrs Thatcher paid a visit but had to leave at the interval on parliamentary business. She confessed this when they met later and Gielgud said mournfully, 'More a quarter of a life, really.'

An American woman visited his dressing room after the first night of *Best of Friends* – a moving evening, but one attended by frequent drying. 'You certainly brought it off tonight, Sir John,' she gushed.

'My dear,' he replied, 'I nearly brought it up.'

Having filmed with Robert Mitchum in *Winds of War*, he reported on the effect on that ravaged face of incarceration after incarceration in the Betty Ford Clinic. 'Oh, Bob's looking so much prettier now.'

At a recording of *Othello*, Ackland returned from lunch to find Gielgud and Richardson sitting alone. Richardson was making pain noises: 'Ohh! . . . ah! . . . ah!' Sir John looked sympathetic.

'Trouble with your shoes, Ralph?'

'Yes.'

'Still going to Peter?'

'Yes.'

'I've been going to Peter for twenty years and I can hardly walk either!'

When Dudley Moore first went to Broadway in *Beyond the Fringe* Gielgud gave him a letter of introduction to Lilli Palmer. It read, 'Darling Lilli, This will introduce to you the brilliant young pianist from *Beyond the Fringe*, Stanley Moon . . .'

On one occasion John Mortimer and his wife arrived at a dinner party with their very young baby in a carry-cot. Sir John was a fellow guest. As the Mortimers left, he spotted the baby in the cot.

'Why did you bring it with you?' he enquired in some surprise. 'Are you afraid of burglars?'

Sir John was not at home on a horse. During the filming of *The Charge of the Light Brigade* in Turkey, he was required to advance his steed five paces and then say his line. For ten takes, he said the words perfectly but the horse failed to move.

'No, John,' said the director patiently, 'I want the horse to move five paces *before* you say the line.'

'I know,' said Gielgud, 'but does the horse?'

The agent, Milton Goldman, told a story of lunch with John Gielgud on the day that the *New York Times* announced that Alexander Cohen had bought the rights of Cornelia Otis Skinner's biography of Sarah Bernhardt with the intention of commissioning a musical.

'I suppose,' said Sir John, 'that Barbra Streisand will play first two acts, and Dame Judith Anderson will take over in the third with the wooden leg.'

Some years ago I took part in a programme for Radio 2 called *Green Room*. Produced by Ned Chaillet, it featured theatre stories recalled by Richard Griffiths, Victor Spinetti, Oliver Cotton, John Moffat and William Hootkins. Spinetti told a tale of Peter O'Toole and Richard Burton on the set of *Becket*. It was early morning and Gielgud, fully made-up, was patiently filling in his crossword. (Popular report was that he just filled it in, irrespective of the clues.) The two stars arrived apparently hung over or still tanked up from a night's carousing.

They playfully punched and thumped each other and rolled around on the ground. Sir John finally looked up from his crossword and said wearily to Victor, 'Oh, why don't they fuck and get on with it!?'

Hootkins claimed to have heard Sir John on a radio arts programme, *Kaleidoscope*, commenting on Olivier's absence from some great theatrical occasion during one of his most challenging illnesses. Rumour had it that he was dying. Asked about this Sir John went into a spin and blurted out, 'Larry . . . he's dead!'. . . 'he's dying!' . . . 'he's getting better!'

Many stories were not broadcastable. My favourite was a new-to-me Gielgoodie. Sir John was directing a play for the West End. On this occasion he was not directing himself – as he often did – he was directing another leading man who, one morning, paused dramatically during a long speech. 'No! No!' cried Sir John. 'Don't pause! We're coming to the West End. Never pause in the West End.'

Disappointed, the actor sought a reason. 'Why not, John? It's a long speech. It gives me a chance to think of what I'm going to say. It gives the audience a chance to consider what I've said. And I think it's rather dramatic.'

'No! No!' insisted Gielgud, 'we're coming to the West End. Never pause in the West End!'

'Why not, John? Why not pause in the West End?'

'No! No! I paused once in the West End and in that awful silence I heard a voice in the gallery say, "Oh you beast! You've come all over my umbrella." Never pause in the West End!'

I'm grateful to Sir Donald Sinden for authenticating, or rather correctly re-assigning one Gielgud classic. A decade or so ago the lavatories at the Garrick Club were redecorated. A fellow member asked Sir John if he liked the grand new loos.

'Oh, no!' he said. 'They make my poor old cock look so shabby!'

Checking this tale with Sir Donald was enlightening. It is another instance of a story handed down to a new generation and tagged on to a new protagonist.

'Did Gielgud say that?' I asked.

'No. It was Seymour Hicks when the loos were redone in 1907.'

Elsewhere in this book ('First Nights') I tell the story of John Gielgud's famous line when Peter Brook asked the cast of Sophocles' *Oedipus* to come to the front of the stage and say something 'obscene'. After others had tried rather feebly, Gielgud came forward and said simply, 'We open next Tuesday.' John Moffat – who is both authoritative and encyclo-paedic – traced it back to rehearsals for another Brook production, *US*, an anti-Vietnam-war polemic for the RSC in the sixties, when it was uttered by an elderly character actress.

'But,' he told me. 'I was rehearsing a radio play with Alec Guinness at the time and when the incident was reported everyone had a good laugh. At the end of the rehearsal Alec pulled me aside and said quietly, 'I didn't like to spoil a good story, but I first heard that line when Komisarjevsky was rehearsing in the twenties.'

**GIMSON**, Naylor. Naylor Gimson was a vaudevillian playing in the early years of the 20th century. He was decribed as 'a Hebrew music-hall artist'. His material was a fifteen-minute sketch, a farce called *Pollock's Predicament*. The farce action was played fast and furious in a set which featured five doors in constant use and with the tag-line: 'Rebecca, if ever

I am unfaithful to you again may all the pictures fall off the wall' at which point every picture fell off the wall and the curtain came down.

At a low period in his early career, Donald Wolfit was engaged to stage manage the act and to play a small role as an Irish policeman. He was puzzled, during the last week, to find Bransby Williams, master make-up man, impersonator of Dickens's characters and an old friend of Gimson's, watching the sketch obsessively from the wings. On the second house on Friday, when Wolfit went to call Gimson, Williams rushed from his dressing room in identical costume and make-up. Gimson was hard on his heels, yelling, 'No, Bransby, you can't do that!' In the confusion Wolfit was never sure which – or both – men he played the sketch with that night.

**GINGOLD**, Hermione. Sandy Wilson has generously pointed out Gingold's bright improvements to revue lyrics submitted to her shows. One of his, originally intended for her 1948 show *Slings and Arrows,* surfaced again in *See You Later* at the Watergate. The sketch was about a 17th century night-watchman. The opening line was, 'Twelve o'clock and everything's ghastly . . .'

Wilson had his man saying 'Hush, hush, whisper who dares, Christopher Wren is saying his prayers.'

Gingold's amendment made it 'Hush, hush, whisper who dares, Christopher Wren is designing some stairs.'

For another number of Sandy's *Medusa,* he had written the line, 'He wooed me in every conceivable shape/As a horse, as a bull, as a bear, as an ape.' This time Gingold's rewrite, again much funnier, ran: 'As a horse, as a bull, as a bear, as a grape.'

Gingold's eccentric appearance was once summed up by a small boy who pointed at her and said, 'Mummy – what is that lady *for*?'

**GOLDMAN**, Milton and **WEISSBURGER**, Arnold. Goldman was a gregarious agent, Weissburger a high-powered lawyer whose clients at various times included Richard Burton, Elizabeth Taylor and Orson Welles. They came to London each summer and gave lavish pre-theatre parties at the Savoy Hotel, hurrying the guests away in good time for curtain-up. It was rumoured that there were A, B and C lists, but the variety of guests on display on different nights belied this.

Arnold was a compulsive photographer, Milton a compulsive introducer – always adding a brief job description with the name. At his memorial service at the Haymarket Theatre, Keith Baxter caught his style perfectly. 'This is Dame Wendy Hiller who is starring in such and such, this is Miss Martha Graham whose company opens a new season next week, this is Keith Baxter who opened in a new play by Christopher Isherwood on Saturday and closed the same night and this is Mrs X . . . [lost for label] . . . who is a very devout Catholic.' Milton was known to have introduced Robert Morley to his son Sheridan, who pretended to have admired each other's work for years. Milton vaguely resented the fact that they already knew each other.

Milton loved to flourish his shaky French and on one occasion, after visiting Princess Grace of Monaco in Monte Carlo, they dined at a restaurant, La Bonne Auberge. At the end of the meal, Arnold thanked the proprietress in English. Milton was more ambitious.

'Madame, vous avez une bonne Auberge et . . . vous êtes une bonne Aubergine . . . Oh my God. Arnold, I called her a fucking egg-plant!'

Arnold's mother accompanied them on their travels for years and was always liable to minister chicken soup to a sick star. Once, at the Savoy, she hurried Arnold to the door because 'Mae West is leaving.' The departing guest was in fact Rebecca West. On another occasion I heard her, on a hot day, trapped on a sofa in strained conversation with Vanessa Redgrave. As they sweated into silence, Vanessa, who was very shortsighted in her pre-contact lens period, gamely tried a new gambit.

'Tell me, Mrs Weissburger, why did you and Arnold never have children?'

After Arnold's death Milton was bereft for a long period, but eventually built a new life with a new devoted friend. In the interim he told me that at last he had nerved himself to ask someone back to his flat. As they entered the bedroom Arnold's picture fell off the wall.

'I thought that,' said Milton, the supreme optimist, 'was a gesture of confidence.'

In his *Broadway Anecdotes*, Peter Hay attributes to Goldman a classic agent story. A cannibal chief asks a butcher for brains. He is offered lawyer's brains at $24 a pound, doctor's brains at $50 a pound and agent's brains at $100 a pound. The cannibal chief asks why agents brain's cost so much more.

'Do you have any idea,' the butcher asks, 'how many agents it takes to produce a single pound of brains?'

**GOLDSMITH**, Oliver. Goldsmith's inspiration for *She Stoops to Conquer* was, according to Leigh Hunt, based on an incident which happened to him as a young man. Asking – in Ardagh – for 'the best house in town', he was mischievously directed to the grandest – the house of Sir Ralph Featherstone. Unlike Mr Hardcastle in the play, Sir Ralph spotted the error and went along with it – taking orders, accepting Goldsmith's condescension and not disabusing him of *The Mistakes of a Night*' until he called for his bill in the morning.

Two dangers attended the first night of the play. The actor playing Marlowe had been so plagued with line-readings and intonation by the author that his performance came out in a strong Irish brogue. Moreover, a friend of Goldsmith's, Richard Cumberland, arranged a meagre claque: Dr Johnson was placed in a side box and whenever he laughed, the house followed suit. Another friend of Cumberland's, Adam Drummond, the playwright, with an infectious, deep, reverberating laugh, was placed in an upper box and told to lead the hilarity.

As Cumberland records, 'He had laughed upon my signal when he found no joke, and now unluckily he fancied that he found a joke in almost everything that was said . . . it was now too late to rein him in.'

They *just* got away with it.

Goldsmith might have relished a mid-Western con-man who attended a performance of the play in the late 19th century on the instruction, 'Pass me in. I am the author.' Knowing no better, the box-office awarded him seats.

**GOODMAN**, Benny. In Irving Berlin's *Alexander's Ragtime Band* movie, Benny Goodman played solos. However, it was the era of big bands and swing – both of which Berlin detested, reckoning that the interpreters flourished at the expense of the composer.

He didn't like being upstaged by a clarinet. When he met Goodman he admitted, 'That was the most incredible playing I've ever heard.' Then he turned the knife. 'Never do that again.'

**GORDON**, Max. Arthur Miller has recorded Max Gordon's disenchantment, as a Broadway producer, with costume drama. A play about Napoleon had failed.

'Never, never, will I do another play where a guy writes with a feather.'

**GOUGH**, Michael. In *Beginning,* his first volume of autobiography (there must be at least five more), Kenneth Branagh retails a story of

Olivier's film of *Richard III*. Gough had been out of work for some time and heard with annoyance rumours that stars like Richard Attenborough and John Mills were in line for the murderers.

'I was enraged. I started moaning about it at parties and complaining to my agent, and generally making a stink.' One night when Gough was already in bed the phone rang. As he picked it up, 'this sinister voice says "You've been stirring it haven't you?"

' "What?" says I, not knowing who the hell it is.

' "A right little shit."

' "Who *is* this?"

' "It's Larry."

' "Oh Christ. Oh Larry, I'm so . . . I mean . . . I'm . . . "

' "Which one?"

' "What?"

' "Which one of the bloody murderers do you want to play?"

'I wasn't sure how I should take this. I jumped in: "Whichever one's got the most lines."

' "Fair enough. You start on Monday week." Then he laughed. "And I hope that's the last bloody trouble we get from you."'

According to Gough, Olivier kept his word and generously broke up the filming of the scene over several days so that Gough, who was counting the pennies, could collect some more cash.

**Greene**, Graham. Michael Meyer tells a fascinating story of Graham Greene, actor, in his autobiography *Not Prince Hamlet*. When François Truffaut was filming *La Nuit Americaine* in Nice, Meyer visited a girl he knew on the set. Needing an actor for a tiny cameo role as an English insurance agent, Truffaut sought to engage Meyer, who was intrigued. Then Truffaut had a rapid change of mind: Meyer was 'trop intellectuel pour le rôle'.

When Meyer told his friend Graham Greene of this, Greene speculated on whether he would be right, suggesting to Meyer that he should be announced as 'Henry Graham, a retired businessman living in Antibes'.

Truffaut was delighted with the stranger's appearance and engaged him. Then Greene got cold feet, but he was finally persuaded not to let Truffaut down: it was a public holiday and there was no alternative available. After Greene had been dissuaded from re-writing his scene – 'You're a small part actor' – he was taken off to be filmed.

As Michael Meyer waited for more than two hours, he became more and more anxious, having heard of Truffaut's terrible temper. Eventually Greene and Truffaut emerged, all smiles. Apparently, Truffaut had become curious after staring at Greene's face through the viewfinder. Had he acted before? Might he have seen him in a documentary? Had he seen his face in a newspaper? Finally, Truffaut realised that the whole set was in on a joke from which he was excluded. An explanation had to be made. For an awful moment, Greene thought he would explode in anger; but then he gave a great laugh and rushed to embrace Greene, saying, 'What a wonderful joke.'

Greene's credit as Henry Graham remains in the film, as does his scene.

**GREENWELL**, Peter. Peter Greenwell was Noel Coward's last accompanist, and in his own right a cultivated composer of musicals, *The Crooked Mile, Twenty Minutes South* and *The Mitford Girls*. He served a long apprenticeship as an actor and musician touring India with the Kendall company and ruling the pit at the Players Theatre during its heyday.

He became an elegant, piano-based cabaret performer late in life, gaining immeasurably from his experience with Coward. It was a revelation to see him beguile a charity audience to laughter with a minor piece of Coward ('Useless Useful Phrases' from *Sail Away*) when an American colleague didn't raise a smile on the same programme with the one Coward song which never fails ('Mrs Worthington'). Alan J. Lerner called him, 'The best Noel Coward since Noel Coward.'

His Coward programme was precise, musicianly and very funny. There was no attempt to force the pace or flag the jokes. Like Coward he had confidence in the material – and the personal anecdotes were cleverly chosen.

Getting the job to accompany 'The Master' at the end was the result of an introduction from Coward's life-long composer, Graham Payn. But Peter won the old boy's confidence by doing his homework. When Coward asked him to play 'Mrs Worthington' at his 'audition' he enquired brightly, 'In E flat?', knowing it was Coward's favourite key.

'Ah,' said Coward, 'I knew we were destined to be lovers.' One night after a show a spooky man met him at the stage-door and said, 'Were you really Coward's lover?'

'No, of course not.' said Peter.

'I was,' said the man and vanished into the night.

Coward had a neat way of giving critical notes. After one rehearsal in his suite at the Savoy he said to Peter, 'I'm going to have a shower. Why don't you amuse yourself having a look at those chords?' Turning back at the bathroom door he added, 'The old boy wrote some rather good ones,' and then, lethally, 'and you're not playing them.'

On another day Peter brought in a copy of the *Evening Standard*. There was a front page article about someone 'coming out' sexually. Coward digested it, looked up and said, 'Well, here's one person who won't be coming out. There are a lot of old ladies in Goring-by-Sea who still harbour designs on my body and I have no intention of disillusioning them now.'

One afternoon Marlene Deitrich was there when Peter arrived. Coward urged him upon her as an accompanist. 'Noel,' she said, 'You know I am a grandmother. If he plays for me, everybody will know I am a grandmother!'

**GUINESS**, Mrs. A forgetful actress in Sir Frank Benson's company, Mrs Guiness once improvised her way off-stage after a scene with a Shakespearean friar saying: 'Then lead the way, for Father, heaven so shine, I can't remember another blessed line.'

**GUINNESS**, Sir Alec. Alec Guinness was an early protégee whom Gielgud cast as Osric in one of his productions of *Hamlet*. It was the end of a particularly thin patch for Guinness, who was shattered when his director suddenly said to him, 'What's happened to you? I thought you were rather good. You're terrible. Oh, go away! I don't want to see you again.'

Alec waited disconsolately until the end of the day and then asked nervously, 'Excuse me, Mr Gielgud, but am I fired?'

'No! Yes! No, of course not. But go away. Come back in a week. Try Martita Hunt [renowned coach]. She'll be glad of the money.'

In 1936, Guinness was in the Old Vic Company when Edith Evans played Lady Fidgett and Ruth Gordon Margery Pinchwife in Guthrie's production of *The Country Wife*. Miss Gordon halted rehearsals one day, advanced to the footlights and demanded of Guthrie, 'Tony, this man is impossible. Can we have another actor?'

Dame Edith and the rest of the cast expected Guthrie to resist but he did not and Lilian Baylis, instead of giving Guinness his full week's severance pay of £12, gave him only £3. Dame Edith, furious with Guinness's treatment, waited behind to say to him, 'Don't worry, everybody has to lose a part some day. Better now than later. Better a small part than a large one.' She was annoyed by Guthrie's weakness and by Baylis's meanness. Years later her biographer, Bryan Forbes, asked her if she ever got to know Lilian Baylis well. Her reply was succinct: 'As well as I wanted to.'

Guinness learnt a lesson from Tyrone Guthrie. He was marking moves in his Temple edition of Shakespeare one day when Guthrie told him, 'Don't. If I give you a bad move, you won't remember it. And that's a very good thing – we'll think of another one. If I give you a good move, you'll remember it.'

Guinness never marked a move after.

**GUTHRIE**, Sir Tyrone. A brilliant, innovative and experimental director with a gift for bravura crowd scenes and for transposing Shakespeare into different periods, Guthrie was an inspiring leader ('A director has but one task: to make each rehearsal so amusing that actors will look forward to the next one') and a sharp shooter with a rebuke.

At Stratford, Gwen Frangcon-Davies played Catherine of Aragon for him in *Henry VIII.* At one rehearsal she came to the front of the stage, somewhat vexed.

'I think I am being masked,' she said distinctly. The ensuing silence lasted a few seconds and then, from the back of the stalls Guthrie murmured simply, 'Lower the prices for the Wednesday matinée.'

In *An Actor and his Time,* John Gielgud remembers an obsessive Old Vic fan, a Miss Pilgrim, an elderly spinster who had a stationer's shop in Islington. She walked from her home to the Cut for every first night and often for other performances. When Guthrie took over the direction in 1933, she violently disapproved his appointment and haunted the stage door until she had obtained the autographs of all the players – who included Charles Laughton, Athene Seyler, Flora Robson and James Mason. Only when she had a set did she reveal that the paper was folded and that on the other side was a demand that Guthrie be sacked.

She was not successful.

Olivier credited Guthrie with 'the most priceless piece of advice I have ever had from anybody'. Feeling that he had not the measure of his Sergius when it opened in Manchester after World War Two, he was disconcerted when Guthrie said, 'I liked your Sergius very much.'

'I snarled and said, "Oh, thank you very much, too kind, I'm sure." And he said, "No, no, what's the matter?" And I said, "Well, really, don't ask . . . please." And he said, "But don't you love Sergius?" And I said,

"Look, if you weren't so tall I'd hit you. How do you mean? How can you love a part like that, a stupid, idiot part?" . . . And he said, "Of course, if you can't love Sergius you'll never be any good in him, will you?" Well, it clicked . . . gave me a new attitude that had been completely lacking in me, up to the time, towards the entire work of acting.'

Guthrie's attitude to directing Shaw was less sympathetic.

'All you can do with Shaw is to fan the actors out in a semi-circle, put the speaker at the top and hope for the best.'

Michael Langham got director advice from him. Langham was making his debut at the Old Vic and Guthrie persuaded him not to sit through his first night: 'Your own rhythm is beating faster at the moment than anyone else's in London: you'll find the whole thing unbearably slow. Come up to my office. We can always slip in at the back every now and then and watch the showy bits.'

The two crowning achievements of Guthrie's career were the opening of the Stratford (Ontario) Festival Theater and the theatre in Minneapolis which bears his name.

**GWYN**, Nell (Eleanor). Nell Gwyn graduated from orange seller under Mrs Meggs at Drury Lane to actress (comedy was, if anything, her forte) to mistress of Charles II, which enabled her to give up the stage. According to Pepys it was Lord Buckhurst who first 'got Nell away from Drury Lane, lies with her and gives her £100 a year, so as she hath sent her parts to the house and will act no more'.

Her descendants are the Dukes of St Albans. On the occasion when the mob attacked her coach under the impression that she was the Duchess of Portsmouth (another of the king's mistresses), she famously shouted: 'Pray, good people, be civil. I am the Protestant whore!'

# *H*

**HALLATT**, May. This extraordinary old character actress, who lived to a great age, was latterly best known for her performance in Terence Rattigan's *Separate Tables,* on stage and on film. She claimed a voracious romantic past and some sexual influence over the Duke of Windsor – 'You see, my dear, I had the *clutch*!'

Donald Sinden, acting with her when she was 91, was surprised, to say the least, when at the first rehearsal the old crone with lank hair and few teeth enquired, 'Now, remind me. Have I slept with you or not?'

**HAMMERSTEIN**, Oscar. The grandfather of Oscar Hammerstein II had a passion for opera and for building opera houses. He stood in his foyer, an impressive figure in a top hat.

'Why do you wear your hat indoors, Mr Hammerstein?' demanded a matron.

'Madam, I sleep in it,' he replied.

Bankruptcy was always on the cards. To one creditor he wrote: 'Sir, I am in receipt of your letter which is now before me, and in a few minutes will be behind me. Respectfully yours, Oscar Hammerstein.'

His star-studded productions (Melchior, Tetrazzini, McCormack, Trentini, Calve, Mary Garden) forced the Met to wheel on Caruso three nights a week. Baffled, they suggested lunch. Hammerstein replied, 'Gentlemen, I am not hungry.'

When eventually his venture foundered, Hammerstein built an opera house in London (later the Stoll Theatre). King George V arrived.

'Pleased to meet you, King,' was Hammerstein's greeting.

**HAMMERSTEIN II**, Oscar. Oscar Hammerstein II promised his father he would not enter the theatre but be a lawyer; however, after his father's death, he joined his uncle as a stage manager. He married early. His future father-in-law had asked if he was a virgin. Hammerstein admitted that he was.

'You mean you're going to practise on my daughter?' was the reply. The marriage was not happy and was short-lived. Hammerstein's first play *The Light* was also a flop. Its author referred to it as 'The Light that failed'.

*Rose Marie* was Hammerstein's first big hit. The London production brought him the bonus of hearing an English rose, auditioning for an understudy to Edith Day, ignoring the 'oo-oo-oo-oo' of the Indian love call and carolling, 'When I'm calling you, double o, double o.'

*Showboat* was the cornerstone of Hammerstein's early career. His new wife, Dorothy – an actress in that she had once understudied Bea Lillie and also played the role of smoke in an ashtray, while Jack Buchanan sang and blew smoke rings – inspired one lyric with a disenchanted throwaway when she told Oscar: 'Life upon the wicked stage isn't ever what a girl supposes.'

The best-loved Hammerstein story, dismissed as apochryphal by Dorothy, concerns the pecking order of words and music. Mrs Hammerstein is supposed to have been at a party where she became irritated by repeated requests to a pianist to play Jerome Kern's 'Ol' Man River'. Finally she interrupted and snapped; 'Jerome Kern did not write "Ol' Man River". All Jerome Kern ever wrote was "Da Da Dee Da" . . .'

The late thirties were a barren time for Hammerstein until a sequence of flops was broken by his new collaboration with Richard Rodgers – *Oklahoma!* Following its success he took a large ad in *Variety* listing his last five disasters, spelling out how short their runs had been and adding the final sentence: 'I've done it before and I can do it again.'

Rodgers and Hammerstein were approached to make a musical of *Pygmalion* before Lerner and Loewe, but found the material intractable. By an odd coincidence, Lerner and Loewe were asked to adapt the story of the Trapp Family Singers for the stage. Loewe cabled his negative response to Lerner: 'Dear boy, what do you want me to write – yodel music? Love, Fritz.' (Later he was to respond to a similar enquiry about *Gone With the Wind* with: 'Vind not funny, Love, Fritz.')

Cole Porter's verdict on Rodgers's music with Hammerstein is revealingly bitchy: 'I can always tell a Rodgers tune. There's a certain holiness about it.' There's an echo of this in Mary Rodgers's reported reply when someone asked her about her father's new score for a musical about Henry VIII, *Rex:* 'Thirty-two ballads and a prayer.'

Hammerstein's verdict on his own style was clear-eyed. Early on he told his protégé, Stephen Sondheim, not to write lyrics about robins and larks; 'You don't believe that stuff,' he said, 'I do.' Similarly, when asked why he didn't write in the easy, elegant, graceful, witty, bitter-sweet, sophisticated manner of Porter or Hart he replied, 'Ah, you mean people who live in New York penthouses. I suppose it's because they don't interest me very much.'

**HARBURG**, EY ('Yip'). Howard Dietz once observed that of all the classic song writers, 'Yip' Harburg was the only one to come up with a protest song: he never stopped asking why, if birds can fly over the rainbow, why, oh why, can't he?

Harburg's introduction to showbiz came when he heard Gilbert and Sullivan songs on the Gershwins' new Victrola; he sat next to Ira Gershwin in class. Hitherto he had assumed Gilbert was simply a witty poet. To keep his family, Harburg worked in an electrical appliance business. Came the Depression, his business became a bubble and poetry his only solution. As his firm went bankrupt, Ira Gershwin sent him a rhyming dictionary with a two-word inscription, 'Start rhyming.'

Gershwin also introduced him to the composer Jay Gorney, with whom he was to write, 'Brother Can You Spare A Dime?' Originally the tune had a torch song lyric on the lines, 'I will go on crying, big, blue tears/Till I know that you're true/I will go on crying big, blue tears/Till all the seas run blue.'

The song divided the producers of the revue which featured it, *Americana* (1932). As is often the way of great brothers and great impresarios, and even more especially of great brothers who are also great impresarios, the brothers J.J. and Lee Shubert did not speak to each other. Mr Lee Shubert heard the song first. He liked what he heard and sent for Mr J.J. Through a third party, Mr J.J. was asked to listen to it.

'Tell him I don't like it,'said Mr J.J. 'He doesn't like it,'said the third party.

'Ask him why,' said Mr Lee.

'He says, "Why?"' said the third party.

Mr J.J. tried to rationalise his dislike of the lyric: 'It's too sorbid [sic],' he managed. Fortunately, the objection was not strong enough to keep the song out of the show.

After her marriage to Jay Gorney, Mrs Gorney married Harburg, whose first wife had left him. It was the proud boast of the second Mrs

Harburg that she never married a man who did not write, 'Brother, Can You Spare A Dime?'

Harburg's first marriage had ended in spectacular fashion. He was writing songs with a composer in an hotel room they had hired. Mid-session there was a knock on the door. Opening it, Harburg faced his two small children escorted by an hotel clerk.

'A woman left these for you,' he said.

'April In Paris' was another song with interesting birth pangs. For the revue *Walk a Little Faster,* Boris Aaronson had created a fetching Parisian scene. Unfortunately, there was neither song nor sketch to go in front of it. Vernon Duke claimed to have hit upon the title in a restauraunt, West Side Tony's. After several scotches had produced maudlin memories of Paris by Robert Benchley and Monty Woolley, Duke removed to a battered upright on the second floor and wrote the melody there and then. Harburg, who had never been to Paris, bought some travel guides and took them to Lindy's to pore over them, completing the lyric a week later. On the first night it created no stir – the singer, Evelyn Hoey, had laryngitis. Mercifully, its eclipse was temporary.

Harburg loved to rhyme whimsically. In 'Speaking of Love', he used the phrases 'I'll be your nincompoop, just be my income poop, speaking of love.' He incurred the sweet acid of Dorothy Parker who asked, deceptively demurely, 'Dear Mr Harburg, *what* is an income poop?' According to Vernon Duke, 'Harburg let out an agonised yell, delivered a poignant address on the subject of Park Avenue parasites and stormed out of the room.'

Harburg and his later collaborator, Harold Arlen, differed over the 'big' song for Dorothy in *The Wizard of Oz.* At first hearing, Harburg thought it too 'important' for the young girl. However, he relented, as long as they could find a bridge to the song which spoke for the child. He remembered a distinctive, rhythmic trill which Arlen used to whistle when calling his dog: the notes of the whistle became the middle of the song and its rhythm affected the whole treatment. The studio's decision – later revoked – to drop 'Somewhere Over The Rainbow' from the score is probably the best known instance of a massive hit nearly getting lost. The other contender is the Mancini-Mercer song, 'Moon River', which was nearly lost from *Breakfast at Tiffany's.*

**HARDEE**, Malcolm. Malcolm Hardee was called more con-man than comic and was something of an anarchic impresario of alternative comedy. In 1970 he was detained for three years at Her Majesty's Pleasure for stealing the Rt Hon Peter Walker's Rolls Royce.

'Well, it had the keys in it. Actually I crashed it in a ditch and knocked over a telegraph pole,' he told John Langdon for his *Comics,* a history of a decade of comedy at the Edinburgh Festival. 'A minute later a police car came round the corner – we ran but didn't get away. The original Bernie the Bolt from *The Golden Shot* – was with me – so if you ever wondered why they changed Bernie mid-series, now you know.'

Other escapades included touring a pornographic version of *Punch and Judy* for adults. During another incarceration he wrote a set of sketches called *The Greatest Show on Legs* and later hoodwinked a feminist group at Edinburgh, called Monstrous Regiment, with an announcement that 'I've just read in this newspaper that Glenda Jackson has died. In the spirit of the Fringe, I think we should observe a minute's silence.' The Monstrous Regiment complied and were furious when, after the reverent minute, Hardee produced the paper again and said, 'I'm sorry, it's not Glenda Jackson, but Wendy Jackson, an old age pensioner.'

Another victim of Hardee's practical jokes was an intense American monologist, Eric Bogosian, now a cult film star. In 1983 Bogosian and Hardee were performing at the Edinburgh Festival in neighbouring tents. Hardee, irritated by Bogosian's heavy metal tape played loudly during his 'quiet bits', decided to retaliate and drove (naked) a small tractor from his tent through Bogosian's, followed by his audience of 44, and out the other side – a lunatic Pied Piper. Bogosian's fury was terrible to behold. According to one witness, 'We had to pin him down in his dressing room because he was screaming and foaming at the mouth, yelling, "They drove a fucking tractor through my fucking show!"'

A year later, when Bogosian was recording a Channel 4 programme at the Albany Empire, Hardee borrowed a fork-lift truck and bribed the staff to open the loading door at the last moment. He tried to drive it in just as Bogosian went on stage – 'But the truck was six inches too tall.'

Hardee's 1989 trick was to file his own review for the *Scotsman,* which had ignored his show. He got a fellow comedian, Arthur Smith, to write a rave and planted the article himself, having worked out the paper's system for filing copy. The *Scotsman* declined to give him more publicity by making a fuss but by that time the damage was done and his show was a sell-out. His final gesture was to drown himself on his way to his houseboat.

**HARDING**, Gilbert. Gilbert Harding, the scholarly but cantankerous panel game personality and occasional interviewer, found himself interviewing the aging sex-symbol, Mae West. After a few voice level tests, Miss West's manager took Gilbert off into a corner and asked him if he couldn't make his voice sound more sexy. 'Sir,' was Harding's reply. 'If I could sound more sexy I should not be reduced to interviewing a faded blonde in a damp basement.'

**HARDWICK**, Sir Cedric. Cedric Hardwick's biography, *A Victorian in Orbit,* turns up some interesting sources for classic theatrical anecdotes. He ascribes to a manager at the Alhambra the exchange most often associated with John Barrymore – 'Did Hamlet have an affair with Ophelia?' 'In my company, always.'

And he gives an earlier provenance for the line so often given to Wilfred Lawson. For Hardwick, it is a touring actor who spends his money not on paying his landladies' bill but on drink, and makes a swaying entrance as Richard III. When the audience yells, 'Get off: you're drunk!' he it is who replied, 'What? Drunk? Me? Wait till you see Buckingham.'

I doubt if this one will ever be resolved.

Hardwick also refers to an old actor who had the ingenious idea of opening *Hamlet* with 'To be or not to be'. When challenged, he explained that he couldn't see how Hamlet could ever speak the lines 'that bourne from which no traveller returns' after he had witnessed the appearance of the ghost, who had plainly done just that.

**HARDWICK**, Paul. Playing Old Siward in Michael Redgrave's *Macbeth,* Paul Hardwick exploited Redgrave's annoying habit of sending frequent corrections to the company on writing paper headed 'A Note from Michael Redgrave'.

The company was rent by dissension and Hardwick sent two actors who were getting on particularly badly identical notes, purporting to come from Redgrave and encouraging each actor to study the other's performance and learn from it. These notes were passed on as the second act started, without giving the players time to check with or remonstrate with Redgrave. Throughout the act they stared in hatred at one another, to the amusement of the rest of the company. After the performance, they were stopped just before they could storm to Redgrave's dressing room to complain.

**HARRIS**, Jed. Jed Harris was a monstrous – and monstrously successful – Broadway producer in the late 1920s and 1930s. Olivier always claimed that he based his characterisation of Richard III partly on Jed Harris and partly on Disney's Big Bad Wolf.

Charles MacArthur and Ben Hecht, who wrote *The Front Page*, one of Harris's great successes, invented a nickname for him – 'Chick' – in response to his oddly pathetic complaint that he had never had a nickname. Harris was enormously pleased and never asked them why 'Chick'. He might have enjoyed it less had they told him the rationale. It is short for 'Chickweed', which rubs your skin raw and is hard to remove.

**HARRIS**, Margaret. Margaret Harris – one of the great trio of Motley, the immensely innovative designers of the very early thirties, together with her sister Sophie, and Elizabeth Montgomery – told me two stories which probably belong under other colours but will remain under hers.

After designing John Gielgud's OUDS production of *Romeo and Juliet*, the girls were commissioned to design his production of Gordon Daviot's *Richard of Bordeaux*. (George Devine, as president of the OUDS, had refused to accept designs from outside the undergraduate circle until Gielgud insisted that he see Motley's design. On sight he capitulated.)

I had always heard that there was a row about 'the fleur de lys'. Margaret Harris's explanation was simple and convincing. The ladies arrived to see that dangling banners had been cut off. Starting to protest, they heard Gielgud's voice. 'Sorry, girls, they had to go, I'm afraid. The gallery couldn't see me.' They understood.

Motley also designed the disastrous Godfrey Tearle–Edith Evans *Antony and Cleopatra*. Ms Harris strayed into the stalls as Evans and Tearle were emoting. She happened upon the handsome black actor who was playing Mardian.

'Hey,' he said. 'Mr Tearle and that old lady – they gonna lose a lot of money.'

**HARRISON**, Sir Rex Carey. Often called Reg by his fourth wife, Rachel Roberts – presumably because that was his given name – Rex Harrison was the definitive survivor of the whole Hawtrey–du Maurier school of naturalistic, easy light comedy. Noel Coward told him that if he weren't the finest comic actor of his generation, the only thing he would be fit for was selling second-hand cars in Great Portland Street. Often an edgy and acerbic man, particularly professionally, he could also be a very generous, concerned and stylish host.

After Robert Morley's *This Is Your Life*, Morley met Harrison in Burlington Arcade. Harrison protested how impossible it would be for him to appear on such a programme – 'Not with my six marriages and all my troubles. But then, Robert, your life has been so different from mine. One wife, one home and, if I may say so, one performance.'

He could be considerably sharper, on one occasion dismissing an agent's wife, who insisted he should listen to her husband's sage advice, as a 'clockwork cunt'. Earlier, in a screaming row with Moss Hart, he changed the adjective to 'Jewish'.

The studied façade which concealed his Liverpool origins made it difficult for people to know the actual Harrison. The late Sheridan Morley recorded an incident at a party given by the agent, Milton Goldman. The host, a compulsive introducer, dragged Harrison across the room to meet his second wife, Lilli Palmer. Forgetfully, Goldman asked her if she knew Mr Harrison. She thought long and hard and then said, 'No, I don't really think I do.'

He learnt an early lesson in comic timing when he played with Marie Tempest in *Short Story*. Tyrone Guthrie, the director, had survived victorious after a furious row with the formidable star. In order to restore her self-respect, he used Harrison's difficulties with a telephone scene. Explaining that the actor was in trouble, he asked Tempest to demonstrate how it should be played. She happily showed off her formidable comic technique. Harrison thought it wonderful.

'I couldn't do that in a hundred years,' he said with uncharacteristic modesty.

'Nonsense, dear boy, of course you can and of course you will.' She also taught him the less admirable trick of starting a round for herself by clapping hands loudly as soon as she had made her exit through French windows.

In the film *The Agony and The Ecstasy*, Harrison played a pope, sharing (if that is the word) one scene with the excellent actor Richard Pearson. They processed down the nave of a cathedral in rehearsal. As they repeated the walk for the shot, Harrison muttered, 'Did you notice we're being lit by only one light?'

'Yes,' said Pearson, 'I had noticed that.'

'Well, get out of it,' hissed Harrison.

For all his other successes, it was *My Fair Lady* which put an indelible seal on Rex Harrison's career. He also contributed the thought behind one of the hit songs. During early rehearsals, when he was unhappy about Higgins's part in the second act, he and Alan J. Lerner were strolling down Fifth Avenue discussing their chequered marital histories. Harrison finally exploded, 'Alan! Wouldn't it be marvellous if we were homosexuals?'

Dismissing the idea as a personal solution, Lerner grabbed something very like it on Higgins's behalf and came up with the line, 'Why can't a woman be more like a man?' – A Hymn to Him.

Harrison's cavalier attitude to conductors during the run of *My Fair Lady* was notorious. When he revived the show and toured it extensively in America, a new musical director joined the company. The director, Patrick Garland, reassured Harrison that he would be able to follow this man's beat easily because he would dress him in a white tuxedo. Harrison flatly forbade it: 'I should be able to see the fellow!'

Patrick Garland also recorded that the conductor explained to Rex how dazzling the new pit musicians were going to be in Chicago, as they were all, he said, veterans of 1950s jazz bands and possessed a bright, brassy sound. On the day of the first band call, Harrison addressed the orchestra 'cowering beneath him' in the pit.

'Ladies and gentlemen of the orchestra,' he said quietly. 'It is a particular pleasure for me to make your acquaintance here, in Chicago, as I am confidently assured by our musical director that you perform with a *bright, brassy* sound. Not one solitary note of which do we want to hear because, as you know, Mr Fritz Lowe, the composer, wrote a uniquely Viennese *string score.*'

Small wonder that when he was filming *Dr Doolittle* on location in England, with a cast largely of animals, the call to fetch him from his trailer was invariably, 'Bring down King Rat.'

In later years he had difficulty with his lines. His last appearance was in *The Circle* with Glynis Johns and Stewart Granger. When an English producer visited him during the pre-Broadway tour, he asked Harrison how Glynis was.

'Glynis who?'

'Glynis Johns.'

'No idea. Lovely girl. Haven't seen her for years.'

Towards the end of his life this much-married man confessed, 'Nobody is as interesting to spend the evening with as a really good part.' Garland concedes that it is half-true, but gallantly points out that Harrison had forgotten himself.

**HART**, Lorenz Milton. The favourite lyric writer of many a buff, Hart has been described as 'A homosexual, a near-dwarf and a drunk, three traits perfectly acceptable in themselves but which, in the period in which Hart grew up, placed an intolerable strain on his sensitive nature.' Hart's pimp had always been a showbiz dentist, 'Doc' Bender. When Hart's biographers asked Howard Dietz if Bender was still alive, Dietz replied succinctly, 'Doc Bender was never alive.'

The birth of the song Hart wrote with Richard Rodgers, 'My Heart Stood Still', has inspired legend and controversy. Legend has it that Rodgers and Hart were in London to contribute to *One Dam' Thing After Another* for C.B. Cochran. Taking a weekend off in Paris, they were hurrying back from Versailles with two girls in a taxi. The cab screeched to a halt, narrowly avoiding a crash.

'My heart stood still!' said one of the girls. It was typical of the collaborators that Hart yelled, 'What a title!' and the methodical Rodgers made a note of it. Back in London, he produced a tune for Hart, who had already forgotten the phrase but, with his usual speed, completed the lyric in an hour.

Benny Green has attempted to disprove this story, largely on circumstantial evidence. I found his demolition job unconvincing and prefer to believe the legend.

Another Rodgers and Hart song with a chequered career was 'Dancing On The Ceiling'. Written for the Ed Wynn vehicle *Simple Simon* (1930), it was anathema to Ziegfeld, the producer. He harangued his writers with all the subtlety of a born impresario. 'Why can't you fellows write an ordinary song?' he bellowed. 'Why are you always so fancy-schmancy?' They wrote him 'Ten Cents A Dance' and set off for England, giving 'Dancing On The Ceiling' to Cochran and Jessie Matthews.

Hart entertained lavishly. His mother, Frieda, was once asked if his friends were not too much. 'Oh, no,' she said. 'Except von time, ven Paul Viteman came mit his whole band.'

The Hart household was run by a black cook and maid, Mary Campbell. When Maurice Chevalier omitted to tip her, she ran after him and gave him a quarter. Josephine Baker, a St Louis girl, incurred her wrath when, after her long transplanted life in Paris, she requested, 'Donnez-moi une tasse de café au lait, s'il vous plaît.'

'Honey,' replied Mary. 'Speak out of your mouth like you was born.'

Hart was irritated by criticism of his rhyming dexterity. One contemporary lyricist said, 'Larry Hart can rhyme anything and does.'

*I Married an Angel* gave Joshua Logan an initial chance to study Lorenz Hart at first hand. The show had a first but no second act and Rodgers despatched Logan to Atlantic City to see that Hart got it written. Hart's charm defeated the work-hungry Logan. Cards, cigars and drink occupied their week. Rodgers was referred to as 'The school master', 'The General' or 'A certain five-foot-eight character back home with a sour apple face'. On the train home, Hart handed Logan a few pages of illegible scribbles – his last-ditch stratagem to avoid work. The punishment was two nights of midnight oil, with schoolmaster Rodgers wielding the big stick and Logan scribbling as he tried to keep up with the improvising, pacing pair.

Hart wanted a number for Zorina, dancing a Balanchine ballet against a surrealist, Dali-esque backdrop. Dali was at the time admittedly about to take New York by storm but what, asked Logan, had this to do with Radio City Music Hall, where the ballet was set?

'Nothing,' said Hart, 'it's so Zorina can dance and Balanchine can fry Dali's ass. What the hell are you trying to do? Make this Ibsen?'

Hart had a peculiar aversion. Logan became aware of it during a Boston rehearsal. To the invitation to the Roxy Music Hall, 'Come with me . . .' a singer kept adding 'now'. Hart, a tiny vociferous windmill, exploded at the back of the theatre.

'No *now*, singers! She's a *now* singer. Did you hear how she began my chorus? It's "Come with me", and she sang, "*Now*, come with me". No *now*, singers!'

You can say the same for 'Well' actors.

Hart's sad end was hastened by the vitriol poured on his masterpiece, *Pal Joey*. Of the subject matter, the *New York Times* enquired: 'Can you draw sweet water from a foul well?' Ten years later, long after Hart's death, the same critic wrote that the show 'renewed his confidence in the theatre.'

Hart attended his mother's funeral just before his own death in 1943. On the way back to the wake he said, 'There doesn't seem to be any reason for Uncle Willie to go home.' Uncle Willie was 92. Six months later Uncle Willie followed his nephew's coffin on the same route.

**HARVEST TIME.** In 1957 Jack Sherman and Geoffrey Vanis wrote a musical called *Harvest Time* at the New Lindsay Theatre, 'an attempt at an English *Oklahoma*'. The cast was part-amateur and part-professional and included a fledgling David Kernan the year before his West End debut in the chorus of *Where's Charley?*

One critic was particularly damning: 'I understand the entire cast is studying to be amateurs.'

**HARWOOD**, Ronald. Ronald Harwood, author of *The Dresser* and a first-class biography of Sir Donald Wolfit, has two stories of obsessive artists. In Morocco he told Dustin Hoffman how much he regretted not having seen his performance in *Death of a Salesman*. Before they could dine, Hoffman insisted on screening a video of his performance in his suite, fast-forwarding all the scenes in which he did not appear.

Entertained at Malibu by Rod Steiger, Harwood expressed similar regrets at not seeing Steiger in his original television performance in *Marty*. Steiger set up a screen and a projector and failed three times to lace it up properly: it always came out upside down. Finally, losing patience, Steiger barked, 'You can watch it this way' and, craning their necks at an awful angle, they did.

**HAWTREY**, Sir Charles. The great light comedian was also a shrewd judge of a vehicle for himself and accepted Ben Travers' first play, *The Dippers*, for production. Then he got to work on the text and cut and cut it to the bone, Travers watching horrified over his shoulder as his 'favourite babies' were slaughtered. Eventually Hawtrey's pencil hovered over Travers' favourite line and then remorselessly struck it out. Travers protested faintly, '. . . I always thought that was rather a good line.'

'It's a very good line, dear boy,' Hawtrey agreed. 'On no account lose it. Put it in another play.'

**HAYES**, Helen. Helen Hayes, for years a leader of the American stage, had a theatre named after her. Some years later it was demolished. When later a second theatre was dedicated to her she commented, 'It's great to be a theatre again!'

The original Helen Hayes Theater was torn down as part of a property development round Broadway, and the Little Theater, next door to Sardi's, was renamed in her honour. An early booking there was Harvey Fierstein's fine homosexual drama, *Torch Song Trilogy*. The neon sign united theatre name with play title: HELEN HAYES TORCH SONG TRILOGY. According to Miss Hayes, two old ladies contemplated the sign and one of them said, 'Well, dear, I hadn't intended to pay thirty dollars just to see a lot of homosexuality, but if Helen Hayes is doing it then it must be all right.'

'So,' added Miss Hayes, 'at least I'm good for something at the box office.'

With commendable modesty, Miss Hayes quotes in her autobiography an early review of her performance in Booth Tarkington's play *The Wren*. It was dismissed by Franklin P. Adams in *The Conning Tower* – 'Helen Hayes was suffering from fallen archness.'

I find her paragraph on her title, 'First Lady of the American theatre', disingenuous.

'The accolade was embarrassing, because there were several other "first ladies" around – Katherine Cornell, Lynn Fontanne and Ina Claire, to name three. But since the label stuck, I began to feel an obligation to live up to it. Poor little me.'

However, in her capacity as first lady, she carried off one ceremony with considerable aplomb. The elderly actress, Irene Ryan – famous latterly as the backwoods Grandmother in *The Beverly Hillbillies* (and to a lesser extent on Broadway as the Queen Mother in *Pippin*) – felt that in return for the rewards of her television stardom she should give something back to the theatre in the shape of a scholarship to the American College Theater Festival. In 1973, when Miss Hayes would have been a stripling of 73, Irene Ryan died, a week before the presentation ceremony. Hayes was drafted in at the last moment and paid a memorably eloquent tribute to Ms Ryan. The audience, and particularly one of the judges, were moved. Bill Woodman, the judge, commiserated with her afterwards on the loss of such a good friend.

'Friend?' said the first lady. 'I didn't know who the heck she was. They told me the old girl had kicked off and asked whether I'd come down. And I told them I'd go anywhere for a trip.'

**HECHT**, Ben. The Hollywood screenwriter, and co-author with Charles McArthur of *The Front Page* claimed that he owed his move to Los Angeles in the 1920s to getting the sack from a Chicago tabloid. His offence? He supplied a headline for a story about a dentist who assaulted a patient in the dental chair. DENTIST FILLS WRONG CAVITY.

Hecht was sceptical of the claims of most Hollywood 'starlets', saying, 'Starlet is the name for any woman under thirty not actively employed in a brothel.'

He was sharp on the subject of David O. Selznick's reading habits too. Selznick loved movies based on books he had enjoyed as a boy, such as *David Copperfield* and *A Tale of Two Cities*. When he mooted the idea of

Little Lord Fauntleroy, Hecht thought he had gone too far and cabled, THE TROUBLE WITH YOU, DAVID, IS THAT YOU DID ALL YOUR READING BEFORE YOU WERE TWELVE.

**HELLMAN**, Lillian. When Lillian Hellman's play *The Children's Hour* opened to rave notices on Broadway, Samuel Goldwyn considered buying it for the movies. An aide hinted that there might be trouble – 'It's about lesbians.'

'Don't worry,' said Goldwyn, 'we'll make them Americans.' (It did get made in 1936 as *These Three* and again, with Shirley MacLaine, after the war.)

**HELPMANN**, Robert Murray. Bobby Helpmann was a witty, wilful, versatile dancer, actor, director and choreographer, born on a sheep station in Australia – a continent to which he returned for the last years of his life.

His first performance outside it was in New Zealand, where he appeared in *Frasquita*. From the stalls, a Miss Everett called out, 'Has your father got any money?' to which the young Helpmann replied, 'I think so.'

Miss Everett said, 'Good, because you're never going to make it in the theatre.'

The end of his life was clouded by a vicious *Times* obituary which unnecessarily characterised him as a 'proselytising homosexual'. In between he achieved eminence in all the fields he invaded, and often scandalous celebrity alongside. He shocked a thirties fancy dress party by appearing with Frederick Ashton as a pair of nuns. Their habits were correct from the front. They did not exist at the back.

Appearing with Vivien Leigh before the King and Queen as Oberon and Titania, they were commanded to the Royal Box during the interval. Bowing and curtseying low, their crowns locked with each other and they were forced to bow out, their heads inextricably joined.

When he choreographed *Adam Zero*, critic Caryl Brahms gave Helpmann a severely bad notice. The next evening they found themselves together in the bar of the Lyric Theatre, Hammersmith. Before his companion, Michael Benthall, could restrain him, Helpmann was across the bar and vociferously protesting.

'Caryl,' he said. 'I never read my notices myself but my mother, who is sensitive to criticism . . .'

A definitive variation of the 'I never read my notices' cry.

In his autobiography, *The Kindness of Strangers,* Bernard Braden records Helpmann's difficulty in finding the Oliviers' country home, Notley Abbey, on his first visit. Lost in the vicinity, he remembered that it was near Thame. Pulling up beside a village policeman, well after midnight, he leant out of the car, pointed ahead and enquired, 'Thame?'

The policeman checked his watch and said, 'Five-and-twenty-past-one, sir.'

I once interviewed him and Pia Zadora on a radio show. He was on first and was, as always, amusing and garrulous. She became a little impatient as Helpmann launched into a long story about Lord Berners entertaining at Faringdon. 'A white horse,' he said, 'stood in the drawing room with them while they munched their tea-cakes.'

Ms Zadora could not wait any longer to be heard. 'What, Sir Robert,' she said, in those cut-through tones, 'is a tea-cake?'

Alan Sievwright's excellent film biography of Helpmann was shown in 1990. In Australia it received one accolade he would have relished from the *Sydney Daily Mirror:* 'A terrific biographical sketch – dropping names like cow pats.'

**Hepburn**, Katharine. In New York Katharine Hepburn lived in Turtle Bay, next door to Stephen Sondheim. In the early days after he moved in, there was some friction, owing to his nocturnal composing habit, but sound proofing brought accord. On one blizzard-beset day Miss Hepburn put on several layers of clothing, shrouding herself in coats, shawls, scarves and headclothes. Smothered in all this, she seized a shovel and started to clear the pavement outside her house. A passer-by started at the energetic apparition and peered through the wrappings to see a face she thought she recognised.

'You're Joan Crawford!' she said accusingly.

Hepburn stopped shovelling for a moment. 'Not any more!' she croaked.

She toured America in an Enid Bagnold play which Sybil Thorndike played unsuccessfully in England. A very young Christopher Reeve was cast in his first Broadway role as a grandson returning from university. In the opening scene, the playwright had him ferreting through a large cupboard in which he stood while Hepburn commanded centre stage. Early in rehearsals Reeve diffidently suggested that it might be more effective if he emerged from the cupboard to play the scene. Hepburn taught him a lesson by taking the idea to the limit and insisting on playing her part from the cupboard. With her inside, so much went on in there that Reeve pleaded to be allowed to go back and the rehearsal resumed with the players in the position which the playwright had intended.

**HESTON**, Charlton. Charlton Heston's ventures into Shakespeare have not been entirely successful: his movie of *Antony and Cleopatra* was reviewed in one tabloid under the headline: 'The Biggest Asp Disaster in the World'. On one of the occasions when he played Macbeth in Los Angeles, Coral Browne rang the box office to ask for seats for the first night. She was told there was none left.

'This is Coral Browne,' she insisted. 'Can I have seats for the first night of Charlton Heston's *Macbeth?*'

'We're sorry, Miss Browne, there are no seats left.'

She tried again. 'This is Mrs Vincent Price. Can I have two seats for the first night of Mr Heston's Macbeth?'

'I'm sorry, Mrs Price, there are no seats left.'

'All right,' she conceded, 'I'll have two for the second half.'

**HICKS**, Gregg. Gregg Hicks has played with distinction in the RSC, the Royal National Theatre Company and with the Glasgow Citizens Company. At the National he featured as an ancient Briton raped by invading soldiers in Brenton's *The Romans in Britain.* His naked form was prominently displayed in newspaper photographs and, as the scandal surrounding the production grew, he was a little worried about what his mother's reaction would be. Eventually she called.

'I saw your picture . . .' (He waited for her chorus of disapproval.) you're not eating enough.'

**HILLER**, Dame Wendy. At the height of the 'method' vogue (1960), Dame Wendy Hiller, appearing with Geraldine Page in Lillian Hellman's *Toys in the Attic,* was asked to define her method.

'Well, I have a bash at it,' she said, 'and if it doesn't go, I have another bash at it.'

**HILLYER**, Lambert. According to Paul F. Beller's book of *Hollywood Anecdotes,* the director Lambert Hillyer, directing *The Shock* in 1923, jumped from a second-storey window during a rehearsal and broke his arm. Irving Thalberg was not amused. 'I told you to hire a double for this stunt,' he shouted examining Hillyer's broken arm. 'I did,' moaned Hillyer, 'but I had to show him how to do it.'

**HITCHCOCK**, Alfred. Recent biographies have emphasised the dark side of Alfred Hitchcock. His attributed attitude to actors summed up in his remark, 'Actors are cattle' is represented in a number of anecdotes. During the filming of *Lifeboat* in 1944, a young actress, Mary Anderson, was anxious to impress Hitchcock with her professionalism and to learn how to gain from flattering photography. 'Which do you think is my best side, Mr Hitchcock?' she asked him early in the shooting. Hitchcock did not even give her a look, 'My dear,' he said, 'you're sitting on it.'

Hitchcock further defined his attitude to actors saying, 'My favourite is the actor who can do nothing well. By that I mean one who has presence, authority and can attract attention without actually doing anything. I suppose I really mean control.'

One of his problems was his passion for cool, blonde actresses – his moods ranging from sweetness to sadism. Tippi Hedren described him. 'Emotionally he had all kinds of frustrations and neuroses . . . He thought of himself as looking like Cary Grant. That's tough, to think of yourself one way and look another.'

Tallulah Bankhead was one actress who earned his respect on *Lifeboat* for her endurance and her salty tongue. She was subjected to a variety of ordeals as ocean storm disasters were reproduced in an enormous studio tank. When she gave up wearing underwear and climbed the ladder to enter the tank there were protests – but Hitchcock declined to reprimand her. 'It could be a matter for wardrobe,' he said, 'or perhaps for make-up – or maybe it's even for hairdressing.'

He met his match in the head of studio music when the question of scoring *Lifeboat* arose. Hitchcock wanted no background music because in this ocean epic people would wonder where it was coming from. 'Ask Mr Hitchcock,' responded his opponent, 'where the camera comes from and I'll tell him where the music comes from.'

*Psycho* is arguably Hitchcock's most famous thriller – especially for the blood-letting scene when Janet Leigh is murdered in the shower. It certainly upset one man, who wrote to Hitchcock to complain that since his wife had seen the movie she could not be persuaded to bathe or shower. What should he do? 'Sir,' replied Hitchcock, 'have you ever considered sending your wife to a dry cleaner?'

I only met the great cockney film director, 'Master of Suspense', on one

occasion. Bernard Levin invited me to appear with Hitchcock and Ian
Fleming's widow, Anne, on a late-night television interview show and in
a sycophantic moment I decided to tell a story that I thought flattered the
starriest guest.

An extremely nervous, indeed claustrophobic to boot, friend of mine
had gone to the cinema to see a movie – an innocuous movie. Somehow
he had got himself into the wrong house. The auditorium was crowded
but he was directed to a single, centre seat and settled down for a good
laugh. The curtains parted and the Censor's Certificate announced
*Psycho* – quite soon the credits revealed that this was an Alfred Hitchcock
film. My friend had heard of Hitchcock and would not have gone near
one of his scarifying shows given the chance. However, he was trapped
centre row so he settled down to behave as beautifully as he could. He
held out until the hushed house was watching the shower scene and Janet
Leigh's stabbing.

Holding the sides of his seat he tried to stay calm but then the silence
was broken by a man sitting next to him who chuckled appreciatively in
a low and sinister register. 'Heh-heh-heh!' My friend forgot politesse and
fled the theatre. I offered this as a tribute to the Master.

He looked down his nose. 'You must have very naive friends, Mr
Sherrin,' he sniffed.

Enough homage.


**HOBSON**, Harold. Harold Hobson was the drama critic of the *Sunday
Times* for years, succeeding James Agate, whose last years in the job had
been jeopardised by a scandal in a male brothel near Gray's Inn Road.
Agate had always encouraged his gay secretary Alan Dent to believe that
he would succeed him but betrayed him by recommending Hobson, an
appointment which suited his publisher, Lord Kemsley. 'Hobson's all
right. Hobson has a daughter, let's have Hobson.'

With his particular passion for French plays and French performers
Hobson fulfilled his long tenure honourably – in spite of Penelope
Gilliat's crack that Sunday mornings were enlivened by 'the sound of
Harold Hobson barking up the wrong tree.'

His passion for France led to a meeting with one of his idols, Jean
Genet, in La Coupole. When they were introduced he showered Genet
with compliments. Puzzled, Genet asked, 'Alors, monsieur, est-ce que
vous êtes pédéraste?' 'Non, monsieur,' Hobson replied, 'Je suis critique.'

Another version has him welcoming Genet at London airport.

Hobson's daughter had come with him to drive the car. In answer to Genet's query, 'Est-ce que vous êtes pédéraste?' Hobson's reply was a flurried 'Certainly not, this is my daughter.'

Because of lameness Hobson was always early in his seat at the theatre and left considerably later than the rest of the audience. Unwittingly I once made a cruel jest about his lameness which he instantly forgave. I was writing a diary in the *Sunday Times* about the opening week of the revue *Side By Side By Sondheim* at the Mermaid in 1976 (only thirty-one years ago and ticket prices were from 75 pence to £5.95 for combined theatre and dinner). I commented on the various reactions of the critics whom I could spot from the stalls and by an unfortunate printing transposition the phrase 'Harold Hobson was first up the aisle' crept into the text – a description which I had applied to another, able-bodied critic.

When the paper arrived on Sunday morning I sped an apology and an explanation round to his flat in Dolphin Square. I got a magnanimous letter back saying that he and his wife had laughed a great deal – especially as she was always chiding him for his tardy exits.

Hobson wickedly captured Robert Eddison's sombre air in a review of his Mephistopheles in Marlowe's *Dr Faustus* in 1948: 'Mr Eddison's haunted Mephistopheles has a fine melancholy. So had his recent Feste, so had his Hamlet. I expect that this rising actor will shortly give us a finely melancholy *Charley's Aunt.*'

At his memorial service at St Paul's, Covent Garden, in November 1992, the critic John Peter recalled Hobson in mischievous mood. Seeing Kenneth Tynan across a first-night aisle at the height of the Cuban Missile Crisis he hobbled painfully to him to say, 'Kenneth, I gather that we may never see tomorrow, so I thought I would come over and tell you that I never really thought much of Brecht' – Tynan's idol.

**HOFFMAN**, Dustin. In an early incident, Hoffman was playing a small part in an Army play, *A Cook for Mr General,* which was in trouble on the road in Philadelphia. A new director, David Pressman, called a ten o'clock rehearsal on Sunday morning. Hoffman turned up fifteen minutes late and was told by Pressman never to let it happen again. On opening day in New York, Hoffman again arrived late for a technical run, but looking a mess – torn shirt, muddy face, in shock. The director asked what had happened. The actor looked agonised.

'I was in an accident – but I don't want to talk about it now.' Concerned, Pressman said no more.

Five years later, after *The Graduate* had made him a star, they met again and Hoffman confessed. He had been so frightened and impressed by the first telling-off in Philadelphia that when on the New York opening, his scooter ran out of petrol in Central Park and he had only 25 cents in his pocket for petrol and he realised he was bound to be late, he had torn his shirt, dirtied his face, mussed his hair and acted in shock in order to escape another reprimand.

'You were so concerned and worried about me,' the actor told Pressman, 'that I've been feeling guilty ever since.'

**HORNE**, David. On *Desert Island Discs,* June Whitfield recalled her first professional engagement as an ASM with this busy actor, who often capitalised on his West End engagements by taking a company, which he headed with his wife, on tour. These ventures were less profitable. June's job was with *Pink String and Sealing Wax* at the Duke of York's Theatre.

As the paterfamilias Horne said grace before and after a stage meal. The latter grace was punctuated by a comfortable belch. One night, a descending bomb, a 'doodle-bug', was heard over the theatre. It cut out just as the postprandial grace was due and landed on St Martin-in-the-Fields some yards down the street.

Horne's immediate line: 'For what we have received may the Lord make us truly thankful' was received first in silence, and then in a relieved wave of laughter.

**HOSKINS**, Bob. Bob Hoskins started his acting career at the Unity Theatre: he liked drinking at the bar there and one night was simply dragged on stage to make up the numbers. He's never looked back.

**HOWARD**, Cy (Seymour Howard). I am indebted to Dick Vosburgh on this occasion as on many others. In his obituary in the *Independent* he reassigned one of the great showbiz chestnuts. The starting point is Alfred Bloomingdale's production of *Allah Be Praised*, a terrible 1944 musical, which was limping to disaster out of town. I have always reported that it was George S. Kaufman who advised Bloomingdale, the store owner, to 'Close the show and keep the store open nights.'

Why is this entry under Cy Howard's name? Well, he was a writer, director, producer, born in Milwaukee, Wisconsin, in 1915. Vosburgh reveals that that piece of counsel was Howard's not Kaufman's. But these stories do attach themselves to famous wits. Vosburgh added two more

Cy Howard stories. He married three times. His second bride was Gloria Grahame, who told Vosburgh in an interview that she called the writer Howard Teichman, who had been Howard's room-mate in college, on her wedding night and asked him, 'What advice can you give me?'

Teichman shouted back, 'Reconsider.'

After her divorce from Howard, Vosburgh says, Gloria Grahame married Tony Ray, who was her former stepson. Howard was up to it. 'If Gloria hadn't divorced me,' he said, 'she might never have become her own daughter-in-law.'

**HOWE**, William and **HUMMELL**, Abraham. William Howe and Abraham Hummell were a pair of Broadway lawyers around the turn of the century. They were so famous for their technique of extortion – usually persuading disappointed young women to sue for breach of promise – that they fathered a regular ad lib. If there was a noise in the wings, straight man would ask comic, 'What's that?' Comic would reply, 'That's Howe and Hummell filing an affidavit.'

It was estimated that between 1885 and 1905 they must have 'taken' hundreds of men in this way. Hummel was eventually disbarred and fled to Europe – but not before he had represented John Barrymore, whom he had failed to frighten with a suit but who grew to admire his cheek.

**HUNT**, Martita. In her later years, the formidable Miss Hunt was rehearsing for a television play. At the end of one day's rehearsal, the PA gave out the calls for the next day.

'Miss Hunt,' she said respectfully, 'you're called at 9.45.'

'Quite impossible!' came the imperious reply.

'Why not?'

'Because my bowels don't move until 10.15.'

This story comes from James Cairncross who adds a footnote: 'The phrase "Just off to see Martita" has long been current in my home when Nature calls. "Martita's taking an extra curtain call", or "Martita's decided to play the matinée after all" come into play whenever a certain "looseness" is being experienced.'

**HUTCHINS**, Geoffrey. A leading classical clown with long service and consistently humorous conduct at the RSC and the National Theatre, Geoffrey Hutchins also has a dry wit. In Peter Nichols's *Poppy* he played a Victorian pantomime dame. Across the river the National's musical,

*Jean Seberg*, was dying a death. Hutchins advanced on his audience to encourage them to join in a singalong. Anyone who did not join in he threatened with two tickets to *Jean Seberg*.

Hutchins also provided what few laughs were going in *Ziegfeld* at the Palladium – backstage as well as onstage. When the hopelessly miscast Topol took over the title role, he introduced an absurd device to distinguish his various entrances as Topol, the narrator and Flo Ziegfeld, the character: he produced a yellow rose in the buttonhole and told the audience, 'When there is no yellow rose in my buttonhole I am Topol. When you see the yellow rose, I am Flo.' Hutchins was apt to wander contemptuously backstage saying 'When I do nothing, I am Geoffrey. When I stick a cauliflower up my arse I am a comic'

During Hutchins's period at the RSC he played Launce, 'clownish servant to Proteus'. John Barton's textual research proved to his satisfaction that Crab, Launce's dog, must be a large one. A huge old English sheepdog was employed, a veteran of Dulux commercials. At the first rehearsal room run-through, Hutchins launched into his opening monologue to find the assembled cast greeting it with disapproving chucklings. Turning round, he saw the dog generously relieving himself. This is a common risk when actors work with animals, but on this occasion the offence was highlighted by the shocked, slightly camp reaction of another player: 'I've got to die there in ten minutes' time.'

**HYDE WHITE**, Wilfrid. The race course always beckoned Wilfrid Hyde White more vigorously than the stage. At his bankruptcy hearing, brought on by a lifetime of living beyond his considerable means, the Official Receiver enquired, 'If you cannot tell us how you spent such a large sum in so short a time, perhaps you can tell us what will win the Gold Cup at Ascot this afternoon?'

Hyde White gave him the tip but only after saying, with a cautionary twinkle, 'Only have a small bet, otherwise we might find ourselves changing places.'

His last years were spent in America. He was asked shortly before his death why he had left England 30 years before and seldom returned. He said it was because of the Inland Revenue and his second wife. After a calculated pause to let the enormity of the remark sink in, he added, 'I'm sorry. That was a very caddish thing I said about the Revenue.'

# — *I* —

**INGE**, William. The American author of *Come Back Little Sheba, Bus Stop* and *The Dark at the Top of the Stairs,* Inge was a melancholy Kansan unable to come to terms with his own homosexuality; he committed suicide in 1973. His biggest hit was *Picnic;* its frustrated women in a mid-Western town belied the comforting Norman Rockwell image they at first presented. The play was a popular success perhaps because of the happy ending the director, Joshua Logan, forced upon it. *Picnic* won the 1953 Pulitzer Prize but Inge continued to tinker with the last act, and revived the play twenty years after its opening, as *Summer Brave.* It flopped and Logan had the last word.

'He would not give up until he had announced how foolish the world was to like this golden play.'

**INNOCENT**, Harold. Harold Innocent was a redoubtable and versatile character actor and raconteur. When he was fourteen, and already an opera buff, he went to the Coventry Hippodrome to see a favourite diva, Margery Shires, as Gilda in *Rigoletto.* After the performance he waited for her autograph at the stage door. She gave it and he precociously asked why she didn't take the high E at the end of 'Caro Nome', 'Like Erna Berger does on the record?'

The unconcerned Miss Shires shook her fur coat contemptuously and flounced away saying, 'I've more to do with my time.'

**IRVING**, Sir Henry (John Henry Broadribb). Garrick, Irving and Olivier are the three actors who have caught the public imagination and will remain household words. Kean perhaps. Mrs Siddons for the ladies – again, perhaps.

Irving reckoned Kean's reputation to be a posthumous one: 'If you read the newspapers of the time you will find that in his acting days he was terribly mauled.' Irving was probably protecting the tail of his own reputation because he, too, was much maligned as well as much praised in his day, but he need not have worried about the legend.

He was plainly disconcerting at first sight. His Hamlet was controversial, modern in its time and disapproved by an older generation of actors and critics for its 'naturalness'. His pronunciation was eccentric and his movement mannered to the grotesque, but Shaw, one of his severest critics wrote, 'Those who understand the art of the theatre and knew his limitations could challenge him on every point except one and that was his eminence. Even to call him eminent belittled his achievement: he was pre-eminent. He was not pre-eminent for this, that or the other talent or faculty: his pre-eminence was abstract and positive: a quality in itself and in himself so powerful that it carried him to Westminster Abbey.'

His first public performance was in Cornwall before he was ten. An old woman had been threatening village children with hellfire; Irving appeared at her bedside in horns, a mask and tail. His 'career' was interrupted while he returned to his parents in London. (He had been sent to Cornwall for the benefits of country air and food.) His headmaster at the City Commercial School helped his stammer by attaching great importance to elocution. His conversion to Methodism at his mother's urging was swiftly followed by his re-conversion to acting by Phelps's performance as Hamlet. He worked as a clerk and acted as an amateur until an uncle's gift of £100 set him free. He took the name Irving when he was paid £3 to play Romeo at the Soho Theatre. He got an engagement in Sunderland at the Royal Lyceum and committed himself to ten years of hardship and starvation. He was raw: Bancroft compared him in those days to Dickens's country actors, Mr Lenville and Mr Folair.

Irving used to tell a story against his early acting. He was giving his Hamlet and was flattered to see an old lady in tears. He summoned her after the performance and told her how moved he was that she had been moved.

'Indeed I was,' she said. 'I've a young son myself play-acting somewhere in the north, and it broke me up to think that he might be no better at it than you.' Years later he would tell apprentice actors: 'Watch, watch always, and if you see nothing worth copying you will see something to avoid.'

Another Irving legend dates from his Sunderland period. After minute roles, he was cast as Cleomenes in *The Winter's Tale* and dried; running offstage to catcalls. His employers and his colleagues stood by him and he thanked them in a promise he would one day keep: 'If ever I rise I shall not forget this.'

In 1866 he had his 'break'. Turned away from the Prince of Wales in Liverpool where there was no work for him, he was called back by the stagedoor keeper, who handed him a letter from Dion Boucicault offering him a part in a new play opening in Manchester. The part was a villian, Rawdon Scudamore, the play *The Two Lives of Mary Leigh*. He came to London in the part and his success was assured.

The incident which propelled him to the Lyceum occurred when he played Digby Grant in James Aubrey's play *Two Roses* and, taking the 291st night of the run as his benefit, he recited 'The Dream of Eugene Aram' by Hood at the end. In the audience was Hezekiah Bateman, an American impresario impressed by Irving's hypnotic power. He invited Irving to join the Lyceum Company where he was to launch his fourth daughter, Isabel. Two quick flops gave Irving a chance to militate for *The Bells*, an adaptation of a French play, *Le Juif Polonais*.

Irving took over the Lyceum and triumphed again in a fully restored *Richard III*. In that tradition of handing on theatrical props, he was handed Kean's Richard sword and Garrick's ring. It was only four years since Irving had invaded London and now he was the undisputed leader of his profession. Of course, another revolution was already brewing, led by Shaw and Ibsen and Granville Barker, a movement which would soon consider him romantic and passé.

It is at this point that we must consider the famous anecdote of the breakup between Irving and his wife. After a long affair with Nellie Moore, a talented actress who died in questionable circumstances, he married Florence O'Callaghan, a smart playgoer, comfortably off, quite unsuitable to be an actor's wife. After the excitement of the first night of *The Bells*, he took her home in a brougham. By this time they had one child and were expecting another. At Hyde Park Corner he said to her, 'Well, my dear, we too shall soon have our carriage and pair.'

Florence Irving turned on him. 'Are you going on making a fool of yourself like this all your life?'

Irving stopped the cab, got out and never spoke to his wife again.

Biographies differ in their stories of Irving's affair with Ellen Terry. To Laurence Irving and Roger Manvell, it was never consummated. Marguerite Steen held that it was on direct information from Ellen: one of his few letters to her is signed 'My own dear wife as long as I live.'

His first nights were haunted by the presence of his implacable wife and two small sons in the stage box. The boys were taught to refer to their father as 'The Antique' and his leading lady as 'The Wench'. Florence attended looking for failure and was overjoyed when she found it: '*Romeo and Juliet* at Lyceum – jolly failure – Irving awfully funny.' Irving was, however, very short-sighted and we must hope that he could not see her.

Sir John Martin Harvey used to tell a story of a theatrical horse, Lily, where Irving had the punch line. The horse's handler extolled her virtues and her roles: 'Rosinante' in *Don Quixote* and 'White Surrey' in *Richard III,* and assured Irving that she never minded any one mounting her, 'Except one gentleman.'

Irving asked who it was.

'Gentleman you may have heard of, sir – Mr Beerbohm Tree.'

'Oh,' said Irving, patting the horse. 'Nice beast! Critic, too, eh?' (Another version has the horse yawning at the mention of Tree's name.)

After a performance by Seymour Hicks in a French farce, Irving came round and said, 'Well, you're at the comedy game, I see, eh? You remind me of Charles Mathews, very like him, very.'

'I'm so glad,' said Hicks.

'Yes,' said Irving, 'you wear the same sort of collars.'

Irving could smile at himself too. With Ellen Terry and her daughter, Edith Craig, he was carrying a large brown paper bag of recently boiled shrimps. Edith Craig noticed that they were leaking into Irving's lap and drew his attention to it.

'Ah,' he murmured. 'Poor things, they're nervous.'

An actor-manager for whom he had worked forgot Irving at the height of his fame. Charles Dillon, by then very old, was in the foyer of the Lyceum when Irving was contemplating the display celebrating his 200th performance of Hamlet. Having failed to remember Irving after many clues, he finally scratched his head, 'Irving, h'm yes, I seem to remember the name . . . And what are you doing now, Irving?'

The honour of Irving's knighthood, the culmination of his crusade for recognition of the actor's art and the respectability of the profession, was preceded by a lecture he gave to the Royal Institution. Its message was put more forcefully by Shaw in print.

'What Mr Irving means us to answer is this question: "The artist who composed the music for King Arthur is Sir Arthur Sullivan; the artist who composed the poem which made King Arthur known to this generation died Lord Tennyson; the artist who designed the suit of armour worn by

King Arthur is Sir Edward Burne-Jones; why should the artist who plays King Arthur be only Mister Henry Irving?"'

In the same year Irving received his knighthood. Max Beerbohm points an inimitable picture of his glimpse of the usually solemn, prelatical actor in a brougham near Marble Arch, on his way to Paddington to catch the train to Windsor.

'As I caught sight of him on this occasion . . . he was the old Bohemian and nothing else. His hat was tilted at more than its usual angle, and his long cigar seemed longer than ever; and on his face was a look of such ruminant sly fun as I have never seen equalled. I had but a moment's glimpse of him; but that was enough to show me the soul of a comedian revelling in the part he was about to play – of a comedic philosopher revelling in a foolish world. I was sure that when he alighted on the platform of Paddington Station his bearing would be more than ever grave and stately, with even the usual touch of Bohemianism obliterated now in honour of the honour that was to befall him.'

It befell him in 1895 and Queen Victoria was reported to have departed from her usual practice by adding, 'We are very, very pleased.'

Irving was to resent Ellen Terry's correspondence of friendship with Shaw ('Pshaw' to Irving, who told his son Laurence that he would 'cheerfully have paid Shaw's funeral expenses at any time') – she was to lose his immediate affection to a Mrs Aria.

In the next century, when Marguerite Steen gave Terry a book by Mrs Aria which contained a passage about Irving, she glanced at the author's name and 'laid the book quietly aside. "Thank you, my dear, Henry left me for Mrs Aria."'

He was reconciled with his sons but not with his wife. The profits at the Lyceum dwindled and then sets for 44 plays were destroyed in a warehouse fire. More tours to the provinces and to America yielded less, and ill-health was taking a heavy toll. In 1899 Ellen Terry was let go on one such tour on which the three plays chosen contained no roles for her. She called it 'the dirty kick-out', but she returned for other seasons at the Lyceum and their farewell *Merchant* together at the end of the 1902 season.

Irving died in the hall of his hotel in Bradford in 1905 after a performance in *Becket*. His last words were, 'Into thy hands Lord, into thy hands.' Julia Hastie, who used to be a long-time character and theatrical landlady in Stratford-upon-Avon, was at that time an artist's model. She had turned down two tickets for what turned out to be that last performance.

The aftermath of Irving's death has not been equalled – except perhaps by the crowds at Marie Lloyd's funeral seventeen years later. Flags were flown at half-mast across the country. In London, the cabbies festooned their whips with black bows. At the Garrick, Beerbohm Tree was dining with a group of friends when the news arrived. Together they rose and left the building. Ellen Terry was playing in Manchester when she heard the news. She collapsed and the curtain was rung down.

Baroness Burdett Coutts arranged a lying-in-state at her London home while awaiting the verdict of the Dean of Westminster about an Abbey burial. The dean, prompted by his virulently anti-theatrical sister, said no. Some years before, Sir Anderson Critchell, an oculist, had saved the dean's sight. Conveniently he remembered that he had been offered any favour in return. He claimed it and paid the ceremony's bill. So Irving was buried in the Abbey beside Garrick, at the feet of the statue of Shakespeare.

Shaw, who received a ticket for the ceremony from Sir George Alexander, declined it with a note: 'I return the ticket for the Irving funeral. Literature, alas, has no place at his death as it had no place in his life. Irving would turn in his coffin if I came, just as Shakespeare will turn in his coffin when Irving comes.'

Bruce Lockhart's diaries contain an Irving-Ellen Terry story of which I gravely doubt the authenticity – however, I like the pay-off.

Conversation between Ellen Terry and Henry Irving after their performance in *Julius Caesar*.

'May I see you home, Ellen?'

'Yes.'

'May I come up and have supper with you?'

'Yes.'

After supper: 'May I undress you?'

'Yes.'

How divine, how beautiful, etc: 'May I undress myself?'

'Yes.'

He does. Ellen looks down. Does not think much of what she sees. Says so.

'Ah!' says Irving. 'You are Cleopatra, Venus, all that is lovable and beautiful! But as for me, I come to bury Caesar not to praise him!'

**IVY, THE**. The great theatrical restaurant which flourished from the twenties to the sixties became fashionable when Cochran's early revues, with Alice Delysia, were running opposite its site at the Ambassadors. It had been a derelict scene store attached to the St Martins and when Cochran took over that theatre he sold it to a restaurateur. His staff and his orchestra began to patronise it. Delysia, always on the look-out for a good meal, became a regular and attracted a larger clientele and made it fashionable. She also found a name for it as she contemplated her crowd of hangers-on: 'Actors cling like ivy, don't you think?' she said, and the name stuck. Mercifully, both the Ivy and the Caprice are now restored to their former fashionable theatrical glory.

# — J —

**JAZZ STORIES**. Jazz has spawned a literature of put-downs and gags. Wally Stott defined it sceptically: 'If you're in jazz and more than ten people like you, you're labelled commercial.'

Louis Armstrong was more downright: 'Hot can be cool and cool can be hot and each can be both. But hot or cool, man, jazz is jazz.'

Unsurprisingly Anthony Burgess used longer words: 'Jazz . . . was illiterate, instinctual, impulsive, aleatoric, unscorable, unprintable – therein lay its charm.' Jazz is religious for Father G.V. Kennars, SJ: 'To swing is to affirm'; or, as Duke Ellington put it in a lyric with Irving Mills, 'It Don't Mean a Thing if it Ain't Got that Swing.'

Of bop Ellington said, 'Playing bop is like Scrabble with all the vowels missing.' Paderewski saw jazz as 'a terrible revenge by the culture of the Negroes on that of the Whites.'

To Charlie Parker it was 'Your own experience, your thoughts, your wisdom. If you don't live it, it won't come out of your horn.'

John Phillip Souza, however, was dubious. 'Jazz will endure, just as long as people hear it through their feet instead of their brains!'

Bill Crow collects some of the most venerable jazz jokes in his *Jazz Anecdotes*: 'How late does the band play?' 'About a half a beat behind the drummer.'

'What's the difference between a bass and a cello?' 'Bass burns longer.'

'How can a jazz musician end up with a million dollars?' 'Start out with two million.'

'What sort of people hang around musicians?' 'Drummers.'

Crow cites an amusing incident when Sid Caesar, not yet a star comic, was playing saxophone with Gene Krupa's band. Teddy Napoleon was playing piano and his sister Josephine was the vocalist. The three of them were in a car on the way to a gig in New Jersey when a cop stopped them for speeding. Examining Napoleon's licence he queried the name 'Napoleon'.

Caesar started to laugh and said, 'Yes, and I'm Caesar!' The cop frowned and pointed to the girl in the back. 'Caesar and Napoleon, eh? And I suppose the girl is Josephine?' 'Yeah, how did you know?'

Drink and drugs feature heavily in the literature of jazz. When the trumpeter Johnny Best saw a sign in a Holiday Inn which read: 'HAPPY HOUR – ALL YOU CAN DRINK FOR A DOLLAR', he made straight for the bartender with: 'Give me two dollars' worth.'

Gene Quill, saxophonist, was playing at Birdland when a picky customer said snidely, 'All you're doing is playing just like Charlie Parker.' Quill made to hand him his saxophone. 'Here!' he said. '*You* play like Charlie Parker.'

I like the response of Bobby Hackett, a man famous for never saying anything bad about anyone, even Hitler: 'Well, he was the best in his field.'

Bill Crow ends his introduction with a classic shaggy dog. Red Kelly, a bass player with the Woody Herman band in the fifties, got drunk at a party and spilt ink on a white rug. He panicked, fled the house and collapsed in bed. Next day he returned in remorse to pay for cleaning the rug and accidentally sat on a small dog and killed it. He fled again never to return. As with all good anecdotes it bucketed around. It was elaborated. It was ascribed to various musicians. Crow checked out the story with Red Kelly at his home in Tacoma, Washington. Kelly explained that he had heard the story in Seattle from a trombone player called Mike Hobi who had read it somewhere. Kelly loved the story and repeated it *ad nauseum* until people assumed it was autobiographical.

'Total strangers would come up and say, "Are you the guy who sat on the dog?"' Finally he got tired of denying it and went along with the legend.

Ironically, he finally returned to Seattle and bumped into Mike Hobi again who said, 'Listen, tell me that story about you and the dog again?' Full circle.

In 2007 I heard the same story – inevitably attributed to John Gielgud! Unlikely.

**JEANS**, Isabel. This exquisite, orchidaceous comedienne was never quite accorded the admiration she deserved. She first appeared in 1909 but found fame in 1924 in a series of Restoration revivals – most particularly as Margery Pinchwife in Wycherley's *The Country Wife*. In 1945, elegantly gowned by Cecil Beaton, she triumphed as Mrs Erlynne in *Lady*

*Windermere's Fan.* When it was revived again in 1966 she said, 'I am playing the Duchess of Berwick and Coral Browne is playing my part.'

Her passion was for the preservation and projection of her beauty. When she took over from Margaret Rutherford in a production of *The Rivals,* she could barely understand why she was being cast as an ostensibly unattractive woman. However, the comedy speed of 'our little comedienne' – Ralph Richardson's words – lopped some fifteen minutes off the playing time.

Her American friend, Burt Shevelove, took her to dinner one evening, having lunched with Irene Browne. As he picked Isabel up, he unwisely remarked that Irene had mentioned that the two actresses had known each other for years but had never been friends.

'I suppose,' Browne had conjectured, 'it was because we were always up for the same parts.'

'Up for the same parts!' Jeans screamed. 'Up for the same parts! I was a star, Burtie! She used to decorate a cameo in the third act.' For the rest of the evening her conversation was punctuated by cries and mutters of 'Up for the same parts!'

**JEFFERSONS, THE**. The theatrical dynasty of the Jeffersons, known in America throughout the 18th century, descended from Thomas Jefferson, an English actor who married a girl invariably known as Miss May, who was described by Tate Wilkinson as 'one of the most elegant women I ever beheld'. Her father, who hated actors, consented to her marriage only if her bridegroom agreed to forgo her dowry if she acted. She did and he did. She lived until 1776 when she was said to have died 'of excessive laughter'.

The first Joseph Jefferson (there were three famous bearers of the name) arrived in America in 1795. His speciality was playing, while quite young, wizened and feeble old men. So convincing was he that one woman offered to start a subscription for his peaceful retirement. His skill earned him the nickname 'Old' Jefferson.

Joseph Jefferson II helped on occasions to paint scenery and in one case, at least, to build a theatre in Springfield, Illinois. Its opening was threatened by a fundamentalist religious revival in the neighbourhood and a crippling licence fee. That paying it was avoided was thanks to the voluntary, unpaid intervention of a young local lawyer who negotiated with the council with a brilliant history of the theatre. A drama enthusiast, he was Abraham Lincoln.

After being carried on at three as a child in Sheridan's *Pizarro* and cutting his teeth under the management of the daunting Laura Keane in her stock hits like *Our American Cousin,* Joseph Jefferson III (born in 1829) scored his greatest success as *Rip Van Winkle* in Dion Boucicault's adaptation of the Washington Irving story. In his autobiography, he tells the story of how he acquired the wig and beard and practised with them in front of a mirror in his lodgings. Unaware that the blind was not drawn, he gestured and grimaced for some twenty minutes until a maid warned him that there was a policeman at the door and that a crowd had gathered, shocked by the antics of a now old man. This gave Jefferson confidence when Boucicault gave him a disappointing note after the dress rehearsal on 4 September, 1865. The actor was told: 'You are shooting over their heads.'

He replied, 'I am not even shooting at their heads. I am aiming for their hearts.' He was to play the part for years.

**JOHNSON**, Dame Celia. One of the best-loved and most vividly remembered actresses, Celia Johnson is etched in everybody's memory for her performance in *Brief Encounter.* Her essentially English quality and her 'un-actressy' approach to acting marked her out from many of her colleagues. Her biographer, her daughter Kate Fleming, allows us an uncharacteristic but enduring glimpse of her being catty *sotto voce* at a TV awards ceremony when her performance in *Staying On,* again with Trevor Howard, was pipped at the post by Dame Peggy Ashcroft (for *Caught in a Train* and *Cream in my Coffee*): 'I thought she was just the teeniest bit hammy,' said Dame Celia.

Her career was organised around her family – though she was an incompetent cook and no great manager – while acting came easily and naturally. At one stage Evelyn Waugh wrote testily to Lady Pamela Berry that Peter Fleming's 'wife has had to leave the stage because they have no cook!' Earlier in her career the impresario 'Binkie' Beaumont said of a new play, 'Oh, Celia will only do it if she wants a new pair of curtains.'

Helping to cast *The Reluctant Debutante*, she insisted on Jack Merivale. 'Is he a good actor?' asked E.P. Clift, the producer. 'I wouldn't know about that,' she answered, 'but he can drop me every night at Henley Bridge on the way home.'

She made her only appearance in New York in 1931 as Ophelia to Raymond Massey's disastrous *Hamlet.* When they arrived in America the producer, Norman Bel Geddes, said ominously, 'I've altered the script a bit.' On the out-of-town opening in Philadelphia the curtain rose to Leon Quatermaine's whispered plea in the wings: 'Forgive us, Master Will, for what we are about to perpetrate,' and the *New York Times* later decided that 'Mr Bel Geddes and Shakespeare disagree most violently about the theme of the play.'

The English cast members amused themselves looking for hidden characters in the text. They unearthed Marshall Storck, a Scandinavian military man, 'with martial stalk'; an Irish Wolfhound, Pat, 'Now might I do it, Pat'; and Horatio's girlfriend, Felicity, 'Absent thee from Felicity awhile.'

During her later years, Dame Celia often played opposite Sir Ralph Richardson. In the partnership, Frith Banbury, the director of *The Flowering Cherry*, found that a good way of getting through to Sir Ralph, 'who was not always amenable to authority', was via her. By the time Lindsay Anderson directed them in William Douglas-Home's *The Kingfisher*, she had refined her own powerful eccentricities and he found both 'pretty well impervious to suggestion . . .' One evening at a preview he muttered to Joe Davis, the veteran lighting designer, 'They've got me licked.'

**JOHNSON**, Dr Samuel. Johnson's forays into the theatre, principally his tragedy *Irene*, staged at Drury Lane by Garrick, were not successful, but his words on Garrick's death have lived: 'I am disappointed in that death which has eclipsed the gaiety of nations and impoverished the public stock of harmless pleasure.' After *Irene* Garrick had said, 'When Johnson writes tragedy, declamation roars and passion sleeps; when Shakespeare wrote he dipped his pen in his own heart.'

Johnson was also generous about Garrick during his lifetime. When asked after they had had some disagreement if the great actor deserved his fame, he replied, 'Oh, sir, he deserves every thing that he has acquired, for having seized the very soul of Shakespeare; for having embodied it in himself; and for having expanded its glory over the world.'

When this was reported to Garrick he was moved. 'Such praise from such a man! *This* atones for all that has passed.'

Johnson also felt that, 'Here is a man who has advanced the dignity of his profession. Garrick made a player a higher character.'

The Doctor's opinion on plays was often solicited and tartly given. Asked about Joseph Reed's tragedy *Dido*, he said, 'Sir, I never did the man injury, yet he would read his tragedy to me.' When a woman playwright insisted he look over her *Siege of Sinope* before it went into production, he was evasive and told her that it would be better for her to re-examine it herself.

She pleaded that she already had 'too many irons in the fire'.

'Why then, madam,' he replied, 'the best thing I can advise you to do is to put your tragedy along with your irons!'

**JOLSON**, Al (Asa Yoelson). The legendary blackface Broadway entertainer, an original 'Mr Showbusiness' was, like Irving Berlin, the son of a Kosher butcher. He went on to amass a fortune through charismatic singing performances and shrewd investments.

He was apt to take over performances by button-holing audiences and asking, 'Do you want the rest of this plot or would you rather have me sing a few songs?' The invariable show of hands sent the rest of the company home while Jolson sang into the small hours.

In 1918, when he was 35, Jolson started singing lessons for the first time – after six he stopped, saying that he thought they were damaging his voice. He provided George Gershwin with his first success, 'Swanee'. The song, with a lyric by Irving Caesar, had failed in one revue elaborately staged with showgirls whose toe shoes lit up; hearing Gershwin sing it at a party, Jolson annexed it and propelled it to triumph. He married Ruby Keeler shortly before she opened in another Gershwin musical, Ziegfeld's *Liza,* in 1929.

In a much-recounted incident on the first night out of town, Miss Keeler is supposed to have suffered stage fright and to have been unable to remember the words of her big number. As the director Bobby Connolly yelled, 'Come on, Ruby!' Jolson jumped up in the orchestra stalls and sang the song at her, restoring her confidence and encouraging her to dance merrily down an elaborate staircase as rehearsed. Legend has it that he continued to practise the stunt until opening night in town, to the delight of audiences. Miss Keeler's memory is different. She says Jolson couldn't resist getting in on the act on the first occasion and that she would have been furious if he had ever done it again.

A frightening thought, Jolson nearly played Porgy in a musical version which did not quite get written by Jerome Kern and Oscar Hammerstein before the Gershwins finally nailed their masterpiece.

To the dismay of producers, Jolson was inclined to leave shows at a whim – particularly if the weather was cold. In 1940 he returned to Broadway in *Hold on to Your Hats* written by E.Y. Harburg and Harold

Arlen and with Martha Raye carried it to a serviceable success. However, twenty weeks into the run, he decided that the cold New York winter did not promise him the sort of weather to which he wished to remain accustomed and while the show still had several months left in it he left for warmer weather and the horse-racing he was missing sorely. The producers might have been warned. Some twenty years earlier, disapproving the chill of Chicago when he was playing in *Bombo,* he had been bewitched by a neon sign flashing, 'It's June in Miami. It's June in Miami.' Without telling his producers, he left for Miami in the morning.

**JUNKIN**, John. When John Junkin toured *The Odd Couple* and opened in Nottingham, he and his co-star celebrated not wisely but too well after their successful first night. When John retired to bed he dropped off into a deep sleep. Half an hour later he became aware of a noise which, as he wrenched himself into consciousness, he recognised as a thunderous pounding on his bedroom door. He groped his way blearily to open it and was confronted by an Irish night porter who looked at him solicitously.

'Excuse me, sir,' he said. 'Are you the gentleman who's locked out of his room?'

# — _K_ —

**KA-NCUBE, SELLO MAAKE**. Sello Maake Ka Ncube is a charismatic South African actor who had a great success at the RSC with his Othello to Anthony Sher's Iago, and in Johannesburg and Britain as Aaron the Moor opposite Sher's Titus Andronicus. He has enormous presence, keen intelligence and an attractive and musical voice – compelling in the lines from Titus:

> '. . . For all the water in the ocean
> can never turn a swan's black legs to white,
> Although she lave them hourly in the flood.'

He is also a soap star in South Africa. When he appeared as Mark Antony he had to quell applause from schools audiences and explain at the outset that this was a play and that they must not cheer every time he entered.

The bloodshed in Titus Andronicus sat famously on South Africa's recent history of violence. School children watched the riot of slaughter intently but unmoved until the curtain calls, when the dead stood up to take their applause. Then one little boy burst into tears. Asked why, he wanted to know if his murdered father too might rise up again.

**KAUFMAN**, George S. Writer, director, wit, Kaufman had a wicked tongue and impeccable timing; he was profusely quoted, not always accurately and often apocryphally, in New York columns and at dinner parties. He had started as a journalist and then drama editor at the _New York Times_ – incorruptible and the bane of press agents: 'How do I get our leading lady's name into your newspaper?' asked one.

'Shoot her,' said Kaufman.

His critical notices often employed the snappy style of the day: 'There was laughter at the back of the theatre, leading to the belief that someone was telling jokes back there'; 'I was underwhelmed.'

Kaufman's biographer says 'He once wrote: "I saw the play at a disadvantage. The curtain was up,"' but this attribution is disputed. Peter Hay in *Broadway Anecdotes* gives the line to Groucho Marx, who mischievously ascribed it to Kaufman in an interview with Walter Winchell. Winchell printed it, giving the credit to Kaufman, with the result that the play's producer did not speak to Kaufman for five years. Then Groucho owned up.

His first wife, Beatrice Kaufman, was not short of stylish comments. When his affair with Mary Astor broke as a major scandal, she said, 'I am not going to divorce Mr Kaufman. Young actresses are an occupational hazard for any man working in the theatre.'

On their fifth wedding anniverary, Alexander Woollcott sent them a telegram: 'I have been looking around for an appropriate wooden gift and am hereby pleased to present you with Elsie Ferguson's performance in her new play.' Kaufman summed up Gertrude Lawrence in *Skylark* as 'a bad play saved by a bad performance'.

In an argument with his first collaborator, Marc Connelly, about a comic line, he made an unanswerable point. The line had made everyone laugh from first reading to final rehearsal, but in its first four out-of-town outings it got not a titter. Connelly still defended it. Kaufman considered. 'There's only one thing we can do, Marc. We've got to call the audience tomorrow morning for a ten o'clock rehearsal.'

His collaboration with Edna Ferber involved two contrasting work routines. Their second play, *The Royal Family,* took, according to Kaufman, two years to write: 'That is because Edna worked from 9am to 3.10pm and I work from 3pm to 9am, which gives us ten minutes a day in which to collaborate.'

He collaborated with Irving Berlin on *Cocoanuts* for the Marx Brothers. Berlin remembered Kaufman walking out into the lobby for the musical items and Kaufman remembered Berlin returning the compliment for the book scenes. After a long run the show, lavishly embroidered by Marxist ad libs, bore little relation to the original. Standing at the back one night, Kaufman interrupted a story Heywood Broun was telling him and edged nearer the stage. When he returned, Broun asked why.

'I had to,' he said. 'I thought I heard one of the original lines of the show.'

When *Strike Up the Band* was in trouble in Philadelphia, two elegant

Old Victorian gents turned up at the box office. Ira Gershwin muttered, 'That must be Gilbert and Sullivan coming to fix the show.'

'Why don't you put jokes like that in your lyrics?' was Kaufman's reply. There was another awkward moment in the lobby at *Strike Up the Band* – a backer spotted Kaufman and mistook him for George Gershwin: 'Mr Gershwin, how could you let this happen?'

Kaufman did not flinch: 'My score is perfect,' he ad-libbed. 'The whole trouble is with Kaufman's book.'

His work with Moss Hart represents his closest collaboration, beginning with *Once in a Lifetime* in 1930. He showed a fatherly delight in Hart's enthusiasm for spending money. The Harts bought a magnificent spread near Kaufman in Buck's County; Moss then improved it with swimming pools, tennis courts and a forest of freshly transplanted trees. Surveying the spectacle, Kaufman growled, 'This is what God would have done if he'd had the money.' It chimes with his remark to Hart: 'I like to be near you, Moss. It comes under the heading *gelt* by association.'

His remark to Howard Dietz, about the Dietz and Schwartz musical, *Beat the Devil*, is a classic: 'I hear your play is full of single entendre.'

Ruth Gordon once outlined a daring new play in which she was to star: 'There's no scenery at all. In the first scene, I'm on the left side of the stage and the audience has to imagine I'm in a crowded restaurant. In scene two, I run over to the right side of the stage and the audience has to imagine I'm home in my own drawing room.'

'And the second night,' Kaufman interjected, 'you'll have to imagine there's an audience out front.' He caught up with Miss Gordon again in Atlantic City. The play he had written with Herman Mankiewicz, a comedy, was trying-out to no laughs. Miss Gordon told him, in tears, that hers, a tragedy, was causing the audience to fall about. Kaufmann suggested a great plan: 'Let's switch audiences.'

When he wrote *Park Avenue*, an unsuccessful musical, with Ira Gershwin and Arthur Schwartz, he was in love at the start of rehearsals with the leading lady, Leonora Corbett, and allowed her contract to give her approval of changes. Out of town the romance soured, and when they rehearsed before opening on Broadway the three distinguished collaborators had to play the new numbers to Ms Corbett at her apartment. She was entertaining her new beau and hardly listened before giving her approval. As she hurried them to the elevator, she asked their opinion of her lover.

'What does he do?' asked Schwartz to cover a conversational hiatus.

'Oh,' she said, 'he's in cotton.' The elevator arrived to allow Kaufman to say with perfect timing, before the doors closed: 'And them that plants it is soon forgotten.' Of Ms Corbett's performance, he was more acid. After a bad show, she swung past him. He asked how it had gone. 'Fantastic!' she said excitedly.

Kaufman turned to his co-writer, Nunally Johnson: 'You've heard of people living in a fool's paradise? Well, Leonora has a duplex there.'

It was not, I think, the Philadelphia try-out of *Park Avenue* which produced his order to a room waiter at 3am after a disastrous preview – 'I want something,' he said, scanning the *carte*, 'that will keep me awake thinking it was the food I ate and not the show I saw.'

Perhaps his most famous line – 'Satire is what closes on Saturday night' – is the one which has dated the most. Kaufman as a director was quiet and considerate. I owe this description of a detailed example to his lively biographer, Howard Teichmann. During one scene in a play he directed, with the starry Jane Cowl in the lead, she had a very long speech after which she put on her hat, gloves, picked up her bag, took some props from the table, put them into the bag and then made a grand exit.

'Miss Cowl,' Kaufman asked, 'wouldn't it be better if instead of saying that speech and *then* doing all that, you did all the stage business while you were delivering your speech?'

'Oh! But that's impossible,' Miss Cowl snapped.

'Why is it impossible?' Kaufman asked softly.

'It just can't be done!' the actress called out.

'Why not?' he persisted, lowering his voice as she raised hers.

'Do you want me to begin,' she demanded, 'and say . . .' and she started the speech, put on her hat, her gloves, picked up her bag, opened the bag, threw the props into it, snapped it shut and walked off, her cheeks blazing with indignation.

She had done precisely what he had asked. When she came onto the stage again Kaufman just looked at her and said, 'My mistake.'

Teichmann cites an early Walter Matthau performance (1952) under Kaufman's direction. Some way into the rehearsal Matthau had developed a storm of 'business'. He sought his director's approval. 'Mr Kaufman, what do you think of the business I worked out for myself?'

'Mr Matthau,' Kaufman said gently, 'not much.'

The business went – to the actor's advantage and, in the long run, gratitude.

According to Teichmann, his notorious director's telegram: 'I am watching your performance from the rear of the house. Wish you were here,' was sent to William Gaxton during the run of *Of Thee I Sing*. Another stricture fell on the composer of that show, George Gershwin, a compulsive player of his new scores at rehearsals.

'If you play that score once more before we open,' Kaufman told him, 'people are going to think we're doing a revival.'

Kaufman was not always recognised. At one stage door he was greeted by an officious stage door man: 'Excuse me, sir, are you with the show?'

'Let's put it this way. I'm not against it.'

In Boston to direct a musical with advance booking of eighty dollars, he observed, 'I've been in this business for thirty years and this is the first time the temperature has been higher than the advance.'

His patience with actors was not inexhaustible as demonstrated to a woman who suddenly called out to him in rehearsal: 'How can I do this with all these interruptions?'

He was terse: 'Don't you know what those interruptions are? Other actors reading their lines!'

Similarly, an entire cast who had been embellishing a Kaufman production, were confronted after an unheralded visit by the director by a note saying; '11am rehearsal tomorrow to remove all line improvements to the play put in since the last rehearsal.' In rehearsal for *Guys and Dolls*, an actor – Tom Pedi – added a couple of lines and Kaufman was instantly on guard. He called Abe Burrows, the book writer, across.

'Mr Burrows,' he said, 'would you consider giving Mr Pedi credit as co-author?' Pedi didn't try again.

Kaufman's second marriage to Leueen MacGrath provoked another of his well-known ad libs. The second Mrs Kaufman moved him from his Park Avenue apartment at 410 to a penthouse 625 numbers up-town. Quite out of character, he went shopping for new furniture with her. In the drapery section of Bloomingdales, a shop assistant, finding him with Leueen bemused by assorted lengths of upholstery, asked if he could help.

'Maybe you can,' said Kaufman. 'Do you have any good second act curtains?'

By this time Kaufman could feel the pangs of professional jealousy. Burt Shevelove used to quote his reaction to the continuing success of Rodgers and Hammerstein. When *South Pacific* opened in Boston, the reviews were spectacular and business boomed. Kaufman's comment was, 'The Shubert Theater is not open on Sundays, but people are so keen on *South Pacific* they're pushing money under the lobby doors. They don't want anything, they just want to push money under the doors.'

Called by the producer, Jed Harris, to a conference with Charles McArthur and Ben Hecht, Kaufman found Harris sitting naked at his desk. This was not a pretty sight: Hecht describes the vision as one of 'hairy and coleopterous [beetle-like] rudity'. They ignored the spectacle, but Kaufman was most irked. As they left, he passed the naked Harris and said casually, 'Jed, your fly is open.' His final word on Harris was more bitter: 'When I die I want to be cremated and my ashes thrown in Jed Harris's face.'

He worked until the end, several heart attacks impeding him in his last years. His last play as a director was *Romanoff and Juliet* starring the author, the young Peter Ustinov, who had directed himself in London. Kaufman was frail and Ustinov spent much time in the stalls directing again. There was a move to sack Kaufman, but David Merrick, never famous for the milk of human kindness coursing through his veins, remained steadfast: 'I would rather have a flop,' he said, 'than fire George Kaufman at this stage of his life and career.' Ustinov concurred.

Kaufman was very generous with hand-outs, particularly during the Depression. The pitch was always the same: 'Don't tell a soul. If you do, I'll never lend you another dime.' He was at it to the end, when an actor pleaded poverty and he said to his last stage manager, 'Give him $100. Tell him it came from David Merrick.'

**KEAN**, Edmund. The great Kean, born in London, deserted by his mother (Ann Carey) and brought up by his aunt, the actress Charlotte Tidswell, became the great star of his day. Coleridge said: 'To see him act is like reading Shakespeare by flashes of lightning.' He also became a byword for the drunken excess and extravagance which colour most of the stories about him. His extraordinary talent marched alongside his wayward temperament – like the time he could not play because he was so drunk and then heckled his understudy from a stage box.

His first stage appearances were as a child in London. His youth was spent in poor circumstances acting in the provinces. He married after a tour in Ireland and was first noticed when playing in Exeter. Drury Lane's talent scout, Mr Arnold, reported his Shylock: 'If the Shylock of the West is right the Shylocks of the great metropolis have all been wrong.' (He also saw him as Harlequin in *Mother Goose* the same night.)

Kean was brought to London but denied work for months and prohibited from appearing elsewhere. Unable to gain access to the stage manager at Old Drury to plead his case and humiliated by a porter who would not let him pass, he eventually owed his interview to Lord Bryon. His demand to make his debut as Shylock was granted, in spite of the fact that two contemporaries, Kemble and Huddart, had emptied the house with it. He opened on 26 January 1814. So great was his triumph that after the trial scene the audience refused to allow the play to continue to Belmont. Next day, the surly porter rushed to open the door for him. Kean laid the man's hand aside with the words, 'Pray do not trouble yourself. I am quite perfect in this part. You have given me enough rehearsals.'

Above all, he celebrated his triumph with the cry: 'Charlie shall go to Eton!' and so his son did. He had no illusions, though, about the vagaries of theatrical fortune. Of an aspiring young actor he asked laconically, 'Can you starve, cocky?'

There were other rewards. Mrs Jordan had once rejected him as her suitor, Don Felix, in *The Wonder* – 'Oh, I can't act with him, he's too little,' she said. Kean looked at her and walked away. Now, years later, he was the talk of London and she wanted to meet him. Recognition was instant. 'Great heavens!' she remembered. 'The little man with the eyes!'

Success soon inspired Kean's wilder drunken escapades. Most famously, he once dined some ten miles out of London and drank so heartily that all thought of his responsibility to the theatre was drowned. An elaborate alibi – a flock of geese by the roadside, an over-turned coach, a dislocated shoulder – was improvised, and when senior sympathisers from Drury Lane came to commiserate, Kean kept up the pretence in a darkened room with pallid make-up and a bandaged arm. On his return to the stage he played his first three roles – Richard III, Macbeth and Othello – with his arm in a sling.

Success took him across the Atlantic. In Canada he was made chief of a Huron Indian tribe. So tickled was he by the honour that he went to great lengths to disguise himself as a fearsome chief, Alanteneida. Only the characteristic intonations of his voice gave him away.

Playing Massinger's *A New Way to Pay Old Debts* in Birmingham one night, for his benefit performance, the evening was a disaster. Kean vented his disapproval on the audience, saying, as he referred to a character's marriage in the play: 'Take her, sir, and the Birmingham audience into the bargain.'

Irving (born five years after Kean's death), recalled his acting style and his conduct towards other players: 'A grand declamatory style was much more suited to a badly-lighted stage than a manner full of artistic minutiae.' The limited range of the light impelled the actor down-stage into the 'focus'. Irving's anecdote has Kean complimented by two admirers who had seen him the previous night. Kean replied that he could not remember anything particular about a performance of Othello.

'Surely you must remember, Mr Kean! . . . You seized Mr – by the throat and got into such a fury. I thought you'd have killed Iago!'

'Ha!' exclaimed Kean, brightening. 'I remember now. Did I seem in a fury, eh?'

The fans insisted that he did.

'No wonder. Damn the fellow, he tried to keep me out of the focus.'

Kean wrenched himself 'out of the focus' on several notable occasions. On one he was due to play Richard III at Drury Lane and hated the thought of abandoning his 'chair' at a convivial occasional club, The Jolly Dogs, which met at The Craven's Head Tavern nearby. At this singing and drinking event, his appearances were rather like an early version of Woody Allen's regular sitting-in at Michael's Pub in New York on Monday nights. The landlord, William Oxberry, bet Kean that he could not get to The Craven's Head to take the chair. Kean played his part at breakneck speed and leapt into the fight with Richmond, usually one of his special effects, whispering to Wallack, who was playing opposite him: 'Kill me quickly tonight, I'm due at the Jolly Dogs.' Still in his royal robes, he just made it. Towards the end of his life, the fight was shortened to accommodate his infirmity.

In Kean's day, the version of *Richard III* which was played was tarted up by Colley Cibber, who added a line, 'Off with his head! So much for Buckingham!' For some reason this line, cut when Irving restored Shakespeare's text, always brought a round of applause. One night a small part player consumed by nerves rushed onto the stage and shouted, 'My lord, the Duke of Buckingham is taken and we've cut off his head.' His thunder stolen, all poor Kean could do was mutter, 'Oh! Then there's nothing more to be said.' In his version of the story, Donald Sinden suggests an alternative improvisation, more suitable in that it conforms to the iambic pentameter – 'Then bury him! So much for Buckingham!'

In his 1933 biography of Kean, H.N. Hillebrand quotes Leman Rede as the authority for a story of Kean and his heavy drinking. His secretary, Phillips, is waiting in another room in a tavern.

*Two in the morning*
Phillips: 'Waiter, what was Mr Kean doing when you left the room?'
Waiter: 'Playing the piano, sir, and singing.'
Phillips: 'Oh, come, he's all right then.'

*Fifteen minutes later*
Phillips: 'What is Mr Kean doing now?'
Waiter: 'Making a speech, sir, about Shakespeare.'
Phillips: 'He's getting drunk. You'd better order the carriage.'

*Fifteen minutes later*
Phillips: 'What's he at now?'
Waiter: 'He's talking Latin, sir.'
Phillips: 'Then he is drunk. I must take him away.'

In Kean's last years he was reduced to poverty, having earned thousands for Drury Lane, educated his son Charles, and excited a generation. His last performance was as Othello opposite Charles's Iago. There is some evidence that his last words, on his deathbed, were: 'A horse! A horse! My kingdom for a horse!'

Fanny Kemble's epitaph on Kean is memorable and moving.

'Kean is gone and with him are gone Othello, Shylock and Richard. I have lived among those whose theatrical creed would not permit them to acknowledge him as a great actor; but they must be bigoted indeed who would deny that he was a great genius – a man of most original and striking powers. Careless of art, perhaps because he did not need it, but possessing those rare gifts of nature without which art is as a dead body ... If he was irregular and unartistic-like in his performance, so is Niagara compared with the Waterworks of Versailles.'

**KELLY**, Grace. The lovely Grace Kelly was known in early life for her discreet affairs with fellow film stars, including William Holden, Ray Milland, Bing Crosby, Clark Gable, Gary Cooper, Jean-Pierre Aumont and David Niven. Niven was questioned once by Prince Rainier about who was the favourite of his lovers.

'Grace,' he said, without thinking. Then thinking twice as fast: 'Er, Gracie,' he added. 'Gracie Fields.'

There may be a grain of truth here as most of the stories Niven tells in his 'autobiographies' are highly imaginatively touched-up bits of fiction.

This one does not appear in either. According to Jane Ellen Wayne's biography, *The Life and Loves of Grace Kelly*, she did not have an affair with Cary Grant when they were filming *To Catch a Thief* on the Riviera, but they did become lovers in the late sixties when Princess Grace was distressed at Prince Rainier's rumoured affairs.

**KEMBLE**, John Philip. John Philip Kemble, the brother of Sarah Kemble Siddons and Stephen Kemble, was an actor/manager of great distinction. His personality and appearance suggested dullness, but his mind was quick and generous. Asthma contributed to his difficulties; he referred to it bitterly as 'drawing on his chest and finding the cheque dishonoured'.

For years he resisted Kean's appearances. After he finally had caught his Othello, he was asked 'if he had seen Kean'. His reply was graceful and generous.

'No, sir, I did not see Mr Kean. I saw Othello. And further, I shall never act the part again.'

Comedy was not his strong point, though there were two views of his performance as Charles Surface in *A School for Scandal*: one celebrated it as Charles's Restoration, the other wrote it off as Charles's Martydom. Kemble was not keen on his own performance in the role, but in 1796 he had to substitute the play swiftly when the first-night reception for *Vortigern* caused him to withdraw that. *Vortigern* was an interesting aberration for Kemble, who announced it as a hitherto unknown five-act tragedy by William Shakespeare. In fact, it was by the hand of William Ireland, who produced other tragedies – a revised *King Lear,* some missing passages of *Hamlet* and a few supposed Shakespearean love letters. The unplayability of the text, and the incompetence of the cast, led to an uproar.

Kemble, like many of the actors of his day, was used to an unruly audience. On 13 April, 1779, he performed *Zenobia* at Drury Lane; a badly behaved woman in a stage box hurled insults at him and his leading lady, Mrs Mason.

Finally Kemble's patience ran out and he addressed the audience.

'I am ready to proceed with the play as soon as *that* lady has finished her conversation, which I perceive my continuing with the tragedy is but interrupting.'

At this, the audience took the actor's side and the woman was ejected. Kemble used a similar technique when persecuted through a performance by a crying baby. This time he came forward with a solemn face and announced in tragic tones, 'Ladies and Gentlemen, unless the play is stopped the child cannot possibly go on.'

In an age when most actors could throw in a song, Kemble found keeping time impossible. In rehearsing him, one musical director, a Mr Shaw, complained: 'Mr Kemble, that won't do at all. You murder time abominably.'

''Tis better, Mr Shaw,' said Kemble, 'to *murder* it than to be continually *heating* it, as you are.'

Kemble's retirement was a great occasion and provoked some jealousy from his even more famous sister. In a feminist outburst at a public dinner in Kemble's honour, Mrs Siddons pointed out that very little fuss had been made when she left the stage. 'Well,' she concluded bitterly, 'perhaps in the next world women will be more valued than they are in this.'

**KENDAL**, William Hunter and **KENDAL**, Dame Madge Sholto. Joint actor-managers, the Kendals acted together under Hare at the Royal Court, under the Bancrofts at the Prince of Wales and then with Hare again, this time in partnership with him, at the St James.

Both acted more frequently and more happily in popular comedy than in the classics, though Mrs Kendal, who became one of the great *monstres sacres* of the Victorian stage, made her debut as Ophelia and played an Amazonian Rosalind opposite her husband. In 1928, on the occasion of her eightieth birthday, she was invited by the BBC to record a speech from the play. Shown a microphone for the first time, she was positioned by the producer, who explained that the mike was her Orlando. She gave him and it a gracious smile and said, 'Ah, my husband was better looking than that.'

Like many older actors, she was more at home in a theatre and therefore liable to behave more wilfully. Her rehearsals could be tyrannical. On one occasion she called for a kitchen chair and placed it centre stage. Then she knelt at it and addressed her assembled company: 'Oh Lord, we pray Thee out of Thy infinite mercy that Thou wilt cause some notion of the rudiments of acting to be vouchsafed this company, for Jesus Christ's sake, amen.' Then she got to her feet and spat out, 'Now we'll see what that will do.'

**KENDALL**, Chrissie. Chrissie Kendall, singer, dancer, actress, is also the champion Malapropper of the British stage. She has been heard to express her admiration for the acting skill of 'Joan Playwright'. Tallulah

Bankhead has been metamorphosed into 'Tallulah Handbag' or even 'Tallulah Bunkbed'. While studying acting, she was advised to read Stanislavsky. She asked her friend Annette how the name was spelt.

'S-T-A-N . . .' Annette began.

'Oh, I know how to spell his *first* name,' Chrissie replied. She habitually refers to the Royal Shakespeare Company as 'The RAC' and lamented once that a friend had gone off to Israel to live on 'a kebab'. During 1979, her fellow dancers heard her express mounting concern over 'the ostriches'. 'What ostriches?' one of them enquired. 'The ostriches in prison in Iran,' Ms Kendall answered. More recently she was concerned about AIDS victims.

'Is he HP positive?' she asked of an ailing friend. Then she corrected herself. 'Sorry, I mean HMV positive.'

Her dismissal of a proposed date with Bob Fosse, who had just auditioned her for *Pippin,* was neat. Her father took the phone call – 'A Mr Fossil' had called her, he said. When Fosse came on the line, he asked her if she would like to be in the show and would she like to have dinner with him that evening? 'Yes and no,' she replied.

**KERN**, Jerome. Jerome Kern's two reputations were as a great composer and as an extremely difficult man. He once greeted a notoriously slippery producer with, 'Good morning, Mr Goodman. I'm Kern. I hear you're a son-of-a-bitch. So am I!'

His masterpiece was *Showboat,* in collaboration with Oscar Hammerstein II. The genesis of 'Ol' Man River' is confused. One report has it that, trying-out in Philadephia, Jules Bledsoe needed a number. B.G. de Sylva, hearing some throwaway dance music, threw in his ten cents and said, 'Slow it down and give it to Bledsoe.' Another version has Hammerstein realising the need for a song to evoke the Mississippi and annexing some up-tempo banjo music in the score which, he felt, sloweddown, would save Kern the task of hunting for a new melody. However, Edna Ferber, on whose book the show is based, records that quite early on Kern turned up at her apartment one afternoon, and played the song. She said, 'I give you my word, my hair stood on end, tears came to my eyes . . . this was a great song.'

A later attempt at collaboration with Hammerstein ran into difficulties. They talked of adapting *Messr Mario Polo!* for the stage. Hammerstein asked Kern; 'Here is a story laid in China about an Italian told by an Irishman. What kind of music are you going to write?'

Kern was unfazed. 'It'll be good Jewish music,' he said.

When Hammerstein heard of the fall of Paris in World War Two, he sent the verses it inspired, 'The Last Time I Saw Paris', straight to Kern in Hollywood, who set them and presented them to Hammerstein as he arrived to work on a movie. The fall of Stalingrad did not produce a similar lyric, but the German strategy did inspire a George S. Kaufman quip to Hammerstein: 'I think the Germans are shooting without a script.'

On Kern's piano stood a basket of pencils and a small bust of Wagner. If Kern or his collaborator was unhappy with work in progress, Kern would turn the bust around the wrong way, saying, 'Wagner doesn't like it.'

Arthur Schwartz, who produced the movie *Cover Girl* with Kern, tells a similar tale of the day he heard Kern's score. One song did not excite him, though he held his peace. However, he noticed Kern pencil a note on the manuscript. Peering to see what it was, he read PNL. Finally, he asked Kern what that signified.

'Producer No Like,' he was told.

**KERR**, Deborah. There is a story concerning Deborah Kerr, who was irritated by constant mispronunciation of her name in Hollywood. 'Kerr' always came out 'Cur' not 'Car'. For one of her premières she was asked what special arrangement she would like by an indulgent studio. She asked for an English commissionaire to call for her limo as she left the première for the party. Her wish was granted and the man functioned perfectly getting everyone's name right including hers. 'Miss Kerr's Car' came out immaculately with both words sounding exactly the same. Unfortunately he then relaxed, lost concentration and called loudly for 'Mr Alfred Hitchcar's cock!'

**KIEPURA**, Jan. The Polish singing star and his wife, Marta Eggerth, played their greatest success, *The Merry Widow,* in New York during the forties. After the opening night, an anxious Kiepura asked a fan if he should polish up his English.

'No,' said the fan. 'English up your Polish!'

**KIMMINS**, Anthony. Apart from his work in films and in the theatre, Anthony Kimmins had a happy meeting with Gerald Hamilton – Isherwood's unpleasant model for Mr Norris, who *Changes Trains.*

Hamilton eavesdropped a conversation in which Kimmins mentioned Sir Alexander Korda. Horning in, Hamilton boasted, 'Did I hear you to say you were a friend of Alex Korda? In that case you must know my good friend, Anthony Kimmins.'

To which the only reply was, 'I am Anthony Kimmins.' A similar incident happened to Laurence Olivier, who was sitting in the Grand Hotel in Rome surrounded by Italian film moguls. They were approached by a British film producer-hustler, who started to boast of his actress-wife's achievements in the London theatre. He cited her triumphs in classic roles at Olivier's National Theatre and the Italians let him hang himself with stories of Olivier's pleas that she should play Hedda, Lady Macbeth, etc – until, somewhat to Olivier's embarrassment and entirely to the hustler's dismay, they unveiled the oracle.

**KING**. There have been two Martin Luther King musicals. Martin Smith wrote and composed one called *King,* which was performed for one night at the Prince Edward in the 1980s. It starred Obba Babatunde and Leilani Jones and it tore the roof off the packed theatre.

Meanwhile, another composer, Richard Blackford, had also embarked on a *King* project and secured Mrs Loretta King's co-operation. When Smith appeared in Atlanta to confirm that he had her blessing, she admitted she had confused the two projects and withdrew her support for his venture. Blackford's version progressed, shedding various collaborators, book writers, lyric writers, directors – particularly as the show went into rehearsal and a strong black lobby in the cast argued for greater black control. One star entered a room to rehearse one of her songs, clapped eyes on the rehearsal pianist, a fine musician, and said, in shock, 'But he's not black!' Wisely, he left. The atmosphere continued to be poisonous and it was not surprising that when the show lumbered to its opening night it was dull and unfocused, where Smith's version had been lyrical, simple and committed.

Simon Estes, an operatic bass appeared on stage in a large, stiff, single-breasted suit with a large, stiff single-hued voice. Mr Babatunde had been all passion, intellect and conviction. In civilian life Mr Estes wears a gold medallion with the legend, 'Try God'. One of the production team suggested he should inscribe 'Try Acting' on the reverse.

The appalling backstage racism was not the only reason why 'We Shall Overcome' dwindled into 'We Shall Underwhelm' but it certainly pole-axed any attempt to drive a wilting piece of work through to success. A writer, Neil Shand, suggested a witty, ironic solution to the producer's dilemma – 'They should bus in audiences.' On the first night, the muddled show was greeted mainly in silence until the usual hyped-up ovation from friends, agents, backers and producers.

Perhaps the last word should go to the unfortunate television writer, Lonie Elder III who was hired (well out of his depth) at the persuasion of the black lobby to re-write during rehearsals. Elder III was incensed by the notices, which accurately reflected an impartial audience's dismayed reaction. Rambling in the foyer before the second night, Mr Elder III moaned that the critics had objected to his conversion of Martin Luther King into 'a plaster saint'. Alistair Beaton was the lyricist who had done most to save the show from shipwreck. 'What,' Elder III asked his fellow writer, 'does 'hagiography' mean?'

**'KNOCK-KNOCKS'** (Shakespearean version). The comedian Arthur Smith has a whole Shakespearean revue in his repertoire. One of his specialities is to boast the only known Shakespearean 'knock-knock' joke.

> Who's there? Mandy. Mandy who?
> Man delights not me; no, nor woman neither.

However, I have to disappoint him.

The obvious one is: Who's there? Toby. Toby who? To be or not to be, that is the question.

Then there are: Who's there? Howie. Howie who? How weary, stale, flat and unprofitable seem to me all those uses of this world.

And: Who's there? Moron. Moron who? More honoured in the breach than the observance.

There is another where the three 'Tamaras' come calling, or the Scottish who's there? Leon. Leon who? Leon McDuff.

Or: Who's there? Ida. Ida who? I'da rather be a dog and bay the moon than such a Roman. (A bit of a cheat, here – the original is 'I had rather . . .')

Then there's: Who's there? 'Tis one. 'Tis one what? 'Tis one thing to be tempted, Escalus, another thing to fall. Then again: Who's there. Otis. Otis who? Oh, 'tis foul in here.

**KRUGER**, Otto. According to Katherine Cornell's account in *I Wanted to be an Actress*, Kruger played opposite her in Clemence Dane's play *Will*

*Shakespeare,* in 1923. As Mary, young Will's girlfriend, Ms Dane had her inspiring Will to tell her that she had already inspired him to write a play about star-crossed lovers who hung out in Verona. At this point, the playwright intended the curtain to fall slowly. However, the curtain puller was himself a romantic and had just strayed from his post in pursuit of dalliance. The two unfortunate actors were stranded, as Kruger improvised desperately . . . 'I shall call it *Romeo and Juliet*' – then outlined and launched into the balcony scene. Getting a second wind, he went on: 'And then I shall write a play called *Hamlet* . . . and I shall have my hero say, "To be or not to be . . . " And then I shall have him say . . . "Oh, that this too, too solid flesh would melt."'

By the time the curtain boy was found and returned to his post, Miss Cornell was a nervous wreck, but she felt that Kruger was beginning to relish tearing off the best bits of *Lear* or prophetically introducing his audience to the racial problems of *Othello*.

**KURNITZ**, Harry. A prolific, wise-cracking American writer and producer, Harry Kurnitz wrote for movies and Broadway, and collaborated with Noel Coward on the musical adaptation of Terence Rattigan's play, *The Sleeping Prince* as *The Girl Who Came For Supper*. However his passion was large cars. En route to Paris on one occasion, his lavish vehicle broke down. He hitched a lift in a Volkswagen and on arrival was asked what he thought of it. He snapped, 'I've been in bigger women.'

# — ℒ —

**Laemmle**, Carl. Carl Laemmle was an early motion-picture tycoon who had such a particular concern for his family that he was known throughout Hollywood as 'Uncle Carl'. Ogden Nash celebrated his concern in a couplet which also serves as a useful aid to his name's pronunciation:

Uncle Carl Laemmle
Had a very large family

**Lancaster**, Osbert. A popular cartoonist and clever theatre designer, especially in ballet and opera, particularly at Glyndebourne, Lancaster was asked how his stage designs compared with his pocket cartoons. 'Bigger,' he said. 'Definitely bigger.'

Sketching one day in the Midi, he was surprised by a French urchin who contemplated his work over his shoulder and said at last: 'Tout de même, je crois qu'il a du talent.'

**Landen**, Dinsdale. Dinsdale Landen appeared with Ronald Squire and Michael Redgrave in *A Touch of the Sun*, directed by Frith Banbury. Squire spotted an opportunity for 'business' during the run and coached Landen, who was about twenty at the time and in awe of both stars. Came the night when Squire judged it right to try the new business. It was a riot. Next day, Banbury called the company and a furious Redgrave held the floor until Squire, unmoved, brought proceedings to a close with one line: 'Don't ever try comedy, Michael, or you'll *starve.*'

Landen remembered an occasion when he was an ASM at Worthing and Wolfit came to 'guest' as Othello. Wolfit took a fancy to him and invented a role as a Nubian boy attendant with loincloth and blackened skin. Landen's instructions as the page were to follow the great man everywhere. Not knowing the play well, and in the flurry of hasty repertory rehearsals, he found himself uneasy on stage at one point on the first night. He very soon found out why when he heard Wolfit roaring: 'Not in Desdemona's bedroom, you cunt!'

**LANDESMAN**, Jay. Jay Landesman, sometime publisher, nightclub manager, writer, Man about Soho and husband of the stylish poet and lyric writer Fran Landesman, recaptured a happy handful of anecdotes in his recent *Jaywalking*. In his early years running a club in America he employed the young Woody Allen and Barbra Streisand, who occasionally baby-sat for his son, Cosmo.

When the Landesmans arrived in England in the early sixties they knew few people here apart from Peter Cook. Needing an agent they considered Cook's, Peter Rawley.

'I'm a terrific lover,' he told Mrs Landesman, 'but a lousy agent.'

'Oh what a pity,' she replied. 'I already have a lousy lover, what I need is a terrific agent.'

The Landesmans brought their own brand of Bohemian living to London and played host to a number of visiting Americans. On one occasion they were with Mel Brooks in the old Pickwick Club. Mrs Landesman invited him to join her in the ladies' loo for a smoke. When she dropped the dope on the floor he bent to pick it up and spotted an intriguing piece of graffiti written in lipstick. 'Terry Cooper is a lousy fuck,' it read. Underneath was the postscript, 'Now you tell me.'

Back in the bar the first person they saw was Terence Cooper. Mrs Landesman made the introduction, 'Mel, this is Terry Cooper, whom you've read so much about.'

I like Jay Landesman's memory of tripping on LSD in bucolic Wales. His host, Jeremy Brooks, was beguiled by his intense conversation with a herd of cows. Jay grew expansive, believing that some kind of affinity existed between him and the cows. Ten minutes later Brooks put his hand round his guest's shoulder. 'Jay,' he said, 'I've seen you empty a room but this is the first time I've seen you empty a meadow!' There wasn't a cow to be seen.

The comic actor Chris Langham tells a similar story of tripping with the now sadly-deceased dwarf actor David Rappaport in a field in Somerset. Rappaport wandered off and could be seen in the distance earnestly addressing a herd of cows. Returning, he said apologetically, 'It was all right, Chris, the cows did most of the talking.'

**LANDLADIES**. Theatrical landladies spawn innumerable stories among touring actors. James Harding, in his biography of George Robey, lists several which are often credited to other performers.

Landlady:   'What will you have for breakfast?'
Robey:      'Can I have a little porridge, some scrambled eggs, a kidney or so and a rasher or two of bacon?'
Landlady:   'No, you cannot. The only thing in the house is a kipper, and you can have that. This isn't the bloody Metropole!'

Robey believed in getting the landlady's interminable conversation over at the beginning of the week.

'I can see you have had better days,' he would say. 'Now sit down in the chair and tell me all about it. I am going to give you half an hour. In that half-hour you shall tell me everything and then – not another word for the rest of the week.'

Not all landladies were of scrupulous honesty. In Harding's account, one pointed out a cupboard with a top shelf where Robey could store his 'little dainties' in safety. However, she asked him to be careful as some of her 'valuable old china' was sharing the shelf. When pots of jam and corned beef unaccountably vanished, Robey attached white silk thread to the china and to the cupboard door, so that if it was opened the heirlooms would be pulled down. The result was a midnight crash, no landlady visible in the morning, the bill presented by her daughter and no charge for breakages.

Robey's method of coping with an over-inquisitive landlady was to set out a row of tins, capturing and installing a fly in each. When he returned, he checked the tins and if the flies had escaped, he knew privacy was to be denied him that week.

One woman defeated Robey, who complained that the level of whisky in his carefully marked private bottle was falling unaccountably.

'Yes,' she said. 'I've been meaning to mention it. You see, I've been putting a couple of teaspoons in your soup every day.'

Robey quotes a quatrain left by a departing comic in the inevitable landlady's Visitor's Book:

> Friends may come and friends may go,
> And friendships often sever,
> But the soup Ma makes with a penn'orth o' bones,
> Goes on for ever and ever!

Another entry puzzled the landlady. It ran: 'Quoth the raven.' She asked Robey what it meant. He said vaguely, 'It looks like a bit of a quotation.' The landlady didn't understand it – 'And he was such a nice young man what wrote it!' she clucked.

A friend of Robey's once offered his Manchester landlady tickets for the show he was in. She was outraged.

'Stalls? Stalls!' she cried. 'Mr Robey always gives me a box.'

Two notable leading ladies were Douglas Byng and Ernest Thesiger, who often appeared in drag, Byng almost exclusively. When they stayed together in the celebrated digs in Manchester run by the extraordinary Miss Wood, for the out-of-town opening of Cochran's revue of 1926, Byng told Miss Wood that his father had died the previous Friday. Miss Wood was ahead of him.

'I knew it, I smelt hyacinths when I came into this room – always a sign. When are they going to bury him?'

'Next Thursday.'

'He'll never keep.'


**LANGTRY**, (née Le Breton), Lillie (Emilie Charlotte). Lillie Langtry, the Jersey Lily, was more socially adroit than theatrically talented, but she did rather hawk her reputation in Britain and the United States. Somerset Maugham recalled two anecdotes. She told him she had loved the doomed Crown Prince Rudolf of Austria, who gave her an emerald ring. When they rowed, she threw it in a blazing fire. After he dived to dig it out of the coals, she knew, 'I could not love him after that.'

Often she referred in conversation to one Freddy Gebhardt. Puzzled, Maugham asked her who he was. She was astonished. She told him, 'He was the most celebrated man in two hemispheres.'

'Why?' Maugham asked. Her answer was wonderfully simple.

'Because I loved him.'


**LANTZ**, Robert. Robert Lantz, the New York-based agent, is one of the wittiest men in that town. He is the son of a Berlin-based film producer, one of whose claims to fame was a life-long feud with a leading critic. For years they cut each other and their wives cut each other. One day they were observed sharing a table in a restaurant. Berlin reeled in shock but the explanation was simple. The restaurant was empty and having no one else to talk to, 'rather than stay silent they had an intermission'.

In Manhattan, Robbie has a regular table at the Russian Tea Rooms.

One day a new *maitre d'hôtel* put him in an identical position but on the opposite side of the room. 'Six people came up to me,' Robbie said, 'and complained of vertigo.'

At various times he has represented Danny Kaye, Burton and Taylor, Marlene Dietrich, Bette Davis, Joe Mankiewicz, Peter Shaffer and a multitude of others. The Lantz office is very big on autobiographies, Elizabeth Taylor's book was a best-seller, so was Michael Jackson's. Lantz had dinner with Jackson but politely declined an invitation to go upstairs after dinner 'to meet the cobra'. Shirley Temple's account of her life followed: 'It's a very thick book and it stops when she is nineteen.'

Back in the period when there seemed to be a new Pope every other week and smoke was regularly puffing out of the Vatican chapel, the actor Frank Langella was having a triumph as *Dracula* in New York at the Martin Beck Theatre. One day he called the Lantz office in a rage. An actor friend had sent him a screenplay some weeks before and had now phoned to ask if he liked it. As he had not received it he could not comment. The Lantz office had omitted to forward it. Irate, he demanded an explanation from Robbie. 'What can we do, Frank?' said Robbie. 'We have no Pope.' When I pressed him to confirm the story he smiled his Berlin Buddha smile and remained non-committal.

Some years ago he escorted Bette Davis to a Hollywood function where the guests were placed eight to a table. At the next table sat the ancient Mae West with seven men. Miss Davis went across to pay her respects. She bent over Mae West in conversation for a few minutes and returned to announce in a voice that carried, 'She's under ether.'

He once reminded me of a much-loved Gielgud story which I had forgotten. Sir John directed Peter Shaffer's early play *Five Finger Exercise*, in which one character owes not a little to Shaffer's mother. Some years later in Venice, Mrs Shaffer spotted Sir John taking the sun on the Lido. She introduced herself, 'I'm Peter Shaffer's mother.'

'That may very well be true,' said Sir John and moved on. There is no reply to that, but Shaffer woke up in the middle of the night for months afterwards having dreamed that he had thought of the perfect answer. Then he would realise that he had not.

**LAURIE**, John. John Laurie, beloved of television audiences for his appearances in *Dad's Army*, had a long and distinguished classical career in the theatre. In 1926 he clashed with Bernard Shaw when Lewis Casson revived *Macbeth* for Henry Ainley and Sybil Thorndike. Shaw came to a rehearsal and suggested that 'Scone' in the final couplet, 'So thanks to all at once, and to each/Whom we invite to see us crowned in Scone,' should be pronounced 'Skoon'. Laurie, who was playing Lennox, strode downstage and said imperiously, 'Mr Shaw, you are talking rubbish. I am Scots born and bred. The place is called Skon. It always has been Skon and no Irishman is going to change it.'

When Ainley's health failed him during this production, his understudy, Hubert Carter, an inordinately strong actor, took over and brought such a different, violent approach to the fight scene that Casson had to place ASMs behind strategic pieces of scenery to remind him, 'Macbeth has to *lose* the fight, Hubert! You have to *lose!*'

**LAWRENCE** (Klasen), Gertrude. Gertrude Lawrence returned to England after World War Two in 1948 to play in Daphne du Maurier's *September Tide* at the Aldwych. She had a famous entrance line. Appearing in a doorway looking impossibly glamorous, she said simply, 'I'm mother.' She did not enjoy post-war London but was heartened to hear that Queen Mary was attending a matinée. However, when The Queen came round to meet the cast, she said sternly, 'You should all speak up.'

Miss Lawrence turned on the rest of the cast: 'You see, I told you.'

But Queen Mary had not finished, 'You in particular,' she rasped.

Lawrence's marriage to Richard Aldridge, an American theatre manager, was celebrated by Noel Coward with a famous telegram: 'Dear Mrs A. Hurray, hurray. At last you are deflowered. On this as every other day, I love you, Noel Coward.' Emlyn Williams's comment on being told of the wedding of middling manager and luminous star was more acid: 'That's about right,' he said.

Coward's other wires to Gertrude Lawrence also packed a punch. When she received the script of *Private Lives* she cabled: 'Nothing that can't be fixed' – probably referring to a current contract complication. Coward misread it to imply criticism of his perfect play, and cabled back: 'The only thing to be fixed is your performance.' When she went into a serious drama in New York, his message was more jocular: 'Legitimate at last – won't mother be pleased!'

One of Lawrence's most extraordinary performances came during the Boston try-out of the Weill-Hart-Gershwin musical, *Lady in the Dark*. Weill and Ira Gershwin had given Danny Kaye a potential show stopper in 'Tschaikowsky' – Gershwin had written the lyric, which included a list of 49 tongue-twisting composers compiled for a magazine years before: 'The names that always give me brain concussion, the names of those composers known as Russian.' Miss Lawrence was to follow it with 'The Saga of Jenny' – who 'would make up her mind'. Both songs looked like being lost in rehearsal but at the Boston opening Kaye produced such an electric performance that he stopped the show. The anxious collaborators watched to see if Lawrence would be destroyed by this ovation. On the contrary, she tore into such a bumping and grinding version of 'Jenny' that she topped even Kaye's moment, and they continued to slay audiences throughout the run.

**LAWRENCE**, T.E. When D.H. Lawrence completed *Lady Chatterley's Lover* he gave a copy of the manuscript to the literary patron Sir Edward ('Eddie') Marsh. Marsh was full of enthusiasm and dismayed that censorship would prevent immediate publication. He thought that his friend T.E. Lawrence, then serving as Aircraftman Ross, would like to read it. So he wrapped it in brown paper and sent it off. Lawrence returned the manuscript some weeks later, saying how grateful he was to have had the chance to read it but adding that he could not understand the fuss about – 'all this sex business. I never met anyone who cared a biscuit for it!'

Lawrence also inspired one of Noel Coward's better-known quips. He opened a letter to the serving airman with the words, 'Dear 228171338 (may I call you 338)…'

**LAWSON**, Wilfred. A legendary actor and character – according to *The Oxford Companion to the Theatre,* 'His well known intemperance, which hampered his career, in no way affected the power of his acting' – Lawson's well known intemperance is the source of everyone's favourite theatrical anecdote. It may pre-date Lawson but with the present generation it is firmly attached to him.

The play is *Richard III,* the occasion a matinée and Lawson and another actor, playing Buckingham, have had a liquid lunch. Lawson stumbles on as the king and before he is far into his opening soliloquy, a voice from the gallery shouts, 'You're drunk!' Summoning all the dignity he can muster, Lawson stares back at the barracker and says, 'You think I'm drunk? Wait till you see Buckingham.'

According to *The Oxford Companion,* Lawson's only appearance in Shakespeare was in *Antony and Cleopatra* at the Old Vic in 1934. One correspondent speculates that the Buckingham was Robert Newton and that the incident was at the suburban Shilling Theatre in the thirties, but his testimony is based on hearsay.

Terence Stamp has a charming vignette in his second volume of autobiography, *Coming Attraction,* which shows how young actors revered Lawson. Stamp found himself sitting opposite him on the Metropolitan Line.

'There he was, sitting opposite me, his shoes gleaming like a guardsman's boots, greeting his fellow travellers with a lopsided grin . . . Eventually, fearing that he might suddenly alight from the train, I seized the moment and found the courage to say, "I'm an actor, just starting. Is there any advice . . . you could give me?"

' "Advice?" The voice – I'd heard it so many times from the anonymity of an audience – chuckled back at me as if speaking it for the very first time . . . His eyes rolled, as though scanning an inner dimension where words didn't exist. A cherubic smile moved on his lips . . . "Oh, I just learn the wordies," he finally said.'

In the early days of the English Stage Company, Lawson was sitting in the pub next door when George Devine entered, followed by a host of associates and assistants. He watched them go by: 'There goes Jesus Christ and his twelve apostles,' he muttered to his glass.

Helen Spencer once played opposite him in *Fanny's First Play;* as Mrs Knox, she had to deliver long religious tirades at him. Lawson wore an enormous black beard and used to deliver lewd and ribald comments about the people in the front row through it.

During a live play in the early days of television he muddled his lines more than usual and dried. A fellow actor turned his speeches into a monologue, as Lawson wasn't taking any prompts. When the scene finally ground to a halt, Lawson breathed a sigh of relief and said, 'Well, I fair buggered that up, didn't I?' not realising that he was still on-air.

**LAYE,** Evelyn. The star of many musicals and plays, she was the daughter of Gilbert Laye, an actor, producer and composer who had worked with Cochran, who became something of a mentor. She spent her childhood backstage in her cot. Her first recorded word to her father was 'Boo' – and she, her family and friends adopted it as a nickname, which has stuck.

**LEHMANN,** Beatrix. On the BBC Radio 4 programme *Loose Ends* the prodigal, but now returned to the fold, actress Helen Burns, recalled a story of Beatrix Lehmann – sister of Rosamund and John.

They were playing together in *The Merchant of Venice*, Lehmann as Portia, Burns as Nerissa. Lehmann's great strength was her intelligence, not her embonpoint and it was decided that the designer should fit her out with two special breasts. One night, perhaps not the first, as the pair were about to make their entrance Helen Burns noticed that Miss Lehmann was only sporting half a bosom; the left breast had gone missing. She pointed it out to the leading lady who started a feverish search. 'Has anybody seen a tit?' she enquired of the willowy actors who surrounded her in doublet and hose. Not one had. 'Surely you know what a tit looks like?' They assured her they did, but no one could find the wanderer.

By now the orchestra had played Portia's entrance music several times and they were going to have to go on. Just before they did Nerissa, appropriately two paces behind Portia, spotted that she had developed a small hunch back. The 'tit' had gone walkabout. Deftly she dragged it around to its more appropriate position – approximately.

The show was saved but Nerissa spent the rest of the scene wishing she could give just one more tug to complete the effect.

**LEONTOVICH**, Eugenie. The famous Russian actress scored a triumph in the London production of *Tovarich*, then went on to play a disastrous Cleopatra at the New Theatre in 1936. She was directed by Komisarjevsky and played opposite Donald Wolfit, who had just had a successful Stratford season.

Komisarjevsky took many liberties with the text.

'Seldom has a play been so tormented and twisted and stifled or a work of genius been so casually scorned' was the verdict of *The Times*. Its critic, Charles Morgan, produced a classic burlesque of Leontovich's performance by a simple phonetic reproduction:

> O, wither'd is the garland of the war,
> The soldier's pole is fall'n: young boys and girls
> Are level now with men,

came out as:

> O weederdee degarlano devar,
> Desolderspo lees fall'n: yong boisenguls
> Alefelnow wimen.

James Agate went for the same effect, but first he headed his review: 'ANTON AND CLEOPATROVNA: A TRAGEDY BY KOMISPEARE'. For his blank verse excerpt he chose:

> . . . When you sued staying
> Then was the time for words,

and reported Leontovich's version as:

> . . . Wen you suet staying
> Den was de time for Wurst.

**LERNER**, Alan Jay. Alan Lerner's life was rich in incident, professional and romantic. He wrote, 'There is no greater fan of the opposite sex than me, and I have the bills to prove it.'

His father, creator of a chain-store fortune, was also a rich character. His passions were literacy, the theatre, ladies and boxing. Confusing the two on one occasion, he romanced a lady and told his wife he had been at a boxing match. Stirring earlier than usual in the morning, she asked him who had won the bout. Tossing a mental coin, he named a fighter. Opening the *New York Times* while she went back to sleep, he found that he had guessed the wrong one. From his office he arranged that his clothes should be removed to the Waldorf, where he was installed, before his wife woke up.

He gave his son eloquent advice on the subject of women: it was always the woman's fault. 'The proof of it is that you will go to bed with one woman on Monday and it will be a failure and another on Tuesday and it will be a success. You are the same person. Only the woman has changed. Therefore, whose fault is it? Hers.'

Lerner used to tell a sad story of the friendship he struck up with Lorenz Hart. One night there was a power failure and he sat in the dark with Hart, listening to the radio. The first station was playing a song from *Oklahoma!*. Hammerstein had just stepped into Hart's shoes as Rodgers's collaborator. Lerner saw Hart's cigar glow brighter in the darkness. He changed to another station. More *Oklahoma!* The puffing on the cigar grew more nervous. He found a third station. They heard the same score. Mercifully, the lights came back on and the twisting knife of melody was never mentioned by its victim.

Just as Lerner was becoming successful – notably with *Brigadoon* – his father's health deteriorated; cancer had forced his doctors to remove his tongue. On a beach in Florida, a neighbour approached him.

'I just heard the reviews of *Brigadoon*,' he said. 'Your son is certainly a lucky boy.'

Lerner's father always carried a pen and paper with him.

'Yes,' he wrote on it, 'it's a funny thing about Alan. The harder he works the luckier he gets.'

After Lerner had enjoyed more theatrical and film successes, his father's health weakened still more. When he signed the official form giving permission for one operation, Lerner saw on it 'number of operations: 49'. His father had written beneath, 'When it gets to 50, sell.'

Lerner's father died a month before Alan started work on *My Fair Lady*. Progress to the first night was fraught with incident, especially at the outset, when Lerner and Loewe encountered Mary Martin. At the time she was Peter Panning her way across the Broadway sky. Having been told of the *Pygmalion* project, she asked to hear the score. Neither librettist nor composer thought her right, but both heeded Lorenz Hart's advice – 'If a star seems interested, do not say "No" for at least twenty-four hours.' She heard the songs and departed. Lerner and Loewe waited anxiously for her verdict. When Lerner pinned down her husband over lunch some days later, the verdict was shattering.

'How could it have happened? Those dear boys have lost their talent.' In Lerner it produced a psychological block which had to be analysed away. Rex Harrison's initial reaction to the first two songs he heard was not much better. He hated them.

'We knew it,' wrote Lerner, 'because he immediately said, "I hate them."' In this case the writers knew he was correct and went happily back to the drawing board.

Working on *Gigi,* they came upon Maurice Chevalier and an incident that oddly echoed one experienced by Rodgers and Hart a quarter of a century earlier. Lerner and Loewe were to play the great man his songs. He arrived exactly on time. He listened to the songs throughtfully. He thanked them and left. Panic struck. Perhaps he had not liked the material? The next day he called for another appointment. Was he coming to tell them just that? Only when he arrived did they learn that he liked the songs so much that he had come back to make sure he had the right phrasing on the middle eight bars of 'Thank Heaven'.

Richard Rodgers tells the story of his encounter in his autobiography, *Musical Stages.* Chevalier sat silent throughout, his usually expressive face without a trace either of approval or of disapproval, 'and when we finished he simply rose and left without saying another word. We were stunned. The next morning we didn't do any work. We simply stared at each other and at the walls like prisoners on Death Row . . . after a couple of hours the door burst open . . . "Boys," Chevalier said, "I just had to come back to tell you. I couldn't sleep a wink last night because I was so excited by your wonderful songs!"'

They might have warned Lerner and Loewe. Chevalier also asked the latter pair if his accent was all right. They said they could understand every word.

'No,' was his response. 'Is it French enough?'

An apocryphal story of Lerner and Loewe has them celebrating the London opening of *My Fair Lady* by strolling through Berkeley Square, past the Rolls Royce showrooms. The apocrypha comes in when it is suggested that Lerner having paid for lunch, Loewe bought them a Rolls Royce each.

Lerner did acquire a Rolls and took it to Paris with a formidable Scottish chauffeur, MacIntosh, as chaperone. There they bumped into the columnist, Art Buchwald, who asked if he could examine the engine. MacIntosh refused: 'If I raise the bonnet people might think there was something wrong with the car.'

'In your opinion,' Buchwald asked the chauffeur, 'is Mr Lerner worth a Rolls?'

'Oh yes, sir,' said MacIntosh.

'Why?' Buchwald pressed.

'Because he's so careless with it.'

Lerner was to grow less careless as familiarity bred concern. He recalled staying at the Waldorf Towers and looking out of the window during a phone conversation with Moss Hart. ' "Goddamn it," I began.

' "What's the trouble?" he asked.

' "The Duchess of Windsor's air conditioning is dripping on my Rolls."'

Lerner's last shows were not as triumphant. Of *1600 Pennsylvania Avenue,* which he wrote with Leonard Bernstein, he said, 'Well, you remember the *Titanic.*' His last show, *Dance a Little Closer,* Broadway wiseguys rechristened *Close a Little Faster.* It did, after one performance.

Lerner had one eye (he lost the other in a boxing accident), a tanned-to-mahogany skin and a penchant for gold chains – all of which led to the famous occasion when a taxi-driver dropped him off at the Dorchester and thanked him for a generous tip by saying, 'I've always enjoyed your work, Mr Davis Jnr.'

Alan Lerner died, after a long spell in hospital, as elegantly as he had written, ordering a last bottle of champagne to share with his loved ones and fading peacefully afterwards.

**LEVANT**, Oscar. Pianist, composer, actor and wit, he was asked if the music of George Gershwin – who was famous for dominating parties by playing his own songs – would be around in a hundred years. He said sharply, 'If George is around it will.'

**LIBERACE.** The American piano and candelabra entertainer of unrivalled flamboyance was a monument of and to kitsch and an occasional, self-deprecating wit: 'I've done my bit for motion pictures. I've stopped making them.'

His stage appearances alone were a spangled carnival:

A first-act finale in Nevada: 'A tribute to the Statue of Liberty centennial with Miss Liberty holding a candelabra and Liberace arriving in a stars and stripes Rolls Royce and wearing an ermine robe and red, white and blue hot-pants to lead the band while the Rockettes kicked and sky rockets exploded.'

At the Radio City Music Hall: 'Soaring above the mammoth stage like Peter Pan, trailing a cape of silvery scales edged in purple feathers.'

At the Easter concert: 'Emerging from a giant Fabergé egg in a 100-lb cape of pink-dyed turkey feathers.'

This sort of thing, allied with jewel-encrusted wrists – 'to shake the hand is to flirt with laceration' – and a saccharin style led to criticism.

'The grave digger of art,' *Krokodil.*

'Nobody loves me but the people,' Liberace.

'A deadly, winking, sniggering, snuggling, chromium-plated, scent-impregnated, luminous, quivering, giggling, fruit-flavoured, mincing, ice-covered, heap of mother love,' Cassandra, *Daily Mirror.*

Liberace won huge damages from the *Mirror* and 'cried all the way to the bank'. In court it was his English solicitor who wore the thicker make-up.

Liberace's success was consistent in spite of ridicule and a palimony action by a gay lover. One of his business managers once offered him advice on a television show. 'You've got to do it,' she said.

'Denise,' he replied. 'I don't gotta do nothin' – ever.'

President Truman greeted one of his performances with a 'Whoop!' – Western-style. Liberace remarked, 'That must be the shortest presidential speech on record.'

He was once asked how he knew that his virgin fox pelts – 'It took forever to find them' – were virgin: 'It takes one to know one.'

The *Washington Post*, while accusing him of 'profiteering in out-landishness', also countered, 'Liberace's sincerity is beyond reproach. He genuinely believes in his fantasy world. Judgement of good taste or bad taste is irrelevant. It's his taste, and his joyful flamboyance is rooted in a child's wonderment.'

Noel Coward was more succinct when they met by chance on the *Queen Mary*.

'I've seen your act.' (Long pause.) 'You do – what you do – very well.'

LILLIE, Beatrice (Lady Peel). Seeing her at the Golders Green Hippodrome on 15 July, 1941, Caryl Brahms wrote: 'The greatest revue artist of her age. She did six numbers – all with a clean, neat, intimate, deadly touch. Her wit is a steely flick. Her sense of fun is sweeping. Her handling of the audience is in the miracle class. She annihilated the space in the vast house while maintaining her aloofness and sophistication.'

Her performance on stage was a distillation of witty clowning. Apocrypha tells us that she was once, unknown to her, billed as Lady Peel in a solo concert somewhere in the mid-West. Misled by her routine about a suburban snob down on her luck ('I always 'ad my own 'orses'), the scanty audience believed that they were witnessing the plight of an impoverished gentlewoman working her passage back to the old country. As each wilder piece of comic invention succeeded each act of immaculate clowning, the baffled but sympathetic crowd managed to keep their faces straight while the perplexed star strove in vain to make them laugh.

Her off-stage cracks were better received. At Buckingham Palace just after World War Two, a footman spilt some soup on her new-look Paris gown.

'Never darken my Dior again!' she cried.

Asked if she had performed during World War One, she commented,

'At the end of the First World War, I was knee-high to a hiccup.' In fact, she had appeared by then and in 1921 she was in *A-Z*, a Chariot revue with Jack Buchanan. Most of her roles were *travestie* parts but 'Backstage I was classified as a girl even if I hardly got into a skirt.'

The girls dressed on one side of the Prince of Wales stage, the men on the other. One night Buchanan, with a different thought in his mind, seeing her in tails, asked her, 'Beattie, how do you dress, left or right?'

At first she didn't catch on. 'I still thought flies were something you swatted.'

Buchanan pressed the point. 'Don't be shy, which side do you dress?' Suddenly the light dawned, or so she thought.

'Oh, yes,' she answered. 'In number five, stage left.'

As the wife and widow of Sir Robert Peel, she would say: 'I'm a lady in my own wrong,' and often answered the telephone 'C'est Lady Parle qui Peel.' To a pigeon which flew into her New York apartment, she enquired simply, 'Any messages?' and paying off a boringly talkative Irish taxi-driver in Manhattan, she said, 'Something for you, driver. Buy yourself a sense of humour.'

Reading in *The Times* that an elderly peer had married a very young woman, she carried on to read the list of presents, concluding with (probably her own invention): 'The bridgegroom's gift to the bride was an antique pendant.' In 1951 she ordered a live alligator from Harrods and sent it to Noel Coward with the message, 'So, what else is new?'

After a long run in a Broadway revue, the lyricist Howard Dietz played a last-night trick on her: he filled the front row of the stalls with friends who during her last number donned long false beards of many colours. Thrown for once, she fled the stage, but by the time she reached her dressing room she had recovered her composure. 'Nobody can appreciate my voice anyway,' she said. 'I never sing above a whisker!'

She delivered an unanswerable rebuke to the wife of a Chicago meat-packing tycoon, a Mrs Armour, who complained to her crimper that had she known so many theatricals would be in the salon she would never have come. Miss Lillie ignored Mrs Armour and told the manageress in cut-glass tones, 'You may tell the butcher's wife that Lady Peel has finished.' Another snob looked hard at her pearls one night: 'Are they real?' she asked.

'Of course.'

The woman grabbed them and tried to bite them: 'They're not,' she claimed, 'they're cultured!'

'How would you know?' smiled Miss Lillie. 'You with false teeth!'

The last twenty years of her life were spent sadly near Henley-on-Thames, her mind wandering, tended by her devoted companion John, who died within days of her own death. In his posthumously published book, Bruce Chatwin has reported a touching incident of her heyday and her decline:

It is 1944 in New York and Miss Lillie, alias Lady Peel, 'Lady Parle-qui-Peel', is sauntering down Madison Avenue in her inevitable embroidered mobcap. She is a big hit in the musical, *Seven Lively Arts* at the Ziegfeld Theater. The war is still on and the art business is slow. Showbiz is booming. I haven't a clue what time of year it was. Let us imagine it was spring. She passes the galleries along Madison Avenue and a picture takes her eye.

'Lawdie Gawdie!' It's the Valentin Gallery. She sweeps in. The assistant sweeps her into Mr Valentin's office. He rises to his feet. 'Miss Lillie. I am honoured you come to my gallery.'

'The room,' says Bea, 'was covered in plum velvet and there was a plum velvet easel.' 'Mr Valentin,' she begins, 'my friend, Vincent Price, tells me you have a beautiful painting by M . . . Mo . . . Mo . . .

'Modigliani.'

'Well, let's shorten it to Modi.'

The assistant goes to the shelves behind the plum velvet curtain and pulls out a painting of a young Belgian boy. He has a mass of blond curls and rosy cheeks: he wears a sand-coloured jacket; I forget the other details.

'Is that a Modi?'

'It is, Miss Lillie.'

'I never saw anything so frrrightful in my life. If that's a Modi, I'm leaving!'

She sweeps out. On the threshold she turns to Mr Valentin.

'And how much were you proposing to ask me for the Modi?'

'Miss Lillie, I have always been a great admirer of yours. I was suggesting $15,000.'

'Fifteen thousand dollars! You can keep it! I could offer you 75 hundred, but 15 thousand!'

'Miss Lillie, if you really like the picture, I give it for 75 hundred.'

She goes back to the plum-coloured office and writes out a cheque. Since the war is still on, Mr Valentin agrees to keep it and ship it when hostilities are over.

He shipped the Modi in a crate. It went upstairs into the attic of Bea's house on the river at Henley-on-Thames and she forgot about it.

The first time I saw Bea and the Modi was in 1963 when the chairman of Sotheby's came into our office with Bea, the Modi and Bea's American friend and protector. He said we would store the picture indefinitely. It would be insured for £50,000.

That Sunday I went for lunch and supper at Henley. We laughed, sang and Bea played the piano. I was Noel and she was Gertie. We had perfect pitch:

> If you were the only girl in the world
> And I were the only boy . . .

The last I heard of the Modi was a telephone call from the chairman's secretary about ten years later, asking me if I knew the details of the insurance on the Modigliani and whether Beatrice Lillie signed the insurance form. Her protector had turned up one day at Sotheby's and asked for the picture back. The porter, supposing it to have been left there last week, let him have it. He took it down the road to Christie's where it sold for over £200,000.

The money went to pay her nursing bills.

I hope that Bea in her dotage remembered the rosy-cheeked Belgian boy.

Helen Hayes also tells a charming story of visiting Blackwell's Island on the East River with her husband, Charles MacArthur, and Bea. The island looked green and inviting but they had forgotten that it housed strictly guarded mental institutions. When the party was about to rejoin the ferry for the East 79th Street Pier, they were confronted by a guide who refused to let them leave without a pass. Bea tried pulling rank.

'My dear sir, I am Beatrice Lillie and this is Helen Hayes. We both have performances to give tonight and we have to get to our theatres.' It made no impression. She tried again.

'I am Lady Peel. Miss Hayes is the first lady of the American theatre and this gentleman is the distinguished playwright, Mr Charles MacArthur.'

The guard refused to be impressed.

'Listen, lady, we've already got some Lillies here and several first ladies and maybe a couple of MacArthurs. So show me a pass or get back to the hospital and take tea with Greta Garbo and Lady Astor. There are a few of them there too.'

Finally they telephoned Richard Rodgers's brother, Mortimer, a doctor, who persuaded the authorities to release them. Bea had the last word. 'One day I'm going back to that island to confront those imposters claiming to be me.'

She got her own titles mixed up one evening after a pub crawl with Tallulah Bankhead. In search of her key, she was confronted by a suspicious desk clerk and asked haughtily, 'Lady Keel's pee, if you please.'

Perhaps this is a good place to squeeze in one of Bankhead's better remarks.

MAN: (Rushes up to Tallulah in a bar) Jesus, Tallulah, I haven't seen you for 30 years!
TALLULAH: I thought I told you to wait in the car.

The great pianist/singer and song-buff Michael Feinstein collected a Beatrice Lillie impromptu direct from Marshall Barer when he worked with her on *The Ziegfeld Follies of 1956*. During rehearsals they went to lunch. Miss Lillie ordered bouillabaise. When the covered dish was presented, she lifted the lid, took one look and quickly replaced it exclaiming, 'Low tide!'

**LLOYD-WEBBER**, Andrew. Andrew Lloyd-Webber, the most successful English composer for the popular musical theatre, is also an impresario of great distinction. He became the butt of more cracks than most because of his marriage to his second wife, Sarah Brightman (Why did Roger Moore leave the cast of *Aspects of Love*? Because as soon as Andrew found out he couldn't sing he wanted to marry him); and because of his alleged cavalier treatment of lyricists ('Andrew changes lyricists like gardeners' – Don Black). On another occasion, Black, who wrote the lyrics for *Tell Me on a Sunday* and collaborated with Charles Hart on *Aspects of Love,* was driving to Lloyd-Webber's country house at Sydmonton with the American lyric writer, Richard Maltby. As they reached the approaches, they saw the drive jammed with an enormous queue of cars.

'What's all that about? asked Maltby.

'Oh,' said Black, 'that's just Andrew auditioning lyricists.'

If Lloyd-Webber is unpopular, it is partly because of his enormous success. He once asked Alan Jay Lerner over lunch why people took an instant dislike to him. Lerner replied, 'It saves time.'

This story may be apocryphal but it's still funny. An article in the *New York Times* suggested that Andrew had lost his way since he stopped writing with Tim Rice.

'Oh God,' he was heard to wail. 'I'm having just the same problems as Giacomo, Wolfgang and Giuseppe!'

Legend has it that he once sent a musical note across the Caprice to Stephen Sondheim's table. Sondheim looked at it and ignored it. When someone pointed out that it was from Lloyd-Webber, Sondheim is supposed to have said, 'I knew it wasn't from a musician.'

**LOCKE**, Joseph. Joseph Locke was an immensely popular tenor who toured the music halls with great success after World War Two. Huge crowds turned out to see him and when two Sunday concerts in Blackpool were announced, both were instantly booked out. On performance day, the manager was horrified when Locke arrived at the theatre and whispered hoarsely, 'My voice has gone. I cannot sing tonight.'

'I'm not telling 'em,' said the brave manager. 'They'll tear the place apart.'

At the first house the supporting acts gave their best and the curtains parted after the interval to reveal Locke, who came forward and whispered sincerely, 'I am very sorry. My voice has gone. I cannot sing tonight.'

There was a shocked silence. Suddenly into it fell a reasonable voice from the gallery: 'All right then, show us your cock.' The atmosphere was punctured. After a roar of laughter, the audience dispersed in good humour.

However, the manager was greedy and decided to repeat the experiment in the evening with a plant. Was it the timing? Had some of the fans brought tickets for both houses? Whatever the reason – they tore the place apart.

**LOESSER**, Frank. Frank Loesser was an enormously talented and temperamental composer lyricist. Burton Lane recalled a typical incident: he had written a tune, Loesser eventually completed a lyric, banged it on Lane's piano and expected him to perform it perfectly straight away – 'Goddamn it, can't you read?'

Loesser had a staff job at Paramount. To his dismay, he was loaned to the less prestigious Republic Pictures and assigned to Jule Styne for a musical, *Sis Hopkins*. He was furious at this demotion and threatened not to work with Styne: 'I'm working with Hoagy Carmichael now. I'm not coming to work with some half-ass piano player who is really a vocal coach!' He was as violent when he met Styne: 'You have demeaned me by asking for me.'

Loesser planned to complete his three-week assignment in four days and then have a holiday in Palm Springs, but when he heard Styne's first tune he was excited. 'Never play that song again,' he shouted, slamming the door shut. 'Don't ever play that song for anyone else. We'll write that song for Paramount.' When Loesser took Styne back to Paramount they did not declare the tune when they crossed the border from Republic, and after five weeks of smoking and pacing Loesser came up with the lyric, 'I Don't Want To Walk Without You.'

In the army, Loesser progressed to writing music as well as words – his real Broadway debut was *Where's Charley?*, his masterpiece *Guys and Dolls*, its birth rich in incident.

He handed his producers, Feuer and Martin, four songs for the Runyon show without any contract. That was the nub of the show. The original book was thrown out and Abe Burrows brought in to fashion a new one around the four songs. Loesser always wanted to hear his music loud. When the choreographer, Michael Kidd, first staged the crap game number, Loesser launched a flurry of four-letter words: he expected to hear his song loud and perfect from the start. When Martin tried to intervene, Loesser rounded on him.

'You're Hitler! . . . I'm the author, and you're working for me!' Kidd had the cast stand still and sing the chorus as loud as possible. As they bellowed the song, Feuer and Martin watched Loesser retreat happily up the aisle and followed him out of the theatre as he bought an ice-cream and licked it happily as he returned to his hotel. He had heard his song and he had heard it loud.

He was happy until the next flurry. He was rehearsing Isobel Bigley, who played the Salvation Army girl, in a song of enormous range – 'I'll Know'. He was so infuriated by the ineradicable break in the middle of her range that he finally leapt on stage and punched her on the nose. Too late, he realised what he had done and had to rush to buy an apologetic bracelet.

His famous argument with George S. Kaufman, his director, centred round his wish to reprise ballads in the second act.

'When are they going to hear my songs? What the hell do you think I'm in this for?'

Kaufman had the last word. He offered to reprise Loesser's ballads in Act Two if Loesser would allow him to reprise his first-act jokes alongside. When Loesser got his first award his response was typical: 'I should have had it three years ago.'

*Greenwillow* was probably Loesser's least successful musical – apart from his last. When it closed he was in London. His wire to the cast read, 'Oops! Sorry!' A compulsive smoker, he died in hospital aged 59 of lung cancer, a breathing machine on one side of him, a packet of cigarettes on the other.

**LOEWE**, Frederick (Fritz). Frederick Loewe was a child prodigy born in Berlin. His father, Edmund Loewe, played Danilo in the original Berlin production of *The Merry Widow*. The family came to America in 1923 but Edmund Loewe died during rehearsals for the show for which Belasco had engaged him. Fritz supported his mother as bus boy, boxer, riding instructor, cowboy, gold prospector and horseback mail deliverer – as well as by very occasional concert engagements.

He remained to the end of his life a great gambler and a monstrously active ladies' man. In Boston for a try-out, a producer told Lerner and Loewe that they only had one hope – someone must go to bed with a powerful lady critic who was remarkably unattractive. Loewe bravely undertook the chore and succeeded so splendidly that not only did she review the show in a rosy glow, but whenever Loewe returned to Boston with a musical she turned up to see him with the new husband she had acquired since seeing the light, and the family they were accumulating.

**LORD CHAMBERLAIN, THE.** The Lord Chamberlain's jurisdiction over the British theatre had its origins in 1494 when the Royal Household appointed a Master of the Revels to supervise court entertainments. After the Restoration in 1660, censorship and the licensing and regulation of theatres became part of the Lord Chamberlain's responsibilities. The Theatres Act of 1968 took all theatrical powers out of the Lord Chamberlain's hands and rendered superfluous the three English readers and one Welsh who were required to read work submitted and report on indecency, impropriety, profanity, seditious content and 'the representation of living persons'.

The establishment of a censoring body for plays written after the 1663

Theatres Act, which had formalised his authority, frequently brought ridicule on the censor. E.F. Smyth Pigott, the Lord Chamberlain's examiner of plays from 1875 to 1895, announced: 'I have studied Ibsen's plays pretty carefully; and all the characters . . . appear to me to be morally deranged. All the heroines are dissatisfied spinsters who look on marriage as a monopoly, or dissatisfied married women in a chronic state of rebellion against the conditions which nature has imposed on their sex.'

Shaw dismissed Smyth Pigott summarily: 'He had French immorality on the brain; he had American indecency on the brain; he had "not before a mixed audience" on the brain; his official career in relation to the higher drama was one long folly and panic.'

By the 1960s the contribution of the Lord Chamberlain was no more constructive. In 1963 a letter from his office said, 'I can say categorically that the Lord Chamberlain would not allow a nude woman to be wheeled across the stage in a wheel barrow.' In 1964 he licensed Joe Orton's *Loot* with the proviso: 'The corpse must "obviously" be a dummy and not be seen by the audience.' The next year, five pages of vetoes greeted Edward Bond's *Saved,* including the instruction. 'There must be no indecent business with the balloon.' John Osborne's A *Patriot For Me* was refused a licence. (It was first produced at the Royal Court which had to reconstitute itself as a club.) The reasons for refusal included: 'There are various scenes in the play which the Lord Chamberlain feels unable to license on the grounds that they exploit homosexuality in a manner that may tend to have corrupting influences. He cannot allow such scenes as a homosexual ball at which some of the men are dressed as women (including one who portrays Lady Godiva dressed in a gold lamé jock strap).'

Noel Coward had battles with the Lord Chamberlain, notably over *The Vortex.* Lord Cromer at first refused a licence point-blank on account of 'the unpleasantness of the theme', but relented when Coward persuaded him 'that the play was little more than a moral tract'. Sir Thomas Beecham clashed when he produced *Rosenkavalier* at Covent Garden.

'It appeared that they had discovered the presence of a bed in a remote part of the stage in the third act and were worried about some equivocal references to it in the text . . . I was given the option of two courses. Either the bed could be exhibited without any reference being made to it, or it could be hidden away from sight and we could sing about it as much as we liked. As it was easier to move the furniture than to tamper with the score, I accepted the second alternative and I have always regarded this as a near-perfect example of our British love of compromise!'

The classic Lord Chamberlain's licence was No. 3133, dated 31 January, 1963, issued for the play *The Bed Sitting Room* by Spike Milligan and John Antrobus.

The licence is issued on the understanding that the following alterations are made to the script:

*[Act I]*

Page 1 – Omit the name of the Prime Minister; no representation of his voice is allowed. Page 16 – Omit '. . . clockwork Virgin Mary made in Hong Kong, whistles the twist'. Omit reference to the Royal Family, the Christmas message and the Duke's shooting. Substitute wording as detailed in Mr Mills's letter of 14th Jan, 1963.

Page 21 – The Daz song: omit 'You'll get all the dirt off the tail of your shirt', substitute 'You get all the dirt off the front of your shirt.'

*[Act II]*

Page 3 – No representation of Lord Home's voice is allowed.

Pages 2-8 – The mock priest must not wear a crucifix on his snorkel. It must be immediately made clear that the book the priest handles is not the Bible.

Page 2-8a – Omit 'the good book'.

Page 24 – Omit 'crap', substitute 'jazz'.

Page 2-10 – Omit from 'We've just consummated our marriage . . .' to and inclusive of '. . . a steaming hot summer's night'.

Page 3-13 – Omit from 'In return they are willing . . .' to and inclusive of '. . . The Duke of Edinburgh is a wow with Greek dishes . . .', substitute 'Hark ye! Hark ye! The day of judgement is at hand.'

*[Act III]*

Page 3-7 – Omit 'Piss off . . . piss off . . . piss off . . .', substitute 'Shut your steaming gob.' Page 3 12/13 – Omit the song 'Plastic Mac Man' and substitute 'Oh, you dirty young devil, how dare you presume to wet the bed when the po's in the room. I'll wallop your bum with a dirty great broom when I get up in the morning.'

Page 3-14 – Omit '. . . the perversions of the rubber . . .', substitute '. . . the Kreurpels and blinges of the rubber.' Omit the 'chamber pot under the bed'.

What was so touching about the censor was the desire to supply alternative readings. There was a similar keenness at the BBC's now outdated guide to what would and would not be acceptable in broadcast comedy. Out were 'animals' habits, eg: rabbits', it said, and 'jokes about making a Maltese cross are of doubtful value'.

One of the writers who faced the censor with some concern was Cole Porter, when his lyric for 'Let's Do It' came under official scrutiny. The song is replete with 'animal habits' and stuffed with sexual innuendo. However, the Lord Chamberlain was carried away by the ingenious rhymes and congratulated the lyricist on his exhaustive and scholarly animal research, especially into the mating habits of grouse, who only 'do it' when they're *out* of season.

A later clash between the Lord Chamberlain's office and the New World occurred when Edward Albee's *Who's Afraid of Virginia Woolf?* was played in London. Uta Hagen, who had been in the original Broadway production, was surprised by six or seven pages of changes. The text had been scattered with 'Jesus Christs', the Lord Chamberlain had conceded three. Her entrance line: 'Jesus H. Christ' was changed to 'Mary H. Magdalen'. Miss Hagen, having played the line as written for a year and nervous of her London first night, blurted out, 'Jesus H. Magdalen!'

'Hump' had a Shakespearean pedigree, so 'Hump the hostess' was permitted, but Arthur Hill's reference to his scrotum was reduced to 'the underside of his privacies'. After one try, Hill simply refused to speak the rewrite. Albee cleverly got round, 'She has his right ball' by simply spelling it 'bawl'.

**LUNT**, Alfred and **FONTANNE**, Lynne. Most stories of the Lunts concern their extreme professionalism and their habit of working on key moments and special bits of 'business' until the very last performance in a run, to be sure that they had got it right – after all, there was always a chance that they might revive the play. When asked how they had coped during the Depression, when actors were out of work with theatres closing and managers going bankrupt, Alfred Lunt replied, 'We played *The Guardsman* for a year on Broadway and two years on tour. We had full houses everywhere and we made ourselves a fucking fortune!'

Their last appearance in England was in Peter Brook's production of *The Visit* by Durrenmatt. The production photographs were taken by Angus McBean. Soon afterwards, H.M. Tennent produced *Bye Bye Birdie* with Marty Wilde, a pop star starring as a pop star. He was taken, with entourage, to McBean's studio for a photocall. The entrance was festooned with large portraits of the Lunts. Sycophantically, everyone raved about the Lunts. 'Wonderful picture of the Lunts!' 'Super snaps of the Lunts!' 'Aren't the Lunts wonderful?'

Finally the still, small voice of Marty Wilde's father, who was not versed in the theatre, was heard asking plaintively, 'Excuse me, Mr McBean. What is a Lunt?'

**LYNN**, Olga ('Oggie'). Oggie Lynn was a singer and social being who was so short that she was once asked to rise to attention for 'God Save the King' when she was already standing. According to Ruth Gordon, she was once imported to New York by Cole Porter, who arranged a society debut for her in an Astor or Vanderbilt drawing room. She approached the piano, stopped and said, 'I don't feel like it' and that was the end of her invasion of America.

According to David Herbert in his 'recollections', *Engaging Eccentrics*, she had been trained by Jean de Reske and had a charming voice. A rich American, Bob Lebus of the Lebus Furniture Company, used her as a social climbing ladder. She, always needing money, received cash and trips abroad for introducing him to the rich, the famous and the well-connected. One of his ambitions was to meet Lady Diana Cooper, whom Oggie Lynn dangled as a carrot, always carefully avoiding the actual introduction. Finally Diana Cooper grew bored with being 'Oggie Lynn's carrot' and gatecrashed a dinner party Lebus was giving for Miss Lynn.

Lynn was diabetic and immensely greedy and was therefore nearly as round as she was short. Her daughter, Maud Nelson, worked as Cecil Beaton's secretary before Eileen Hose. When, during World War Two, Beaton managed to get hold of a fresh salmon, he decided to give it to his mother, but on going to take it to her, he found that it had disappeared. Furious, he asked Maud what had happened to it. The devoted daughter burst into tears, fell on her knees and sobbed, 'Forgive me, forgive me, but Oggie had to have it.'

# — _M_ —

**MacArthur**, Charlie. MacArthur's name will survive, not only attached to plays like *The Front Page,* but for one witticism about a gay critic who savaged one of his few disasters, *Ladies and Gentlemen* (1939), another play which he wrote with Ben Hecht. It starred MacArthur's wife, Helen Hayes. The critic disliked her performance, too, saying snidely that 'The trouble with Miss Hayes is that she has been seeing too much of Charlie MacArthur.' Asked how he intended to avenge his wife, MacArthur was straightfaced.

'I've already taken care of him. I am sending him a poisoned choirboy.'

**Macklin**, Charles. Macklin, actor and playwright, was a notable Shylock, a good early teacher and a precise and demanding actor. He rescued the role of Shylock from the dictates of low comedians, being the first actor of his age to play the part with dignity. Pope complimented him with the couplet:

> This is the Jew/
> that Shakespeare knew.

He was particularly hard on improvisers and when Lee Lewes added some dialogue of his own during a rehearsal of Macklin's *Love à la Mode* at Covent Garden, Macklin stopped him.

'Hoy! Hoy! What's that?'

''Tis only a little of my own nonsense,' said Lewes.

'Ay,' said Macklin, 'but I think *my* nonsense is rather better than yours; so keep to that if you please, sir.'

Authors down the ages will sympathise.

Playing Shylock with one Bobby Bates as Tubal, Macklin instructed Bates not to speak until he placed his right foot upon a certain nail. Bates obeyed but Macklin had by the time of the performance forgotten his order. After an embarrassing stage silence, he hissed, 'Why the devil don't you speak?'

'You haven't put your right foot down on the nail,' said Bates, throwing Macklin for the rest of the scene. Bates was lucky to escape Macklin's more violent strictures: he once killed a fellow actor in a quarrel over a wig.

Macklin continued to play until he was very old – 85 and probably older. However, in November 1788 (he would have been at least 89) his memory began to go and the next year, when he was to play Shylock for his own benefit, he could not remember which play was advertised or which role he was to play. Eventually he was led on to speak a couple of speeches and then, mumbling, 'I can do no more', retired from the stage.

He survived another nine years, outliving all his children.

**MAC LIAMMÓIR**, Micheál. Before translating his name, Mac Liammóir was a child actor, Alfred Willmore, who played with Noel Coward in *The Goldfish*. Master Willmore had the title role, King Goldfish and, at £2, 9s 6d more a week than Coward, who remembered him clearly singing, 'I lived within my bowl of glass – Heigh ho – a prisoner I.'

In 1913 they were together in *Peter Pan,* during which Coward told him the facts of life. Next week someone else gave him a different version and when he remonstrated, Coward, aged fourteen, replied in an already perfectly formed Coward way: 'It's no use your waggling that extremely suggestive piece of greasepaint at me. What I've told you is the exact truth.'

Fourteen years later, Mac Liammóir joined Anew McMaster's Shakespeare Company and then, in 1928, the Galway Theatre for Gaelic drama with his lifetime partner, the English actor-director, Hilton Edwards.

Mac Liammóir was often credited with the 'Sodom and Begorrah' description of the two Dublin theatres – the Gate and the Abbey – reflecting the Mac Liammóir /Edwards regime at the Gate and the heavy emphasis on native Irish plays at the Abbey. However, many claim credit. One reader of my *Times* column gave it to Lionel Hale, but I suspect simple reportage here. More promising was Brian Inglis's ascription to Jimmy Montgomery (the late Irish film critic who defined his job as 'a sinecure watching Californication'). The Irish actress, Genevieve Lyons, gives it emphatically to Seamus Kelly, for a long time drama critic of the *Irish Times*. Does the case rest?

There are many stories of the jet-black wig Mac Liammóir wore, which turned out at the end of his life to conceal a rich white thatch and which in turn was often, in the service of the drama, covered with a bald wig, providing three layers of covering.

The devotion betweem Mac Liammóir and Edwards was constant but spiced with violent artistic rows. Apologising after one at rehearsal, Mac Liammóir said lethally, 'And I promise you, Hilton, it's not your wild Irish boy you'll be dealing with tonight – but a *dedicated artist!*' His last tour de force was his one-man show, *The Importance of Being Oscar*, directed by Edwards. 'Life,' he said, in a phrase that could have been Wilde's, 'is a long rehearsal for a play that is never produced.'

When he was appearing in the show in London, he came on to the *Tonight* show which I was directing. I picked him up from an hotel near Green Park and he was fascinating about his first acquaintance with Wilde, as an author. As a child, he was entranced by Wilde's fairy stories but dimly aware that there was some awful secret about Oscar which caused grown-ups to shy off the subject. He plucked up courage and asked his father what was Wilde's crime. Mr Willmore asked why he wanted to know. The child replied that he was enjoying the fairy stories so much. The father came up with an inspired answer, which Mac Liammóir recalled with rich, rolling relish.

'Well, you see, my boy, the trouble with Oscar Wilde was that he wanted to turn boys into girls.'

**MacMillan**, Sir Kenneth. Nicholas Hytner spoke the eulogy at Sir Kenneth MacMillan's farewell in Westminster Abbey on 17 February, 1993. Nicholas directed MacMillan's last new work, the dances for *Carousel* at the National Theatre. He had been nervous, he confessed, when he approached the great man to enlist him for the job, and having rattled on, finally blurted out, 'The point is it's all about sex and violence.' At this MacMillan smiled and said quietly, 'That's what I do.'

The last dance which MacMillan made for the show was for the exuberant 'June is Bustin' Out All Over'. He was unmoved by the fulsome excitement which the first run-through generated, until the dialect coach said, 'It's like an orgy on *speed.*' Kenneth spent the rest of the day happily repeating the phrase.

**MacNeice**, Louis. The poet was also a keen pub-goer. In an Oxford saloon bar, with Max Miller and Peter O'Toole, they played a game of inventing fictitious pub names. MacNeice won with 'The Dog Returns'.

**MACRAE**, Duncan. Macrae to Kenneth Williams, on the occasion of constant complaints about the dialogue in Joe Orton's *Loot:* 'I've heard the same things from people in the dressing room. Och, they're all carpers, moaning minnies with no stomach for anything new in the theatre. It was the same thing when I did my fireman sketch in Scotland: a very distinguished critic, Mamie Crichton, came backstage and said it was scandalous what I was doing with the hose-nozzle between my legs – I said to her, "Och, Mamie, the precedent for phallic comedy goes right back to [Macrae's pronounciation] Aristo-far-knees." There wasn't a peep out of her after that.'

**MACREADY**, William Charles. Macready's great legacy is the compelling theatrical pause – a 'Macready' – and his instinct to regularise his profession – adequate rehearsals and restoring Shakespeare's texts, in spite of an innate distaste for it. His early touring reminiscences show an uncharacteristic sense of humour. Playing in a barn as a young actor, he supported Conway in a touring *Macbeth*. After Duncan's murder, the exigencies of a fit-up tour left Macbeth on the wrong side of the stage with no servant to clean his hands in a hurry. Macready improvised soap and water and, finding no towel, grabbed the nearest cloth to hand. Moments later Lady Macbeth was faced with a similar dilemma and Macready again obliged. Next day there was a hue and cry for an elderly actor's 'small clothes'. Simkins, the actor in question, reported them stolen. Only then did Macready remember that this was the garment he had grasped and thrown away the moment he had 'saved the situation'.

Apart from Shakespeare, he had a great success in *Virginius* by James Sheridan Knowles at Covent Garden in 1920. He also toured the play with varying success, remarking in his memoirs that at one performance in Louth, which virtually no one attended, 'I never acted Virginius better in my life. Mr Robertson [the manager] was astonished at what he thought my philosophy, being accustomed as he said, to be "blown up by his *Stars* [sic: see how early the word encroaches] when the houses were bad."'

He shows no great love of Bath, where a woman declined to buy tickets, preferring to wait for 'something entertaining for the children. When will *Aladdin* be done?' One day he went to Bath in a coach. A fellow passenger assured him that 'Macready would not act if they did not applaud him.' On that occasion he gave an apology. He failed to do so once in Norwich when he played Hamlet and the Claudius, to whom he had given a critical note, decided to die centre-stage, where Macready had intended to expire. To Macready's hissed, 'Get up and die elsewhere, sir,' the actor replied by sitting up and saying loudly, 'Mr Macready, you've had your way at rehearsals; but I'm king now, and I shall die just where I like.'

His Shylock was once enormously enhanced by the presence of a fan in the wings, who foolishly approached him just before he went on to rant about 'his ducats and his daughter'. Macready exploded and nearly decapitated the unfortunate before making his cue. After the performance, he assumed that the stage manager had planted the victim in order to inspire him to greater rages, and asked if he could give him a little something.

'At present, sir,' said the stage manager, 'they have conveyed him to the hospital.'

In Manchester, finding no servant waiting with a bowl of cochineal to incarnadine Macbeth's hands, he punched a fan lurking in the wings on the nose and helped himself to the blood which resulted. The victim got £5 for his pain.

There is a story that Macready, subject to criticism for excessive mannerisms – apart from the pauses – would rehearse in binding strings. If he burst his bonds then he knew that the gesture which broke them was essential. To Wallack, he confessed that he liked to rehearse in a glass after his wife had tied his hands behind his back. Wallack, a naturally graceful actor, suggested he tried tying his legs as well.

Macready's fellow artists were sometimes frail fellows and sometimes much put upon. In *Virginius,* one could not remember his name 'Numitorius'. Macready gave him a mnemonic – 'Think of numbers – the book of Numbers.'

That evening, in reply to the inquiry 'Who asks the question?' the unfortunate actor replied, 'I, her uncle – Deuteronomy.' Which would have been all right a couple of hundred years later in *Cats.*

John Cooper, playing the Ghost in Macready's *Hamlet* after Macready's return from America, was dressed in a suit of armour which had done duty around the States. In the middle of the battlement scene, the unfortunate actor began to cry out.

In response to Macready's, 'What the devil is it? Go on, sir!' he could only say, 'I cannot. I am ate up alive by something.' The audience laughed. The star was furious and the victim fell through a trap, screaming, 'Remember me!' – to tear off the armour, which had only been unpacked that afternoon and was swarming with hungry American cockroaches.

The most sensational events in Macready's life took place in America. As the veteran of the London stage, he had welcomed Edwin Forrest, America's rising star, to Drury Lane in 1836. When Macready visited America in 1843 he was welcomed and entertained by Forrest, who refused to accept rival engagements. Nonetheless, Macready was possessed by jealousy of Forrest on his return to Britain.

Perhaps the press had fanned the flames of rivalry. When Forrest next visited England, a row was brewing. In Edinburgh, where Macready was playing Hamlet, Forrest hissed his 'mad business'. On Macready's next visit to America in 1848, he was pelted with eggs on his opening in Philadephia. Forrest was not responsible and urged his supporters to let 'the superannuated driveller alone'. Macready's farewell at the Astor Place Opera in Greenwich Village amid disturbances was advertised for 10 May, 1849. Macready's fans filled the theatre. Forrest's crowded the streets outside. Eventually the two sides clashed and Macready narrowly escaped with his life. Two dozen rioters were killed and over three dozen wounded.

Macready retired to Cheltenham and, although not overly rich as a result of his tenancy of Drury Lane, resisted the operatic gesture of constant returns to the stage for lavishly paid farewell performances. J.L. Toole visited him there and reported '. . . he said he did not believe in an actor remaining on the stage after his powers were at an end; he thought a man should retire in the zenith of his strength: and he believed that he had played Macbeth on that last night as well as ever he played it. I confirmed this; and it pleased him very much when I told him that I had stood at the entrance of Drury Lane on his farewell appearance for five hours.'

**MADONNA** (Ciccone, Madonna Louise Veronica). When Madonna was recording Stephen Sondheim's songs for the Warren Beatty movie, *Dick Tracy*, the session was held up because Sondheim was not happy with the tone of the piano. It had to be changed and a new one tuned. Headlines had been screaming that Ms Ciccone earned between $30 million and $50 million a year. An impatient Madonna Louise Veronica sighed, whined and drummed her fingers at the delay and finally moaned: 'I wanna *earn* my money,' eliciting from Sondheim a bitter, 'Impossible.'

**MAHAR**, Joseph. The clever Irish actor, who had never appeared in England until John Tillinger's production of Orton's *What the Butler Saw* in 1990, had an early experience with Tillinger when both were acting in a Shakespearean repertory season in America. They were playing two conspirators in *Julius Caesar*, on the point of knifing Caesar, when a stage manager's phone rang obtrusively in the wings. Unfortunately the house heard Mahar's muttered, 'What shall we do if it's for Caesar?' as clearly as the ringing.

**MAMET**, David. David Mamet, the fine Chicago-born author of *Sexual Perversity in Chicago, American Buffalo* and *A Life in the Theatre,* is a master of authentic colloquial low-life dialogue – a facility which has spawned a classic American theatrical joke.

A bum asks a well-dressed businessman for a hand-out. The businessman rejects him, saying, ' "Neither a borrower nor a lender be" – William Shakespeare.'

' "Fuck you," ' the bum replies – 'David Mamet.'

According to Harold Pinter 'He sent me, unforgettably, *Glengarry Glen Ross* with a note saying, "There is something wrong with this play. What is it?" I wired him immediately, "There is nothing wrong with this play. I'm giving it to the National".'

**MANKIEWICZ**, Joseph Leo. Joe Mankiewicz, among the more literate of Hollywood writers, faced one of his biggest challenges when he was called upon in his directorial capacity to put some drama in the epic *Cleopatra.* He had to update the script constantly during shooting – spending Sundays and nights writing. Such was the pressure he began compulsively to bite his fingernails. In the end he had to wear gloves to cover the unpleasant effect. But before that Elizabeth Taylor had caught him chewing his nails on the set. 'Joe,' she ordered, 'don't bite your fingernails.'

'I'm not,' he said, 'I'm biting my knuckles. I finished the fingernails months ago.'

Before the nightmare of *Cleopatra*, Mankiewicz made a rather good job of Shakespeare's *Julius Caesar*, starring Gielgud, James Mason, Marlon Brando, Edmund O'Brien and Louis Calhern. According to John Gielgud, one of his assistant directors did not match his superior's sensitivity. The man was trying to encourage some uninspired extras into some signs of life before shooting the forum scene: 'All right, kids,' he yelled. 'It's Rome, it's hot and here comes Julius!'

Mankiewicz was a notoriously difficult man – when Katharine Hepburn finished shooting *Suddenly Last Summer* she was so furious with Mankiewicz's treatment of Montgomery Clift, who had been ill throughout shooting, that, having positively assured herself that she had no further commitment to the picture – shooting, retakes, dubbing, voice-over – she spat full in his face and walked out of his office.

Robert Lantz, who was at one time Mankiewicz's agent, was later breakfasted in Hollywood by two producers who wanted a director for a particularly difficult movie project. He suggested Mankiewicz – 'the only possible man for the job.' The two producers were amazed. They pointed out that Lantz no longer represented Mankiewicz. 'No,' Lantz replied, 'It's a rare case of the fan hitting the shit.'

Many have claimed the phrase since.

**MANNINGHAM**, John. Manningham was a seventeenth-century lawyer and diarist who recorded that *Twelfth Night* was commissioned by lawyers at the Middle Temple and performed in hall at a feast on 2 February, 1602.

Manningham's diaries also contain the only known contemporary anecdote about Shakespeare. A woman fell for Burbage when he was playing Richard Crookback and made a date to see him (under the name of Richard III) at her house after the show. Shakespeare overheard this, got to her house before the play had ended and, in Manningham's words, 'was at his game 'ere Burbage came. The message being brought that Richard III was at the door, Shakespeare caused return to be made that William the Conqueror was before Richard III.'

**MANSFIELD**, Richard. Richard Mansfield, born in Berlin, the son of a German opera singer and a British wine merchant, was one of the outstanding American actors of the late nineteenth century. Versatile and civilised, his personality denied his modest height, 5ft 6ins – 'They see what I make them imagine that they see' – and his voice was a distinctive and wonderful instrument, trained from an early age.

His early career was in London and in light opera. He played the great Shakespearean roles and also Cyrano, Jekyll and Hyde and Monsieur Beaucaire. Clayton Hamilton, an actor who played with him, remembered vividly his quarrel scene in *Julius Caesar*.

'When he played Brutus . . . he sat inconspicuously in a darkened corner of the tent, while Joseph Haworth, cast as Cassius, was allowed to take the stage, with the limelight full upon him, and pour out his lines in a tremendous torrent. Mansfield remained quiescent – till a single sudden phrase. But when he roared out, "Away, slight man!" the walls of the theatre shook as with an earthquake. It was as if Cassius had been blown bodily out of the tent and off the stage.'

Mansfield had a favourite story on the old debate about whether Hamlet was mad.

'One morning in the West I met a young friend of mine and asked him where he had been the night before.

"I went," my friend replied, "to see so-and-so's Hamlet."

"Aha, did you?" said I. "Now tell me – do you think Hamlet was mad?"

"I certainly do," said he. "There wasn't a hundred dollars in the house."'

Mansfield was a pioneer of Shaw in America but his relations with Shaw were not always cordial. When he played *The Devil's Disciple* in New York, a woman reporting on the performance to Shaw said, 'Mansfield ought to get down on his knees and thank God for such a play.'

Shaw replied, 'Yes, but he wishes to God someone else had written it.'

In his last season, encouraged by his wife, Beatrice Cameron, who had already played Ibsen's Nora in *A Doll's House*, he introduced *Peer Gynt* to New York. Percy Hammond, a stage-struck youth who was to become a critic ('I have knocked everything but the knees of the chorus girls and nature has anticipated me there,') managed to get a job giving bird cries. After the first night, Mansfield took his stage manager aside.

'This youth is at heart a critic, not an actor. Dispose of him as constructively as you can.'

**MARSHALL**, Arthur. Arthur Marshall's favourite memory of Gladys Cooper's *Peter Pan* (1923) was provoked by a remark from Wendy. (Already that year's Peter had been dismissed by one professional critic: 'Peter Pan has grown up at last – into a pantomime principal boy.') However, when Wendy asked the Lost Boys about Peter's age, a voice from the stalls said clearly and cruelly, 'Thirty-five.'

**MARSHALL**, Norman. Norman Marshall's career as a theatre director and manager continued from 1926 until his death. He pioneered a series of Gate revues in the thirties and was associated with many first performances, including *Marco Millions, Victoria Regina, Parnell, Of Mice and Men, The Petrified Forest, The First Gentleman* and *The*

*Indifferent Shepherd.*

In the 1950s and 1960s, he held a senior post in the drama department of the television company, Associated Rediffusion. A homosexual, particularly shy with women, Marshall sometimes unnerved actresses who had given good performances by seeming subsequently to avoid them. A fellow executive at AR took him to lunch at the Dorchester to point out that his shyness was disconcerting for actresses who, having expected a friendly smile and a compliment, were ignored in apparent disapproval. Marshall thanked him profusely and promised to mend his ways. He vowed to start immediately. As he walked away down Park Lane he saw an actress approaching him with a winning smile. Acting on his new resolution, he steeled himself to smile back and engage in small talk.

'Hello, darling,' he tried. 'What are you doing nowadays?'

The 'actress' smiled even more invitingly.

'Hoping you're coming home with me, dearie.'

**MARTIN**, Mary. There are many references to Mary Martin through this book but in none is she quite set centre-stage. However, in 1949 she had one of her two great successes in Rodgers and Hammerstein shows. In *South Pacific* she appeared opposite the Great Metropolitan opera basso Ezio Pinza. In a small role was American actor Don Fellows, who later had a busy career on the English stage. It is to him that I owe this account.

According to Don Fellows, the charismatic operatic heart-throb pursued his leading lady relentlessly but fruitlessly. And there was one major bone of contention between them. Pinza was convinced that he sang best in a warm atmosphere – like his sunny Italy. Martin was equally certain that dried her throat and that she could only sing properly in a cool environment. The show opened in April. Fearful of the onset of summer, Mary had a huge air-conditioner installed in her room. Ezio gloried in the summer heat. Battle was joined in the autumn.

Inside the stage door of the theatre was a cast iron steam-radiator which stood midway between the two star dressing rooms. At the first chill Ezio had the house engineer turn it up full. If Mary arrived to find it on, she turned it off. Ezio coming in later and finding it cold turned it back on. During his 'Some Enchanted Evening' she would slip away to turn it off. Her 'I'm Gonna Wash That Man Right Out of My Hair' was his chance to turn it back on.

As the contest esculated and both were on stage, she got her maid, Gladys, to turn it off. He then briefed his dresser, Peter, to reverse the process with both hands. On stage in their love scenes his ardour escalated. Backstage the cast would hear her remonstrate, 'Ezio, you must kiss me nicely.' His response? 'When I keeess, I keeess.'

Meanwhile, Gladys's hands could not match the strength of Peter's so Mary bought her a strong pair of pliers. Ezio bought a monkey wrench. The iron maiden won. One morning she arrived with a plumber who dismantled the entire radiator.

There was no such problem with *The Sound of Music*, though its enormous success could hardly have been prophesied after John Gielgud's account of the Dress Rehearsal.

*28th Sept, 1959, New York*
The Mary Martin/Rogers [sic] and Hammerstein run-through was ghastly. I thought Ivor's ghost would come down on a wire to bless it. Cute and appallingly sentimental by turns – *seven* children, singing nuns, and M looked as old as God and was frisking around as if she was 17. Hideous men, no dancing or chorus and an endless boring plot.'

**MARVIN**, Lee. As well as giving many great screen performances, the actor Lee Marvin became an unwitting legal pioneer when Marvin Mitchelson, the American divorce lawyer, sued him for palimony on behalf of Michelle Triola (Marvin), his mistress. An odd piece of evidence about the closeness of the relationship, which was not given in court, was an encounter in the green room of *The Johnny Carson Show* on which Marvin was appearing. Ms Triola was inviting all in sight to join them for a weekend on 'our yacht': 'Come on our yacht. We have a lovely yacht. Come on our yacht.'

Finally, Marvin said grumpily, 'Our yacht? She might as well talk about our cunt.'

**MARX** (Leonard), 'Chico'. Chico Marx was a keen backgammon player. Playing Sam Goldwyn, who was less good, he was irritated when Goldwyn's small son knocked over the board three times, forcing them to start again. Losing his patience, he asked Sam Senior to send Junior out of the room. However, Junior kept returning until Marx took him by the hand and led him from the room. It was some few minutes before he returned. Amazed, his father asked how Chico had brought it off. 'Simple,' he said proudly. 'I taught him to masturbate.'

**MASCHWITZ**, Eric. Eric Maschwitz, the underrated lyricist of 'A Nightingale Sang in Berkeley Square', 'These Foolish Things' and 'Room 504', was also a head of BBC Light Entertainment and bravest of all the three husbands of Hermione Gingold, to whom he was devotedly unfaithful. In her posthumous biography, *How to Grow Old Disgracefully*, Gingold describes a period vignette: 'I remember rushing from the BBC where I was doing a radio play to His Majesty's Theatre to catch the final curtain of Eric's musical *Balalaika*. I discovered Eric at the back of the stalls shouting "Author Author!" and, having started it off, rushing round to take a bow.'

Maschwitz's own favourite anecdote – much retold and re-written in the telling – concerns another of his musicals, *Goodnight Vienna*. As he told it to me, he was driving back from Brighton, passed through Lewisham and saw that a production of the play was at the Hippodrome. He stopped the car and went in to see what business was like.

'How's it doing?' he asked the commissionaire.

'About as well as you'd expect *Goodnight Lewisham* to do in Vienna,' the man replied.

**MASSEY**, Anna. Anna Massey had a great overnight success in the West End in *The Reluctant Debutante* by William Douglas-Home. She was virtually straight from drama school and Emlyn Williams invented a nightmare story to reflect this astonishing rise. When I told it to Anna at a Foyle's lunch some twenty-odd years later she said she had always been vaguely aware of it but that no one had ever quite dared to go into its details for her.

Emlyn Williams said that he had dreamed he was a very old actor, forgotten by his profession and living in poverty in a bedsit in Notting Hill Gate. Every day he called his agent to be told there is no work. Then one day the agent surprises him by saying that he has at last found him a part – not a good part, just a walk-on as a waiter carrying a tray of glasses, but a part none the less, in a new play opening in the West End.

Dutifully the old actor rehearses and as the first night approaches grows more and more nervous. At the actual opening he hears his call, collects his props, throws open the door, trips and sends the tray and contents flying, scattering glass at the feet of the stars.

Dismayed and dejected, he trudges up to his freezing dressing room at the top of five flights of stairs and waits to be told that he has been given the sack. Eventually there is a knock on the door and the ASM enters and says, 'Mr Williams, Dame Anna Massey will see you now.'

At the time that Williams created this story it was a wonderfully witty reflection on the sudden access of fame to a beginner. Now that time has passed and Anna Massey's patient and skilful progress has brought her success in a variety of roles – most notably fine performances in *Hotel du Lac* on television and as Lady Utterword in *Heartbreak House* at the National Theatre – there is a sort of double irony in the fact that she might very well qualify for the honour which Emlyn Williams mockingly bestowed on her.

**MATTHAU**, Carol. Walter Matthau's widow – previously married to William Saroyan – had a sharp line when her husband took too great an interest in other women. According to Truman Capote in *Answered Prayers*, when a Swedish starlet with a pretty face, an overpowering bosom and unusually heavy legs took her flirting too far and Walter Matthau asked her age his wife snapped, 'For God's sake, Walter, why don't you chop off her legs and read the rings.'

**MATTHEWS**, A.E. There are many versions of the 'disowned telephone call' story, but perhaps its attribution to A.E. Matthews is the most thoroughly attested. The veteran actor, who half a century before had created the role of Algy in *The Importance of Being Earnest*, became notoriously forgetful in later years. All sorts of *aides-memoires* were concealed around the set and often in the wings, so that Matthews could pop off-stage and remind himself. However, on one occasion, Matthews's memory deserted him at a critical moment: on stage a telephone rang and he could not remember what he had to say. Turning to an unfortunate debutante who was sharing the stage with him, he simply said, 'It's for you.'

William Douglas Home's play, *The Manor of Northstead* – a follow-up to his great success, *The Chiltern Hundreds* – found Matthews's memory very frail and the part very long. Seeking to reassure producer and director, Matthews protested, 'Don't worry, chaps. I promise you, even if we had to open next Monday, I'd be all right.'

'Matty,' countered Wallace Douglas, the director, 'we do open on Monday.'

**MATURE**, Victor. When Victor Mature's application for membership of a smart Californian golf club was turned down on the grounds that actors were not allowed to be members, his letter of reply was succinct:

'I am *not* an actor,' he wrote back, 'and I have my notices to prove it.'

**Maxim**, Ernest. Most of Ernest Maxim's work has been in television, but he has written for the theatre and choreographed and directed there, most recently *Bernadette*, 'the people's musical' and a grand failure.

Wags suggested that Maxim was hoping to add drama to the last act of *Bernadette* by introducing a new scene. The ridiculous grotto would be brought back on and miracles would start to happen. First a blind man would enter the grotto and emerge seeing. Then a cripple would limp in and come out doing somersaults and handsprings. Finally, a man would go in in a wheelchair and come out with new tyres.

A few years ago he was the moving spirit behind *Barnardo*, a show about the founder of the charity homes. It was such a comprehensive disaster that the word at the BBC was that Dr Barnardo's homes were taking up a collection for Ernest Maxim.

The opening dialogue exchanges were not promising. They went something like this: 'Where's Dr Barnardo?'

'Oh, he's out picking up boys.'


**McCartney**, Paul. Along with Linda McCartney, Paul of that ilk is now a famous vegetarian. It was back in the sixties that he became one for the first time. Gerald Asher, the imaginative boss of the adventurous (now sadly defunct) wine-shipping firm, Asher Storey, used to host particularly entertaining lunches in his offices in the City. There would usually be a City person or so there, a wine or food expert and a couple of entertainment people. Asher noticed McCartney's name appearing more and more often on his order lists, and invited him and Jane Asher, with whom he was walking out at the time, to lunch. Such was the fame of the Beatles in those heady days that no one was surprised when they were late – the other guests sat down to lunch and to taste the wines Gerald had carefully selected. They had finished the quiche and were about to move on to the lamb when the famous couple arrived, made their apologies and surveyed the table. Their faces fell.

'Oh dear! Didn't you know?' they said. 'We became vegetarians this morning.'

A more bitchy story circulated when McCartney was rumoured to be missing, kidnapped or murdered. A double was said to be standing in for him. The story was blown by a manager working for Brian Epstein.

'I might be fooled by the face,' he said, 'but I could tell that breath anywhere!'

**McGOWRAN**, Jack. Jack McGowran erupted splendidly in Peter Hall's first Stratford season; among other parts was his Old Gobbo, to Dinsdale Landen's Young Gobbo. At the time, the convention in the theatre was that the company be brought down to look at the set – to see the problems, understand their environment, feel a part of the place – whatever!

Hall made a company call for Michael Langham's production of *The Merchant* starring Dorothy Tutin as Portia and Peter O'Toole as Shylock. The entire cast loyally assembled – except McGowran. Peter Hall sent for him, and sent again. He did not show. Finally, the embarrassed ASM was sent again: he returned as reluctant as any messenger in classical tragedy who felt that bad news might bring about his summary execution. Still he hesitated to convey the reason why McGowran was declining to view the set he had to inhabit. Much pressed, reluctantly he finally lisped out: 'He said, Mr Hall, if you read the play, you'd know Old Gobbo was blind.'

During that season he was sometimes sharper in his approach to Hall, remonstrating on one occasion, 'Peter Hall, there's a lot of people in the world – but you're not one of them!'

On another occasion Dinsdale Landen watched him arrive so much the worse for wear that he doubted he could play. Hall said he had an infallible remedy which would make McGowran throw up and sober up – I think it was 'an old RAF cure'. He sent Dinsdale to get a cup, some water, a lot of salt and a couple of cigarettes. He scrambled the salt and tobacco in the water and handed the potion to McGowran, who swallowed it at a gulp. The two younger men waited for the bomb to strike. McGowran gulped and blinked and as they enquired how he felt, said, holding out the cup, 'I'm all right, but could I just have one more?'

Peter O'Toole played in an O'Casey revival in Dublin with McGowran. Like many of the best Irish plays, this one featured a meal, and like most Irish actors McGowran took the heavy consumption of real food in his stride. O'Toole had to cook a massive fry-up for McGowran to demolish. During rehearsals O'Toole had ordered himself a huge pair of bushy eyebrows. They failed to arrive until a few days after the opening night, by which time O'Toole had grown into the part and no longer wanted them. He flung them into the pan with the rest of the food and McGowran devoured them happily.

**McKELLEN**, Sir Ian. It is, perhaps, too soon to collect McKellen stories, though his early career with The Actors' Company yielded an attractive one. People were interested to see if the democratic nature of the company – leading actors alternating leading roles with small parts – would survive. McKellen himself tells of a tale that was going around, about how marvellously the venture was working.

'In the next production Ian McKellen's playing the third waiter.'

'What's the play called?'

*'The Third Waiter.'*

He was also quoted disarmingly about his reason for wanting to become an actor: 'Because I thought I'd meet a lot of queers.'

On one of Ian McKellen's visits to the White House for a theatre fund raiser, Ronald Reagan was the incumbent. Reagan recalled the words of some 'wise old man': 'If only we could understand everything in Shakespeare's plays, the world would be a better place.' McKellen was reluctantly impressed until a few days later, when he heard Reagan on television, addressing a Baptist audience. The President recalled the words of a wise old man: 'If only we could understand everything in the Bible, the world would be a better place.'

McKellen also described the Reagans' running entrance: 'Two septuagenarians telling us they are not old.' He watched from the sofa as they kissed, slapped backs, reached out and touched cheeks, finding an appropriate response for each person. 'It was utterly exhausting and an utter waste of time. He could have signed a cheque and got on with being President!'

**McMASTER**, Anew. This powerful, idiosyncratic last of the grand Irish touring actor-managers is magically evoked by Harold Pinter in a monograph – Pinter was a member of McMaster's company. When I produced the movie *The Virgin Soldiers,* I bought two dozen copies as end-of-picture presents for the young actors who had played the principal title roles but the gesture rebounded when one of the boy's girlfriends tried a spot of blackmail. She sent a grubby solicitor with the news that she was about to contact a Sunday paper alleging misconduct – which had not happened. I asked the solicitor the basis for the allegation. He produced Pinter's McMaster book which I had inscribed 'Love, Ned' and suggested that things looked highly suspicious. I told him I had signed all 24 copies in the same way and heard no more.

Niall Toibin tells a story of McMaster which echoes one of Edith Evans's elsewhere: 'I think,' Toibin heard him say in his highly mannered voice, 'that Micheál [Mac Liammóir] is very affected, don't you?'

Pinter tells the story of McMaster booking a cinema in Limerick because he heard the projectionists in the town were all on strike. They opened with *Othello* on a Monday, which was St Patrick's Night, in a movie house which held 2000. The play began two-and-a-half hours late at 11.30 and finished at half-past two in the morning. The house was full, fully drunk and unaccustomed to Shakespeare. The first half was pandemonium but in the second, McMaster suddenly gripped them with the fit: 'By the time he had reached "It is the very error of the moon; She comes more near the earth than she was wont. And makes men mad" (the word "mad" suddenly cauterised, ugly, shocking), the audience was quite still. And sober.' Pinter congratulated McMaster, eliciting a perfect piece of self-conscious actor comparison:

'Not bad, was it? Not bad. Godfrey Tearle never did the fit, you know.'

Pinter also records the way McMaster teased him remorselessly when he slipped up on Bassanio's lines in *The Merchant of Venice*. Instead of 'For thy three thousand ducats here is six,' Pinter had come out with 'For thy three thousand buckets here are six.'

Shylock replied, quietly and with emphasis: 'If every *bucket* in six thousand *buckets* were in six parts and every part a *bucket* I would not draw them – I would have my bond.'

No one else on stage could continue, 'But Mac stood, remorseless, grave, like an eagle, waiting for my reply.'

**MEMORIAL SERVICES.** My sole claim to being unique is that I am, to the best of my knowledge, the only critic of memorial services in the world. I review them once a month for *The Oldie* magazine. They are fertile soil for the anecdote hunter. Keith Waterhouse and Victoria Mather were lunching with the editor, Richard Ingrams, when he said that he felt that his magazine's name and brief demanded that attention be paid to these 'Celebrations of' and 'Thanksgivings for' the lives of the great and the good, actors and the artists. Who should he ask to fulfil this important role? Together they chorused 'Well, Ned goes to a lot' and so my new job was invented in 1992.

The life of Helen Hanff, author of *84 Charing Cross Road*, was celebrated at the hardy perennial – St Paul's, Covent Garden, 'The Actor's Church'. Valerie Grove recalled taking Miss Hanff on a literary pilgrimage to Hampstead to where John Le Carre lived. She had already visited Keats' home. As they lingered outside in the car Le Carre appeared at the front door. Hanff was impressed. 'This is something!' she enthused.

'They showed me Keats' house, but they never showed me Keats!'

Patricia Eddington bravely brought alive her husband Paul's last moments. On hearing the word 'oxygen' he had opened one eye and whispered, 'Did you say "gin"?' When Paul was in David Storey's play *Home* they engineered a meeting in Paul's dressing room between Storey's miner father and Sir John Gielgud, resulting in 'Mutual incomprehension never seen before or since.'

The impresario David Land, the man behind *Jesus Christ Superstar* and *Evita* and manager of The Dagenham Girl Pipers, was celebrated in his own Theatre Royal, Brighton. The critic Jack Tinker reminded us of David's dismissal of his Rottingdeane home as 'early ugly', of his decision to call his firm 'Hope and Glory', so that he could answer his telephone, 'Land – of Hope and Glory'; and of his induction as a Doctor of Literature at Sussex University when he gazed at his black hat and yellow robes and protested, 'They'll think I'm a rabbi with jaundice.'

At St George-the-Martyr in Queen Square, Paul Nicholas, Britain's first *Jesus Christ Superstar*, led off a service for his father – Oscar Beuselinck, a famous showbiz solicitor, reputedly an inspiration for John Osborne's Bill Maitland in *Inadmissible Evidence*. One eulogist, Arthur Davidson, QC, imagined Oscar's reaction to his presence in the pulpit; 'What's he doing up there? I could have got somebody much better. I could have got George Carman!' Carman, the more notorious Queen's Counsel, read a lesson.

In remembering 'Jak', the *Evening Standard* cartoonist, we were reminded of his picture of Hugh Grant, subsequent to his encounter with Ms Divine Brown, coming down the steps of LAPD with the caption, 'She swallowed the evidence.'

Clement Freud's address for the actor-comedian Derek Nimmo mentioned the coat of arms on the buttons which decorated the cloak which often enveloped Nimmo's uniquely grand chauffeur. He drove the actor's coffee-and-cream Rolls Royce. 'Your coast of arms?' Freud had once asked. 'No,' came the reply. 'The chauffeur's.'

On another day, we learnt that the dancer and Shakespearean actor Leslie French was the model for Eric Gill's naked statue of Ariel – one of his famous roles – outside the BBC's Broadcasting House; and that the Director General had demanded that the sprite's member be made smaller before it went on public display.

From Joan Sims's long *Carry On* career Ronnie Cass selected one exchange:

'Care to join me in the arbour?'

'I didn't know we were so near the sea.'

Looking down on a packed Westminster Abbey Jimmy Tarbuck reckoned that though Sir Harry Secombe would 'have been delighted to see a full house, his first thought would be, "Don't let Ken Dodd take the collection".'

We sent off Spike Milligan the year after Sir Harry. Spike had always hoped to outlive Harry so that the Welsh tenor could not sing at his memorial service. David Secombe outwitted him by producing a recording of his father in full voice with 'Guide Me O Thou Great Redeemer', which echoed through St Martin's-in-the-Fields.

In the same church we heard from Ian Wooldridge of the sports broadcasting editor John Bromley's successfully cavalier attitude to contracts. In a court battle with an American fight promoter, the boxing man's QC asked Bromley, 'If it is your custom to draw up a contract of this complexity on the napkin of a night club called [pause for maximum effect] the Rififi Club?'

After some consideration Bromley smiled broadly and answered, 'Certainly.'

In 2002 Kevin Whately evoked John Thaw's humour on the set of *Inspector Morse*.

'I can't say this rubbish, I'm a Commander of the British Empire.'

To another ebullient director yelling, 'Cut!'

'What did he call me?'

And in an imaginary imitation of schedulers casting a future programme, '... that little, fat, white-haired one – that John Thaw.'

Barry Took was the writer, presenter, comic and occasional BBC executive who midwifed the birth of *Monty Python's Flying Circus* – whimsically nicknamed by his head of department 'Your children by Greer Garson'. His memorial service was held appropriately in the St John's Wood Church. Alan Coren often picnicked with Took in the churchyard 'between Lords and the Lord.' Barry always ordered 'two rounds of salt beef, and make it lean,' simply so that he could hear Sam, the delicatessen assistant, say, 'Lean? Which way?' In the churchyard they 'laughed until the crumbs flew.'

Brian Pringle's passing produced a rich crop of theatrical memories. 'Pringle, son of a vicar – not always a good start in life;' Pringle on Pringle – 'I was born with a face nobody could think well of;' Pringle drunk in charge of a tandem going the wrong way up a one way street – 'I'm looking for my passenger, officer'; Pringle's explanation for many castings, 'Bernard Cribbens not available.' Pringle's favourite theatre story. Two old actors discuss a forthcoming provincial tour, 'Not much of a play. Not much of a tour. But there's a cake in the third act.'

Alan Tagg was a distinguished theatre designer who came to notice in the early days of the Royal Court when he designed the first production of John Osborne's *Look Back in Anger*. At his memorial service, Edward Fox produced a vivid image of him in Fox's mother's garden in Sussex. He found some old footballs. Children had abandoned them. Tagg filled them with concrete and painted them pink. As Fox put it, 'His soul is with God. His balls are in Sussex.'

Lord Runcie was the prince of eulogists. One of those most eagerly heard after his own death is Alan Bennett. At John Schlesinger's service at the Liberal Jewish synagogue, he homed in on the Queen's Award of a CBE to the gay film director. Adjusting his medal ribbon Her Majesty said, 'Now, Mr Schlesinger, we must get this straight.' John took it as a coded acknowledgment of his sexuality.

Referring to Dame Thora Hird from the high pulpit in Westminster Abbey, Bennett spoke warmly of the confused end of her long life (she died at 92), quoting her daughter Janette. Thora had phoned her to say she was filming with John Wayne but that he had left her alone on the set. Jan said it was unlikely.

'Look out of the window, Mum. Can't you see the mews?'

Thora (doubtfully) : 'Yes, but they can do wonderful things with scenery these days.'

Julie Walters also spoke at the service, from the same high pulpit – a vantage point which allowed her to remark with reference to one of Thora's popular advertisements, 'that they might have installed a Stannah stair lift.'

Ronnie Corbett, celebrating Ronnie Barker, actually 'milked' the same pulpit. At first barely visible (big laugh) he then climbed on to a box, the better to be seen (bigger laugh). I doubt if he knew that Bishop William Walsham How, who wrote the first hymn, 'For All the Saints . . .' in the 1870s was, like Ronnie, less than five feet tall. Being too short for most pulpits he travelled with a specially-built platform wherever he preached.

It is difficult to go on working longer than the delightful, dizzy comedienne, Patsy Rowlands. 'Two days before she died,' her son, Alan, said, 'she decided to retire. The next day she was planning a comeback.'

The classic pantomime dame is a dying breed. One of the last to go was

Jack Tripp, a magically neat dancer, irrepressibly droll, embodying the
true comic spirit of Christmas past, present and future. For all that, he
could also cut down pretence with a sharp aside. At his memorial Service
Roy Hudd told of an occasion when one Ivan Owen ('the hand up Basil
Brush') told him that his home had been burgled '. . . but they didn't take
anything.' 'Oh dear!' said Tripp, 'how humiliating!'

His *bête noir* was the engagement of so called celebrities in pantomime.
Jonathan Cecil once told Tripp that he didn't think one such was too bad.
'Well,' said the resigned dame, 'at least he was boring.'

Remembering Graham Payn, companion of Noel Coward, brought up
a splendid exchange between them. At Coward's Jamaican home Payn
put on an impromptu poolside show. Amused, Coward heckled. Graham
stood his ground and said, 'I'll have you know people have paid good
money to see me sing and dance.'

Coward could not resist. 'Yes, but not so very many and not so very
much.' Graham had held his peace. 'I wanted to say, "Well, it was mostly
your material,"' but he forbore to do so.

We also heard the story of his first audition for Coward. Newly arrived
from South Africa in 1932, his ambitious mother submitted him for
Coward's revue *Words and Music*. Knowing the time allotted would be
short she insisted he showed of all his talents at once. Accordingly he sang
'Nearer My God to thee' in a pure treble and tap-danced at the same time.
'He must be in the show!' Coward shouted. And he was.

One of the perennial favourites for reading at memorial services is
Canon Henry Scott Holland's sentimental lesson about 'having only
slipped away into the next room,' a quotation taken horribly out of
context from a serious sermon delivered while Edward VII lay in state at
Westminster. The Canon's point was that this was escapism, 'denial of a
real and fundamental change which he believed should be understood in
terms of redemption and ultimate satisfaction.' Not nearly so cosy.
However, as I emerged from one memorial the actor Keith Baxter wittily
parodied the sentimental extract as, 'I'm not dead. I've just popped
round to Harrods!'

**MERMAN**, Ethel. Ethel Merman, whose voice inspired Porter, Gershwin
and Berlin to some of their most memorable songs, was above all a
Broadway broad. She leapt to fame in *Girl Crazy* by the Gershwins in which
she sang 'Boy! What Love Has Done For Me', 'I Got Rhythm' and 'Sam
And Delilah'. The pit orchestra, led by Red Nichols, included Benny

Goodman, Gene Krupa, Glenn Miller, Jack Teagarden and Jimmy Dorsey – not a bad backing group for a debutante. When she sang 'I Got Rhythm' at her London debut, this assured, no-nonsense, superb technician opened with 'I'm so excited . . . I'm so nervous . . . I'm so afraid . . . *I Got Rhythm!*'

'But Not For Me' was also in the score and at charity benefit shows in later life, Ginger Rogers, who first sang it, could be heard complaining, 'Ethel's singing my song!'

Merman's assurance was legendary. When a chorus girl asked her in the wings at the first night of *Annie Get Your Gun* if she was nervous, she said simply, 'Why should I be nervous? I know my lines!' There is some dispute over whom she notoriously first refused to learn new material for, either Irving Berlin, late on in rehearsals for *Annie,* or Jule Styne and Stephen Sondheim, when they offered her a new verse for a song in *Gypsy.* Maybe having found that it worked once she used the line again? Anyway, she greeted the proferred new verse with a majestic, 'Call me Miss Birdseye, the show is frozen.'

On one of her visits to England she dined with Victor Spinetti. After a series of Rabelaisian stories – she loved swapping blue jokes with old vaudevillians – she announced that she was doing *The Killer Black Show.*

'It's Cilla,' said Victor.

'I know,' she snapped, 'that's why I'm calling her Killer.'

During rehearsals, the choreographer had asked her to move downstage at one point.

'Why?' she demanded.

'Oh,' he said, 'when you sing "There's No Business Like Show Business", I'm going to bring on the dancers – there's choreography behind you.'

'The hell there is,' said Merman. 'When I sing "There's No Business Like Show Business", the only thing behind me is the American flag.'

When she made a disco version of the song, she told me touchingly that Berlin (well into his nineties) had called her to say that he'd heard her sing it on breakfast television and she'd never sung it better. Equally touchingly, she said, with some puzzlement: 'And you know he never asked me to his house.'

One of her late triumphs was a two-woman gala with Mary Martin. Cyril Ritchard was the narrator. The two ladies had a little difference over what he should be called. Merman was for 'narrator', the director suggested *'conferencier'.* Neither lady liked that. Martin suggested 'Compère'.

'Compère?' said Merman. 'Compared to what?'

As she stood in the wings during one of Martin's numbers, she muttered to a friend of mine, 'Isn't she wonderful? Isn't she great? What a performer! She's a dyke, of course!'

Perhaps Merman's most devastating verdict on her disastrous marriage to Ernest Borgnine was the fact that she devoted one empty page to the union in her autobiography. Her much-quoted riposte to Borgnine when she returned from meeting a movie studio head goes like this:

'How did you get on?' Borgnine asked.

'Swell,' said Ethel. 'He said I had the eyes of a teenager, the complexion of a twenty-year-old and the legs of a twenty-five-year-old.'

'How about your sixty-year-old cunt?' her husband grunted.

'You were never mentioned.'

**MESSEL**, Oliver Hilary Sambourne. A distinctively decorative designer from the twenties, Oliver worked on Cochran revues and the famous white bedroom for *La Belle Hélène*. On the first night of *My Fair Lady* at Drury Lane, when the curtain rose on Oliver Smith's front cloth of Edwardian London, he hissed across me a disapproving, 'Greetings telegram!'

His exquisite Book of the Hours costumes for *Twang!*, Lionel Bart's Robin Hood musical, were given short shrift by the director Joan Littlewood, who told the cast to jump on them for starters. Messel watched in tears.

**MEYER**, Michael. Michael Meyer, playwright and the senior translator and biographer of Ibsen and Strindberg, was capable of a gaffe of Gielgudian proportions. In the loo at a revival of *Hassan* (directed as the original had been by Basil Dean) he met an elderly gent in a dinner jacket. Chattily he said, 'Isn't it a splendid play.' The old gentleman conceded that it was 'interesting'.

Meyer expanded: 'But what a ragged production.' The old man said nothing. Just then the critic Ivor Brown entered.

The old man greeted him, 'Hello, Ivor.'

'Hello, Basil,' said Brown.

**MILLER**, Dr Jonathan. The good doctor's production of *Measure for Measure* for the National Theatre toured widely and eventually reached

Barrow-in-Furness, where it was to play in a theatre not too unlike a working man's club. The manager-compère greeted the great man with, 'Will you need the microphone to introduce your acts, Mr Miller?'

My favourite Miller story comes from earlier in his career when he was at his best as a happy stand-up comic. Appearing on the Cliff Michelmore *Tonight* show in the fifties, he launched into his monologue in medium close-up. Directed to track back, the cameraman crooked his finger to signal his dolly-pusher to retreat a fraction. Miller caught sight of the finger and took it as an invitation to advance, which he did. This produced another pull-back by the camera and that in sequence brought Miller forward again. This stately progress continued in and out of the lit areas until the camera finally hit an unyielding wall at the other side of the studio.

**MILES**, Sir Bernard. For all his experience in music hall, in repertory and in the classics, Sir Bernard's name will always be associated with the Mermaid Theatre which he first founded in 1951 and which he created at Puddledock later in the decade. While the Mermaid was in construction, I paid regular visits to the site because Bernard had expressed an interest in a musical adaptation of *No Bed for Bacon,* which Caryl Brahms and I had adapted from the novel she wrote with S.J. Simon: a commuter to the City, whence Bernard drew most of his funding, had given him a tape of an amateur performance.

We were summoned to Puddledock where he enthused about the Elizabethan setting and the plot – 'Bloody girl, dressed up as a boy – going to work with bloody Shakespeare!' He proudly showed us over the rubble with Josephine Wilson, his wife, and Gerald Frow, his son-in-law and PR assistant. Josephine wore a permanently worried look, as though in constant anticipation of the next brick which Bernard would surely drop. She kept her distance, rather like the English lady five yards behind her husband in *Monsieur Hulot's Holiday.*

Administration was carried on in a small hut on the building site and we finished up there with the Miles family, sausages and some very sharp white wine, which played hell with our digestion on this and subsequent visits – these stretched to saga proportions. At first Bernard was expansive. What a perfect play to open the Mermaid, a play about Shakespeare and about the City of London. He retold us our plot with immense enthusiasm, a habit he fell into whenever we returned. However, he wanted some changes to the script. He was glad we had written as we did because, he said, it enabled him to see clearly where we had gone wrong. He sent us off to re-write while he went to America to appear in a remake of *Wuthering Heights.* 'A great man of the theatre,' we told each other. 'We can learn from him.'

Some four weeks later we submitted the re-writes and went down to hear his verdict.

'I'm so glad you did those re-writes,' he said. 'It's all wrong, but I can now see exactly what to do about it.' More sausages, wine and indigestion and we went away to do more work. Two weeks later we were back again.

'I'm glad you did those re-writes. Now I can see exactly how to bloody do it.'

He told us the plot again and, with rich enthusiasm, centred on a new scene he had invented.

'Nothing bloody like it has ever been seen on the stage. Just bloody think – she's rehearsing with bloody Shakespeare and he gives her this speech. Remember, he thinks she's a boy and she knows she's a girl. So she gets to this line, "Bare thy bloody breast," and she can't, but he doesn't know that so he keeps after her. "Bare thy bloody breast," and she doesn't, so he rips her shirt off and he sees both of 'em and he knows. Never been seen on the stage. Bloody marvellous!'

Beginning to despair, we had another go. Returning, we found Bernard in an exultant mood.

'Bloody marvellous! It's all wrong, but I'm glad you did it. Now I know what to do. Throw out all your dialogue. Every bloody word! Go back to Shakespeare. Shakespeare had a word for everything. Find 'em all. I don't want a word of yours. All bloody Shakespeare's. I want an under-water-over-air tapestry of Shakespeare's language.' Then he had a vision: 'I can see the opening night. We'll have the Queen and we'll have bloody Philip! Both at the Mermaid, London's theatre! She'll come down by barge, sailing down London's river, and she'll get out of the barge and she'll sit herself down and when the play starts every bloody word'll be Shakespeare's – not one of yours – just bloody Shakespeare's for bloody everything, and after about five minutes Philip'll get the idea and he'll dig her in the ribs and say, "That's where the bugger got it from!"'

We made our excuses and left. Bernard, like any sensible manager, was discussing alternative openings with several other teams. He finally chose his own adaptation of Fielding's *Rape upon Rape* to open The Mermaid, with songs by Lionel Bart and Laurie Johnson. It was a huge hit. We had two attempts to make *No Bed for Bacon* work, at Bristol and Croydon. Neither was a success.

**MILES**, Sylvia. Victor Spinetti swears that this clever American character actress was once walking down a street in New York with Tennessee Williams when the playwright spotted an alarmingly thin woman on the opposite sidewalk.

'She's so skeletal!' he exclaimed.

'Oh, Tennessee,' said Miles, 'that's anorexia nervosa.'

'Oh, Sylvia,' said the playwright. 'You know everybody.'

Rumour has it that Ms Miles once had a disastrous love affair with a homosexual. She was understandably distraught when he broke it off. Nightly, she drowned her sorrows in Joe Allen's restaurant in New York. On one occasion a large, witty, black waiter asked her if she would like a cup of coffee. She would. How would she like her coffee? Ms Miles looked him up and down and rolled out the old chestnut: 'Like my men!' The waiter's voice went up a register.

'Oh! Miss Miles, we don't serve no gay coffee here!'

Poor Sarah has been unfairly saddled with this tale, which has nothing to do with her. Nor has the one about the party at which Sylvia is supposed to have said, in the presence of lots of younger actesses, 'I've got the best body in this room.' To be greeted with, 'Why didn't you bring it with you, then?'

**MILLER**, Ann. Ann Miller was a tap dancing American icon from the great American musicals. MGM's *On The Town* with Sinatra and Kelly, *Easter Parade* with Garland and Astaire and *Kiss Me Kate* with Howard Keel. She was a warm, friendly, broad in the Merman mould but making her best effects not with her voice, but her legs. She later tapped her way around America for nine years with Mickey Rooney in a big, bawdy, burlesque musical, *Sugar Babies*. Born in Texas her ancestry was French, Irish and Cherokee. She trained in dance at five to rectify rickets. At eleven she was dancing at five dollars a night for audiences of Rotarians, Elks and Shriners. Her mother told them that she was eighteen. Perhaps they believed her.

After a film apprenticeship which involved George Cukor, Katharine Hepburn, Frank Capra and the Marx Brothers she played on Broadway in the 1939 edition of *The George White Scandals*. The show flopped but first she stopped it with a number called 'The Mexiconga'. Back in Hollywood she appeared with Rudy Vallee and the cowboy star, Gene Autry. 'I was the first girl he kissed apart from his horse.'

Her jet black hair stretched down to her waist but on stage it was tucked away under a stiff, heavily lacquered half-wig. During the run of *Sugar Babies* one crack was 'Ann Miller fell today and broke her hair.' A New York weathercaster was moved to say, 'There was a high wind in Manhattan today – a hair moved on Ann Miller's head.' In 1972 when she was opening a tour of *Anything Goes*, a steel curtain fell on her head. 'There was blood all over the stage, but there could have been more,' she said. 'This dumb wig saved my life.'

In her book, *Tapping into the Force*, she describes an hypnotic regression into Ancient Egypt where she believed, she and a half sister had been murdered by their brother. No specific names were ever mentioned but she had already identified herself as Queen Hatshepsut in a previous incarnation. She visited modern Egypt on four occasions. Each time she caught some mysterious sickness. The last time she got to Luxor to take a look at her tomb. She took one glance and announced, 'The body was never in that tomb.'

Later evidence suggested that she may very well have hit the mark. Apparently her father's tomb was found to be severely overcrowded, with no fewer than three mummies in it. As she emerged from the site she was bitten by a scorpion, 'or some such thing,' and saved by her guide who threw himself at her feet and sucked the venom from her ankle. She took some days to recover but the famous legs were unimpaired.

One of her greatest triumphs was a famous commercial for Great American Soups. In a whimsy of Stan Freeberg's she tapped on top of an eight-foot soup can encircled by twenty-foot water fountains, a twenty-four-piece orchestra and an array of chorus girls.

A few months before she died, she appeared in a revival of *Sondheim's Follies*. Movement and tapping were no longer possible, but she produced an appropriate 'I'm Still Here'.

**MILLS**, Sir John. When John Mills and John Gielgud appeared in Brighton in the pre-London tour of Charles Wood's fine play, *Veterans*, the conservative Brighton audience were shocked by the flurry of expletives which assailed them. In the circle, one irate man stood up and shouted that the two knights should be ashamed of associating themselves with such filth. So saying, and dragging his 'lady wife' with him, he barged along the row to the exit, shouting at Mary Hayley Bell (who he did not know was Lady Mills) as he pushed past her: 'Out of my fucking way!'

**MILTON**, Ernest. A challenging and eccentric American born actor, he first played in London in *Potash and Perlemutter* in 1914. While at the Old Vic, he married the critic Naomi Royde-Smith, who had reviewed many of his performances. When he broke the news to Lilian Baylis, she said, 'Very nice, dear. Come to me in your joys and come to me in your sorrows, but not in between because I've no time for chit-chat.'

In 1955, he and Donald Wolfit appeared in Hochwalder's *The Strong Are Lonely*, eliciting from Kenneth Tynan the suggestion that they were 'upstaging each other for the greater glory of God'.

**MINSTER**, Jack. In spite of a predilection for directing West End comedies, Jack Minster had a permanently mournful expression. He managed a great grumpy note at one rehearsal. 'Don't keep looking at the floor, boy,' he told an actor. 'You won't find anything down there . . . except the bloody play.'

**MINSTRELS**, Black and White. During the long run of *The Black and White Minstrel Show* at the Victoria Palace, there was a power cut which meant that the recorded musical playback for the Minstrels could not continue, no matter how effective their often luminous costumes might have been. Pros to the last, George Chisholm and Leslie Crowther, the only 'live' acts, rushed to the darkened stage and entertained for nearly an hour, using two torches to illuminate each other's face. It was not until the lights came on again that they remembered they were both wearing only briefs.

**MISS SAIGON**. During rehearsal, the Cameron Mackintosh office rang the Vietnamese Embassy to check on local wedding rituals. The researcher was asked what the information was for. She confessed it was for *Miss Saigon*. 'There is no such place,' said the embassy man. 'That is Ho Chi Minh City.' The spectacular opening night party, which cost more than the entire budget for an earlier Mackintosh show, *The Card*, was held at the Cotton Centre across the Thames. Champagne flowed but not fast enough for Peter Cook, whose ingenious way of grabbing a bottle from a passing waitress was to say, 'Excuse me, Melvyn Bragg is causing a bit of a disturbance over there, I think this will pacify him.'

**MISTINGUETTE**, (Jeanne-Marie Bourgeois). Perhaps we should add Mistinguette to the short list of famous Belgians – she, like Maurice Chevalier, had *some* Belgian blood – though she was born in 1874, in grim circumstances, in Enghien, then a small, rural town outside Paris (now an outer suburb).

She was to go on to be an immense star in France, insuring her legs for 500,000 francs – the 'million-dollar' claim was a publicity gimmick. In her love affairs she rivalled the great courtesans of the day – La Belle Otero, Emilienne d'Alençon, and Cléo de Mérode, who had a highly publicised affair with King Leopold of the Belgians, becoming known as 'Cleopold'. Mistinguette notched up the 60-year-old King Edward VII when she was 26.

She also charmed King Alfonso XIII of Spain, although her first meeting was not promising. The Spanish King and Queen were expected to attend her performance at the Eldorado Theatre. They did not show up, but sent a courier to apologise and explain that they had gone to another theatre. He asked Mistinguette to join them for supper. He had kept a carriage waiting. 'Good, then you can drive me straight home,' said Mistinguette.

'But what shall I tell His Majesty?' asked the distraught courier. 'What will the King say?'

'I imagine he'll use the same word I used when I realised he had stood me up,' said Mistinguette. 'But I imagine he'll say it in Spanish.' Later the affair flourished.

When overtures were made just before the outbreak of World War One on behalf on the German Crown Prince she declined, 'He doesn't need Mistinguette to increase his popularity in France and Mistinguette doesn't need the Crown Prince to help her with her publicity in Germany.'

Chevalier was the great love of her life but the two egos could not sustain a lasting affair.

**MITCHELL**, Margaret. The one-hit-wonder author of *Gone With the Wind* kept firmly away from participation in the preparation and shooting of the movie. She did, however, agree to attend the Atlanta première in 1939. She was seated next to Gable and was amazed when the camera pulled back from Vivien Leigh tending wounded soldiers to reveal an enormous mass – thousands – of Confederate troops. 'Mah Gawd,' she hissed, digging Gable in the ribs, 'if we'd-ah had as many soldiers as that we'd-ha won the woah!'

According to Howard Deitz, the MGM publicist, it was while Gable was filming in Atlanta that a woman asked to take his hotel room the day he checked out, making it a condition that the sheets should not be changed.

**Mitchum**, Robert. Mitchum's cavalier, or to say the least, casual approach to his craft was best summed up when an earnest interviewer asked him what he looked for in a script. He said promptly: 'Days off.'

**Mitford Girls, The**. *The Mitford Girls* played triumphantly at the Chichester Festival Theatre in 1981 and less successfully when it transferred to the Globe in the West End. Diana Rigg wrongly attributes its funny nickname 'La Triviata' to the surviving girls. It was in fact the comment of the Duke of Devonshire, Andrew Cavendish, who married Deborah Mitford and is deeply suspicious of too much emphasis on Mitford mythology.

**Mizner**, Wilson. Mizner, already an outsize character in California, invaded Broadway at the age of 29 and embarked on a career as self-confessed con-man and playwright-collaborator. *Alias Jimmy Valentine*, written in collaboration with Paul Armstrong, who put in most of the work, was the most successful. Mizner coined the phrase, 'Never give a sucker an even break' and also said, 'I never worry about money unless a rich man comes anywhere near me. Then I can't sleep until I find a way to get in on the take.' During his Broadway heyday he managed the Strand Hotel, finding room for 50 homeless. The rules he posted to preserve some sort of order included, 'No opium smoking in the elevators!' and 'Carry out your own dead!'

When Mizner returned to Hollywood, he became the owner of the famous Brown Derby restaurant. Sitting there with Joseph L. Mankiewicz, they watched a Paramount executive, Rufus Le Maire, enter, decked out in an Inverness cape. Taking in the spectacle, Mizner whispered to Mankiewicz, 'That, my boy, sets the Jews back six hundred years.' Ushered into Jack Warner's office on commencing an engagement to write scripts, he dropped an LA telephone directory on the boss's desk, saying, 'This might have been good for a picture, but there are too many characters in it.' Another Miznerism has been much appropriated: 'When you steal from one author it's plagiarism. If you steal from a lot, it's research.'

**MOORE**, Victor. Victor Moore was a great Broadway comedian in the twenties and thirties and moved on to success in Hollywood. He was the star comic of *Oh, Kay!*, a Gershwin musical with a book by Wodehouse and Bolton. On the opening night in Philadelphia, he had a triumphant first-night scene. Moments later he heard even louder laughter inspired by events on the stage he had just left. Assuming that his co-star, Gertrude Lawrence, had improvised some piece of business to top his triumph, he rushed back to see what it was. He found that a stray mongrel dog had wandered into Miss Lawrence's scene, leaving her no option but to watch it as it crossed the stage in leisurely fashion, leaving through the fireplace which was apparently full of a roaring fire, against which it nonchalantly cocked its leg before departing.

**MORE**, Kenneth. In *More or Less,* Kenneth More recalls a charming encounter with Noel Coward. He was playing in *Power Without Glory* (along with another emerging actor, Dirk Bogarde) when he received a summons to meet the Master, who was starring in *Present Laughter* at the Haymarket and preparing *Peace in Our Time.*

After a dinner in Coward's flat in Gerald Row, Coward played the piano for a time and then advanced upon More, apparently with romance in his eyes. Kenneth More jumped up, alarmed, and blurted out, 'Oh, Mr Coward, sir, I could never have an affair with you, because – because – *you remind me of my father!*'

With his usual perfect, deflationary timing, Coward smiled enigmatically, said, 'Hello, son,' and collapsed with laughter. Ever after he greeted More with 'Hello, son,' to the mystification of onlookers.

**MORLEY**, Sheridan. The son of Robert Morley, grandson of Dame Gladys Cooper, Sheridan Morley was immersed in the theatre as critic, commentator and biographer of the stars all his life. One of his subjects was Sir John Gielgud, whose biography he put off publishing for as long as possible hoping to avoid having to describe Sir John's private life while he was still alive. One useful device was to answer the Knight's enquiries with 'I've only got you to 21 so far.' On one occasion Gielgud telephoned him with urgent news, 'You'll never believe this. In America they are about to name a theatre after a dramatic critic!' Then, remembering to whom he was talking he said, 'Oh my God! You are one!' and slammed down the phone.

As Coward's godson, he was also his authorised biographer. The book was called *A Talent to Amuse*. When he embarked on it Coward gave him two sets of telephone numbers saying, 'These are my friends and those are my enemies. Start with the enemies, dear boy and you'll get a better book.'

Very late in Olivier's life, Morley interviewed him about his 1939 film of *Wuthering Heights* in which David Niven and Merle Oberon were co-stars. He was researching his biography of Niven, *The Other Side of the Moon*. He asked Olivier if Niven and Oberon had been lovers. Olivier confirmed it but added, 'There's one thing you have to understand, that although Niven and I were both in love with Merle Oberon, I was the one who married her.'

'No you didn't,' said Morley, 'you married Vivien Leigh.'

'My dearest boy,' was Olivier's response, 'you are so right!'

Not usually much concerned with politics Sheridan Morley did one interview with Mrs Thatcher when she was a junior minister for pensions. He began, 'It has been said, Mrs Thatcher, that England is a great place to live if you are neither very poor or black.'

She replied with finality, 'Well, I'm not, am I?'

Morley was christened Sheridan after his father's role as Sheridan Whiteside in the Kaufman and Hart comedy *The Man Who Came to Dinner* in which Robert Morley was playing at the time of his birth.

There was a favourite canard that Sheridan often slept in the theatre during plays which he was reviewing, the blanks filled in by his devoted wife, the critic Ruth Leon. On the sad occasion of his death a collegue was told that he died in his sleep. 'What was the play?' was the question. An honourable tradition for a critic – when James Agate died someone made the same crack.

**MORTIMER**, John. Although John Mortimer, barrister, playwright and creator of *Rumpole of the Bailey*, does not claim this legal anecdote, current in chambers and in El Vino's, he has propagated it enthusiastically. The case in question was a complicated commercial affair and the parties involved had gathered in the High Court to hear the verdict. It was a Monday and the embarrassed judge confessed to the court that although he had written his 8,000-word judgement over the weekend he had left it at his home in the country so he could not deliver it till the next day. 'Fax it up, m'lud,' suggested the helpful junior counsel.

The judge considered this and replied, 'Yes, I suppose it rather does.'

Another of Mortimer's fancies is to compare marriage with the hurricanes which threaten America in the South. 'It starts off with all that sucking and blowing and you end up losing the house.'

**MOUNTFORT**, Mrs Susannah. Poor Mrs Mountfort, a successful seventeenth-century Ophelia, went mad in later life. Hearing that *Hamlet* was to be played, she gave her guardians the slip and concealed herself in the theatre until Ophelia's mad scene, whereupon she leapt on stage before the girl who had played the part so far. Unfortunately, the effort was too much for her and she died soon afterwards.

**MUNI**, Paul. The great American actor Paul Muni (bom in Austria), who graduated from the New York Yiddish theatre and played the leading role of Willy Loman in Arthur Miller's play *Death of a Salesman* in London, was a specialist in the biographical films which were particularly fashionable in Hollywood in the thirties and forties. Muni was Louis Pasteur in a 1936 film which celebrated the pasteurisation of milk. In spite of Jack Warner's prediction that the film would flop Muni picked up an Oscar and luckily fought off a suggestion that the movie should end with a voiceover solemnly saying 'And to this day, housewives all over the world are grateful to this man, because he invented pasteurised milk.'

Later Warner toyed with the idea of a life of Beethoven for Muni, having seen the latent possibilities of 'biopics'. Muni was an early method man and as Beethoven was deaf so he was deaf to his neighbour's over-the-garden-wall chatter. As the neighbour was Mrs Mischa Auer, wife of another Hollywood star, she reported the fact that he had ignored her to Mrs Muni.

'Oh,' said Mrs Muni cheerfully, 'he probably didn't even hear you. Today he's Beethoven, so he's deaf as a doorknob!'

Later Warner decided against the Beethoven project, telling his producer Hal Wallis to look for a different biographical subject. 'Anything but Beethoven,' he said. 'Nobody wants to see a movie about a blind composer.'

At the end of the craze Wallis was quoted as saying, 'Every time Paul Muni parts his beard and looks down a telescope, this company loses two million dollars.'

Muni's obsessive concern for developing his character lay more in his mental preparation than his attention to make-up. On one movie, on a day when he had not expected to be called to the set, an assistant director asked him how long it would take him to get ready, 'Four hours,' said Muni. 'Two hours for the outer man, two hours for the inner man.'

Muni's wife, Bella, kept a vigilant eye on the film set, both to approve his scenes and to make sure his leading ladies did not get too involved. When he shot *The Commandos Strike at Dawn*, the director told his co-star, the British actress Anna Lee, not to make physical contact with him – 'Paul doesn't like it.' It was not until they got to shoot some publicity shots and Mrs Muni was not present that Miss Lee found the true reason she had to keep her distance. She was suddenly hauled into a passionate embrace and was so surprised that she found it difficult to respond with enthusiasm.

Muni let her go muttering, 'Oh, you English women are so cold!'

With his theatrical background, Muni brought an old theatrical tradition to the movies. He called it 'The Five Day Test'. He had observed that in newly assembled theatre companies romances broke out quickly between members of the company. 'Boys and girls; girls and boys; boys and boys.' Usually the old character actor falls for the prettiest young chorine. Very exceptionally a youngster falls for a lucky oldster. Muni's advice was to give it five days. 'At the end of that time, if you still want it, *then* do something about it. But usually you don't.' And, with Mrs Muni on the warpath, usually he couldn't.

**Murray**, Don. Don Murray played the cowboy opposite Marilyn Monroe in Joshua Logan's 1960 film of William Inge's *Bus Stop*. Ms Monroe had been checking out Freud in the years that lay before – including, in 1954, asking Robert Mitchum when they were filming *River of No Return* to explain an entry in her Freudian textbook. The chapter she was devouring was 'Anal Eroticism'. First she had asked her co-star 'What's eroticism?' and then some time later, 'What's anal?'

She had majored by the time it came to *Bus Stop*, according to Logan.

At one point, Murray spoke a line incorrectly, 'Wake up, *cherie,* it's nine o'clock – the sun's out – no wonder you're so pale and scaly.' It should have been 'so pale and white.'

Logan called 'Cut!' and Ms Monroe made her informed comment.

'You just made a Freudian slip,' she explained to her co-star. 'You must be feeling right in the scene. That was a Freudian slip about a phallic symbol. Unconsciously you were thinking about a snake. That's why you said "scaly". A snake is a phallic symbol. Do you know what a phallic symbol is, Don?'

According to Logan, Mr Murray did. 'Know what it is?' he said. 'I've got one.'

**MY FAIR LADY.** This musical produced the definitive story about theatre-goers reluctant to relinquish prized tickets. When *My Fair Lady* fever was at its height, the house manager spotted a woman with an empty seat beside her. He asked if it belonged to her. She admitted sadly that, 'My husband was coming but he was killed in a car accident.' The manager sympathised and wondered why she hadn't invited another member of the family or a friend. The woman said she couldn't: 'You see, they're all at the funeral.'

That certainly tops one I witnessed in New York when we were playing *Side by Side by Sondheim* at the Music Box. There was a disturbance in the mezzanine (or circle): a man had a heart attack and was carried out, accompanied by two companions. He died and they returned to their seats.

Two more members of the Drury Lane audience arrived at the theatre on a pair of complimentary stalls tickets: the covering note explained they had won them in a charity raffle. They returned home to find their house comprehensively burgled. Tickets for *My Fair Lady* were a sure way of getting people out of the house.

The farewell appearance of Margaret Halstan was one of the odder facets of the run. A much-admired actress and the original Gloria in *You Never Can Tell*, she was over 80, frail, nearly blind and poor. Hugh Beaumont engaged her for the one-line role of the Queen of Carpathia to whom Eliza Doolittle is introduced at the ball at which she could have danced all night. Her single line was 'Charming. Perfectly charming.'

When she asked Binkie exactly what she said he replied, 'Charming, charming,' to which she said sharply, 'Yes, I'm sure it's charming, but what does she *say*?'

He arranged a nightly taxi to take her home. When it failed to arrive one night, another member of the cast gave her a lift. Graciously, Margaret Halstan enquired, 'And what part do you play, dear?'

'I play Eliza Doolittle,' said Julie Andrews.

# — 𝓝 —

**NATHAN**, George Jean. Nathan was an American dramatic critic and editor whose first work was for the *New York Herald,* which he joined in 1905. He also edited *The Smart Set* with H.L. Mencken, championing modern European dramatists – Shaw, Strindberg, Ibsen, Hauptmann and O'Casey. He published Eugene O'Neill's early plays and praised Saroyan's first works.

However, he will probably be better remembered for dismissive witticisms. On Vincent Price's Abraham Lincoln, in Paul Horgan's *Yours, A Lincoln* in 1942: 'The Price Lincoln, had Booth not taken the job himself, would have been shot on the spot by every dramatic critic in Ford's Theater on that fateful night.'

More perceptively: 'A musical show is like another fellow's wife or sweetheart. For one man who shares his taste there are always those who wonder what he sees in her.' He called Tallulah Bankhead's Cleopatra, 'Queen of the Nil', making sure the compositors did not correct an imagined misprint. *Tonight or Never* produced one of those infuriating one-sentence reviews: 'Very well, then: I say, Never.'

He made Katharine Hepburn a regular target. In 1950 he wrote of her Rosalind; 'Flat and dry of voice, except for a periodically manufactured tremolo that suggests she studied vocal shadings not with Constance Collier but Al Jolson, inflexible in gesture, and as bare of Shakespearean lilt as Arden's winter trees of foliage, the Bard's heroine becomes merely a schoolgirl's recitation and a lesson learned.'

In the same year he destroyed an early performance by Charlton Heston in *Design for a Stained Glass Window:* 'Charlton Heston, a pretty fellow whom the moving pictures should capture without delay, if they have any respect for the dramatic stage, duly adjusts his chemise so the audience may swoon over his expansive hirsute chest, and conducts his prize physique about the platform like a physical culture demonstrator.'

Back in 1943 he had been to see *Richard III*: 'To the multiplicity of the play's murders, Mr Colouris and his company added another. The play itself.'

Probably his most arrogant quote was, 'There are two kinds of dramatic critic: destructive and constructive. I am destructive. There are two kinds of guns: Krupp and pop.'

**NEAGLE**, Dame Anna. Poor Dame Anna, a much loved actress of limited ability but great popularity attracted, perhaps, an unfair share of criticism – notably from Kenneth Tynan who, when she appeared in a musical accused her of 'shaking her voice like a tiny fist at the audience'; and Noel Coward who once dismissed her, 'never a terribly good actress but then she never got any worse.' Leaving the New York première in 1938 of *Sixty Glorious Years* in which Dame Anna played Queen Victoria, he said, 'I never realised that Prince Albert married beneath him.'

Later he was to make two retractions. In 1950, visiting *Odette*, the Herbert Wilcox film about the wartime heroine Odette Churchill, he admitted to his diary, 'Anna extraordinarily good.' In 1964 he read Wilcox's autobiography, *Twenty-five Thousand Sunsets*. 'His unquestioning adoration of Anna shines through every page. You would think from reading it that dear Anna is the greatest actress, singer and dancer who ever graced the stage and screen. The fact that this is not strictly accurate never for a split second occurs to him . . .' However, 'she has a vast and idolatrous public. It is a very, very strange phenomenon.'

**NEILSON-TERRY**, Phyllis. Phyllis Neilson-Terry, the daughter of Fred Terry and Julia Neilson, was a notable actress over many years. The title role in *Trilby* was one of her early triumphs and later she toured in some of her parents' triumphs, notably *The Scarlet Pimpernel*. In the thirties, she played many Shakespearean roles, often in the Open Air Theatre, Regent's Park. One of her more surprising roles was Oberon, where her commanding height and powerful coloratura voice were regally authoritative. Legend has it that each evening as she soared into 'I know a bank', her voice cleared the spaces in the park and reached the zoo, some hundred of yards away, waking the entire dog family, wolves and hyenas especially, and setting them off in loud howls.

I once asked her about her performance as Lady Macbeth, enthusiastically received by James Agate.

'Ah, yes,' she said. 'That was at Stratford-upon-Avon – with Donald

Wolfit. I don't know if you are aware,' she went on, 'but Donald had a reputation as a very selfish actor. When we came to the scene after Duncan's murder at the dress rehearsal, I was supporting him in his hour of need. I stood behind him and placed my hands on his shoulders – but Donald hissed at me, "Don't touch me" – because he thought I was distracting from his performance. Now, this was very silly – because I was playing his wife and I had to support him and if I couldn't touch him the only thing I could do was to listen – and . . .' Here, in an extravagant gesture, she stretched one arm out to its very full length and cupped an ear with the other: '. . . and when I *listen,* everybody looks at me.'

**NESBITT**, Cathleen. Initially celebrated for her romance with Rupert Brooke, Cathleen Nesbitt's long and distinguished career ended with her second tour of America as Rex Harrison's mother in My *Fair Lady.* She was nearly 90 and, Rex reckoned, the only actress who could appear convincingly as his mother. By then she was frail and when the revival opened in New Orleans, a chair was placed on the side of the stage so that she was spared long trips to her dressing room. She soon complained to the director, Patrick Garland, 'that the changes to the show were not improvements'. As no changes had been made, he was puzzled. He soon discovered that she was seeing and hearing parts of the show she had never registered before.

'There's that new song,' she protested. 'It's terrible. Something about the rain in Spain.'

When the tour reached San Francisco she celebrated her 90th birthday. The papers made much of the event and, on her first entrance, the audience gave her a standing ovation. Thinking that this must be the curtain call for the end of the show, she gave a stately curtsey and made an immediate exit.

When the company reached Los Angeles, she met Harrison in an hotel lobby.

'Dear Rex,' she said. 'What are you doing in California?'

**NEWMAN**, Sidney. Sidney Newman, the innovative head of drama of ABC TV in England in the late fifties and sixties, looked, according to Paul Ferris, like a Mexican but was in fact a Canadian. He came to England after a successful career as a drama producer in Canada and triumphantly introduced 'the new drama' – 'kitchen-sink theatre' – to British television. Accusations of philistinism were crystallised in the story of a producer, who suggested the production of a play by Ionesco.

'Ian who?' Newman is said to have replied.

He moved from ABC to the BBC as head of plays and fought a long, noisy battle to retain the 'one-off' play. His enemies used to tell the story that when his contract expired, a large black limousine with smoked glass windows drew up at Television Centre, collected him and drove him back to the ABC studios, where he jumped out, saluted the chairman and reported, 'Mission completed, sir', before returning to Canada.

**NICHOLAS NICKLEBY**. The RSC's marathon performance of *Nicholas Nickleby* transferred from the Aldwych to New York amid great excitement. Passers-by would wait for audiences to emerge at half-time to ask if it was all it was cracked up to be – rather like earlier generations of Americans anxiously waiting on the New York waterfront to learn if Little Nell was dead.

One bookshop advertised the fat original novel with the legend – 'If you haven't got time to see the play, buy the book.'

**NICHOLS**, Mike. A classic encounter – perhaps apocryphal, but I hope not – took place when Mike Nichols directed Walter Matthau in Neil Simon's comedy, *The Odd Couple*. As their disagreements became more acrimonious, the insults flew more wildly until Nichols, from the stalls, put an end to the row with a crushing riposte. There was an awkward pause before Matthau, accepting defeat, stepped forward and said quietly, to break the mood, 'Hey, Mike, can I have my prick back?'

Nichols snapped a lordly finger and then called, 'Props!'

**NIGHTINGALE**, Annie. Annie Nightingale has become a very successful popular music journalist and radio disc-jockey. My favourite Annie Nightingale incident is, however, perhaps not one of which she is particularly proud. She was interviewing the song writer Paul Simon, whose initial success was achieved as half of a singing duo with Art Garfunkel. The combination of the two voices is beguiling but the songs are all written and composed by Simon.

Some years ago the singers split up and Simon went solo. It was at this moment that a sympathetic Nightingale was asked to interview him for BBC 2. Was it hard, she asked, for him to carry on writing without his long-term collaborator?

'No,' he said. But surely they had been singing together for a very long time? He agreed. So, must it not have been traumatic to have to write on alone? No. But surely if you have been writing songs with a partner for all that time and he suddenly splits . . .

Eventually Simon explained coldly but politely to the pop expert that Garfunkel had written none of the songs – only sung them with him. Simon had written them all himself.

It was here that poor Annie finally buried herself, 'Is this a scoop?' she asked hopefully.

'No,' said Simon, 'I guess most people know.'

**NOVELLO**, Ivor (David Ivor Novello Davies). Actor-manager, matinée idol, playwright, and composer, Novello was a friend and something of a thorn in the flesh of Noel Coward – his romantic musicals had a habit of long out-running Coward's later work. On one occasion, Coward tried to gain entrance to a theatre where one of his own shows was playing. Refused admission by a commissionaire, who failed to recognise him, he protested angrily that he had written the play, directed it and composed the music.

'Regular little Ivor Novello, aren't we?' said the commissionaire, unimpressed.

One of Novello's long-time affairs was with the son of a wealthy book-maker, who did not approve the relationship. Having had a few drinks at the races, he is said to have driven home past Novello's home, Redroofs, and to have shouted in maudlin fashion, 'Give me back my son!' In Novello's circle the incident was quickly referred to as 'Calling the sods'.

**NUNN**, Trevor Robert. During Trevor Nunn's stint as the artistic director of the RSC at his base in Stratford, he perfected an art which became known as 'Trevving'. It consists of asking an actor to his office or to dinner – perhaps at a round table in the inner restaurant of The Dirty Duck – fixing said actor with an intense gaze and persuading him to play a part which he had no intention of accepting. Towards the end of his tenure, he was much in demand to direct expensive commercial musicals. So long were his absences that a group of actors petitioned Jimmy Saville (elevated to Sir James in 1990 for charity work) to 'Fix it', on his television programme of that name, for them to meet their leader.

**NUREYEV**, Rudolf. As Nureyev diversified his career as he grew older, he expanded Nureyev Enterprises into the legitimate theatre, or at least into musicals, touring *The King and I* in America with Liz Robertson as Mrs Anna. On one occasion, in a cold, full theatre, the King of Siam arrived on stage with a poncho round his bare shoulders, clogs on his bare feet, muttering, 'Now I am warm' and turned the 'Shall we dance' polka into a clog routine.

In Miami, they were playing the end of Act One when Rudolf barely made the stage in time for his entrance, and was immediately distracted. Mrs Anna is subtly advising the king on how to convince the British that he is not a barbarian. To each of her suggestions he replies that that is exactly what he had intended.

To Mrs Anna's and the audience's confusion, the king's lines were peppered with frantic calls of, 'Matt – the phone!' to the stage manager in the wings, accompanied by bizarre miming. There was no way the man was going to bring on a telephone so that Nureyev could conduct a 20th century conversation in 19th century Siam.

Eventually the curtain fell and Nureyev sped to his dressing room. It transpired that in his dash to get on stage he had interrupted a long-distance call to Paris and left the receiver off. And he was paying for the call!

The anecdote which circulated most plentifully after the great dancer's death told of a boy whom he had picked up at a nightclub but dismissed when he got home, saying, 'Your beauty has faded.'

In a letter to the London *Evening Standard* Jim Kelsey suggested that this is a typical bastardisation of a tale which changes its character totally in retelling and mistelling. According to Mr Kelsey, back in the sixties Nureyev was dining in the King's Road with Erling Sunde, then a teacher at the Royal Ballet. They left the restaurant late at night and Nureyev, resplendent in fur hat and coat, tried without success to pick up a young stranger. The boy rejected him and Nureyev, dismayed, turned to Sunde and said: 'My beauty am fading.'

Very soon it became a catch-phrase at the Royal Ballet.

# — O —

**OFFENBACH**, Jacques (Jacob Eberst). Offenbach took as his professional name that of the town of his birth, Offenbach-am-Main. His death produced perhaps the favourite Offenbach anecdote. On the morning he died, an old actor from one of his companies, Leonce, called on him to enquire of his health. Offenbach's faithful, long-serving manservant Matharin explained, 'Monsieur Offenbach is dead. He died quite peacefully, without knowing anything about it.'

'Ah!' muttered Leonce, as he moved on. 'He will be very surprised when he finds out.'

Just before his death, Offenbach handed a colleague an old musical sketchbook full of melodic ideas with the words, 'Here, take this. Give it to Saint-Saëns [a frequent critic of his music] when I am dead.'

In his charming book of food and music stories, *Foie Gras and Trumpets*, Charles Neilson Gattey retells a story of Offenbach (on a tour of America) and an old waiter at Petry's famous restaurant in Philadelphia. The waiter grimaced at the suggestion of a julienne – 'I don't recommend that. The vegetables they use up – how can they do it?' Offenbach decided to forgo soup and asked if they had salmon.

'Certainly we have. We've had it a long time.' Offenbach suggested a steak.

'The cook will ruin it.'

'Strawberries?'

'Mushy and tasteless.'

'Cheese?'

'I'll ask it to come up,' said the waiter; 'won't need any help. It can walk alone.'

Offenbach protested at the man's disloyalty to his employer. 'If I were your employer I would fire you.'

To which the waiter said, 'He already has. It's my last night here.' He bowed low and left the table.

Offenbach eventually dined well.

**OKLAHOMA!** The breakthrough musical for Rodgers and Hammerstein, which broke on Broadway in 1943, produced a little slew of stories even before its debut. Its original title when it played New Haven was *Away We Go!* It was given the thumbs-down by Mike Todd and by one of Walter Winchell's stringers with the snappy verdict, 'No girls, no leg, no jokes, no chance.'

It provided Nunnally Johnson with a witty wire when, soon after, his play *The World Is Full of Girls* flopped disastrously. He cabled his producer Jed Harris: 'Change the title immediately to *Oklahoma!*'

Rodgers is said to have declined a drink on the opening night because he wanted to blur no single moment of a triumphant evening and Hammerstein, of course, took his famous advertisement in *Variety* listing his last five major flops above the legend, 'I've done it before and I can do it again.'

Perhaps apocryphal but nonetheless endearing is the single-minded verdict of the wardrobe mistress, whose four-word verdict on the greatest triumph since *Showboat* was, 'You call those seams?'

**OLIVIER**, Lord. Olivier's career as a front man for a brand of cigarettes – in the tradition of du Maurier – amused him. As he started to rehearse one production, he spotted a particularly nervous young actor fumbling with a packet of cigarettes – Craven A. He strolled over and offered the actor an Olivier. The embarrassed young man declined, still spilling his Craven A packet.

'Why not?' Olivier asked.

'Oh,' stuttered the confused beginner, searching for an appropriate answer. 'They give gifts with these.'

'Ah,' smiled Olivier. 'They give parts with these.'

In his *Confessions of an Actor*, Olivier has told the story of his debut at the Brighton Hippodrome after everybody in the theatre, from call boy upwards, had warned him until he was bored stiff about a tricky 'sill' at the foot of the door where he was to make his entrance. He still managed to trip over it in the excitement and flew arse over tip, landing at the footlights under the unsurprised gaze of Ruby Miller.

Of all the Olivier stories, perhaps the one which best sums up his unique mixture of inexplicable inspiration and dazzling technique is the one the cast of *Othello* told after a particularly brilliant performance, when the cast were as one in wonder at his power and splendour. So moved were they that they clapped him from the stage to the dressing room, only to hear him slam the door in obvious distress. When someone plucked up courage to knock on the door and say 'What's the matter, Larry? It was great!' he supplied the explanation.

'I know it was great, but I don't know how I did it so how can I be sure I can do it again?'

Tarquin Olivier's biography of his father throws up a couple of stories about Olivier which have not hitherto had an airing. He was, apparently, so jealous of Vivien Leigh's Oscar for *Gone With the Wind* that he tore it from her hand on their way home from the ceremony. He had lost out for *Wuthering Heights*.

More inventively he dined one night at the Garrick Club with Tarquin and two friends when a club servant was showing off the club's portrait collection to some visitors. 'These,' he indicated, 'are the Zoffanys' – Olivier leapt to his feet. He bowed. 'I am the Poppa Zoffany – and these are my sons, Rocco, Luigi, Paolo . . .'

Many Olivier stories do not demonstrate the same awareness. Tarquin quotes his mother, actress Jill Esmond, who was Olivier's first wife and more sophisticated. When they were in Berlin, she told him to meet her at the famous art gallery the Kuntshalle. His arrival was delayed because, panicking in German, he asked the cab driver to take him to the Fuchshalle.

One Laurence Olivier story turns up in Barry Humphries' autobiography. At an official reception in Sydney in 1948 for Olivier (not yet knighted) and Vivien Leigh during their theatrical tour of Australia, the Lord Mayor introduced them as 'Sir Oliver and Lady Leigh'. In reply to a subsequent correction, he remarked amiably, 'Shit, you can't win 'em all.'

**O'NEILL**, Eugene. O'Neill's theatrical pedigree was derived from his father, James O'Neill, the model for the actor James Tyrone in *Long Day's Journey Into Night*. Before becoming a writer, Eugene O'Neill had served as a merchant seaman. After his last voyage in 1912, instead of giving his out-of-work son a hand-out, James O'Neill gave him two small parts in his fustian, touring production of *The Count of Monte Cristo*. The ex-sailor hated acting, hated his roles and above all hated the creaking vehicle his father never tired of touring. At Ogden in Utah,

O'Neill senior gave his son a note: 'Sir, I am not satisfied with your performance.'

'Sir,' was the reply. 'I am not satisfied with your play.' However, the experience encouraged O'Neill junior to start writing his own plays and very soon to boast of them to a newspaper editor in Connecticut, who had told him that were he not James O'Neill's son he'd be in the gutter with other bums. Though drunk, O'Neill was able to reply, 'The day will come when James O'Neill will be remembered only as the father of Eugene O'Neill.'

O'Neill was born in James Square on 16 October, 1888 in an hotel on the corner of 43rd Street. His career as an able seaman inspired a number of his plays and a couple of anecdotes. One old sea-faring colleague gave him a concerned note after seeing *The Hairy Ape:* 'For God's sake, tell number four stoker to stop leaning his prat against that red-hot furnace.'

O'Neill had a great success with *Strange Interlude* in 1928. He alleged that the play was inspired by Lynn Fontanne, who had complained eight years earlier about too many speeches in praise of mothers in *Anna Christie.* (She had had trouble with her own and with Alfred Lunt's, finally forcing her husband to choose between his mother and her.) At the height of his fame, O'Neill ran into another ex-sailor. They exchanged pleasantries and O'Neill asked how the other was doing. He said he had married and settled down.

'And you, Gene. Are you still working on the boats?'

Like many successful playwrights, O'Neill had to face plagiarism suits. In one involving the authorship of *Strange Interlude,* the critic George Jean Nathan gave evidence that the playwright had described the plot, purpose and treatment of the play to him during an evening of heavy drinking some years before. An over-clever attorney for the plaintiff painstakingly elicited from Nathan a detailed account of exactly what they had drunk that night. Then he pounced, demanding how, if the critic had drunk all that, he could possibly remember so clearly the conversation he alleged he had with O'Neill. It was Nathan's turn to score.

'If I can recall exactly the number and character of the drinks, which you assent were enough to intoxicate anyone, why should I not be able to recall exactly the conversation before I had so much as even one?'

In 1946, O'Neill had a memorable meeting with Irving Berlin. The pair were introduced by Russell Crouse. Berlin was overawed at the prospect of facing O'Neill until he found that the playwright knew all the old songs, and the evening developed into a singalong until three o'clock in the morning. Emboldened, Berlin invited O'Neill to a performance of *Annie Get Your Gun*, which gave *him* an excuse to feel nervous: O'Neill hated going to the theatre, bad plays and being recognised. He had reckoned without Ethel Merman, who steam-rollered him into helpless approval.

**OSBORNE**, John. John Osborne's second volume of autobiography, *Almost a Gentleman*, yields a crop of vivid vignettes. Subjected to the thick charm of 'Binkie' Beaumont's blandishments he 'was made to feel like a mud wrestler being complimented by a Duchess'. He appears to have preferred the 'awesomely unlikeable' American producer David Merrick – 'He liked writers,' said Osborne, 'the way a snake likes live rabbits.'

George Devine, his mentor at the Court, is vividly evoked smoking cigars in heavy drag for his transvestite role in Osborne's *A Portrait for Me* and lovingly remembered for his 'fixed bayonet relish' in taking on the philistines. Ex-wives get short shrift but perhaps once again it is his mother, Nellie Beatrice, who provides the most colourful memory. They were at dinner at Stratford-on-Avon during a run of *Othello* with Paul Robeson as the Moor and Mary Ure (then the younger Mrs Osborne) as Desdemona.

The Osbornes were entertaining Robeson after a performance. 'Oh, Mr Robeson, it's such an honour for us to meet you, especially for my son,' said Mama. 'He's such an admirer of yours. You see, Mr Robeson, he's always been so sorry for you *darkies.*'

**OVERHEARDS**. The classic overheard is believed to be by a member of the London audience, whispering loudly during Sarah Bernhardt's tempestuous *Cleopatra*: 'How very unlike the home life of our own dear queen!' Some 80 years later, when Mart Crowley's gay play, *The Boys in the Band*, played at Wyndham's Theatre to a deserved success, one camp spectator emerged, saying, 'How very unlike the home life of our own dear queens.'

Peter Hay believes that when Joan Greenwood played in *Peter Pan*, Hermione Gingold greeted the line 'Do you believe in fairies' with a *basso profundo:* 'Believe in them, darling? I know hundreds of them!'

I vividly remember coming out of a Stratford *Julius Caesar* to hear an American lady intone; 'Geez, that Brutus, was he *noble.*'

'Jonathan Miller's *Three Sisters* at the Cambridge Theatre produced a great audience comment from another American woman: 'It's more a play than a show.'

The 1969 production of *Antony and Cleopatra* was directed by Peter Dews, and starred John Clements and Margaret Leighton. Dews heard one West Sussex lady leaving the auditorium saying, 'Yes, and the funny thing is, *exactly* the same thing happened to Monica.' Various *Macbeths* are said to have inspired remarks on the lines of 'something very similar happened to Monica'. Others in the same vein are 'Rather an unpleasant family, these Lears' and the comment of a woman who was watching Alec Guinness and Simone Signoret in *Macbeth* at the Royal Court; leaning across to her companion she pointed out loudly, 'You see how one lie leads to another!'

When the Lunts played Durrenmatt's *The Visit* at Brighton – their last appearance together – a keen-eyed patron at the Theatre Royal said wisely, "Course, you can tell her age when you get to the hands.' When Olivier played David Turner's *Semi-Detached* in a Birmingham accent, two old ladies were overhead tut-tutting in the interval at the Saville Theatre.

'Hasn't he gone off?' said one.

'Yes,' replied the other. 'He's not the same since he married that Joan Playwright.'

In a revival of *The Seagull* at the New Theatre, the Trigorin wore a purplish tweedy suit in the last act. As one couple left the theatre, the woman said, 'Well, dear, how did you like it? Did you jump when the poor man shot himself? I did.' Her escort, who had obviously not enjoyed it and probably had not wanted to be dragged to the play in the first place, was brusque. 'If it had been me, I'd have shot the fellow in the purple bags.'

When we were playing *Side by Side by Sondheim* (again at Wyndhams), a woman looked long and hard at David Kernan, who was singing a beautifully heartfelt 'Anyone Can Whistle' and then turned to her companion, pointed at David's legs and said loudly, 'Oh, look. Turn-ups are coming back.'

During the same run, while I was sitting on the side of the stage intro-ducing the songs, I noticed a group of Germans in the front row talking in loud whispers to one another. Eventually, just before the interval, they got up and left, asking the anxious company manager, 'Vy does von talk and ze ozzers sing?' Had they heard me sing they might have understood.

Sybil Thorndike had her own verdict on audiences: 'Some nights they're porridge; some nights – electricity!'

One of the ordeals of performing is people who insist on 'coming round' and putting in their tuppence. This can be kinky. When I was at the Music Box with *Side by Side,* convinced that my heavy dieting had worked wonders, one dressing room visitor insisted on comparing me to Orson Welles, and Carol Channing told me I was 'the spirit of Robert Morley'.

Earlier, at the Mermaid, I took two American friends-of-a-friend round to see Millicent Martin, at their insistence. They seemed short on charm and sure enough the lady's opening line, her face dropping, was 'Oh, but you looked beautiful on stage.' (An echo of Sarah Bernhardt's maid, perhaps, who once said, 'Oh! Madame was so lovely tonight, I didn't recognise Madame!') Perhaps hoping to repair the damage, her husband wagged a finger at Milly and said, 'You can't fool me. You've done solo work before,' and, even more encouragingly, 'You'll do solo work again.'

I dined one night at a neighbouring table to Milly and another guest who had been to see the show and at whom I must have been chattering from the stage for nearly two hours. I joined them for coffee and we talked for some time before a dim light began to shine in her eyes.

'Wait a minute,' she said. 'Aren't you the guy who reads out the announcements?' On another night the management entertained the staff of various London ticket agencies. They had a drink with the cast afterwards and I worked hard for twenty minutes with a young woman who had a ticket booth somewhere along the Strand. At the end of it, she asked what I did.

'I work here at the moment,' I said.

'What as?'

'Sort of on stage.'

'Oh,' she said, reluctantly accepting the evidence. 'You look more sophisticated up there.'

This pales before the reactions of two rather precious men who were coming out of a performance at the Music Box in New York. Leaving the stage door (quite sober), I slipped and fell in the gutter. They surveyed my prostrate figure with little enthusiasm.

'Well,' said one, 'it's funnier than anything he did during the show!'

The classic case of the naive audience is the man who bellowed 'You great black fool!' as a nineteenth-century Othello was being duped with the handkerchief. Bennett Cerf has a story – perhaps apocryphal – of Olivier playing Othello in the open air in America. In the interval, a woman invaded his dressing room and asked when the next bus into town left. He expressed surprise that she wasn't staying to see the rest of the play.

'Frankly,' she told him, 'I saw it years ago back in Brooklyn. It was in Yiddish and it hurts me to hear how much it loses in translation.'

When a very young Judi Dench and a very young Ian McKellen were playing *The Promise* at the Oxford Playhouse with a very young Ian McShane, they made their entrance for Act Three swathed in furs from head to foot. They had matured during the course of the action from Russian teenagers into middle-aged Russians. This modern Russian play had concentrated on conditions in contemporary Russia for all its considerable length. However, the sight of Dench and McKellen, peering out of their fur cocoons and contemplating one another in Russian silence for some considerable time, produced a sniff from one woman in the front row: 'Anybody'd think they were in Russia,' she said loudly to her companion.

David Hare reports a man who, at the end of the first act of a play of his at the Bristol Old Vic, turned to his companion and said, 'If this was on TV, I'd turn it off.' On a later occasion he heard a woman put her arm consolingly round her boyfriend as they walked away from another of his shows, saying, 'I'm sorry, darling, that was my idea.'

Almost as bad as a direct depreciation is the ritual delivery of an equivocal remark to cover embarrassment. W.S. Gilbert is supposed to have entered one actor's dressing room with the line, 'My dear chap! Good isn't the word,' and he certainly greeted Beerbohm Tree after his Hamlet with, 'My dear fellow, I never saw anything so funny in my life, and yet it was not in the least vulgar.'

Standard equivocations are 'Well, you've done it again' and 'How about you?' A sign of danger is a back-stage visitor who waxes too enthusiastic about scenery and costumes. When the Chichester Festival revived Sandy Wilson's exquisite musical *Valmouth* in a rather lacklustre production, my friend Caryl Brahms had Sandy Wilson pointed out to her at a restaurant after the show. She rushed across to tell him how good it was to see the play again. When she returned to her companion, he pointed out to her that she had already bumped into Sandy unknowingly at the interval and said to him in darkest tones of doom, 'My dear, what can we possibly say to them when we go round?'

Maybe audiences should simply stay away. Ovid had a poor opinion of them: 'Adulterers, whore-masters, panders, whores and such-like effeminate, idle, unchaste, lascivious, graceless persons were the most assiduous Play-hunters in their time.'

# — *P* —

**PAIGE**, Elaine. Elaine Paige, star of *Evita*, *Cats*, *Chess* and *Anything Goes*, served a long tough apprenticeship before landing *Evita*, her break-through role. She has told how on the first day of rehearsals she was taken out to lunch by the director, Hal Prince. 'He was hugely successful and I was deeply in awe of him.' In the course of conversation Prince said that he was going out that evening to see *Peter Grimes*. Battling bravely and aiming at casual awareness, Miss Paige put her foot in it. 'Of course, I know who he is, but I've never met him.' Prince's reply, as he was off to Covent Garden to see Benjamin Britten's opera is not recorded.

**PAPP**, Joseph. Joe Papp, the dynamic moving force behind the Public Theater and the New York Shakespeare Festival, was sensitive to criticism and tried the age-old exclusion 'disinvitation' gauntlet on Edith Oliver, the off-Broadway critic of the *New Yorker*. Ms Oliver replied in the equally traditional way by paying for her own ticket and crouching anonymously near the back row of the public theatre where some Beckett one-acters were in performance. Papp spotted her and asked why she was so far back – there were empty seats up-front.

'But I thought you were mad at me?'

'Hell – that was three days ago!'

Papp also employed the disgraced Broadway producer Adela Holzer for a time between incarcerations: 'She was on the phone a hell of a lot – but she never raised a cent.'

John Simon launched one of his most vicious attacks on Ruth Gordon, who played the title role in *Mrs Warren's Profession* when Papp produced it at the Lincoln Center. 'It is a generous role for womanly and impassioned actresses, and many performers have essayed it. I can think of four, however, who have not: Totie Fields, W.C. Fields, Tutankamun's mummy and a trained monkey. Not until now that is; Miss Gordon's performance combines elements of all four.' Of Papp he added: 'Was this just a piece of errant commercialism to pull in the crowds that grooved on the witch of *Rosemary's Baby?* Or, worse yet, sheer tastelessness and incomprehension of the work's meaning? *Mrs Warren's Profession* may or may not be described as a problem play; Mr Papp is certainly a problem producer.'

Papp produced several plays in collaboration with the Royal Court Theatre. One which he commissioned was Sam Shepard's *Curse of the Starving Class* (1978). When Papp offered the commission, Shepard asked him: 'How much?'

'Two hundred dollars.'

'Two hundred dollars . . . sheee!'

Shepard hiked the commission to $500 and then enquired what sort of play Papp was anticipating. Papp, who had just had a hit with David Rabes's *Sticks and Bones,* knew just the sort of play he wanted: 'A family, two sons, one stays home, one goes off to Vietnam, or anyway to war, and gets fucked up!'

**PARENTS.** The reactions of lay parents to the achievements of their theatrical children yield a rich harvest.

The late Ray Cook was a musical director of many West End shows and an arranger and composer. Among his credits were *A Chorus Line* and *Side by Side by Sondheim.* He was Australian and during the London run his parents came over to witness his success. After *A Chorus Line,* with its ultimate audition plot, they came round and agreed that they had enjoyed it: 'But,' said Mrs Cook, 'do the same people get the parts every night?'

'Yes,' said Ray.

Mrs Cook was unimpressed: 'Hardly worth the rest coming in, is it?' she said.

Shortly afterwards, André Previn recorded a television interview with Sondheim, illustrated by songs from *Side by Side.* The senior Cooks viewed a video alone. When Ray saw them, he asked the same question: had they enjoyed it?

'It was all right,' said Mrs Cook, 'but why is that Sondheim climbing on your bandwagon?'

David Hare was apprehensive of his parents' reaction to his outspoken play, *Slag.*

'I enjoyed it,' his mother told him, 'but I think your father, who was of course in the Navy, understood more.'

Victor Spinetti was once in an avant-garde feminist play. His mother rang from Wales to ask, 'What's this *Vagina Rex and the Gas Oven*?

Spinetti told her: 'It all takes place in a woman's vagina.'

'Oh,' she said. 'Your father'd like that.'

Dame Judi Dench probably wins the admiring parent stakes. When playing her Juliet at the Old Vic in 1961, her parents came from York to see the play. When she came to the line, 'Where is my mother and father, nurse?' her mother leapt up and cried, 'Here we are, darling, H27 and 28!'

Robert Anderson, the American playwright, had sympathetic parents. When his mother heard that Deborah Kerr was to play the lead in *Tea and Sympathy* (unread by her), her comment was, 'It must be a much better play than I thought it was.' After her death, Anderson's father escorted Anderson's wife-to-be, the actress Teresa Wright, to the première of his play *Silent Night, Lonely Night*. Before it had even got under way, he said loudly to her, 'No matter how bad this is, I'm going to tell the poor boy I like it.'

Parental interest is not a new phenomenon. As long ago as 1904 George Ade had a success with his Broadway comedy, *The College Widow*. When his mother came to see it, she had only one question: 'George, do you really get more than $500 a week for doing that?'

'Yes, I do, Mother,' he replied.

'George,' she said, 'you keep right on fooling them.'

**PARKER**, Charlie ('Bird'). Charlie Parker's evolutionary saxophone-playing brilliance and his career of excess, figure side-by-side in the anecdotes of those who remember him. He once pointed out the veins in his arm saying sadly, 'This is my Cadillac,' and pointing to another, 'and this is my house.' Towards the end of his life when, according to Bill Crow in his *Jazz Anecdotes* he had 'inhaled, imbibed, ingested and injected monumental quantities of every form of stimulant, euphoric, narcotic, soporific, hypnotic and hallucinogen known to modern man,' he was treated by a doctor for what turned out to be his final illness. 'Do you drink?' asked the ill-informed doctor.

'Sometimes,' confessed 'Bird', with a wink at a friend, 'I have a sherry before dinner.'

In Clint Eastwood's film celebrating him, made 33 years after his death, the trumpeter Red Rodney is portrayed. He was telephoned by a reporter on a Nebraska newspaper. He gave her an interview. Before signing off she said, 'Thank you, Mr Rodney. And, by the way, can you give me Charlie Parker's phone number?'

**PARKER**, Dorothy. Dorothy Parker's witticisms – in reviews, in sketches, in passing – are scattered through the histories of Broadway and Hollywood. In 1933 she reviewed Katharine Hepburn's performance in *The Lake* at the Martin Beck Theater with the famous and much repeated condemnation; 'Watch Katharine Hepburn run the gamut of emotion from A to B . . .' Less quoted is the fresher image with which she continued. Complimenting a splendid supporting actress, she noted that Miss Hepburn always put a certain distance between herself and her distinguished colleague – 'lest she catch acting from her'.

She failed to stifle Rudolph Besier's *The Barretts of Wimpole Street* in the *New Yorker* in 1931, in spite of writing: 'Now that you've got me right down to it, the only thing I didn't like about *The Barretts of Wimpole Street* was the play.' She dismissed A.A. Milne ('Whimsey-the-Pooh') and his *Give Me Yesterday* in her best, casual button-holing style: ' "Ah!" I said to myself, for I love a responsive audience, "so it's one of *those* plays." '

Bored to tears with listening to a woman who hadn't acted for years and who yet went on and on about her love for the theatre – '. . . I'm so wedded to it' – she said sharply, 'Why don't you sue, then, for non-support?' On an occasion when she stood in for Robert Benchley, she told her *New Yorker* readers that, 'The all-star cast, as is the manner of all-star casts, held ham's holidays and did every line, every bit of business, for all it was worth and just that little touch more . . . I have, happily for me, never seen upon one stage so many discourteous, patronising and exaggerated performances.' She concluded: 'Robert Benchley, please come home. A joke's a joke.'

Her reputed telegram to Uta Hagen –'A hand on your opening and may your parts grow bigger' – was the birth of a cliché. On a domestic level, Frank Case, during his reign at the Algonquin Hotel, was said to have tapped at the door of her room and enquired suspiciously, 'Do you have a gentleman in your room?'

'Just a minute,' was her reply, 'I'll ask him.'

Ms Parker was also mistress of the quick dismissive verbal thrust: '*House Beautiful* is play lousy'; 'Guido Natzo was natzo guido'.

Kay Strozzi, in *The Silent Witness* by Jack de Leon and Jack Celestin, in 1931 suffered a more delayed execution: 'Miss Strozzi . . . had the temerity to wear as truly horrible a gown as ever I have seen on the

American stage. There was a flowing skirt of pale chiffon – you men don't have to listen – a bodice of rose-coloured taffeta, the sleeves of which ended shortly below her shoulder. Then there was an expanse of naked arms, and then, around the wrists, taffeta frills such as are fastened about the unfortunate necks of beaten white poodle-dogs in animal acts. Had she not luckily been strangled by a member of the cast while disporting this garment, I should have fought my way to the stage and done her in myself.'

She was once required to specify the essentials of her trade. She settled for truth. 'There's a hell of a difference between wisecracking and wit. Wit has truth in it. Wisecracking is simply callisthenics with words.' She was not above wisecracking and her wit was not confined to the theatre. 'This book should not be tossed aside,' she wrote, 'but hurled with great force.' She homed in on women writers: 'As artists they're not – but as providers they're oil wells. They gush!' She aggravated her offence by saying, 'It's a terrible thing, but I can't think of good women writers. Of course, calling themselves women writers is their ruin; they begin to think of themselves that way.'

She skewered half a profession with, 'Scratch an actor and you'll find an actress'. She wired Robert Sherwood's wife congratulating her on the arrival of a much-worried-over baby: 'Dear Mary, we all knew you had it in you.' Judged by the available evidence, her favourite straight woman was Clare Booth Luce, who once stood aside for her saying, 'Age before beauty' – to be countered by 'Pearls before swine.' Later, when Ms Parker was told that Miss Luce was always kind to her inferiors she enquired innocently, 'Where does she find them?'

She attempted to conceal a beguiling vulnerability when she married Alan Campbell: 'People who haven't talked to each other for years are on speaking terms today – including the bride and groom.' She was more often sharp than supportive. 'That woman speaks eighteen languages and can't say No in any of them.'

I like her putdown to an American actor who had come back from a season in London and had lost some of those hard American consonant sounds ('skedule' for 'schedule' and other betraying mannerisms). 'If you don't mind my saying so,' she said, 'I think you're full of skit.'

She ran off Basil Rathbone as 'two profiles pasted together,' and a political witch-hunt with 'the only "ism" in Hollywood is plagiarism.' Into the chestnut class of wisecracks have gone: 'And I'll say of Verlaine too: he was always chasing Rimbauds'; more nonsensically, 'There I was, trapped like a trap in a trap,' more truthfully, 'Scratch a lover, find a foe'; eventually, 'If all those sweet young things present were laid end to end I wouldn't be at all surprised.'

She was perhaps too keen on the *double-entendre* which the word 'lay' offers. When she was apartment hunting her requirements were simple: 'All I need is room enough to lay a hat and a few friends.'

She inspired one of Tallulah Bankhead's confessions by asking her to a particularly wild party. 'The more I behave like Whistler's Mother the night before the more I look like her in the morning,' said Bankhead. Dorothy Parker called her 'Whistler's Mother' ever after.

In another famous party phrase she commented, 'Enjoy it! One more drink and I'd have been under the host.' More soberly, she generalised on successful American writers. 'It is our national joy to mistake for the first rate, the fecund rate.'

To the American Horticultural Society she announced: 'You can lead a whore to culture but you can't make her think.'

Alexander Woollcott called her 'a mixture of Little Nell and Lady Macbeth'; but she wrote her own epitaph: 'Excuse my dust. This is on me.'

**PARSONS**, Louella. The two rival Hollywood gossip sisters were Hedda Hopper and Louella Parsons – with space in the papers and time on radio. Can it be possible that, when Ingrid Bergman shocked Hollywood by leaving her husband for Roberto Rossellini and making *Stromboli* in Italy and the news came through that she was pregnant, Ms Parsons, when on her radio show, wept into the microphone: 'Oh, Ingrid, Ingrid! Whatever got into you?'

Ms Parsons did have an inside line to the news. She was married to a doctor who specialised in venereal disease and urology. For a long time he was head of the medical department at Twentieth Century Fox.

Such was Hopper's power that she occasionally called her Beverly Hills home 'The house that fear built.'

**PAVLOVA**, Anna. The great ballerina was about to make her entrance for 'The Dying Swan' on one occasion when an English member of her company brushed past her and performed the solo before she could be restrained. She was greatly surprised when Madame sacked her on her exit. She said the music had inspired an irresistible desire to dance.

Dame Ninette de Valois remembers being berated by an irate matron

during a war-time tour of Scotland for cutting 'The Dying Swan' from
*Lac des Cygnes* – in which ballet, of course, it never had a place.

**PECK**, Gregory and Véronique. The Hollywood couple Gregory and
Véronique Peck came to see *Side by Side by Sondheim* when we were
playing it on Broadway at the Music Box Theatre. I was writing a piece for
*The New York Magazine* at the time and was delighted to detail how Mrs
Peck had struggled valiantly against an overpowering desire to sleep and
in spite of every bit of help – nudging and prodding – from her embarrassed husband and daughter sitting on either side, had finally dropped
her head and succumbed. I wrote that I assumed that the Pecks had just
flown in and excused her lapse as the unjust consequence of jet lag.

It was not until 1992 that I finally met the Pecks at a function organised
by Carl Foreman's widow Eve. 'Weren't you the man . . . ?' Mrs Peck
opened in friendly fashion. I confessed that I was and they said that *all*
their friends had sent the cutting to them. They had laughed rather a lot
at it. There was only one thing she wanted to make clear. She did not have
jet lag!

**PERCY**, Esme. Esme Percy, famous for his association with Sarah
Bernhardt and for his youthful beauty, was in old age cast in Christopher
Fry's *The Lady's Not For Burning*. By now he had acquired a glass eye,
which one night plopped out and rolled round the stage, leading to a
frantic search by other actors who included John Gielgud, Pamela Brown,
Peter Bull, Richard Burton and Nora Nicholson.

Percy was very anxious: 'Oh, do be careful,' he whispered, 'they cost £8
each.'

It was Richard Leech who retrieved it.

**PERELMAN**, S.J. *Monkey Business* was the first of two films co-written by
Sid Perelman for the Marx Brothers. Perelman had to read the script to
them in their New York hotel suite. They arrived (late), attended by their
wives, producers, agents, accountants, gagwriters and Zeppo's dogs – 27
people in all, plus five dogs.

There was a deathly silence after Perelman finished reading. Finally
Chico asked Groucho what he thought of it. Removing his cigar Groucho
said, 'It stinks.' At which all the guests including the dogs left the room.

*Monkey Business* – rewritten – was to become not only a hit movie but
a classic comedy.

One morning in Hollywood, Perelman saw John O'Hara's Rolls Royce parked by the curb, outside a doctor's surgery. As a mild joke he wrote on a piece of paper 'Dear John, it's no worse than a bad cold' and put the note on the windscreen. Later, in New York, Perelman heard that O'Hara was furious because he thought Perelman was spreading rumours that he, O'Hara, had gonorrhoea. Recalling what he had written, Perelman asked why that should have upset him, 'Well,' said someone, 'because he did have gonorrhoea.'

As an English aside, Perelman always claimed that what made him take *The Times* (of London) regularly was reading the account of a man who was arrested for shoplifting when he fainted at the cash desk because he had hidden a frozen chicken under his hat.

**PERLMAN**, Itzhak. At a promotion for a Japanese car firm at Carnegie Hall ('How do you get to Carnegie Hall?' – 'Practise'.), various illustrious musicians, including John Dankworth, Cleo Laine and Itzhak Perlman, contributed. Perlman caused confusion among his Japanese sponsors when he announced that his first piece was by Kreisler.

**PETTINGELL**, Frank. The splendid character actor Frank Pettingell lives in one of Kenneth Williams's stories. 'I adored Frank; he was an imposing figure, striding about in a travelling coat invariably armed with books. He once told me, "I've got so many books in the house they have to be stacked on the landing. The floor is sagging under the weight. The architect says I've got to reinforce the timber joists or the bedroom floor will give way."

' "What's below?" I asked.

' "The dining room," laughed Frank. "I'll be able to read and eat in bed."'

**PINTER**, HAROLD. Harold Pinter's extraordinarily influential career in the theatre began less grandly as a small part actor in the touring companies of Anew McMaster (in Ireland) and of Donald Wolfit. He has written an illuminating monograph on McMaster and spoke eloquently about Wolfit in a BBC television programme celebrating the great actor's life.

In Wolfit's troupe, he was in the company of other fledgling playwrights – Alan Ayckbourn, Ronald Harwood and Alun Owen. He acted under the name of David Baron, which slightly spoils a story of a quirky piece of casting which Wolfit imposed on him. It has been suggested it was because he was irritated by all these eager young playwrights, Pinter among them, submitting plays to him, that Wolfit revived, in 1953, Matheson Lang's prodigious touring success, *The Wandering Jew*, in which he had played with Lang at the outset of his career. At the first rehearsal, he told the company that he needed a young man for the thankless role of carrying the cross past a window in the first scene. His baleful eye surveyed the collection of actor dramatists and finally it lit on the hapless David Baron.

'Pinter,' he said in his deepest tones. 'Pinter shall carry the cross.'

At one point during his difficult early struggles Harold Pinter worked as a waiter at the National Liberal Club. He heard two elderly members discussing when Franz Kafka's novel, *The Trial* was published. According to Pinter he stopped and said, 'You've got that wrong. It wasn't published in 1923. It was 1929.'

The members said, 'Thank you very much' but 'the head waiter dragged me into the kitchen and said, "You're fired. You don't speak to the customers."'

In later life, Pinter has acquired a reputation for taking himself as seriously as Wolfit. He is almost as committed to cricket. He wrote a poem about Sir Len Hutton. It was characteristically economical:

> I saw Hutton in the prime;
> Another time, another time.

The story goes that he sent the couplet to Simon Gray, who read it and left it at that. However, Pinter pursued a critical evaluation and phoned Gray to get it.

'I'm sorry, I haven't finished reading it yet,' was Gray's witty evasion.

Pinter poses peculiar problems for his translators with some of his more colloquial English. In one German production of *The Birthday Party* the audience was justifiably puzzled by the line, 'Who peed against the city gates in Melbourne?' What Pinter, the cricket enthusiast, had written was, 'Who watered the wicket at Melbourne?'

Pinter's reputation as a combative cocktail party or dinner guest grows. Another source suggests that he no longer dines outside London without establishing the distance of the venue from a railway station. This is said to be because on one occasion he stormed out of a dinner party after a political row and, finding it was too far to walk to the station, had to creep back in humiliation.

His separation from his first wife Vivien Merchant and his affair with Lady Antonia Fraser (later his second wife) prompted one of the bitterest remarks from a rejected spouse: 'He didn't need to take a change of shoes. He can always wear Antonia's. She has very big feet, you know.'

Justin Mortimer's portrait of Pinter, painted in 1991, caused some comment when it was unveiled at the National Portrait Gallery that August.

His father-in-law, Lord Longford, said, 'He looks frightfully sad.'

'Yes,' agreed Lady Antonia Fraser, 'he's thinking about the Kurds and the people of East Timor. It's his human rights face. Terribly appropriate.'

**PLATO**. An early critic, Plato was also as a young man a playwright, but he burnt his tragedies at the instigation of Socrates. This may have been because he had read them, but that is probably an unworthy thought.

Plato on actors is unqualified: 'And therefore when any of these pantomimic gentlemen, who are so clever that they can imitate anything, comes to us, and makes us a proposal to exhibit himself and his poetry, we will fall down and worship him as a sweet and holy and wonderful being: but we must also inform him that in our state such as he are not permitted to exist: the law will not allow them. And so after we have anointed him with myrrh, and set a garland of wool upon his head, we shall send him away to another city.'

In other words, 'Get out of town!'

**PORTER**, Cole Albert. Porter was born in Peru, Indiana, into a rich family. His mother was much the most important influence on him. She added his middle name in childhood because a gypsy had told her that his initials should spell a word (CAP). From his father, a druggist, he derived an interest in poetry and particularly in Browning's complicated rhymes. Another early influence was a dirty book shop which he passed on the way to school and which generated a life-time facility for off-colour rhyming jokes – relentlessly exploited in songs like, 'But in the morning? No!'

He was sent eastwards to a snob school where the headmaster preached the doctrine, 'A gentleman never eats. He breakfasts, he lunches, he dines, but he *never* eats.' Yale merged into Harvard, where Porter read law, continued to write for undergraduate revues and progressed to Broadway with a semi-amateur Society revue, *See America First.*

Moving on to Paris, Porter was variously reported as a Foreign Legionnaire, an officer of the Zouaves, a member of the French Army, a corporal, a captain, an American aviator and AOC to the head of a relief organisation behind the lines in World War One. He probably spent most of his war behind a piano.

He married Linda Lee Thomas – eight years older, a beauty and the woman who administered the final finishing touches to his French polish. Her first husband had given her the Hope Diamond which she returned after 24 hours because she disliked its 'dirty blue colour'. He also had the distinction of being the first American known to have killed a man in a car accident. Linda eventually divorced him when his infidelities became too blatant. Porter later met the girl who precipitated the critical action: 'Oh,' she said. 'I don't know whether I should meet you or not. You see I was your wife's ex-husband's mistress.'

Established in the Rue Monsieur, the new couple were known as *Les Coleporteurs.* Porter worked hard at his music and at giving the opposite impression. By 1927 he had decided to make a purposeful assault on Broadway. Irving Berlin, whose wife Ellen Mackay was a friend of Linda Porter (her father had been a suitor while Linda was between marriages), introduced him to an agent, Louis Schurr, who presented him to E. Ray Goetz (Berlin's first brother-in-law), for whom he wrote the score of *Fifty Million Frenchmen Can't Be Wrong.* Later, when a horse rolled over on Porter, crippling him into agony for the rest of his life, he said, 'Fifty million Frenchmen can't be wrong – they eat horses.'

With theatrical success, his life became more extravagant – bouts of composing interspersed with world tours and cruises, including the costly chartering of a Japanese train to get to Nagasaki – all at the height of the Depression.

These sorties often lent colourful explanations to his sources of inspiration. 'Night and Day' he claimed sprang from a Mohammedan call to prayer heard in Morocco. The verse may have originated at a rain-swept beach luncheon in Newport, where Mrs Astor's complaint that 'The drip, drip, drip, is driving me mad' sent him racing to the piano. 'Begin the Beguine' he claimed was born in Kalabahi Island, New Guinea; 'The Kling-Kling Bird in the Divi Divi Tree' in New Zealand; and 'It's Delightful, it's Delicious, it's Delovely' reflected the three reactions of Porter, his wife and their travelling companion, Monty

Woolley, to the spectacle of the dawn rising over the harbour at Rio de Janeiro.

Some of his lyrics provoked protest. 'Love For Sale' was frowned upon and the white girl who introduced it was quickly replaced by Elisabeth Welch. In 1926, the critic Gilbert Seldes gave his thumbs-down to one of Porter's funniest narrative lyrics, 'The Oyster', pronouncing it indelicate. It was withdrawn and not revived until Ben Bagley rediscovered it in the sixties.

Porter held Hollywood in some contempt, boasting that he had made Louis B. Mayer weep when he played him 'In The Still Of The Night' – 'Who could possibly top that?' he laughed. On the other hand, he used his trips to Los Angeles to escape from Linda Porter, who did not approve the louche Californian life-style or Porter's easy access to beach boys.

Towards the end of the thirties, Porter's scores pleased the public more than the critics, but his greatest success came after the revolution in musical taste wrought by *Oklahoma!* Porter's contribution to the New Wave was *Kiss Me Kate,* a commission which he accepted against his better judgement on the urging of the book writers, Sam and Bella Spewack. The final result was a triumph and balm to Porter's battered ego. His pleasure was short-lived. Rodgers and Hammerstein opened *South Pacific* a few months later and the airwaves echoed with 'Some Enchanted Evening'. Entertaining an out-of-town guest at the Waldorf, Porter's ears were assaulted by constant requests for the song. Eventually his ill-informed friend asked who wrote it.

'Rodgers and Hammerstein,' said Porter bitterly, 'if you can imagine it taking two men to write one song.'

**PORTER**, Eric. Eric Porter's fine Shakespearean theatre work is often overshadowed in the public mind by his performance on television as Soames in *The Forsyte Saga*. His first Lear was at Bristol. Peter O'Toole, who was in the company, confirms that at the dress rehearsal the director, having given detailed notes to the rest of the company, turned playfully to his leading actor and said, 'A touch ham, Eric.'

Porter who was, not unnaturally, tense, chased him out of the theatre and all the way up King's Street to the tramway centre, still in his flowing white beard and billowing robes. Oh, to have been a witness.

**PORTER**, Nyree Dawn. Nyree – originally Ngaire when she arrived in Europe from New Zealand – was a sterling actress and singer who achieved great fame as Irene in BBC television's *The Forsyte Saga*. She had the misfortune to cop an inaccurate, sub-standard Noel Coward quip: 'Nyree Dawn Porter? The three worst actresses in the English language!'

**POTTER**, Mrs Brown. James Cairncross supplies this anecdote:

'While working at the Salisbury Playhouse in the late forties, I became acquainted with the late Sir Reginald Kennedy Cox, whose knighthood had been awarded some years before for his excellent work with deprived boys in London's East End. By the time I met him he had been retired for some time, was living in a beautiful house in the Cathedral Close and took an active interest in the affairs of the theatre.

'One day, over morning coffee in his house, he revealed that in his youth he had written a play on that well-known recipe for theatrical disaster, Mary, Queen of Scots; and not only written it but had had it performed in London (I think perhaps for some kind of Sunday night performance), with Mrs Brown Potter in the leading role.

'I know little of this lady, except that she was a kind of touring version of the much better known Mrs Patrick Campbell and that she is said to be among the select few actresses who have played Hamlet. I asked Sir Reginald how she had fared as the ill-fated queen. "My dear fellow," he replied. "What is one to make of an actress who, on a London first night, turns to one of the Four Marys and hisses under her breath, 'Say my next line for me dear, I've never liked it!,'" '

Mrs Brown Potter also had some celebrity as a picture postcard beauty. In the novel *Trottie True,* a character whose profession was colouring these cards asks for a moment's grace because 'I'm just touching up Mrs Brown Potter.'

**POTTER**, Dennis. Dennis Potter, the playwright whose credits need not be recited here, sprang a new story on his faithful public during the launch of his television show *Lipstick on Your Collar* – the third instalment in his song-and-dance trilogy.

He recalled an old officer from his days as a National Service other rank. 'Pottah!' the major bawled.

'Sah!' responded Potter, coming running.

'How do you spell "accelerator"?' asked the old boy. 'I've been through all the blasted ex's in this bloody dictionary and I can't find it.'

**POTTER**, John S. A fit-up manager of innumerable short-lived mid-West and Californian theatres and companies, he is immortal if only for his reply to an actor who foolishly asked for a couple of dollars against his unpaid salary. 'What! Ask for a salary when blackberries are ripe!'

**PRICE**, Dennis. At one point in his movie career, Dennis Price was constantly irritated by being confused with Michael Denison, simply because they were both young, handsome leading men with Denis – differently spelt – somewhere in their names.

On one promotional tour for a film, the cinema manager yet again introduced Dennis Price as Michael Denison. Price took it in his stride until the manager added suggestively, 'And what do you suppose your dear little wife Dulcie Gray is doing at this moment?'

'She's probably in bed with Dennis Price,' was the swift reply.

**PRIESTLEY**, John Boynton. Playwright, novelist and critic, his first stage success was a dramatisation of his novel, *The Good Companions*, then he dabbled neatly and successfully with Ouspensky's theory of six dimensional space-time, which impressed his middle-class audience. He moved on to 'experimental forms' with less success (via well-made plays, some gentle, some hilarious). One of these was *The Dragon's Mouth*, written in collaboration with his third wife, Jacquetta Hawkes. In front of a starkly formal set, actors wore evening dress and read their roles. Arriving after the curtain went up on the first night, he was faced by an angry colonel and his lady leaving early.

'Sensible fellah, I see you are leaving too,' said the departing colonel.

In 1939 his play *Johnson over Jordan* looked a certain hit. It starred Ralph Richardson, was directed by Basil Dean, had music by the young Benjamin Britten and a revolutionary lighting technique so that Richardson could walk over Jordan into an azure empyrean as the curtain fell. The reading went well and Priestley left for the Continent full of confidence. He returned to watch the dress rehearsal into which all this beauty and talent had been poured by Basil Dean. He watched it without comment until the curtain fell, then he turned to Dean.

'Well, Basil,' he said, 'you've buggered that.'

It didn't run.

J.B. Priestley was inordinately proud of his plays, his novels and the money he had made from them. At the Savile Club, he was asked what he would do if he won £100,000.

'I've got £100,000,' he replied grumpily.

'Yes, but what if you won another £100,000?'

'I've got another £100,000.'

**PRINTEMPS**, Yvonne. The enchanting French singer-actress appeared in London in *Conversation Piece* and treated audiences to this unusual rendering of a Coward line: 'A cloud 'as pissed across the sun.'

**PROCTER**, Patrick. There was a plan for Patrick Procter to design the production of Sandy Wilson's *Valmouth* at the Chichester Festival. Procter was introduced to Wilson and told him how excited he was. Wilson was pleased. 'Oh, yes,' said Procter. '*Salad Days* is my favourite show.' *Salad Days* is by Julian Slade. *Valmouth* at Chichester was designed by the team Mr and Mrs Andrew Brownfoot, known in the theatre as 'the Brown-feet'.

**PRODIGIES**. Master Betty (William Henry West, 1791–1874), born in Ulster, was known as the Young Roscius; he took London by storm in the season 1804–5. His Hamlet at Drury Lane caused Fox to whisper to Samuel Rogers, 'This is finer than Garrick.' Also present were Canning, the Duke of Devonshire and Pitt, the Prime Minister. After a few seasons, the public tired of him and his Richard III was hissed off stage. He went to Cambridge, attempted a comeback and afterwards lived in obscurity, his fortune squandered by his father.

He led to a rash of imitators. There was Miss Feron, aged eight, known as the Infant Billington (after an opera singer, Miss Billington); Miss Lee Sugg, aged seven, called the Young Roscia; Master Brown, aged thirteen, the Ormskirk Roscius; Master Fori, aged eight, the Young Orpheus; Master Byrne, aged nine, the Infant Vestris; Master Saunders, aged fourteen, the Infant Clown. There was an Infant Hercules, an Infant Candle-snuffer, a Comic Roscius and an eight-year-old, Miss Mudie, who played adult roles – as wife and mistress.

Even dogs got in on the act and in 1784 Scalioni's troupe of performing dogs broke records at Sadler's Wells acting *The Deserter* under their leader, Moustache!

**PTASZYNSKI**, André. The enterprising producer of *Return to the Forbidden Planet* showed great resilience when he suffered the cruel misfortune of seeing the Savoy Theatre burn down before he could start the run of his production of *Thark,* for which he had record bookings. Bravely, he contemplated an advertising campaign boasting, 'The Hottest Seats in Town' and 'Not a Seat in the House'.

# — 2 —

QUILLEY, Denis. Denis Quilley was a fine actor and singer, who often crossed my path. He and Jane Wenham starred in a radio musical I wrote with Leopold Antelme for BBC West in the 1950s; but I think I only *helped* his career on one occasion. When he was rehearsing the bitchy Sir Benjamin Backbite in Jonathan Miller's production of *School for Scandal* for the National Theatre, he couldn't seem to find the character. He took his troubles to the good Doctor.

'I can't find Benjamin Backbite.'

Dr Jonathan thought for a second.

'Do you know Ned Sherrin?' he asked.

'Of course! Now I understand exactly,' said Denis and had no further trouble with his characterisation.

# — $\mathscr{R}$ —

**RACHEL** (Eliza Felix). One of the greatest French tragediennes, Rachel was born into a poor Jewish family and discovered, Piaf-like, singing in the streets. Her big successes were in Corneille and Racine, in a revival of *Marie Stuart* by Lebrun and as *Adrienne Lecouvreur* by Scribe and Legouvé; her farewell was in this role at Charleston, South Carolina. It was an odd spot for a farewell to a career of immense financial and artistic success, given at the request of a few fashionable members of Southern society on the announcement that at only 38 she was ravaged by tuberculosis.

The actor Chery, who played Michonnet in this production, recorded its pathos. It was, he wrote, 'The most painful spectacle I shall ever experience . . . I saw her barely able to remain on her feet, barely able to speak, coughing at each word, holding her breath to stifle this cough, gripping my arm in order not to fall, and despite her suffering, I saw her find the energy to carry on to the end of her part with indomitable courage.'

An extreme example of the old tradition of 'Doctor Theatre' injecting enough energy to give a performance.

**RAPPAPORT**, David. The best known British dwarf actor capitalised on a successful career in England to make an initial hit in America. It ended in disappointment and suicide and a last engagement on *LA Law* defending a 'dwarf throwing' club in court, a brave and splendid performance.

Faced by a chat show host in America, Rappaport answered the obvious question, 'Do you find any difficulties here with being, um, unusual?'

'With what? Do you mean my accent?'

The interviewer was not as inventive as Jack Paar, who greeted Michael

Dunn, a famous American dwarf, who hopped up beside him on an interviewing stool with, 'Tell me, Michael, how do you put people at ease?'

**RATTLE**, Simon. Simon Rattle's combination of rapport and control of an orchestra was never better demonstrated than when he conducted the Berlin Philharmonic, still fumbling for a musical identity in the vacuum left by von Karajan. Finding the musicians talkative at rehearsal, he easily got away with, 'Gentlemen, I have been told you had an amazing sound. I hadn't realised it could be heard when you weren't playing.'

**RAY**, Ted. Ted Ray had a computer-like memory for jokes and a tremendous aptitude for the quick retort. On the occasion of his installation as King Rat at a Water Rats dinner dance, the toast-master announced that the new King Rat would now say grace.

Somewhat embarrassed by this unfamiliar chore, Ray mumbled. The domineering toast-master shouted, 'Speak up, sir. Your guests cannot hear you.'

Ray was back on his own ground: 'You mind your own business,' he said. 'I'm not talking to them.'

His big break came just after World War Two when he supported Danny Kaye in his record-breaking engagement at the Palladium and scored a huge success. His real family name was Olden and in his early days he reversed it to provide his stage name 'Nedlo' – gypsy violinist. At one stage he re-named himself Hugh Nique. Addressing a daunting audience of fellow pros in an after-luncheon speech, he opened with, 'You will be wondering why I sent for you

**RAYMOND**, Cyril. The solid, reliable Cyril Raymond was always dismissed mockingly by Kenneth Tynan as 'that-very-good-actor-Cyril-Raymond'.

**REAGAN**, Nancy. Nancy Davis, as she was when an actress, attracted far more attention as First Lady than as a theatre and film performer: by the end of the Reagan reign in 1989, there was an industry in Nancy Reagan jokes. On television, Johnny Carson suggested that her religion was Christian – Dior. On being asked if she understood poor people, she is supposed to have said, 'Yes, if they speak very slowly.'

A BBC commentator, watching her teetering on stiletto heels, her hair impeccably coiffured, echoed the hoary crack about Ann Miller and said, 'I hope she doesn't fall and break her hair.' Robin Williams commented that when Nancy was drinking a glass of water, he had never seen Ronnie speak.

In her scabrous biography, Kitty Kelley tells the story of an elderly actor who danced with delight after the inauguration saying, 'I screwed the First Lady in summer stock!', but fails to recount the story of the distinguished character actress, previously married to an agent, who was presented to the Reagans when her play opened in Washington. As Nancy came down the line, she embraced her. When the presidential entourage moved on, the playwright, also in the line-up, reproved her.

'You can't do that now she is First Lady.'

'Why not?' she queried. 'My first husband fucked her.'

**REDGRAVE**, Sir Michael. The splendour of Michael Redgrave's illustrious career was dimmed towards the end of his life by the cruel onset of Parkinson's disease, which dictated his last appearances – in a play of Simon Gray's at the National, where he sat through the performance as a noble, dominating presence; and in John Mortimer's *A Voyage Round My Father* at the Haymarket Theatre, where he was helped by a radio prompter in his ear. This worked well for the first couple of performances, until Redgrave found himself the involuntary relayer of taxi instructions which invaded the frequency on which his prompter was transmitting.

However, in his earlier career he had performed prodigious feats of memory. In one of his finest film achievements, as Barnes Wallis in *The Dam Busters,* he was faced with a long, solo briefing to a formidable array of stage senior Army and Air Force officers. The master shot was to be some ten or fifteen minutes long. Redgrave and his director decided to go for it in one take. The performance was impeccable and Redgrave relaxed, exhausted, as the director called 'Cut!' The star found himself beside an extra who confided to him helpfully, "Ere, 'ave you worked for this company before? You wanna watch 'em. They're very bad at payin' for extra dialogue.'

Redgrave, who played Hamlet at Stratford at around 50, is reputed to have been in receipt of one of Glen Byam Shaw's subtlest notes. After giving detailed criticisms to the rest of the company after dress rehearsal, he turned to Sir Michael.

'Splendid, Michael, splendid – but just a touch too young.'

**REID**, Beryl. Beryl Reid was first a music-hall artiste and a popular broadcaster with two cast iron characters – Monica, an impossible schoolgirl – and Marlene, a Birmingham teenager. Beryl Reid graduated, via revue to a secure position as a leading comedienne. Her breakthrough was in *The Killing of Sister George* on stage and in the cinema.

She also had a big success as Madame Arcati in Coward's *Blithe Spirit*, at the National Theatre. She was, however, unhappy during rehearsals and one night retreated in tears to her home on the Thames at Wraysbury – Honeypot Cottage. So distraught was she that when her friend Barbara Evans approached the house from the river with a companion, Beryl shouted out of the window, 'Oh I'm terribly sorry -I can't ask you in. I'm in bed with someone I don't know very well.'

As she writes in her memoir, 'I couldn't *believe* the words that were coming out of my mouth, because I had nobody in the house!'

**REITH**, Sir John. The puritanical first director of the BBC inspired a favourite story which went the rounds of Broadcasting House. As Sir John walked the corridors one day, he met Jesus. He asked what he was doing there. Jesus explained that he had come to deliver the epilogue.

Sir John demurred in some embarrassment.

'I'm afraid not,' he grunted. 'There was always some little doubt about your mother.'

Recent accounts have revealed Reith as something of a bottom-pincher – which ill accords with his puritan image. On one occasion he wanted to sack an announcer who had been divorced, but finally compromised, saying 'At least he shall never read the epilogue.' Another time he happened upon a senior engineer and a famous West End actress having it off on a studio table. His first instinct was to dismiss both, but persuaded that the scandal would be too great, he compromised again: 'Very well, then – burn the table!'

**RICH**, John. John Rich was the son of Christopher Rich, manager of the Drury Lane Theatre, who died in 1714. His son's career in management produced the spectacular success of John Gay's *The Beggar's Opera* at Lincoln's Inn Fields in 1728, after it had been rejected by Cibber. Gay boasted that it has 'made Gay rich and Rich gay'. On the whole, though, Gay's reputation was not for neatness in conversation. He had an irritating habit of addressing everyone as Mister rather than by name. This irked Samuel Foote, the actor-playwright, who asked him to call him by his name. 'Don't be angry,' said Rich. 'I sometimes forget my own name.' Foote was surprised. 'I knew you could not write your own name, but I did not suppose you could forget it.'

**RICHARDSON**, Sir Ralph. Sir Ralph Richardson judged the exact moment of his conversion to acting as an ambition to seeing Sir Frank Benson, as Hamlet at the Theatre Royal, Brighton, scratch his sword on the stage floor during the ghost scene, in an eerie, spine-tingling effect.

One of Richardson's Waterloos was Joe Orton's *What the Butler Saw*. According to Coral Browne, his difficulty in learning it stemmed from not knowing what a lot of it meant. He never got 'nymphomaniac' right, always referring to it as 'nymphzomaniac'. When Peter O'Toole and Peggy Ashcroft went to see the play on its pre-London tour, he greeted them in his dressing room after the performance with, 'Do either of you have a little cyanide?'

Richardson and Donald Wolfit were both, as very young men, members of Charles Doran's touring company. When Richardson played Shylock in an H.M. Tennent production of *The Merchant* at the Haymarket – opposite Angela Thorne – I told Donald Wolfit I'd seen it. He was all alert – a detective of theatrical 'business', those tricks of playing which, it is hoped, enhance the text.

'Did he,' asked Sir Donald, 'drop his knife with a clatter as he left the trial scene?'

'Yes,' I said, 'it was a wonderful moment.'

'Ah,' sighed Wolfit, his point proved. 'Doran's business!'

Richardson, who enjoyed his reputation for eccentricity – ferrets as pets, a vicious parrot called José, motorcycling in his eighties – was also a skilful theatre politician, adept at outflanking directors and authors. When he was appearing in John Osborne's *West of Suez*, Michael Meyer asked him about Osborne's reputation for not allowing a line to be cut.

'I've cut a lot. I just leave things out and when he comes round afterwards, before he can open his mouth I say, "Old chap, you've got to forgive me, my memory's going."'

His professed requirement from directors was that they let *him* think of the character: 'I just want *them* to give me a decent place to stand with a bit of light.'

Meyer points out that more than any actor he could think of, Richardson knew when he had failed. There are infinite variations on his plaintive query to a young actor in the wings after one disaster – was it in

*Macbeth* at Stratford in 1952? – 'If you ever come across a little bit of talent with the name Richardson on it, let me know. I'd like to have it back.' (Another version relates it to his *Othello,* with the wording, 'Has anyone seen my talent? It was always small, but it used to be shining.') When he played Othello to Olivier's Iago in 1938, Olivier sold Guthrie, who was directing, on the Freudian idea that Iago was secretly in love with Othello. They agreed not to reveal this motivation to Richardson but Olivier prepared to plant a kiss on him during his fit. The gesture was reserved for the first night. After it, a very puzzled Richardson took Guthrie aside and asked, 'Tony, have you noticed anything odd about Laurence recently?'

During his disastrous Macbeth he had trouble memorising the moves for the final duel with Macduff. He learnt it painstakingly in rehearsal, relying on his personal mnemonic, 'One, two, clash your swords, three, four, round we go.' Unfortunately, he absentmindedly kept these un-Shakespearean lines in at full volume on the first night.

His disgust at a bad show sometimes communicated itself directly to the audience. In one pre-London tour, he stopped to ask if there was a doctor in the house. The eager reply was 'Yes.'

'Oh, doctor,' he said mournfully, 'isn't this a terrible play?'

To a fellow actor he once muttered as they walked offstage: 'If I was a member of the audience, I'd ask for my money back.'

Michael Meyer, in his affectionate memoir of Richardson, lists two spectacular dries. One was on the opening night of *The Alchemist* in 1947. He was playing Face. The opening scene shows Face and his master, Subtle, barely achieving their refuge and slamming the door in the face of their pursuers. Richardson should have said, 'Believe it, I will', to which Subtle replies, 'Thy worst, I fart at thee.'

Richardson blanked completely, arguably the first time in the history of the theatre when a play opened with a prompt. On another occasion, when playing John of Gaunt before an audience of schoolchildren who were studying the play as their set book, he dried after '. . . this earth of Majesty, this . . .' until 800 unbroken voices chanted 'seat of Mars'. As he grew older, he took prompts in his stride. On one pre-London tour, when he failed to hear a first prompt and only took the line after a second reminder, he also took the audience into his confidence. 'Jolly useful chap, that,' he said, nodding to the wings.

On another occasion John Gielgud was deputed to break some unpleasant news to him which everyone else knew about, but not Sir

Ralph. He tried to do it over dinner at the Caprice, speaking even more rapidly than usual in his nervousness. He finally got nearly to the point and explained that at certain ages, people were apt to do something totally uncharacteristic, '. . . to do something that may even seem slightly desperate . . .' Richardson took his hand and stopped him in full flood.

'Johnny! You're thinking of getting married at last.'

Not long before his death Sir Ralph was asked to appear in a charity programme in support of imprisoned writers. 'No,' he said wickedly, 'on the whole I think all writers should be in prison.'

**RIGBY**, Harry. Ghostly visitations have always given me a miss so perhaps I am being fanciful in claiming this experience as supernatural. In New York for a couple of days, staying on the West Side in the apartment of my friend Glen Roven, a dazzling composer-lyricist, I lunched at the Russian Tea Rooms on 57th Street, just by Carnegie Hall.

One of the most regular diners there – virtually a fixture – was the whimsical old theatre producer, Harry Rigby. Harry was the man who revived *No, No, Nanette*, *Irene* and *Good News* and also gave you *Sugar Babies*. At about 12.30pm, I watched Harry pass down through the other side of the restaurant. I made a mental note to say hello before I left the room.

Lunch over, I looked around and couldn't find Harry, so, thinking no more of it, I went back up to town to be met by a glum Glen. He was a friend of Rigby's and, at a very young age, the conductor of *Sugar Babies*, which had starred Ann Miller and Mickey Rooney,

'Harry died,' he greeted me. 'He had a lunch date at the Russian Tea Rooms and when he didn't make it they phoned his apartment. When they got no reply the janitor went in and found him. He died about 12.30pm.'

Did I see Harry keeping his date or some other distinguished-looking Broadway producer? I like to think I saw Harry.

**RIGG**, Diana. Diana Rigg's early classical years were spent with Peter Hall's Royal Shakespeare Company, during which time she played in Giraudoux's *Ondine* with Hall's then wife, Leslie Caron. As the story goes, she was included in the Halls' party for Christmas luncheon. The conversation turned to 'corpsing' – breaking up with involuntary laughter on stage. Ms Rigg confessed that sometimes she found the instinct to corpse irresistible.

'Why don't you think of something serious,' Ms Caron suggested, with iron sweetness, 'like getting the sack.'

Diana must have found it hard not to corpse when she played Cordelia to Paul Scofield's Lear in Peter Brook's production at Stratford. In the reunion scene in Act Five, they are mutually sympathising. To her tender suggestion: 'Had you not been their father, these white flakes did challenge pity of them' Scofield/Lear replied *sotto voce:* 'Are you suggesting I've got dandruff?'

**ROBBINS**, Phyllis. Phyllis Robbins shot to rapid stardom in the 1940s and achieved national celebrity with the song 'How Much Is That Doggy In The Window?', a novelty number which she recorded and which became a big seller. As a result, she was persuaded to embark on a variety tour, topping the bill with a hastily assembled act – a couple of songs and, as climax, her hit number. She opened at the Metropolitan in the Edgware Road and got through the first part of the week without untoward incident. However, on the Friday night, a fuller first house was less indulgent and as she began her second song, a bored voice from the gallery cut through the restless murmurings from the rest of the house: 'Come on, Phyll, give us the dog and piss off!'

**ROBERTS**, Rachel. Rachel Roberts, the exraordinarily talented Welsh actress who starred in the films *Saturday Night and Sunday Morning* and *This Sporting Life* as well as in many stage successes in the fifties and sixties, had a volatile personality which could not cope with the different lifestyle which she inherited on her marriage to Rex Harrison. Working with him in Paris on the disastrous film version of Feydeau's *A Flea in Her Ear* she confided to her diary, 'Rex grew more and more stiff and distant from me. I suppose I drank more and more.' In her cups she was likely to disappear and make love without taking much care over her choice.

During the filming of *Flea* her part in the shooting schedule finished early and she decided to while away the spare time learning French. One night she did not return to their hotel and when she did turn up the next evening still drunk, she reported proudly, 'Hier soir, j'ai fucke le chauffeur de mon mari.'

In later years she was asked if she missed Rex's way of life – in particular the use of his chauffeur-driven car.

'No,' she said, 'but I miss the use of the chauffeur.'

**Robey**, Sir George. Robey, known as the Prime Minister of Mirth, was generally considered the funniest man in England for the first half of the 20th century. His trademarks were huge black eyebrows, a little cane, a shabby bowler and a seedy clerical costume. His voice was powerful, his attack prodigious. His habit was to confront an audience which spotted dreadful double meanings in his unctuous polysyllables delivered with the blandness of an archdeacon. Through it all there yet ran a wild anarchy. Laughter doubled as he pretended to reprove the audience with the words, 'Desist! Really, I meantersay! Let there be merriment, by all means, let there be merriment, but let it be tempered with dignity and the reserve which is compatible with the obvious refinement of our environment.'

A complex man, he had also an affected side, pretending to more education than he had actually received. One of his many hobbies was making violins. He achieved a high standard but played execrably. However, on one occasion a fellow artist in a neighbouring dressing room heard beautiful sounds emanating from Robey's. Later he congratulated Robey on the strides he had made. Robey pretended to accept the compliment before pointing out that the virtuoso was in fact the great Belgian violinist, Ysaye, who had been trying out an instrument Robey had just finished making.

Perhaps the saddest anecdote of Robey is that in retirement in Brighton he would sit before a looking glass each evening at seven, making-up, as he had done every evening for a lifetime.

**Robson**, Dame Flora. A powerful, emotional actress. I once asked her how she managed instant tears on stage, and she said, 'I think of those poor young men going down in the submarine *Thetis* before the war and the tears just come.' (This was some twenty years after the tragedy of the sunken sub.) She might perhaps have remembered instead her early service in Sir Ben Greet's company. She arrived one morning to be asked by the stage manager: 'D'ye know Ariel?'

'No,' she said.

'That's a pity, yer playing it tomorrer night!'

In 1934 she acted with Oscar Homolka in a low-tension, two-handed thriller, *Close Quarters*, at the Haymarket. In the second act the door bell rang.

'I wonder who that can be?' she asked.

A voice from the stalls replied, 'Whoever it is, let them in.'

She showed a surprising flair for high comedy on the occasions when she was allowed to use it, as in her Miss Prism. She was also capable of the occasional *faux pas,* but not slips of Gielgudian proportions. In one award acceptance speech, she pleaded modestly, 'You shouldn't give awards to me. I am an established actress. You should be thinking of unknowns – like Eileen Herlie.'

**ROGERS**, Peter. The immensely successful producer of the *Carry On* movies got a gratuitous blast of criticism from Barbara Windsor when they were making *Carry On Camping* in a particularly wet, cold, dank location. Unaware that Kenneth Williams was wearing a concealed microphone, she inveighed about their working conditions. 'It's disgraceful! Freezing cold in PT clothes with sludge up to your ankles, pretending it's summer. Of course it's all right for Peter Rogers. He drives down here in his great Rolls Royce, gets out in his cashmere coat and his Wellington boots, sits in the producer's chair calling "Carry on, girls", then departs to the bar for his glass of vintage champagne. We're treated like a load of rubbish but he falls with his arse in the marmalade.'

The first intimation that Rogers had overheard came when he passed her soon after and said, 'Thank you for those few kind words,' the second some days later when she received a large but anonymous consignment of marmalade from Fortnum and Mason.

The *Carry On* producer countered one actor's complaint – 'I should have more funny lines. I'm a comedian' – with the simple sentence, 'Your secret is safe with me.' This is, of course, a recycling of a popular theatrical retort. Mrs Patrick Campbell is supposed to have been bested in a similar exchange with Charles Frohman, In her case, she had reminded Frohman that she was 'an artist'.

**ROMBERG**, Sigmund. Most Romberg stories concern his murder of the English language or his acts of musical thievery from classical sources. He once accused Jerome Kern, who was wearing a chequered cap, of 'looking like a race course trout'. On another occasion he shouted at a rehearsal pianist, 'The trouble with you, Miss, is that you haven't enough shows behind your belt!'

**ROSCIUS**, Quintus. Roscius, the most famous of Roman actors, was a slave granted his freedom because of his skill and celebrity. After him, various 18th and 19th century actors were given nicknames – the infant

Roscius; the Brighton Roscius; the Hibernian Roscius. Master Betty – whose London celebrity from 1804 to 1806 was the best known – was so adored that one fan, who heard he was staying in Dymchurch en route to perform in Coventry, waited at table in the inn at which he was staying to catch a glimpse of him.

The original (died 62 BC) is said to have had some deformity in his face which encouraged him to wear a mask, but often audiences would ask him to remove it that they might hear his beautiful speaking voice.

His most celebrated reference is in *Hamlet* Act II, Sc 2. when Hamlet, teasing Polonius about his age, says '. . . when Roscius was an actor in Rome'.

**ROSE**, Billy. Robert Russell Bennett, one of Broadway's great orchestrators, was involved in Billy Rose's production, *Seven Lively Arts.* The concept involved ballet, opera, Broadway, vaudeville, jazz, concert music and modern painting.

Stravinsky was commissioned to write *Scenes de Ballet* for Markova and Dolin. After the Philadelphia opening, Rose cabled Stravinsky: 'Your music great success stop. Could be sensational success if you would authorise Robert Russell Bennett retouch orchestrations stop. Bennett orchestrates even the work of Cole Porter.'

Stravinsky's reply was: 'Satisfied with great success!'

**ROYALTY AT THE THEATRE**. Early stories about royalty and the theatre are sketchy. The Earl of Essex (or one his followers) is said to have hoped to have fuelled his revolt against Queen Elizabeth I in 1601 by commissioning The Lord Chamberlain's Players to mount a production of *Richard II*. It had obviously had little or no effect. Let us hope the actors got their money. The unconcerned queen is supposed to have commanded another production soon after. There is little evidence to suggest that she enjoyed Falstaff so much that she ordered Shakespeare to depict 'the fat Knight in love' in *The Merry Wives of Windsor*.

The Puritans suppressed the theatre but came the Restoration under Charles II and his suggested plea on behalf of his actress-mistress, Nell Gwyn – 'Let not poor Nelly starve.'

It is with the Georges that theatre becomes a fairly regular pastime of monarchy. George I deemed it advisable to order court entertainments and was supposed to go along with Shakespeare's histories and to point out the subtleties to the Prince of Wales. When George II was king, the news that the Young Pretender had been defeated reached him when he was in his box at Drury Lane. As the news spread through the theatre, the audience began to sing a new hit, an anti-Pretender song called 'God Save the King'.

George II's preference was for music but he was persuaded to attend a performance by Garrick as Richard III. Unfortunately, the actor who took his fancy was the lowly impersonator of the Lord Mayor of London. Right up to Richard's search for a horse on Bosworth field, the king was still asking, 'Will dat Lord Mayor not come again?'

However, George III's tastes were low-brow. When his father, Prince Frederick, talked of sponsoring a Shakespeare season – a new play a week until he had run through the entire canon – George was against the idea. 'Was ever such sad stuff as a great part of Shakespeare?' he protested, 'only one must not say so.' He thought Garrick 'a great fidget who never could stand still'. However, he allowed Mrs Siddons to read to the princesses and enjoyed theatre as long as scenes of great unhappiness were avoided. He loved low comedy; clowns inspired enthusiasm in him. He even relished jokes about 'Farmer George's' interest in agriculture. 'Hee, hee, good, they mean my sheep!' he would chuckle, when topical references were inserted.

George III was a Drury Lane regular, but in 1800 his arrival in his box for a performance of *She Would and She Wouldn't* was greeted by a would-be assassin's bullet. It missed and landed in a pillow at the side of his box. The would-be assassin, Hatfield, an ex-soldier, was grabbed by the mob. Later a medal was struck to commemorate the king's escape, but on the spot Sheridan ran up an extra verse for the National Anthem which the loyal cast sang for their king.

A public row in the foyer at Drury Lane between George III and his son is the origin of the tradition that one entrance from foyer to auditorium there is known as 'King's Side' and the other as 'Prince's Side'.

Like Charles II, George III's younger son, the Duke of Clarence, had a long affair with an actress, a much better one than Nell Gwyn – Mrs Jordan. So rocky were the royal finances that Mrs Jordan frequently subsidised her lover and their children. When George III heard that the duke was making her an allowance of £1000 a year, he told his son to reduce it to £500. Mrs Jordan had the last word. 'No money returned after the raising of the curtain.'

Queen Victoria relished theatrical performances and when Buckstone ruled the Haymarket demonstrated twice that she enjoyed his catchphrase 'Now just look at that!' He always escorted her to her box, walking backwards in front of her, bearing a lighted candelabra. On one occasion, the candles blew out and on another he tripped and fell arse over tip. Both times a cry of 'Now just look at that!' amused the queen.

Sir Frank Benson was knighted by George V, during the tercentenary Shakespeare celebrations at Drury Lane, with a stage sword – the only actor to receive the accolade in a theatre. When Noel Coward's patriotic play, *Cavalcade*, at Drury Lane, was visited by the king and Queen Mary, the rumour ran round the house that he too had been dubbed. However, it was not until 1970, at the urging of Queen Elizabeth the Queen Mother and her two daughters over luncheon, that he accepted the rank.

Some (sketchy) evidence suggests that as a potential royal bride, in the first instance for the hand of the Duke of Clarence, Princess May of Teck asked for a performance of *Romeo and Juliet* to celebrate her wedding in 1893 to the future king. Although it was her favourite play, she disapproved the ending which demanded the death of both 'star-crossed lovers' – upping the ante on *West Side Story*, she wished both to survive.

I am inclined to sympathise with Princess May. Unfortunately, I have not been able to substantiate this story: but I am fairly sure that her eventual husband, King George V, would have preferred to avoid such a celebration entirely.

Charlie Chaplin, one of whose earliest legitimate stage appearances was a supporting role in William Gillette's adaptation of *Sherlock Holmes*, remembered an occasion when the Royal Box contained Queen Alexandra, the King of Greece and Prince Christian. During one moment of suspense, Prince Christian leant across to the king in a mood of explanation, eliciting a booming, guttural, 'Don't tell me! Don't tell me!' from the king, which echoed through the theatre.

In 1918, when Queen Mary was late for a gala matinée at the Old Vic, Lilian Baylis greeted her in a kindly but impatient fashion: 'I'm glad you've turned up at last, dear,' she said. 'It's not your fault being late. But we've got a long programme to get through, so let's get on with things.' As the orchestra dashed off a quick National Anthem, she gossiped proudly, 'We always play your husband's tune here, right through.' Backstage after the second act of *The Cherry Orchard*, Queen Mary remarked, 'I suppose it all ends very badly.'

In the 1950s the Duke of Edinburgh, recently married, addressed the lineup backstage after a three-hour Old Vic *Romeo and Juliet*. 'What was that about two hours' traffic on the stage?' And Queen Elizabeth the

Queen Mother, asked if she would like to see the musical, *The Mitford Girls,* replied, 'Oh, no, I've met them all in real life, I don't think I need to see them on stage.'

Some years later Princess Diana confessed to the director of Penelope Keith's *Hay Fever,* 'It's my first Noel Coward.'

Director (shocked): 'You've never seen a Noel Coward play before?'

Princess Diana: 'Well, I am only twenty-one.' (And she was.)

**RUDMAN**, Michael. Michael Rudman's career as a director on Broadway, in the West End and at the National Theatre started in Texas and proceeded via University College, Oxford, Nottingham, the Traverse, Edinburgh and the Hampstead Theatre Club. In 1990 he became briefly the eighth director of the Chichester Festival Theatre.

He deprecated the magnitude of the task of programming a festival of ten plays in over six months. 'The entire season took fourteen minutes to plan. Two minutes to dictate a letter to Sir Peter Hall, four minutes to offer a play to producer Peter Wood, two minutes to thank Penelope Keith for her congratulations on my getting the job and recruit her for *The Merry Wives of Windsor,* four minutes to get Neil Simon on the phone, one minute to get his delighted approval for a British première, and one minute to remember Graham Greene's *The Power and the Glory.*'

He told *The Times* that his inspiration was an overheard conversation from a neighbouring table while dining in a New York club. One man was telling another, 'Shut up and pretend to look as though you know what you are doing.' An essential skill if you are running a theatre. Unfortunately, the directors of the Chichester Festival relieved him of his post before the following season could commence.

**RUSSELL**, Ken. Ken Russell – brilliant film maker, particularly of music documentaries – Elgar, Delius, and also of cinema movies like *Women in Love* came up with the most extraordinary bit of personal juvenilia in the mid nineties. He asserted that he bought his first condom from his local chemist in Southampton. The chemist was Benny Hill's father who advised Ken, 'Wash it with Lifebuoy after each use and it'll last you a lifetime.'

It does sound like one of his son's sketches.

**RUTHERFORD**, Dame Margaret. A fine comedienne and an under-estimated, versatile dramatic actress, memories of Dame Margaret's features will illuminate this story. When she heard that Edith Evans was to play Cleopatra she said, 'There, Edith has beaten me to it again.'

In *Serious Pleasures,* his biography of Stephen Tennant, Philip Hoare tells a bizarre story of Margaret Rutherford's infatuation for Tennant, who led her on and is thought to have proposed marriage to her. Having treated her with reverence, he invited her to stay the weekend and then refused her entry to his house.

'She was terribly upset – she nearly had a nervous breakdown. The butler felt sorry for her and let her in, only to find her later, in the cellar, eating coal.'

# S

**SAINTHILL**, Loudon. A talented, highly decorative designer born in Tasmania and trained in Australia, his early English successes at Stratford led increasingly to opera and ballet commissions, to lavish musical spectacles and to pantomime. He designed Robert Helpmann's production of Cole Porter's *Aladdin* for Harold Fielding at the Coliseum. At an open audition for Nubian slaves at which all (except Cole Porter) were present, Helpmann, confronted by a line-up of enormous, muscular black men, leaped from his seat, turned to the auditorium, flung wide his arms and announced: 'Loudon Sainthill, This Is Your Life!'

**SALBERG**, Derek and **SALBERG**, Reginald. Derek and Reggie Salberg owned and managed theatres. Derek's prime concern was the Alexandra, Birmingham, and Reggie's the Salisbury Playhouse. Their other passion was cricket in the tradition of Sir Frank Benson. Derek was famous for a remark which Michael Green, in his second volume of autobiography, claims to have inspired. They were playing in a scratch team near Birmingham. Salberg was captain and Green felt that a promising young bowler was being ignored because Salberg was not aware of his potential. At the end of one over he suggested, 'Why not put on Shakespeare?'

The reply was instant: 'Last time I put on Shakespeare I had to remortgage the house.'

**SALEW**, John. John Salew understudied Alec Guinness in the fifties' production of *Hotel Paradiso* and went on for Sir Alec for two performances. According to Kenneth Williams's autobiography, he was much put out not to be thanked by the star for filling the breach. Williams put him up to complaining to Guinness which, incredibly, he did. He received a gracious apology and a crate of whisky. He then protested to his colleagues that whisky was not his drink. Gin was.

Williams wickedly egged him on to go back to Guinness and point out the error.

'Douglas Byng looked shocked. "Telling people to return presents? No good can come of it." However, the long-suffering star dutifully changed the bottles and Salew got his gin.' According to Kenneth, he 'returned, pronouncing himself entirely satisfied with the course of events, in spite of my reminders that but for me he wouldn't have had any bottles at all.'

**Sallis**, Peter. After years of distinguished character performances Peter Sallis found different fame as a 'voice' in the animated comedy series, *Wallace and Gromit*. In 2006 he published a charming memoir, characteristically modest, *Fading Into the Limelight*.

Typically four of the intimate theatrical occasions he records are observations – Sallis as reporter, not principal. He was acting with Gielgud in *Venice Preserved* when Sir John's knighthood was announced: 'We queued up outside his dressing room door to go in and congratulate him. I've never felt such a happy feeling anywhere and he was standing there in the dressing room with the tears running down his cheeks. One by one we went in and we either shook him by the hand or were given a hug or a kiss, depending a bit I suppose on your billing . . .'

Gielgud entered that night to a standing ovation. On stage, 'I can see him now, his head is back, the tears are cascading down his face, his smile is radiant. Well, I thought he looked happy in the dressing room, but this, he just stands there and he stands there and he laps it all up and the cheers go on and the clapping and the stamping. They won't let it stop. But it does stop eventually, and he says his first line, which is "My lord, you shall hear me, I am not the arrant knave you think me!" And they all erupted again.'

Then there is his involvement with Ionesco's *Rhinoceros* at the Royal Court – starring Olivier, directed by Orson Welles. A glimpse of Noel Coward, backstage after the first night: 'The door burst open . . . and this time it was Noel Coward who said, at the top of his voice, "What a perfectly bloody play! This is the author." He turned round and there was Ionesco, all five feet of him, ears sticking out, smiling broadly and Noel said, "He can't speak a word of English."'

A vignette of acting opposite Olivier.

'I had one scene in particular with Olivier where we both had a row. A few days into the run, Olivier got angry plus. He got angry squared, even, and I swear his face turned a shade of green. It is quite possible that he might have had a word with the lighting man and said, "Look, I'd like you to try a bit of green on me tonight, see what you think?" I don't know, but that is the impression I had at the time, and I remember it still. It frightened the life out of me. He didn't actually advance on me physically and the pallor of his face was this dark green.'

Finally in 1963 and the American director of *A Shot in the Dark* demanded of a young Judi Dench the performance her Broadway predecessor had given.

' "No, Judi, excuse me," he would say, "Miss X would always rise at this point and she'd move towards the settee, almost as though she was . . . no, no, no. I've got that wrong. Yeah. I'm getting it Judi, I'm getting it, almost as if she's forgotten something and then she carries on. You understand me, Judi?" Stuff like that was going on all the time.'

I'd like to see him try it now!

**SANDS**, Diana. The late John Dexter used to tell a wicked story about the Lincoln Center's attempts to broaden the repertoire for black artists and break the pattern of servant roles. Recognising the immense talent of Diana Sands, they decided that she should not be denied the chance to play the great classical parts – why not her Millamant, her Duchess of Malfi, her Lady Macbeth? They settled on *St Joan* and rehearsals were exciting. The snags only set in with the first preview, when the actress replied to the question of her identity with the Shavian line, 'Ah'm the Maid,' and the house rocked. Post-mortems followed and it was decided to cut the line. However, amid the laughter the line which followed it had been obscured. Next night it stood out loud and clear:

'What's your name?'

'D'Arc'

**SARDI'S**. Sardi's, the traditional Broadway theatrical place to eat, is the equally traditional scene of nail-biting waits for reviews. In other restaurants the ritual is now echoed – nervous producers slam down the serving hatches when the thumbs-down sign arrives from the *New York Times*; sycophants melt into the night; victims search for each other or their erstwhile lovers.

Sardi's was opened just after World War One. At about the time that the Shuberts built the St James Theater on 44th Street, the restaurant moved along that street. In the thirties it served as a sort of cut-price Algonquin for a group of press agents, reporters and other newspaper men who occasionally tried to hype a favourite into stardom. One young woman nearly achieved fame until too many of the group vied for her favours, and some, feeling that they had missed out, torpedoed her chances. They called themselves the Cheese Club and at least once had a modest success when they advocated that an up-and-coming actor, William Gargan, appear with Leslie Howard in *The Petrified Forest*. Howard's response was that Gargan was not sufficiently well known. Accordingly, they showered the public prints with tit-bits about Gargan, who got the part and went on to modest success.

**SCALA THEATRE**, The. The Scala Theatre near Goodge Street Station saw many famous productions, not least Donald Wolfit's *King Lear*, the most famous Lear of the 20th century, and countless annual *Peter Pans*. It was also host to some opera seasons, one being of Benjamin Britten operas. After one first night, a critic was leaving the theatre when he was assailed by a highly excitable middle-European member of the audience who said passionately, in an almost impenetrable accent, 'Vera guid orchestration!'

The critic, feeling he should not pre-empt his notice, nodded dismissively. The man would not be dismissed. He said again, 'Vera guid orchestration!' The critic, trying to escape, agreed that Britten was a master of orchestral colour. The man grew more agitated.

'No! No! No! Ver-guid orchestration!' He had to say it about five times before the critic realised that he was actually trying to say 'Where is Goodge Street Station?'

**SCHNEIDER**, Hortense. Schneider, the queen of Second Empire operetta, was born in Bordeaux to a Jewish immigrant tailor. She joined Offenbach's company at the Bouffes-Parisiens in 1885 on an introduction from Barthelier, whose mistress she had become. (He was one of the two stars of Offenbach's first success at the Bouffes, *Les Deux Aveugles.*) When Offenbach first heard her sing he asked if she was going to take singing lessons. To show keenness, she said she was. Offenbach then threatened that if she did he would tear up her contract and smack her bottom. He gave her 200 francs a month. When, much later, she left Offenbach's company in a huff over her salary, she was engaged elsewhere for less. After another row, when she was working at the Palais Royal, she announced her retirement – not for the first time.

Offenbach, who was angling to produce *La Belle Hélène*, called on her to persuade her to reconsider. Although he played her some songs from his new operetta, she refused to change her mind, damned the Palais Royal and departed for Bordeaux. On the journey, Offenbach's melodies stayed in her head and she began to regret that the role of Hélène might go to a rival. Soon after her arrival in her home town, according to Alexander Faris in his biography of Offenbach, the following exchange of telegrams took place:

Offenbach to Schneider: 'All off Palais Royal, possible Variétés.'

Schneider to Offenbach: 'I want 2000 francs a month.'

Cogniard (Manager) to Schneider: 'Agreed, come quickly.'

Schneider to Cogniard: 'Marvellous! I just want a week's rest.' Two days later she was in Paris.

When Offenbach died in 1880, Schneider, nearly 50 years old, walked the full two miles behind his cortège in steady rain. Her lovers included Edward VII, who, as Prince of Wales, was sometimes employed to walk her pet dog during her performances: 'What a good and faithful Prince of Wales he was! Did you know that he loved to walk my dogs in the Passage des Panoramas while I was on stage?'

Schneider outlived her lover by ten years, dying in 1920, having become a religious recluse who devoted her days to good works.

**SCHWARZENEGGER**, Arnold. I once met Arnold Schwarzenegger, the ex-Austrian body-building Charles Atlas of his day, ex-film star in violent spectacles, a Kennedy son-in-law and now Governor of California. We came together in 1977 in Chicago in a lift or, as they say in that town, an elevator. I don't know why Arnold was in a Chicagoan elevator. I was there to preside over the American regional opening of the musical revue *Side by Side by Sondheim*. It starred Cyril Ritchard – born 1895 – who was playing the narrator's role which I had written and originated in London and New York. (Others who followed in my footsteps in America included the Mesdames Hermoine Gingold, Arlene Francis, Dorothy Lamour and Peggy Lee.)

Ritchard moved from the West End to Broadway in the fifties. In both places he clashed frequently with Noel Coward. When he played *Private Lives* in New York he proudly drew Coward's attention to his new toupée, demanding approval. 'Oh, my God,' said Coward, 'I thought it was a yachting cap!' Back in England, they had differed over a Coward lyric in the revue *Sigh No More* (1946). The song referred indelicately to three nuns. Ritchard, a devout Catholic convert, protested, 'My aunt was a nun.'

'Very well,' replied Coward, 'Make it four nuns.'

Unfortunately Ritchard died on stage in the middle of a matinée of *Side by Side* and the company manager, an ex-dancer in his mid-sixties, couldn't wait to clear away the corpse, grab the script, dash on and finish the show – which must, of course, go on.

There was, however, a regular understudy, a charming actress based in Chicago, Brenda Forbes – who had no time to get to the theatre. Her birth date is unrecorded but she is of a similar generation, made her first appearance at the Lyric Theatre, Hammersmith, in 1927 and supported Catherine Cornell with distinction on Broadway in the 1930s. She had also given her Lady Montague (an unrewarding role) and understudied Edith Evans' Nurse in the Cornell *Romeo and Juliet*.

For the Chicago production Cyril Ritchard had insisted on adding two songs to the narrator's role – singing is not one of my accomplishments but he considered it one of his. When we arrived Miss Forbes was in a tizzy. She had been sent neither script nor song copies from which to learn her part. I rushed off to the top of the hotel (the theatre was in its basement) where there was a photocopying machine. Having produced a complete score and script I brought them back to a delighted Miss Forbes. 'Oh! What a relief,' she cried. 'Now I can study the script *and* the songs. I'm so glad about the songs,' she trilled with all the secure pity of an old pro, 'I'm told that the poor boy who played it in New York wasn't allowed to sing them!'

It was on the way down in the elevator with the script that I met Mr Schwarzenegger. As I got out I said, 'Good morning,' to which he replied, 'Have a nice day.'

**SCOTT**, George C. The powerful American actor and film star George C. Scott was the principal player in an anecdote which David Susskind used to tell. It may be apocryphal – if it is, apologies to Mr Scott – but it perfectly illustrates the self-absorption of some great actors.

Scott was starring in a New York cop series produced by Susskind. During the filming of one episode a disagreement between Scott and the director escalated to reach an impasse and threatened to bring the production to a halt. Susskind called the opponents for a meeting at the close of the shooting. The discussion began around six and ended inconclusively and acrimoniously. In the early hours Susskind was awoken to be told that the director had just had a heart attack and was dead.

Waiting until six, when he knew Scott would be preparing for shooting, he called the actor and broke the news to him.

'Ya,' said Scott. 'I don't feel too good myself.'

**SCOTT**, Ridley. In an earlier incarnation, the highly successful director of *Alien* and other major movies was a young designer in BBC television, attached to the *Tonight* programme which I directed. He had not long left art school and told a charming story of bumming his way round the United States during vacations. He got mightily drunk one night in a border town in the South and awoke to find himself on the steps of a Mexican brothel. Pulling himself together, he dragged himself inside and demanded student rates.

**SCRAMBLED TITLES**. Many a play has been helped to an early grave by a frivolous parody of the title. *Flower Drum Song* may have survived Ken Tynan's inspired *The World of Woosie Song* but the monolithic and boring *Children of Eden* in 1991 did not benefit from being known as *Children of Neasden;* and Joshua Logan's Deep South *Cherry Orchard, The Wisteria Trees,* quickly became known as *Southern Fried Chekhov.* Noel Coward called it *A Month in the Wrong Country.* When the interminable *Showboat* first opened way back, it was dubbed *Slowboat* and that was before Frank Loesser's great song, which would have consigned it to China. Carson McCullers's *Ballad of the Sad Café* had a new life as *The Salad of the Bad Café.*

I am indebted to Alec Graham – a fine revue writer and a collector of theatrical frivolities – for more examples.

Ivor Novello's musicals were always fair game – and many of the spoof titles were traced to Novello himself. For *Glamorous Night* read *Amorous Bite;* for *Careless Rapture, Careless Rupture;* for *The Dancing Years, The Prancing Queers; Perchance to Dream, Her Chance to Scream; King's Rhapsody, Queen's Bounty.* Novello's last musical, *Gay's the Word,* needed no scrambling.

A revue writer, Arthur Macrae, dismissed Coward's musical version of *Lady Windermere's Fan, After the Ball,* as *I'll See You All Over Again.*

Robert Helpmann, who appeared in the H.M. Tennent revival of *Antony and Cleopatra* with Godfrey Tearle and Edith Evans, re-christened it *The Old Lady Shows her Nipples. The Lady's Not For Burning* became *St Joan With a Happy Ending; Joyce Grenfell Requests the Pleasure* was *Never on Sunday;* and the musical about Queen Victoria and Albert, *I and Albert,* was dubbed *The Royal Cunt of the Hun*. Another play about Victoria, *Portrait of a Queen*, held its place in the small ads columns alongside John Osborne's play about a homosexual Austrian officer, *A Patriot for Me*. Wags suggested that the titles could be swapped.

More recently, *Bernadette* was known to a few as *Raise The Titanic*; *Time and the Conways* aka *Doing Time with the Oliviers*; and Barry Cryer thought that Andrew Lloyd-Webber's revival of *Joseph and His Amazing Technicolour Dreamcoat* should be re-named *Jason Donovan Superstar? – Jesus Christ!*

In America, Bette Davis's revue *Two's Company* was *An Evening Without Beatrice Lillie*; and Cole Porter's *Out of This World*, which featured a nearly naked male chorus line, soon became *Gentlemen Prefer Gentlemen*.

In the movies, Vivien Leigh's *Anna Karenina* became *Long Encounter*, and Olivier's movie *Hamlet, Prince of Denham*; Doris Day's *Calamity Jane* was dubbed *Hopalong Chastity*; and a rumoured project to film Miss Day (whom Groucho Marx knew 'before she was a virgin') was to be called *Maidenhead Unvisited*. *High Society* became *Play It Again, Samantha*; *Pandora and the Flying Dutchman*, *Pandora and the Flying Dutch Cap*. The inventive Dick Vosburgh found a new name for an Alan Ladd epic called *The Iron Mistress – Ouch!*

**SELZNICK**, Irene Mayer. Mrs Selznick, the daughter of Louis B. Mayer and later a successful producer of Broadway and West End plays – *A Streetcar Named Desire* and *The Chalk Garden* – escaped from Los Angeles after a marriage to David O. Selznick which followed one of the most extraordinary proposals. It took the form of one of the memos for which the producer was famous: 'I have been thinking of you and have decided to marry you if you will have me. I am a little middle-aged, to be sure. I have a hammer toe and I run into things. I am extravagant and once I wanted to be a big-shot. I snore loudly, drink exuberantly, work excessively and my future is drawing to a close. But I am tall and Jewish and I do love you.'

Cautioned in England, when Laurence Olivier was tinkering with Tennessee Williams's script for *Streetcar*, that the Oliviers were king and queen of the English theatre, she was happy to draw herself up and reply, 'And I am the daughter of an emperor.'

**SEYLER**, Athene. A peerless comedienne, she summed up the frustration of mature actresses with bright new directors when one such summoned her to Television Centre, having apparently looked through *Spotlight* and, unaware of her reputation, thought the face looked right for the role he was casting. Having settled her before his desk, he revealed his ignorance with a single question.

'What have you done?'

Athene Seyler was having none of that. She simply said, 'You mean since breakfast?' (A similar question to Frank Pettingell produced a flood of every play he had done since 1910, which he refused to stem.)

Athene Seyler herself told of going to the Caprice for a professional lunch wearing an elaborate hat of which she was particularly proud. She was mortified to see another woman across the room wearing an identical hat. Making the best of it, she performed an elaborate pantomime, smiling and pointing at her own hat and the other woman's. She was greeted with puzzled stares, then with irritation, annoyance and finally a head turned away.

'Oh, well,' she thought, 'I did my best.'

On getting home she looked into her mirror to find she was wearing a quite different hat.

As a young actress, conscious that beauty was not her strong suit, she was one of Mrs Patrick Campbell's victims in a society comedy. Mrs Pat entered with a group of swells and bearing down on Ms Seyler, said disdainfully, 'Isn't she pretty?' which was not part of the text. She did it for three nights, to the younger actress's discomfiture and annoyance. On the fourth night, Athene Seyler was ready. In response to the line, she put out her tongue and made the ugliest face she could. She did not have to do it again.

At 101, Athene Seyler became the oldest actor to appear at the National Theatre, eclipsing the previous record of Douglas Byng (94). She gave a platform performance in the Cottesloe auditorium on Thursday, 31 May 1990. Previously, attending the National as a member of the audience, she had inadvertently up-staged two actors who were on stage in a singularly dull play. One had occasion to yawn. Athene Seyler's voice, trained in the Edwardian era, couldn't manage a whisper.

'I do so agree,' she boomed, delighting her neighbours.

**SHAFFER**, Peter and **SHAFFER**, Tony. Peter and Tony Shaffer are twin sons of Jack Shaffer, a Yorkshire patriarch and property owner who always hoped he could persuade the immensely rich and talented boys to give up writing and settle down to a proper job. This attitude seems to run in playwrights' families. Tony Shaffer once bumped into Harold Pinter's father at the first night *of The Homecoming.* Dad asked Shaffer to have a word with Harold and tell him the public obviously didn't enjoy his work and 'couldn't he brighten it up?'

Old Shaffer's most famous property was Earl's Terrace, where flats were occupied at various times by Peter Wyngarde, Sir Donald Albery, Sir Raymond Leppard, some Russian embassy staff, Ivan Yates, James Mossiman, Ian McKellen and Anthony Besch. Visiting one tenant, he surveyed the fading Victorian floral print on the stairs.

'This place needs redecorating,' he said, 'but my son Tony tells me the wallpaper is genuine Colin Morris.'

Mrs Shaffer, having enjoyed Peter's first West End play, *Five Finger Exercise,* was dismayed a couple of days later to read in the *Daily Mail* that the monster mother was based on her. The author has spoken more carefully to the press since then.

A famous story is Binkie Beaumont's reaction to *The Royal Hunt of the Sun.* According to Richard Huggett's 1989 biography of Beaumont (quoting Brook Williams as his source), Shaffer was weekending at Knotts Fosse. He gave Binkie's partner, John Perry, his new play and when he came down in the morning heard them discussing it in the breakfast room.

'You wouldn't believe it, Binkie darling, but it's set in the Andes mountains in South America and there's this Spanish army marching over them, and there's a big battle scene and they find this Inca king and all his Indians and there are blood sacrifices and torture and mutilation and dozens of scene changes and a cast of hundreds.'

According to Huggett, 'There was a horrified pause and then Binkie whispered, "She's mad."'

The story is, in roughly these terms, in most people's repertoires. I thought it was worth checking it out with Shaffer and according to him, the inapposite pronoun 'she' was not used. The exchange went, 'Now they go up the Andes, dear.'

'Then what happens?'

'Now they go down, dear.'

'Fancy!'

Shaffer points out that there was no way H.M. Tennent could have mounted a production on that scale and that Binkie was most helpful in introducing it to the National Theatre, of which he was a director.

Perhaps the most poignant Shaffer twins story is of the first-night party for Tony's play, *Sleuth,* at Sardi's in New York. The twins are almost identical and when Peter Shaffer entered the restaurant he was given a standing ovation – being mistaken for Tony. When Tony arrived, the whole room, believing that they had saluted him already, stayed firmly in their chairs.

**SHAW**, Dennis. Between them, Jeffrey Bernard and Keith Waterhouse have immortalised the late Dennis Shaw in the play *Jeffrey Bernard Is Unwell.* Shaw, known as Den-Den, was a sometime agent (in an office which was furnished with a desk, a chair and a gin bottle) and an actor who, to quote the script, was 20 stone and encrusted in warts and played B-picture villains and Gestapo officers back in the fifties. He was notorious for his bad behaviour, 'banned from every pub within a square mile of Piccadilly Circus'.

Waterhouse left out one of his favourite 'Den-Den' sagas in the play. They were dining in a Soho restaurant and Shaw ordered *duck à l'orange.* When the dish arrived he prodded his fork into the rather dry petit pois and asked the waiter what they were. 'They are peas, Mr Shaw,' said the waiter. 'These aren't peas,' rasped Den-Den. 'These are the pellets you shot the fucking duck with.'

'Mr Shaw, I have been a waiter here for thirty-five years, and never has a customer spoken to me in that fashion.'

'You've been a waiter in the same place for thirty-five years? I'm not surprised, when you serve used ammunition as a vegetable!'

A woman once approached Shaw in Shaftesbury Avenue and stuttered, 'Excuse me. Could it be . . . ? Are you . . . ?'

Shaw: 'Well, come on, out with it. I'm in a hurry. What do you want?'

Woman: 'Are you Dennis Shaw?'

Shaw: 'Of course I am. Why the hesitation?'

Woman: 'Well, it's such an awful thing to ask anybody.'

**SHEARER**, Norma. Norma Shearer hardly seemed the stuff of movie stars – ankles too thick, waist too wide, eyes a pale blue which D.W. Griffith said would photograph blank in a close-up, and one sporting a cast. Robert Morley once asked her, 'How did you become a movie star?'

She replied, 'I wanted to.'

She came to New York from Canada with her mother and sister, determined to make her way modelling for ads for dental pastes, soft drinks and car tyres, posing as 'Miss Lotta Miles'. She developed her screen poise by staring at a looking glass: 'I could smile at a cake of laundry soap as if it were dinner at the Ritz.'

Her determination included marrying Irving Thalberg, the whizz kid who wielded power at MGM: she had to sit it out while Thalberg's interest in Constance Talmadge was not returned. When the marriage finally happened, Joan Crawford, also an MGM actress, moaned, 'What chance do I have, now Norma Shearer's sleeping with the boss?'

Anita Loos said, 'Norma was bent on marrying her boss and Irving, preoccupied with his work, was relieved to let her make up his mind.'

She was established as 'Queen of the Lot'. They had two children and she made few films after Thalberg died young in 1936. She had affairs with Mickey Rooney and George Raft before marrying her ski instructor, twelve years her junior.

Mrs Patrick Campbell has, as so often, a last word. She told Shearer she found her 'So sane for a movie star.'

**SHERIDAN**, Richard Brinsley. The son of the prominent Irish actor/ manager, Thomas Sheridan, Richard Brinsley's three great comedies, *The Rivals, The School for Scandal* and *The Critic* are his legacy, but he left codicils of wit and anecdote as a parliamentarian and as a manager. He dismissed Dundas, a member of William Pitt's cabinet, with: 'The Right Honourable Gentleman is indebted to his memory for his jests and his imagination for his facts.' Accused by Pitt of being drunk in the House of Commons, he recalled an epigram written to commemorate an occasion on which Pitt and Henry Dundas staggered into the House together, both incapacitated:

> 'I can't see the Speaker,
> Pray, Hal, do you?'
> 'Not see the Speaker, Bill?
> 'Why, I see two.'

Two dukes told him one day in St James's that they had been trying to decide if he was a greater fool or rogue. Insinuating himself between them and taking an arm of each, he said solemnly, 'Why, i'faith, I believe I am between both.' When his son announced his intention of entering the House and proclaiming his independence of party by writing clearly on his forehead the words, 'To Let', Sheridan suggested, 'And under that, Tom, write "unfurnished".'

His wit was brightest in adversity. Always in debt, he once mused on why, since he was Irish, he was not O'Sheridan – 'For in truth we owe everybody'. When he owed Mrs Siddons, she sailed in to beard him and emerged satisfied. Quizzed as to how this came about, she explained that he had promised to pay her the next month on condition that she lent him £50 – 'So you see I have attained my object.'

His finest hour came in the House of Commons in 1809 when it was announced that his theatre, Drury Lane, was on fire. He opposed a motion to adjourn the House: 'Whatever the extent of the private calamity, I hope it will not interfere with the business of the country.' Later, watching his theatre burn from a neighbouring Piazza coffee-house, with a drink in his hand, he repulsed sympathy, saying, 'A man may surely be allowed to take a glass by his own fireside.' His resolve only cracked when he heard 'that the harpsichord, on which his first wife [Elizabeth Ann Linley] was wont to play, was gone too. Then he burst into tears.'

He spent his last years in dire poverty and then was buried in great style in Westminster Abbey. 'France,' commented a French newspaper, 'is the place for a man of letters to live – England is the place for him to die.'

**SHEVLOVE**, Burt. Claudette Colbert was driving through Hyde Park with the American writer, director and wit.

'What are those trees, Burt?' she asked.

'They're plane trees, Claudette.'

'And what are those pink flowers?'

'Rhododendrons.'

'Oh yes, and what are those little white things?'

'Those are Englishmen.'

**SHOR**, Toots. Peter Hay, in his *Broadway Anecdotes,* lists some of the insults in which Toots Shor, who owned a celebrity restaurant in New York in the thirties and forties, indulged. He exaggerates Shor's claim to have invented the character of the insulting inn-keeper – John Fothergill at The Spreadeagle at Thame at least has a prior claim. However, Shor's independence was bold. His respect was reserved for athletes and sports writers. When Chaplin, at the peak of his fame, turned up, Shor was unimpressed: 'It'll be twenty minutes, Charlie,' he said. 'Be funny for the people.'

He declined to be patronised by Louis B. Mayer, dismissing Mayer's 'A nice big room you've got here, I hope the food is good,' with 'I've seen your pictures.' To the skinny young Sinatra he said, 'Don't tell anybody you eat here, ya bum, you're no ad for the joint.'

**SHOWBIZ TELEGRAMS.** The short sharp prose of telegrams often brings an anecdote into sharp focus.

Evelyn Waugh scored heavily over his editor when told to investigate the alleged death of an American nurse in Abyssinia. The message he received was: REQUIRE EARLIEST NAME LIFE STORY PHOTO-GRAPH AMERICAN NURSE UPBLOWN ADOWA. Waugh checked the facts and his reply was considerably shorter: NURSE UNUPBLOWN.

Gary Grant's reply to a magazine query – HOW OLD GARY GRANT – is justly famous. He wired: OLD CARY GRANT FINE HOW YOU?

There was a classic exchange in 1898 between the war artist Frederic Remington and the newspaper magnate William Randolph Hearst. Remington cabled: EVERYTHING IS QUIET. THERE IS NO TROUBLE HERE. THERE WILL BE NO WAR. WISH TO RETURN. REMINGTON. It is Hearst's reply which sticks in the mind: PLEASE REMAIN. YOU FURNISH PICTURES AND I'LL FURNISH THE WAR, HEARST.

Noel Coward was a great telegram sender and the outbreak of World War Two inspired one to Jack Wilson, his partner: GRAVE POSSIBILITY WAR WITHIN FEW WEEKS OR DAYS IF THIS HAPPENS POST-PONEMENT REVUE INEVITABLE AND ANNIHILATION OF ALL OF US PROBABLE. When the revue *Set to Music* went ahead, Coward followed up with: SUGGEST YOU ENGAGE EIGHT REALLY BEAUTIFUL SHOW GIRLS MORE OR LESS SAME HEIGHT NO PARTICULAR TALENT REQUIRED.

Coward also sent whimsical wires to his staff. From Florence he cabled: HAVE MOVED HOTEL EXCELSIOR COUGHING MYSELF INTO A FIRENZE; and: AM BACK FROM ISTANBUL WHERE I WAS KNOWN AS ENGLISH DELIGHT.

Gertrude Lawrence caught the habit. When an estate agent in Bermuda said the house she was considering there came with a maid, a secretary and a chauffeur, she telegraphed: AIRMAIL PHOTOGRAPH OF CHAUFFEUR.

Florenz Ziegfeld, the American impresario, sent the most and the longest telegrams – however, they mostly lacked wit and therefore have no place here.

The impresario Billy Rose cabled Stravinsky, who had contributed to a dance interlude for Markova and Dolin for a Broadway revue. He suggested that although the ballet was 'a great success' re-orchestration by the Broadway master Robert Russell Bennett might make it even better. Stravinsky replied: SATISFIED GREAT SUCCESS.

The Queen, of course, used to send telegrams to centenarians. However, a consultant doctor who was announced as Honorary Physician to Her Majesty got this (not from her): CONGRATULATIONS. GOD SAVE THE QUEEN.

Eddie Cantor to Norma Shearer, whose husband was the movie producer Irving Thalberg: CONGRATULATIONS ON YOUR LATEST PRODUCTION STOP SURE IT WILL LOOK BETTER AFTER IT'S BEEN CUT.

The painter Whistler missed Oscar Wilde's wedding with this apology: AM DETAINED. DON'T WAIT. G.K Chesterton's wire to his wife has passed into legend: AM IN MARKET HARBOROUGH. WHERE OUGHT I TO BE? A one-word reply was enough: HOME. Best of the self-conscious wires was Robert Benchley's from Venice to the *New Yorker*: STREETS FULL OF WATER. PLEASE ADVISE.

I had not come across one of the ruder wires until I read Angus McGill and Kenneth Thomson's book *Live Wires*, which celebrates this branch of literature. Another film figure, Carl Laemmle Junior, cabled his father who had founded Universal Pictures: PLEASE WIRE MORE MONEY AM TALKING TO FRENCH COUNT RE MOVIE. Daddy got back to him quickly: NO MONEY TILL YOU LEARN TO SPELL.

In 1916 Norman Douglas, the novelist, slipped bail when charges were pending over an indecent offence with a young man. Twenty-five years later he came back, cabling a friend: FEEL LIKE A BOY AGAIN.

The final wire is probably fiction. It is an exchange between a Foreign Editor and his reporter:
WHY UNNEWS?
UNNEWS GOOD NEWS
UNNEWS UNJOB.
Alas, the telegram is no more.

**SHURLOCK**, Harold. Harold Shurlock was a censor on the staff of the Breen Office in America in the fifties and sixties. Acting on the advice of the Twentieth Century Fox censorship consultant, Frank McCarthy, George Cukor, the director of *Let's Make Love*, a movie starring Marilyn Monroe, Yves Montand and Frankie Vaughan, invited Shurlock to visit the set to witness the shooting of a scene which he thought might raise problems. It was a romantic encounter between Monroe and Montand. Monroe turned her formidable little-girl charm on Shurlock: 'This is the first time I've ever met a censor,' she breathed before playing the scene. Shurlock was shocked by the scene and objected to it. Open-eyed she asked why. He told her he could not allow her 'wriggling and rolling in a horizontal position.' Monroe affected not to understand. 'It's horizontal,' repeated Shurlock; 'It's as though you were getting ready for the sex act.'

'Oh, that!' smiled Monroe. 'You can do that standing up.' She kept her scene.

**SIDDONS** (née Kemble), Sarah. A matchless tragedienne who declined to play comedy, her refusal to wear men's clothes as Rosalind contributed to her failure in the role. She was one of the twelve children of Roger Kemble, a provincial actor-manager. Her early marriage to William Siddons, an actor in the company, gave her the name by which she is still popularly known.

After touring, she flopped at Drury Lane with Garrick and went on to join Tate Wilkinson's company in York and John Palmer's in Bath. She returned to London in 1782 and two years later Gainsborough celebrated her success, painting her as 'The Tragic Muse'. Handsome and dignified, with a beautiful, commanding voice, she did not improve with age and became somewhat stout. She made her farewell as Lady Macbeth on 29 June, 1812. The audience would not let the play proceed after the sleep-walking scene. Her return for her brother's benefit seven years later as Lady Randolph in Home's *Douglas* was not a success.

Hazlitt had a story of her domestic life: 'No man is a hero to his valet-de-chambre is an old maxim. A new illustration of this principle occurred the other day. While Mrs Siddons was giving her readings of Shakespeare to a brilliant and admiring drawing room, one of the servants in the hall below was saying, "What, I find the old lady is making as much noise as ever."'

Sidney Smith also observed her off-stage: 'She was an excellent person, but she was not remarkable out of her profession and never got out of tragedy even in private life. She used to stab her potatoes and say, "Boy, give me a knife!" as she would have said on the stage, "Give me a dagger!"'

In drapers'shops her demand of a bolt of calico – 'Will it wash?' – was as awesome as when she spoke to Macbeth about the bloodstains.

Recalling this incident herself, she laughed, 'Witness truth, I never meant to be tragical.' Sir Walter Scott used to imitate her blank verse to a Scottish provost: 'Beef cannot be too salt for me, my lord!' And to a servant at the dinner table: 'You've brought me water, boy; I asked for beer.'

Exhausted and dry during one performance, Mrs Siddons did send out for a pint of beer. The pot boy, delivering it to the theatre, asked for her and a stage-hand pointed her out onstage. Unused to theatres but conscious of his duty, the boy went straight to the tragedienne in mid-soliloquy and tried to hand her her pint. It is suggested that there was a Broadway echo of this when Sandy Dennis, who was appearing there, ordered a steak dinner from Frankie and Johnnie's, which was then a popular upstairs steak house on 45th Street. However, the lad who delivered the package – though not quite so naive – did spot her on his way to her dressing room and innocently blundered into her scene. Still not spotting the audience, he apologised for interrupting her conversation and added, 'Here's your steak, Miss Dennis.'

Siddons held some fascination for the Scots. On one occasion, five elderly Scotswomen forced their way into her drawing room.

'A very awkward silence took place: when presently the first lady began to accost me, with a most inveterate Scotch twang, and in a dialect which was scarely intelligible to me in those days . . . "You must think it strange," said she, "to see a person entirely unknown to you intrude in this manner upon your privacy; but, you must know, I am in a very delicate state of health, and my physician won't let me go to the theatre to see you, so I am to look at you here." She accordingly sat down to look, and I to be looked at, for a few painful moments, when she arose and apologised; but I was in no humour to overlook such insolence and so let her depart in silence.'

On her first appearance in Scotland, Mrs Siddons grew impatient for some sign of reaction from her audience. Getting nothing from them, 'She coiled up her powers to the most emphatic possible utterance of one passage, having previously vowed in her heart that if this could not touch the Scotch, she would never again cross the Tweed. At the end of the passage, she faced a silence broken only by a single voice arguing, "That's no' bad."' Laughter was followed by thunderous applause.

**SILLY**, Mademoiselle. I have really included Mlle Silly because of her name: but she was a French operetta star who feuded with Hortense Schneider in Offenbach's *La Belle Hélène* in a *travestie* role – this was a form of typecasting, because her everyday boulevard costume included trousers and a monocle.

**Sinden**, Donald. Donald Sinden played Sir Peter Teazle memorably in a revival of *The School for Scandal.* After a triumphant London run, the distinguished cast were booked for a European tour. Sinden went ahead to prepare the way and to talk up the very senior cast of players. In Norway he was received with open arms and after his hosts had listened with respect to the litany of famous theatrical names he was promising to bring with him, a man with his eye on the box office ventured a request.

'Mr Sinden, would it not be possible for you to include among the smaller parts some of the actors from *The Brothers* and *Emmerdale Farm?*'

**Smith**, Sir C. Aubrey. Sir C. Aubrey Smith was, along with Nigel Bruce, the epitome of the cricket-mad English gent in Hollywood. Mrs Patrick Campbell is said to have dismissed him as a possible Higgins in the original production of *Pygmalion* with, 'Nonsense, I couldn't possibly act with a cricket bat.'

In *A Hundred Different Lives*, Raymond Massey recalls a touring company in Cardiff which played a midweek matinée to an audience of six. The company numbered seven. Aubrey Smith, who was one of them, claimed that it was a record, but another actor remembered a similar occasion when the company had outnumbered the audience by two to one. However, the play had been *Henry IV, Part II* and according to Massey, Smith bellowed in triumph, 'Good God, sir, that play has a cast of thirty – two to one means an audience of fifteen. Ours is the victory by a margin of nine, sir, nine!'

According to his biographer, Richard Huggett, the young, aspiring Binkie Beaumont completely rejigged his flat to entertain Smith and a group of hearty fellow actors in an impressively 'butch' manner. He moved in heavy leather armchairs, pipe racks, sporting prints and a portrait of W.G. Grace and fed them brown Windsor soup and mutton chops washed down by beer and claret. As a reward, the fledgling impresario was invited to spend a day at Lords – surely a first and last, if it happened.

Golf was another of Aubrey Smith's passions. On one occasion he was practising in the wings with his stick and a ball of paper before making an entrance. He accidentally chipped the paper through the French windows of the set and on to the stage. Seeing his embarrassment, Massey reassured him that it would not be noticed. He was not pacified.

'I know, but I shanked my shot,' he boomed in a reply that echoed around the theatre.

**SMITH**, Harry B. Harry B. Smith was probably the most prolific American librettist and a fertile lyricist to boot. He claimed, alone or in collaboration, the books of over 300 shows and the lyrics of more than 6000 songs.

He wrote the book for *Watch Your Step* (his fourth that month and credited as 'book, if any'), Irving Berlin's first complete Broadway score – a Dillingham vehicle for Vernon and Irene Castle based on a French play, *Round the Clock.* On the disastrous tour (Dillingham sacked W.C. Fields, who was overshadowing the Castles), Smith heard a classic chorus-girl moan at dress rehearsal.

'I went to church this morning and I burned candles for the success of this piece; but, personally, I think it will be a fucking failure.' Berlin's score and the verdict that it was original and native American made it a smash.

Smith has the odd distinction of being the first American lyric writer to have his lyrics published in book form without the music.

**SMITH**, Dame Maggie. I always feel a little proprietary about Maggie Smith, because I wrote the first lines she spoke on a London stage in a fifties revue at the old Watergate. It was a monologue and she was playing an usherette on her first night, carrying the ice-cream tray down the aisle at a local Odeon.

'It's my première tonight and I'm thrilled as thrilled can be . . .' was her opening line. I have long forgotten the rest but, when last checked, Dame Maggie could go on for ages.

She had been at the Playhouse when I was up at Oxford: a student, then an ASM, then in small parts alongside Ronnie Barker and then a notable Viola in an OUDS *Twelfth Night,* with John Wood as Malvolio and Patrick Dromgoole beating me to Sir Toby at the audition. During the run she was spotted by Leonard Sillman and transported to New York for *New Faces.* Her notable return to London was in Bamber Gascoigne's *Share My Lettuce* for Michael Codron. Her co-star, Kenneth Williams, has remembered giving her a lotion – 'a balm to soothe the pupils of your eyes . . . Some sort of alkaline solution,' he called in explanation across the courtyard between their dressing rooms at the Comedy Theatre when she asked what is was. 'Why?'

'Well,' she called back, 'I just spilled a drop of it on the window sill and it's gone clean through the paint.'

When Codron moved the show for the third time – to the Garrick Theatre – she moaned, 'This must be the longest tour in town.'

Many of her glory days were under Robin Phillips's direction at Stratford, Ontario, where she was an unsurpassed Millamant, Cleopatra, Lady Macbeth, Amanda in *Private Lives* opposite Brian Bedford, and exquisite as Rosalind, playing it at an older age than had Dame Edith in the thirties.

At the National Theatre, she was notoriously discomfited by Olivier's notes about her diction and her strangulated vowels when she was Desdemona to his Othello. Her fury increased when the notes continued after she had had excellent notices. She bided her time until she could be sure that he 'would be in his dressing room, wearing a loin cloth and blacked up all over. Then she put her head round the door and said, "How now, brown cow?"'

When she played in Ronald Harwood's *The Interpreters,* the playwright was nervous of her, but felt impelled to pay his respects every so often. After the play had been running a few weeks – a mezzo success – he went round to her dressing room. After the initial pleasantries, she asked him what he was doing.

'Struggling with a new play,' he said.

'Aren't we all?' she countered.

Her triumph in Peter Shaffer's *Lettice & Lovage* took her equally successfully to Broadway, where she starred at the Barrymore, which backs onto the Longacre, or is it the other way around? Some time after the opening a lively, noisy, all-singing, all-dancing black show moved into the neighbouring house. At the first matinée, she could hear them loud and clear on her stage. The Shuberts, who owned both theatres, were summoned and were full of apologies – they should have realised, they had heavy black velours which could be hung on the back walls of both theatres, not a sound would come through. She returned for the evening performance. The stage manager greeted her: 'I think you'll be very happy, Dame Maggie. We've hung the blacks.'

'There was no need to go that far,' she said.

According to Kenneth Williams, Maggie Smith was once aghast at the prices in Fortnum's lingerie department: 'Seven guineas for a bra!' she complained. 'Cheaper to have your tits off!'

When her son Toby Stephens was cast in the title role of Coriolanus at the RSC she called his father, her ex-husband, Sir Robert, to tell him; 'Toby's got Coriolanus – and it's not catching.'

Michael Coveney's excellent biography of Dame Maggie, *A Bright Particular Star*, puts on record a few more Maggie Smith stories.

In another of her runs in Ronald Harwood's *Interpreters*, she took violent exception to the bilious green set and the acid green carpet which matched it. 'Invoking the name of one of the outstanding snooker champions of the day she would complain . . . "When I get out on that stage I feel like Hurricane Higgins."'

She also disliked the factory aspect of the National Theatre building in which she could easily lose her way between dressing room and stage. She always carried a poem sent to her by John Moffat which read, 'Fuck and bloody arsehole, shit, bugger, damn; I don't know where the fuck I am.'

The only story I know of Maggie Smith and Coral Browne in conversation took place when Maggie was about to play Lady Macbeth for Robin Phillips in Stratford, Ontario. Meeting Coral in Hollywood before rehearsals, Maggie asked for advice. 'It's a fucker, darling,' Miss Browne told her encouragingly, 'and all I can say is keep your eyes open in the sleepwalking scene. For some reason it rivets the fuckers.' She was riveting. I saw her.

Filming *Sister Act* with Whoopi Goldberg, a film she did much to lift into fitful laughter, there was a script problem on location in Reno. Maggie was playing a Mother Superior; Ms Goldberg a night-club singer on the run, disguised as a nun. On the set actors were querying a message supposedly sent by the Pope to his subordinates. There was no plausible means by which he could have sent it. Looking up from her chair on the sidelines Maggie offered, 'By *fax vobiscum*, I presume.'

Coveney supplies another Smith story but omits the punchline. Some months into the run of the famous National production of *Othello*, Olivier was trying to persuade Maggie to play Vivien Leigh's old role in Thornton Wilder's *The Skin of Our Teeth*. She was resisting the idea and all the other suggestions he was making.

So incensed was Olivier that during the performance that followed her rejection of the part, in the scene where he should have hit her with Lodovico's proclamation, he slapped her with particular force. Maggie was knocked out cold. Edward Petheridge, who was playing a small part, let out an involuntary cry, 'Oh, Mag!' Frank Finlay had to improvise a new piece of business for Iago: carrying an unconscious Desdemona from the Senate House.

What Coveney does not record is that as she came to on her way into the wings, she muttered laconically, 'First time I've seen stars at the National.'

**Smith**, Martin. Martin Smith was a much missed West End all-rounder who died of an AIDS related illness in 1994. He was a composer, actor, singer, orchestrator, arranger, accompanist and conductor, his musical skills having been nurtured early in the Salvation Army. He was the leading man in musicals which flopped – often the fate of home grown talent. But he did play Che in *Evita*, in *City of Angels* and both Marius and Jean Valjean in *Les Miserables*. He was volatile, promiscuous, loyal, very talented and extremely attractive. At a memorial concert titled after his one-man-at-the-piano show *A Handful of Keys*, a friend recalled one of his blazing rows with Martin. The climax had Martin shouting at him, 'You're a nasty, evil, deceitful person – and don't you ever forget, I made you what you are today!'

**Spewack**, Bella. A formidable American dramatist and screenwriter, she was best known for working on the book *Kiss Me Kate* with her husband, Sam. The adaptation of *The Shrew* was conceived by Saint Suber, an ambitious stage manager, and Lemuel Ayres, the distinguished designer. Bella Spewack, having first rejected it, came up with the idea of the play within a play and held out for Cole Porter as composer against the opposition of her producers and Porter himself. She persuaded both camps. Backers were the next hurdle. Once convinced, Porter was prodigal in composition but 75 backers had to be tapped to raise $180,000. One backer's mother ran a ticket agency. At half-way during the first run-through, the man approached Mrs Spewack: 'Mother says this is *schwatz* [weak].'

'Tell your mother to go home and sell tickets,' she snapped. She continued to promote and defend *Kiss Me Kate* for the rest of her life.

**Squire**, Ronald. Ronald Squire, a delightful comedian in the apparently effortless, 'laid-back' du Maurier tradition, had, on stage or on film, a sly, casual manner, but one which was not achieved without backstage stress.

The favourite tale of other actors is his clash with Yvonne Arnaud (empress of gallic chuckle and charm) after a pre-London performance at the Theatre Royal, Brighton. Sparks flew and they stomped to their adjoining star dressing rooms. As they huffed and puffed their way through the opposite doors, Squire turned on the English epitome of Parisian chic and snapped, 'And I tell you, Yvonne, if you do it again I'll let everybody know you were born in Brussels.'

**STAGE DIRECTIONS**. Stage directions can be a burden, a delight or an impossibility. Alec McCowan, on deciding to do a play, regularly crosses out all suggestions of phrasing or intonation. John Dexter claimed to have undertaken to direct Peter Shaffer's *The Royal Hunt of the Sun* because of the direction 'They cross the Andes.'

J.M. Barrie was a master of beguiling whimsy, particularly in *Peter Pan,* where many of the stage directions were added to the text in the Nunn Caird version, adding tiresomely to the length of the play. Shaw, too, could be whimsical. The opening of *Back to Methuselah* reads: 'The Garden of Eden. Afternoon.' Elsewhere we find 'The youth he has jostled accosts him without malice, but without anything that we should call manners.'

Shakespeare was no stranger to excess in stage directions. Lavinia must enter in *Titus Andronicus* 'hands cut off, tongue cut out and ravished', while in *The Winter's Tale,* in 'Bohemia, near the sea', Antigonus exits 'pursued by a bear'. Modern correspondence in *The Times* suggests that Shakespeare was not as geographically ignorant as he appeared for centuries to be: there is a case made that Bohemia did in fact stretch to the Baltic.

Ibsen could be demanding, particularly at the end of *The Master Builder.* The ladies on the verandah wave their pocket handkerchiefs and the shouts of 'Hurrah' are taken up in the streets below. Then they are absolutely silenced and the crowd bursts out into a shriek of horror: 'A human body, with planks and fragments of wood, is vaguely perceived crashing down behind the trees' (Archer's translation). Not easy to stage convincingly, but not as hard a direction as the American Sadakichi Hartman's (1869 – 1944) – 'The universe gropes towards a new phase of self-realisation,' or Wagner's 'The Rhine overflows its banks.'

Some demands are self-conscious jokes, like Ring Lardner's 'To denote the passage of time the curtain is lowered for seven days,' or Beckett's:

D: 'Are you suggesting that the painting of van Velde is inexpressive?'
B (a fortnight later): 'Yes.'

Max Beerbohm was probably the master in this field; and the Master's piece was the directions for *Savonarola Brown:* 'Enter MICHAELANGELO. ANDREA DEL SARTO appears for a moment at a window. PIPPA passes. Brothers of the Misericordia go by, singing a requiem for Francesca da Rimini. Enter BOCCACCIO, BENVENUTO CELLINI and many others, making remarks highly characteristic of themselves but scarcely audible through the terrific thunderstorm which now bursts over Florence and is at its loudest and darkest crisis as the curtain falls.'

**STAGE DOOR KEEPERS**. The stage door keeper who has seen it all is best summed up in a Peter Cook sketch where the old boy mutters, 'I've seen 'em all. They've all come through my stage door. All the greats – Vesta Victoria, Dan Leno, Max Miller, Gertie Gitana . . . (long pause) . . . They were terrible.'

There was a splendid nonagenarian at the Criterion Theatre who always seemed to materialise in actresses' dressing rooms with a message just when they had least clothes on. When Julia McKenzie was starring at the Vaudeville in Alan Ayckbourn's play, *Woman in Mind,* under Michael Codron's management, she had an enormous critical success and won the most prestigious British award – the *Evening Standard* gong for Best Actress. Her co-star was Martin Jarvis and the stage door keeper was an old man who spent most of his time with his head buried in a television set. Every night when Julia came in – even after her rash of raves and awards – he would mutter, 'Evenin', Miss Jarvis!' 'Evenin', Miss Jarvis!'

After weeks of 'Evenin', Miss Jarvis', she finally lost her patience and said, 'It's McKenzie! I'm not the blonde, I'm the redhead!'

He did not even lift his head from the television. He just said, 'You can't expect me to know that. The set's black and white.'

**STAGE FRIGHT**. The Concise Oxford Dictionary defines 'stage fright' as 'nervousness on facing an audience – especially for the first time.' Experience does not entirely bear this out. Often it is those who have worked longest and borne most who find it harder to face the audience – and not only on first nights. There was a case in 1995 when John Sessions, a supremely talented performer, suddenly lost his way in the middle of a performance of *My Night with Reg* at the Criterion just when he was relishing his ebullient, extrovert, life-of-the-party role.

Some weeks later Stephen Fry disappeared a few days after opening to lukewarm notices in Simon Gray's play *Cell Mates*, leaving notes for his parents, his sister, his co-star and the author/director saying that he had 'let them down'. Apparently he did a church charity the next night (a Sunday) in Islington. Dark suspicions were aroused when no trace of him could be found. 'Has something terrible happened to him?' were the words on many lips. Then to everyone's relief he was reported spotted on a cross-channel ferry and at Dunkirk. In the end he conquered his demons and returned to a very successful career. One of his most successful ventures was a television series on the nature and treatment of depression.

There have been less sensational exits from the stage. David Langton, who went on to become the master of the house in the TV series *Upstairs, Downstairs*, disappeared from the West End hit *Seagulls Over Sorrento* in the forties and turned up much later in Canada. A star Irish actor left the stage in Dublin, wandering up the aisle and out of the building during a performance of *HMS Pinafore* in the 1980s. Alcohol was blamed. But the trusting management still brought him to the Old Vic a few years later, adding a frisson of excitement to a dull production.

Early in the 20th century, an actress, Maude Gill, once revived a costume drama and engaged an actor who felt more comfortable in modern clothes. So unhappy was he on the first night that the prospect of playing a love scene with Miss Gill in fancy dress threw him into a panic. When the time came for them to embrace he lost his nerve, forgot his lines and blurted out: 'I fain must leave thee.' Then he walked off the stage and was never seen again.

There have been two classic cases among great actors in recent years. One of the most public was Ian Holm's withdrawal from O'Neill's *The Iceman Cometh*. It was years before he brought himself back with an award-winning performance in a difficult Pinter piece and later a triumphant *King Lear* at the National Theatre.

Laurence Olivier appears to have resisted the trauma with difficulty. Victor Spinetti once recalled Olivier telling him that in a well documented period of stage panic, while he was running the National Theatre and playing Othello, 'All I could see, my baby, were the exit signs, and all I wanted to do each night was to run off the stage towards them.'

Five years later, in 1970, Jonathan Miller directed Olivier's Shylock. Miller is quoted by Olivier's flashy biographer, Donald Spot.

'Almost paralysed with stage fright, the perspiration flowed heavily, his breathing irregular. His eyes went blank and there was a dreadful silence backstage for it seemed that Olivier might not continue. But he did, and from the second performance on, he obtained a generous prescription of the tranquiliser, Valium.'

There was a classic case of temporary memory loss when an excellent actor, Paul Greenwood dried so many times during an ASC first night of *The Happiest Days of Your Life* that the curtain was dropped and they started again. Unfortunately, when they resumed, stage management had not replaced the essential props which had been moved already and on which the cues depended. For the rest of the performance Paul's nightmare was redoubled. Mercifully he made a complete recovery and went on to play more and bigger parts with the company.

It can happen in America too. Imagine a nervous chorus boy about to enter opposite the formidable Lauren Bacall.

Stage Manager: 'Get on, it's your cue!'

Chorus Boy: 'I'm not going out there until they feed her.'

Perhaps the last word comes from Noel Coward, impatient at people who find the discipline of the theatre too much:

'If you lose hope, take dope, and lock yourself in the john.
'Why must the show go on?'

**STALLONE**, Sylvester. Rumour has it that Elton John thought Sylvester Stallone would be amused by his first glimpse on video of Stallone's *Spitting Image* puppet. He turned up at Stallone's mansion and played it. The television set was promptly hurled through the window.

**STAMP**, Terence. There is a Terence Stamp anecdote I longed to authenticate but which I was unable to confirm until I interviewed him on *Loose Ends* in April 1993. Stamp was in the first flush of cinematic beauty when he stayed overnight with an actress who was filming a Crippen movie. She had to leave early for the studio. She crept out leaving him asleep. Some hours later he awoke to hear the maid banging about in the next room. Then she came into the bedroom. Terence's aureole of Billy Budd curls appeared over the coverlet. 'Don't worry,' she said, unimpressed; 'we've 'ad Albert Finney 'ere.'

It is only fair to say that Terence insists that, after the maid had barged in, the conversation went, 'Morning, Albert.'

Terence, blearily, 'It's not Albert, it's Terence!'

**STANDING OVATIONS**. The standing ovation has virtually become a required reaction for modern audiences, especially on first nights at musicals, when it is led by family, friends and agents. This depreciation of what was once a thrilling rarity can be traced to the fifties and sixties habit in the United States of sending ageing movie actresses into the hinterland of America in musical vehicles. So excited were regional audiences by the sight of their legendary favourites, and so moved were they to find that they could still stand, that they rose to them at the end of the evening. After they had done this a few times, it became an accepted practice. When they went to New York, audiences felt cheated if they didn't observe the ritual there: the evening was not complete without it, they felt they had not had their money's worth. Sadly, there seems no way of stopping this pernicious habit.

**STANISLAVSKI**, Konstantin. The lavish rehearsal schedules at the Moscow Art Theater have long been envied by Western directors. When Stanislavski's company came to New York in 1923, Theresa Helburn of Theater Guild made overtures to see if the Russian master would direct a play for her company. Stanislavski was encouraging. She enquired, 'How long do you need to rehearse a play?' Stanilavski said two years.

'Two years for one play? But that's impossible.'

'In that case,' said Stanislavski, 'how about two weeks?'

**STEIN**, Joseph. The prolific playwright and musical book writer had ample proof of the universality of the theme of *Fiddler on the Roof* when it opened in Japan. He and the lyricist, Sheldon Harnik, had been doubtful until the run-through, when the Japanese producer turned to them and said, 'Tell me, do they understand this show in America?'

Surprised, they asked what he meant. His reply? 'It's so Japanese!'

**ST JOHN**, Adela Rogers. Adela Rogers St John was usually wheeled out in old age to reminisce for TV documentaries about the old Hollywood. Her father, Earl Rogers, an American lawyer who died in 1922, was perhaps an even more interesting subject. Many of his clients were Californian Chinese. As a young woman Adela was sitting in his office when a distinguished, impeccably dressed old Chinaman entered and asked her father how much he would charge to defend him on a murder count. When Rogers told him he paid out the money in gold, bowed and began to leave. 'Hold on!' said Rogers. 'Where are you going?'

'I go kill the man now,' said the Chinaman. 'Then I be back.'

**ST JUST**, Maria Lady. Maria St Just, previously the actress Maria Britneva, was a great friend of Tennessee Williams, who shrewdly and imaginatively made her one of his literary executors; after his death she farmed and protected his work zealously. She also edited a book of the playwright's letters to her. Gore Vidal asked her what had happened to her letters to Tennessee. She said he seemed not to have kept them. 'That's Tennessee!' said Gore. 'So sentimental.'

**STOPPARD**, Tom. Tom Stoppard was a journalist before his career as a playwright blossomed. After working in Bristol, he was interviewed by an editor, Charles Wintour, for a job on the *Evening Standard*. Wintour asked him his special interests, and he said 'politics'. Who, Wintour enquired, was currently the Home Secretary?

'I said I was "interested".' Stoppard replied. 'I didn't say I was obsessed.'

He didn't get the job but he did get to tell the story when he won an *Evening Standard* award.

**STRITCH**, Elaine. In her one woman show, a cascade of anecdotes pour out of Elaine Stritch, demanding her inimitable delivery. However, on *Loose Ends* she told a story of the West End first night of Noel Coward's musical *Sail Away*. The play was at the Savoy Theatre; the party at the neighbouring hotel. Aware of her somewhat exuberant behaviour in those days, Coward warned her to be on her best behaviour at the celebrations. She dressed conservatively and was surprised to find herself going up in a lift with a very drunk Kenneth More and Vivien Leigh. Stepping out of the lift she was admonished by Coward's wagging finger. 'I told you to behave properly, Elaine. I didn't tell you to come dressed as a fucking nun!'

Having told the story, she turned to me and said, 'You can edit that out on the tape, can't you?'

'No,' I said, 'this is live.'

'Oh, my god! Live television!'

'No, Elaine, live radio.'

'Radio? You mean I didn't need to put on my face?'

**SULLIVAN**, Barry. Bernard Shaw often used the Irish tragedian Barry Sullivan as a stick with which to beat Irving. He played with great success on both sides of the Atlantic and in Australia. Early training made him adept at dealing with unruly audiences. In the middle of *Hamlet* at Plymouth, a group of sailors 'who had drink taken' demanded a hornpipe. Sullivan, who had often played William in Douglas Jerrold's nautical melodrama, *Black-Ey'd Susan,* promptly gave them an expert hornpipe and then returned to the *Hamlet* in hand.

He could, however, be pompous. When he opened the Memorial Theatre in 1879 for Charles Edward Flower of the brewing family, it was with Helen Faucit, giving her farewell performance as Beatrice. Grateful for this one-night appearance in his new theatre, which London would not take seriously, Flower decked out the green room as a special dressing room for her. Sullivan demanded exactly the same treatment. According to J.C. Trewin, Flower turned to his wife and said solemnly, 'You, my dear, must send across silver candlesticks, vases of flowers and a lace pincushion for Mr Sullivan.'

**SUPERSTITIONS.** The unfortunate effect of *Macbeth* – 'The Scottish play' – constitutes probably the most famous theatrical superstition. Actors down the ages have been wary; the incidents below are the tip of the iceberg.

Sybil Thorndike, touring it in Wales during World War Two, thought it unleashed something evil. Michael Redgrave had a bumpy ride with it in 1947 – unhappy with his Lady Macbeth, Ena Burrill; elaborate stage effects going wrong when the play opened in Liverpool; and a major scene with Hugh Beaumont of H.M. Tennent when he lost his patience with a giggling school audience at one matinée and threatened to 'go home'. Edith Evans refused to play the Lady. She could not understand her ruthlessness and tradition has it that she dismissed the idea saying, 'I could never impersonate a woman who had such a peculiar notion of hospitality.' Gielgud tried to play Macbeth more than once and was never satisfied with his performance, though on the first occasion, at the Old Vic in 1930, the critic James Agate visited during the interval and told him he was so good in the first half he did not think he would be up to the second. Two actors died of heart attacks before the Manchester opening. A third (a witch) collapsed on stage dancing round the cauldron, to be replaced by a reluctant Ernest Thesiger. On the first night of Godfrey Tearle's *Macbeth* at Stratford, Diana Wynyard sleep-walked her way off a high platform and broke an arm. Peter O'Toole, who superstitiously called his character Harry Lauder, had adventures with his first night which became *the* theatrical incident of the eighties. The origin of the superstition is obscure, but its source is supposed to lie in the death backstage of the boy who played Lady Macbeth at its first performance in 1606.

Mention of *Macbeth* backstage is as unlucky as whistling or putting shoes on a dressing-room table. The whistler's crime is counteracted by his leaving the dressing room, turning round three times and knocking to secure re-admission. Green is an unlucky colour for stage decor and especially for costumes – possibly because the light in old times was green and could cancel out a green figure on stage. The rhyming slang word for stage – green (gage) – seems not to affect the luck of the show. Peacocks and peacock feathers are considered unlucky in stage decor, but so they are indoors in civilian life. Peacocks once decorated the boxes of the Palace Theatre, Leicester. When Sir Oswald Stoll bought it, he had them hacked away.

A play called *The Clock Goes Round* at the Globe Theatre had thirteen in the cast and a star who wore a green dress and carried a peacock fan. It closed after only thirteen performances. It is unlucky to wish actors good luck on first nights. '*Merde!*' or 'Break a leg!' are acceptable.

Cats have a place in the history of theatrical tradition. A black cat is a good omen during rehearsal but can presage ill-luck if it appears during a performance. However, George Hoare, the archivist of the Theatre Royal, Drury Lane, records interventions by Ambrose, the theatre cat, during *Billy* and *A Chorus Line,* both of which enjoyed long, happy runs.

The tradition of not speaking the last line of a play until the first performance ends has died out; but Dressing Room 13 is still not a favourite and knitting on stage, spilling wine, unscripted bells ringing or gongs banging have all been cited as unlucky phenomena.

**SWEENY**, Fred and **DUFFY**, James. There are many anecdotes of actors caught 'off' mid-performance. Sweeney and Duffy were an American double act. On one occasion James Duffy forgot a matinée and was discovered by a distraught stage manager in a Turkish bath. 'Duffy!' he yelled in despair, 'what are you doing here? You're on!'

'I am?' said the absentee. 'How'm I doing?'

# — T —

**TANDY**, Jessica and **CRONYN**, Hume. The English actress and Canadian actor who became two of America's leading theatre stars and film favourites – Ms Tandy won an Oscar for *Driving Miss Daisy* – have taken a share of ribbing as well. 'I never miss a Hume-Cronyn movie' was one wit's comment on *Cleopatra,* the Burton-Taylor-Harrison extravaganza in which Cronyn had a small role. But their extreme devotion to the theatre was never better demonstrated than in *The Gin Game* on Broadway in 1977, when both insisted on playing though Cronyn had a raging 'flu temperature and Tandy was consumed with anxiety. The director, Mike Nichols, had the last word. He suspended performances 'to save my stars from death by professionalism'.

**TAYLOR**, Samuel. Sam Taylor was a dedicated Hollywood and Broadway craftsman whose place in history he owes to a movie credit for one of the earlier talkies to emerge from Hollywood. It was *The Taming of the Shrew* and it read: 'by William Shakespeare, with additional dialogue by Sam Taylor'.

**TEMPEST**, Dame Marie. Dame Marie was a frequent and fascinated visitor to Noel Coward's bedside when he was laid low with piles (he used the time to write the second act of *Bitter Sweet).*

'Other visitors seldom referred, except obliquely, to the mortifying nature of my complaint . . . she came on several occasions to see me and we discussed every detail with enthusiasm.'

One of the great *grandes dames* of the British theatre from the 1880s until her sad decline over 50 years later, Dame Marie Tempest first appeared in 1885 in Suppé's comic opera *Boccaccio* at the Comedy Theatre. She was a pretty little pouter pigeon with a sweet soprano voice and a mischievous gift for comedy. She played with great success in musical comedy until the turn of the century when she left Daly's and the musical theatre after a row with George Edwardes. At 35 she made the switch before time told on her voice, and indeed liked to feature it with subsequent interpolations in comedies.

She was the essence of metropolitan chic and grandeur, on-stage and off, and was a terror to young actresses as well as to her less starry contemporaries. On hearing that Sybil Thorndike had been made a Dame, she commented tartly, 'That's what comes of playing saints. Nobody asks *me* to play a saint.'

Crammed in the tiny H.M. Tennent lift with a young actor, Dame Marie finally got out saying, 'After that experience, young man, there's nothing for us but marriage.' In her entertaining autobiography, *Looking Forward, Looking Back,* Dulcie Gray gives a new insight to this story. She has Marie Tempest closely closeted in the tiny space years earlier with A.E. Matthews, with whom she was touring and to whom she was not speaking. Matthews raised his hat, kissed her on the cheek and said, 'Good morning, Marie.' She ignored him and they ascended in silence. When the lift arrived, he stepped out, doffed his hat, bowed and said, 'After such proximity, Marie, I can only offer you marriage.' Perhaps she recycled it later when trapped in the same lift with the young actor.

At the peak of her career, she preferred to rehearse (only in a theatre) for two hours in the morning and two hours in the evening, from seven to nine. Evening rehearsals were conducted in evening dress and at nine she was inclined to put down her book and adjourn to a central table at the Savoy Grill for dinner.

Although reluctant to give interviews, she once, according to Richard Huggett's biography of Binkie Beaumont, enthused publicly at his insistence about playing in Manchester, a town she did not enjoy. 'I cannot speak too highly of the *water* in Manchester,' she said, 'it's so good for washing and so good for the complexion. If I had my way I would take *barrels* of it to London. Oh yes, it is so soft and tastes delicious. I wish all the provincial cities had such beautiful water.'

**TEMPLE**, Shirley. Shirley Temple, whose career took off in 1931, set off an anthology of stories. Her father, a bank teller in Santa Monica, complained that women were writing to ask him to father their child. He reported the fact to Darryl Zanuck, asking him to promise not to tell Mrs Temple – 'She'd be ashamed of her sex,' he told the studio chief.

Little Shirley soon had an inflated idea of the importance of Hollywood. When she met Pershing, a World War One general, she showed him her autograph book full of Hollywood stars. Pershing was unimpressed, having heard of few of them. 'How did he ever get to be a general?' was the brat's comment.

Nor was she pleased when Santa Claus asked for her autograph in a Los Angeles department store. She knew he could not be Santa – 'He said he's seen all my movies.'

She was equally clear-eyed after meeting H.G. Wells. She was told he was the most important person in the world. 'God is the most important person in the world,' was her verdict, 'and the Governor of California is second.' Darryl Zanuck, her studio boss, was dismayed that she was not encouraged to name him as the third.

**TERRISS**, William. Terriss's main claim to fame lies in his unfortunate end. Known as 'Breezy Bill' for his popularity and athleticism in melodrama, he sacked a 'super', Richard Price, from his Adelphi Theatre Company, who promptly assassinated him outside the stage door. He had been in Irving's company and was a particular favourite of the actor-manager. Sir Seymour Hicks tells a story of Irving teasing him about the meaning of two lines at the end of a fine-sounding speech which he was declaiming handsomely at rehearsal. After the third time of asking and Terriss's third halting, 'Well, guvnor, what they mean, of course, what they mean . . .' Terriss finally confessed, 'So help me, guvnor, I'm blowed if I know what they do mean.'

On Irving's genial 'No, I thought not,' he joined in the general laughter.

Irving favoured moonlight duels but in the one he fought with Terriss in *The Corsican Brothers,* Terriss, no respecter of persons, asked whether some of the moonlight might not fall on him, 'as nature is impartial'.

**TERRY**, Dame Ellen Alice. Ellen Terry's long career began at the age of nine, playing Mamillius in *The Winter's Tale* in Charles Kean's company at the Princesses Theatre. At seventeen she left the stage for marriage to the artist, G.F. Watts.

'I got ill and had to stay at Holland House – and then he [Watts] kissed me – *differently* – not much differently but a little and I told no one for a fortnight, but when I was alone with Mother . . . I told her I *must* be married to him because I was going to have a baby!!! *And she* believed me!! OH, I tell you, I thought I knew everything then ... I was *sure* THAT kiss meant giving me a baby.'

Watts now had a live-in model and instructed her not to cry – 'It makes your nose swell.' On her return to the stage, she acted *The Shrew* with Henry Irving, but their great partnership did not begin for another eleven years after she had left the stage again for her liaison with the architect Edward Godwin. It was at this time that her parents identified the body of a young suicide as Ellen. Her family went into mourning until she heard the news and rushed to reassure them.

Towards the end of her life, Dame Ellen played Portia for the umpteenth time under a new young director, who upset her usually placid temperament with meticulous directions. Eventually, her patience cracked and at a run-through of the scene she asked, with deceptive innocence, 'Now, when do you want me to do that little something for which you are paying me all this money?'

In 1919, at the age of 72, she played the Nurse to the Romeo of Basil Sydney, the Mercutio of Leon Quatermaine and the Juliet of Doris Keane. By now the Terry memory, always vulnerable, was shot to pieces, but such was her reputation for bubbling naturalism that, according to John Gielgud, they were able to whisper her role into her ear line by line so that she could repeat it with every appearance of spontaneity.

**Terry**, Fred. The young brother of Ellen and, of course, an uncle of John Gielgud, Fred Terry epitomised the handsome romantic actor. He was married to the beautiful Julia Neilson, who long outlived him. The dignified actress Violet Fairbrother, busy in stern matron roles in later life, was an autumn love. His daughter, Phyllis Neilson-Terry, tells how he once mounted a production of *Romeo and Juliet* in which, according to Gielgud, he intended to play Mercutio. However, though illness prevented that, it did not stop him casting a shy and inexperienced actor as Paris. Senior members of the company took advantage of the boy during their preparations for the dress parade and persuaded him that he needed more make-up. He already had 'an elaborate Carpaccio costume – parti-coloured tights and an Italianate wig falling to his shoulders'. They encouraged him 'to add mascara to his eye-lashes, rouge to his lips and a dangling pearl to his right ear'. When the boy presented himself, Terry roused himself from his slumbers in the stalls, stared hard at the stage, burst out laughing and cried, 'My God, it's a tart I once slept with in Bury St Edmunds.'

Donald Sinden, who memorably revived Sir Percy Blakeney in Fred Terry's perennial touring hit *The Scarlet Pimpernel*, in Nicholas Hytner's production at Chichester, scored a similar *coup de théâtre* in his first appearance disguised as an old hag. However, he suggests that after opening nights, Terry used to pay an old actress in his company to impersonate this role so that the moment she appeared, knowledgeable playgoers would nudge each other and say wisely, 'That's Fred Terry!' while the actor/ manager himself was preparing for his first dandy-ish entrance as Sir Percy.

**THESIGER**, Ernest. An emaciated, eccentric, versatile actor, he began with Alexander and Tree and created the role of the Dauphin in *St Joan*.

He had a passion for petit-point and was the author of *Adventures in Embroidery*. He was awarded a CBE, probably because he shared his passion with 'dear Queen Mary'. Thesiger once asked Somerset Maugham why he never wrote him a part in one of his plays. 'Oh, but I do,' said Maugham, 'but Gladys Cooper always plays them.' He was the object of that traditional put-down by a passer-by. 'Excuse me, but weren't you Ernest Thesiger?' He is said to have replied: 'Madam, I was.'

Visiting his old school, Marlborough, the wizened, cadaverous, mincing-mannered old needle-worker spotted a particularly well-built sixth former. To his host, the Senior Master, he confided, 'I'd give anything to be that boy's mother.'

Uncharacteristically running for a bus, laden down with parcels, he was caught with one foot on and one foot off. 'Stop! Stop!' he shrieked. 'You're killing a genius!' Fortunately the conductor heard him and his genius remained intact.

During the war he was reported as hurrying down a side street and muttering, 'I'm off to see if X Mansions is really razed to the ground, as I have an uncle who lives there and I know I'm in his will!'

**THOMAS**, Dylan. Rayner Heppenstall recalled a visit to Mousehole in Cornwall with the bucolic poet Dylan Thomas and his wife Caitlin. They stayed at a guesthouse called The Lobster Pot and after one evening of heavy drinking, Thomas railed against a classically beautiful sunset making 'savage remarks about picture postcards and visual *clichés* and continuing to talk and drink copiously, he stopped suddenly and said, "Somebody's boring me, and I think it's me."'

**THORNDIKE**, Dame Sybil. My favourite memories of Dame Sybil are personal, so I'll get them over first before rehashing the famous stories. We had met during radio plays when I sent her a comedy script by Keith Waterhouse and Willis Hall for an early episode of *That Was The Week That Was*. She had not seen the programme, as she had been acting in a play about St Teresa of Avila – the saint who levitated. It was a particularly unlucky production in that during it Dame Sybil, who was 79 at the time, jumped for a Number 11 bus in the King's Road and, failing to levitate sufficiently, missed the platform and set off the arthritis which was to persecute her so cruelly for the last fifteen years of her life.

The sketch in question was a device for cabinet ministers, played by regular members of the company, to submit their problems to an Agony Aunt, who gave appropriately simplistic answers. I got the script on a Friday and biked it immediately to Dame Sybil in Swan Court, Chelsea. It was to be performed the next day. I was surprised but delighted to get a call from her agent to say that she would do it. It transpired that when it arrived, Sir Lewis Casson had shown some interest in the buff-coloured envelope and she had told him that it was some pieces of television nonsense she had no intention of doing. When he enquired further and she told him it was for *TW3*, he said, 'But you must do it for that programme. It's practically Communist!' He had been watching it while she was at the theatre.

She arrived to rehearse for the live show, having virtually learned her lines overnight, but was relieved to be introduced to the teleprompter, a new device for her. All went well in rehearsal, but when I cut to her for the first time on transmission I could see her right hand shaking alarmingly. The convention was that she spoke her answers into a dictaphone. There was an electrifying moment as the dictaphone dithered in her hand and then, with a magisterial slap with her left hand, she grabbed her errant right and steadied it. It was a magnificent lesson in professional control asserting itself. She sailed through the rest of the sketch to enormous laughs.

Dame Sybil's penultimate television appearance was as Charles Dickens's grandmother in a biographical play which I wrote with Caryl Brahms, and which was broadcast in 1970 on the occasion of the Dickens centenary. By then, arthritis was crippling her, and as I put her into her car after one rehearsal, she groaned savagely, 'The spirit is willing but the flesh is disgustingly weak!' When we recorded her cameo scene, she was obviously in pain and fluffed a couple of lines. I sent my assistant down to tell her we would have to do it again – with the excuse that there had been a technical error. It wasn't her fault, he reassured her.

'You're a liar,' she smiled at him, 'but I like you.'

Of all her great roles, St Joan, which she created, will be vividly associated with her. She and her husband had commissioned Laurence Binyon to write a play on the subject when they heard that Shaw had the character in mind. He had seen her in Shelley's *Cenci* and had gone straight home to his wife to announce that he was starting work on a long-contemplated play about the saint, now that he had met an actress who could play her. When the Cassons told him that they had invited Binyon, he despatched one of his peremptory postcards. 'Nonsense, Sybil is playing my Joan. Let so-and-so play Binyon's.' She always insisted that the first night of *St Joan* was the one occasion when she had no nerves.

'I was exalted. God was there and I didn't care a hoot for anything except getting over what Shaw had written.' Shaw inscribed her copy, 'To Saint Sybil Thorndike from St Bernard Shaw.'

Dame Sybil's saintly image did have some cracks in it. When Marie Tempest invented ostentatious business down-stage during one scene in Robert Morley's *Short Story* in 1935, Dame Sybil played a flamboyant game of patience up-stage during Tempest's big scene the next night. They met in the wings.

'You're a very clever actress, aren't you?' said Tempest.

'Not especially darling, but clever enough to act with you,' was Sybil's reply.

She looked on playing horrible parts as a sort of personal catharsis. She appeared in *Grand Guignol* and, after performances of *Medea,* felt 'I'd been in a bath.' I have heard her use with relish the phrase 'slap-bang like the Greeks', which suggests the enthusiasm she put into a role.

'All the foul tempers, wanting to knock my husband's block off, to spank the children. I got rid of them, all. The family used to say I was angelic after playing Medea!'

Theatrical expectations were high when she and Edith Evans were cast together in N.C. Hunter's *Waters of the Moon* at the Haymarket in 1951. Frith Banbury, who directed them, tells a good story, the only record of friction between the two dames. Dame Edith complained that Dame Sybil had overacted criminally at a matinée. Banbury spoke to her about it. She was contrite. 'Yes, I was rather naughty on Saturday afternoon but I had two grandchildren in front and I was determined they should know what the play was about . . . Consequently too much underlining . . .

However, I've pulled myself together now and if you come again I think you'll find all is in order.'

Stories of Dame Sybil and Sir Lewis rising early and learning a passage of Greek over breakfast abound. However, in 1960, when Michael Redgrave and Fred Sadoff produced Noel Coward's *Waiting in the Wings*, the first day of rehearsal coincided with a lightning transport strike. The producers called the Cassons in Chelsea to arrange for a car to pick them up. There was no reply, so they drove to the rehearsal room in the Tottenham Court Road to find them both there. They had walked from Chelsea to WC1 as they had always intended, unaware that there was a transport problem at all.

John Gielgud movingly recorded Dame Sybil's last public appearance, albeit as a member of the audience – she was a devoted and conscientious theatre-goer – at a farewell night at the Old Vic.

'She was wheeled down the aisle in her chair to smile and wave for the last time to the people sitting in the theatre she had always loved so well. Lively, passionate, argumentative, always travelling, acting, learning a new language or a new poem, a magnificent wife and mother, she was surely one of the rarest women of our time.

' "Oh, Lewis," she cried once, "if only we could be the first actors to play on the moon." '

I have never heard the concern for good works demonstrated throughout their lives by Dame Sybil and Sir Lewis better summed up than by their daughter, who, Emlyn Williams reported, one day answered the telephone by saying, 'They are neither of them in. Daddy is reading Shakespeare Sonnets to the blind and Mummy's playing Shakespeare to the lepers.'

**THRING**, Frank. This extravagant Australian actor made a stir on stage in Olivier's Peter Brook production of *Titus Andronicus* at Stratford, the Stoll and on a European tour.

He made an impression regally ordering lunch in a Stratford restaurant, concluding . . . 'And I'll 'ave the *hors d'oeuvres* to start with.'

**TIEGS**, Cheryl. Some years ago Cheryl Tiegs, the American model, was paid a ludicrous $70,000 for putting her name to a book she had not written entirely herself. 'The problem with writing,' she complained, 'is that there's not much money in it.'

It sounds like small change now.

**TIOMKIN**, Dmitri. Tiomkin, the Russian-born Hollywood composer, will always be remembered for his Oscar acceptance speech for Best Musical Score in 1955. 'I would like to thank Beethoven, Brahms, Wagner, Strauss, Rimsky-Korsakov . . .'

Nine years earlier David O. Selznick had engaged Tiomkin to compose the score for *Duel in the Sun* – a picture which was soon known by its nickname, *Lust in the Dust*. Selznick peppered him with the characteristic memos asking for a Spanish theme, a ranch theme, a love theme, a desire theme, and an orgasm theme. Tiomkin was sanguine about the love theme and the desire theme: 'That I can write; but how do you score an orgasm?' Selznick demanded that he try. Tiomkin worked hopefully on an interesting dramatic crescendo and proceeded to orchestrate it with Selznick's permission. When Selznick heard it, after praising the other theme he begged Tiomkin to work on the orgasm theme again. The composer agreed and eventually his final version was married to the print of Gregory Peck making passionate love to Jennifer Jones. Selznick gave it a thumbs down. It was, he said, too beautiful. 'It isn't orgasm music. That's not the way I fuck!'

'Mr Selznick,' yelled Tiomkin, his patience finally exhausted, 'you fuck your way! I fuck my way! To me, *that* is fucking music!' Disarmed by Tiomkin's outburst Selznick finally agreed the orgasm theme.

Another legacy that Tiomkin left the world was the Russian Tea Room in New York which he founded with his wife, the Broadway choreographer Albertina Rasch.

**TRACY**, Spencer. Spencer Tracy's long relationship with Katharine Hepburn is said to have started explosively when they met to make their first film together. To Hepburn's 'I'm afraid I'm a little tall for you, Mr Tracy,' he replied 'Not to worry, Miss Hepburn, I'll soon cut you down to size.'

Told by a young actor that method acting was the coming thing, Tracy simply responded 'I'm too old, too tired and too talented to care.'

**TREE**, Sir Herbert Draper Beerbohm. It is hard not to warm to an actor/manager who was wont to cry, when asked how he felt, 'Radiant! Absolutely radiant!'

Beerbohm Tree first appeared professionally in 1878 after having some success as an amateur. He managed the Comedy and Haymarket Theatres before building Her Majesty's largely out of the profits he made from *Trilby,* his equivalent of Irving's *Bells,* a play Paul Poler adapted from du Maurier's novel. Tree saw it in New York after his brother Max had dismissed it as 'utter nonsense . . . which could only be a dismal failure in London'. Tree played Svengali and Dorothy Baird (who was to marry Irving's son, H.B.) the title role.

He was inordinately proud of his new domain and one day took a taxi to it. The driver asked for the destination.

'Do you think,' Tree asked, 'that I am going to mention the name of my beautiful theatre inside a common cab?'

He continued Irving's tradition of spectacular Shakespeare – real rabbits in *A Midsummer Night's Dream,* real splashing waves in *The Tempest,* real horses in the lists in *Richard II* – and he inspired one of W.S. Gilbert's more memorable put-downs. After one show in which Tree had given his energetic all, Gilbert contemplated the rivulets of sweat and said, 'Your skin has been acting, at any rate.'

Shaw was as vicious in print about his Falstaff in 1896 (Coquelin had admired his make-up inordinately, incredulous that he could fatten his cheeks using only skilful greasepaint). He wrote, 'Mr Tree wants one thing to make him an excellent Falstaff, and that is to get born over again as unlike himself as possible. Mr Tree might as well play Juliet.' In a New York production of *Henry VIII,* he was overheard supervising some American women extras whose legitimate stage experience was negligible.

'Ladies,' he demanded. 'Just a little more virginity, if you don't mind.' When *Chu Chin Chow* enjoyed a long run at His Majesty's during World War One the scanty costumes of the chorus girls provoked his comment, 'More navel than millinery.' On one occasion he was contemplating a production of *Macbeth* and became obsessed with the idea of casting 'Secret black and midnight hags' who were literally black. A few candidates turned up in the flesh, and one replied by letter:

Dear Sir,
    I hear you are looking for dark people. I would like to see you.
Signed Sardanapulus.
P.S. I can lift a grand piano with my teeth.

Grasso, an Italian Othello much given to foaming, frenzied overacting, he decided was far from Shakespeare's ideal: 'Grasso's Othello would never have wanted a pocket handkerchief.'

He was vivid (if nurturing a strain of anti-Semitism) about the fine Jewish actor, Israel Zangwill: 'his face shining like Moses, his teeth, like the Ten Commandments, all broken'. For his *Merchant,* Tree recruited crowds from the East End at two shillings a night. Unlike the Christians in the Hall-Hoffman production, Tree's only pretended to spit at the Jews. After the first night, one crowd member, ahead of his time, sought an audience with Tree. 'Make it a round guinea a week, guvnor,' he requested, 'and them Christians can really spit at me.'

Tree appears to be the originator of a long-running joke about billing. Some importance is given to 'and' before an artist's name. One aspiring actress asked Tree for this prefix.

'Yes, my dear girl,' said Tree. 'But why "and"? Why not "but"?' He had a variation for a cockney low comedian who made the same request.

'I'm so sorry, my dear chap,' was Tree's response. 'How can I do so? You know it is so 'ard to give the 'and where the Art can never be!' I wonder if the comic got the joke?

An over-genteel actress was rebuked with, 'Oh my God! Remember you are in Egypt. The skay is only seen in Kensington.' Of another, who had risen via the nineteenth-century version of the casting couch, he said, 'She kissed [sic] her way into society. I don't like her. But don't misunderstand me: my dislike is purely platonic.'

He was dismissive of a fellow member of the Garrick Club who complained that when he joined all the members were gentlemen. 'I wonder why they left?' Tree enquired. Of fans, 'The only man who wasn't spoiled by being lionised was Daniel.' Of critics, specifically A.B. Walkley, 'A whipper-snapper of criticism who quotes dead languages to hide his ignorance of life.' And of British decor, 'The national sport of England is obstacle racing. People fill their rooms with useless and cumbersome furniture, and spend the rest of their lives in trying to dodge it.'

At one rehearsal, Tree kept asking a young actor to take a step backwards until the boy finally said in despair, 'But if I do I shall be right off the stage.'

'Yes,' said Tree, 'that's right.'

Tree's wit was not always vicious. Sometimes it took a whimsical turn. In a post office he enquired of a girl if she sold stamps. She said she did. 'Then show me some.' She produced a large sheet. Tree pointed to one in the middle: 'I'll have that one,' he said. On another occasion he passed a man groaning under the weight of the huge grandfather clock on his back.

'My poor fellow,' Tree sympathised, falling in step with him, 'why not carry a watch?'

Tree anecdotes don't dry up with Tree's witticisms. His father was an immigrant German corn merchant who tried to dissuade his son from going on the stage 'lest he should fail to get to the top of the tree'. The theory is that this was his inspiration for his stage name.

His engagement to an actress, Maud Holt, was full of drama. Miss Holt had regular misgivings about Tree's fidelity. He had admitted that his past life 'had not been entirely unworldly'. Once they were married she became more tolerant. Indeed, one story suggests extreme tolerance. Tree had a set of rooms at the top of Her Majesty's where he entertained. Esme Percy, then a young and decorative member of his company, was invited up to the manager's suite for supper after a performance. An elaborate table for two had been prepared as a prelude to seduction. As they sat down to dinner the door was flung open. Lady Tree took in the situation at a glance.

'Enjoy your dinner, Mr Percy,' she is supposed to have said, 'the port is on the chim-a-ney piece and it's still adultery.'

However, when the matinée idol Lewis Waller fell in love with Lady Tree, her reaction was exactly the reverse, though most reports suggest that although she was grateful for Waller's affection she did not return it. Sir John Gielgud has suggested that in fact Lady Tree competed with Madge Titheridge for Waller's love and that a story circulated that both went to his funeral in widow's weeds. Presumably Mrs Waller made a third.

An accident in which Lady Tree broke her jaw halted her career but brought her and her husband together again. She, too, had a neat turn of phrase. Seeing Tree enter Her Majesty's with the elderly Ellen Terry and Mrs Kendal, whom he had persuaded to play Mistress Ford and Mistress Page to his Falstaff, a fellow actor said, 'Look at Herbert and his two stars.'

'Two ancient lights,' she said. According to Madge Kendal, Maud Holt was an eager, raw recruit to acting when she married Tree and bitterly resented an actor's attempt to help her when she took over at short notice a part which was to have been played by an older woman. He offered to 'give her all the wrinkles'.

'Don't talk to me about wrinkles,' she snapped, unaware that it was a stage term for traditional business.

The common *canard* about Tree is that he always remained an amateur. He certainly approached his roles with enthusiasm and with fresh emphasis each night, but this technique did make him vulnerable in roles requiring long sustained passages – hence his failure as Hamlet. His daughter Viola noted his intensity when she played the queen to his Richard II: 'I looked instinctively to see my father come out, very simply and rather tired, dressed in black, and each time it seemed as if he were surprised to see me standing there, and as if we were really to say goodbye to each other for the first and last time. Then I fell on his neck, and said my speech sobbing, because at that moment I was not Richard's queen but my father's daughter . . . He never could begin his speech at once – he was so worried by my tears.'

At one performance of *Richard II*, Tree shed his own tears. Returning from Ireland, the king lands on the coast of Wales and throws himself on the ground 'to tell sad stories of the death of kings'. Tree's passion for realistic detail in his spectacle led him to order real broom to be strewn on the stage. On this occasion, broom was in short supply and prickly gorse was delivered.

In *Pygmalion*, Shaw reports that when the moment came for Mrs Patrick Campbell as Eliza to throw the slipper at Higgins, she scored a bull's eye. Although Shaw had secured a particularly soft pair, Tree was so immersed in the play that he had forgotten that the incident was scripted and had been rehearsed: 'The physical impact was nothing, but the wound to his feelings was terrible.' It was necessary to produce the prompt book before he was convinced. Mrs Pat took care never to hit him again, a rare restraint on her part.

Shaw and Tree exchanged sharp letters after the first night. Shaw's has been lost – or destroyed – by Tree. His own reply survives: 'I'm not saying that insulting letters of eight pages are always written by madmen, but it is a most extraordinary coincidence that madmen always write insulting letters of eight pages.'

Towards the end of his career, Tree's interest in management seemed to outrun his enthusiasm for acting. He died, aged 64, after a fall on the stairs at Birchington where he was staying. Lady Tree contrived to act after his death, notably with Seymour Hicks in a play called *A Certain Loneliness* at the St Martin's Theatre. The play would have lost money had not Cochran, the producer, bought the oak-panelled drawing room set as a job lot from a Scottish castle and sold it at a profit to America after the run. When Hicks deferentially tried to direct her and define her moves, she said, 'Don't worry, Mr Hicks, it will be quite all right. You do your little bit of acting wherever you like. It won't worry me and I shall be ready when you want me.'

**TRINDER**, Tommy. Tommy Trinder's brand of comedy was the essence of cockney backchat – he was the wittiest taxi driver who never steered a cab, the epitome of the lightning Londoner getting the last word. During his cabaret act, he used to roam the room, handing out cards and saying, 'Trinder's the name.' One evening, at the Cafe de Paris, he happened upon Orson Welles's table. Welles was drunk and as Trinder handed him the card saying, 'Trinder's the name,' Welles snarled, 'Why don't ya change it?'

'Is that an insult, Mr Welles,' asked Trinder, 'or a proposal of marriage?'

I remember an edition of *Beat the Clock* which he was hosting in the course of *Sunday Night at the London Palladium*. An appallingly bad-tempered woman was a contestant, and as she got more and more objectionable, Trinder struggled not to insult her. Bending over backwards to appear gracious, he let her into the final round, which she won. The big prize was wheeled on. It was a hair dryer.

'I've got one already,' she said, sourly.

Trinder's will to be pleasant snapped at last. 'Never mind, madam,' he hissed. 'One day you may have a two-headed baby.'

**TUTIN**, Dorothy. Playing in the opening scenes of *The Chalk Garden* with Googie Withers in the eighties, Dorothy Tutin was surprised when a woman suddenly emerged from the 'vom' – the subterranean passages leading from foyer to auditorium – brandishing a pair of tickets and saying loudly, 'This isn't *Annie Get Your Gun*! Stop this and put on *Annie Get Your Gun*! My tickets are for *Annie Get Your Gun*!' Eventually she was removed by theatre staff and no more was heard for a few minutes when suddenly Ms Tutin and Ms Withers, playing a scene on a sofa, were aware of a third presence. Somehow the woman had found her way back onstage and was still protesting. Finally she was removed and the play proceeded without further interruption.

# — 𝒰 —

**URBAN**, Joseph. Joseph Urban was a scenic designer and architect who moved from Vienna to America and became indispensable to Ziegfeld's spectacular revues; he also designed the lavish Ziegfeld Theater. His annexation by Ziegfeld was fortuitous. Urban had come to America to produce scenery for the Russell Opera Company of Boston. As the company staggered towards collapse, he got a job painting the sets for an horrendous disaster called *The Garden of Paradise*. Gene Buck, one of Ziegfeld's right-hand men, recognised an original talent and insisted that Ziegfeld see the show at the Park Theater against his better judgement. Ziegfeld eventually conceded a visit and was bowled over.

**USTINOV**, Sir Peter. Peter Ustinov was so much the definitive anecdotalist that it is perhaps impertinent to offer Ustinov stories. However, I believe these are worthy of wider currency.

Ustinov was at a reception at 10 Downing Street for the President of Iceland – an actress. He owed his invitation to the fact that his play *Half Way Up the Tree* had just been a great success in Reykjavik. Mrs Thatcher said innocently to him, 'We don't see you here very often,' to which he snappily replied, 'The President of Iceland doesn't come here very often!'

He played his own Beethoven's Tenth in Berlin, in German. He enjoyed the discipline of acting in a language he knew well, but not well enough to allow him the luxury of forgetting his lines. He found it exciting to be kept on his toes every night and not be able to talk his inimitable way out of it if he dried. He also appreciated the way the German audience received a witty line with a sound which is not quite a laugh. 'There is a short, sharp intake of breath. I call it a wine-tasting noise.'

He did a brilliant impersonation of King Hussein of Jordan – not many people *do* King Hussein but I assume it was brilliant. 'He speaks so quietly you have to lip read him,' said Ustinov. He also once visited a Bedouin in a palatial desert tent. The hospitality was generous but the host had a preoccupied air.

'You visit us on a bad day,' he told Ustinov. 'One of our young men has eloped with a girl from another tribe and they are asking for twenty thousand dollars American for her virginity. We have offered eight thousand dollars American and we are awaiting their reaction.' Outside, said Ustinov, a wife sat weaving a length of tent cloth with her feet and a gleaming Mercedes waited to take the children to school.

Ustinov was a book-signing buff. At Hatchard's on one occasion a friendly American in large, dark glasses and a green golfing hat pulled well down came up and asked him to sign a book. 'To whom shall I make it out?'

'Don't you remember me, Peter?' asked the purchaser.

'Remember you? I can't see you!'

'It's Bing Crosby.'

Crosby was followed by a lady who asked, 'Would you sign this for Rosalind, please?' Ustinov started to sign 'Ros' when she stopped him. 'No! No! It's *Rozalynde* – you see I'm from New Zealand.'

Once in Glasgow, a young man flung a book down in front of Ustinov the author and said abruptly, 'Would you sign it to "The Auld Fools," it's for my parents.'

On an early visit to America, Ustinov was trying out a play in Boston when he was interviewed by the formidable gossip columnist Louella Parsons. 'You must spend a lot of time on your feet in this play, Peeder?' she said abruptly at one point.

'Yes, well, I walk about quite a lot in the first act,' he replied innocently.

'And what about the second act?' she pressed.

'Oh, I do get to sit down a bit in act two,' he countered, puzzled.

She pounced: 'What about the third act?'

'I stand all through act three.'

'There!' she said, swinging round triumphantly to the camera: 'That is the problem for so many housewives. You are on your feet all day, but get Preparation SE39 and soothe your aches and pains away.'

In Canada he made a commercial himself for American Express. A Canadian journalist asked him why he did it. 'To pay for my American Express,' was the neat explanation.

In New York a cabbie once wished him 'Have a nice day.'

'Thank you,' said Sir Peter, 'but I have other plans.'

# V

**VALK**, Frederick. Frederick Valk, a great German-Jewish actor who came to England in 1939 as a Czech national to escape the Nazis, had gifts spectacular enough to secure him many leading modern classical roles. His Othello was particularly highly regarded. Tynan wrote of it: 'I have seen Mr Valk in the part and there, in the simple equation Valk–Othello, is an end of it.' Agate called it 'the best Othello since Salvini'. In the late forties he played it again with Donald Wolfit, a great Iago. Again Agate wrote lyrically, 'If Valk is not a great Othello, and if the duel with Wolfit is not magnificent throughout, then let me retire.'

Valk, a generous actor, nevertheless reported tartly the experience of being directed by Wolfit.

'Oh, Donald's a nice fellow.' Pause. 'Mind you . . .' Another pause.

'Yes?'

'Sometimes he gave me rather difficult positions . . . I said: "Donald, could I deliver this speech standing up?" He put his hand on my shoulder, and said, "Freddie, I have played Othello myself, and I know all the best positions."' Pause. 'He did. And he was making sure that I didn't have any of them.'

**VAN DRUTEN**, John. Dorothy Tutin tells a charming story of the London production of Van Druten's *I Am a Camera,* the Sally Bowles saga which received one of those clever-clever dismissive notices when it opened in New York: 'Me no Leica.' During the dress rehearsal, a cry rang out from Van Druten to move a piece of furniture. The stage manager couldn't work out which piece. Finally she cottoned on.

'Oh! You mean the pouffe!'

She earned the quick reproof from Van Druten. 'That's not a pouffe. It's an Ottoman!'

He also had to cope with the voluptuous Austrian actress, Marianne

Deeming, who played Madame Schneider and was particularly proud of her bosom – indeed she was known to have auditioned it, fully frontal, when determined to impress a producer or director. She refused to wear the heavy period clothes which covered her best feature until Van Druten put the dress on himself and became so intent on showing if off that she grew fascinated and was won over.

**VAN DYKE**, Dick. Dick Van Dyke, the American comedian best known in England as a butt for his appalling cockney accent in *Mary Poppins*, really has no place in my personal volume of theatrical anecdotes. However, I am short of Vs, so here goes.

A young actor was applying to American Equity for membership. The interviewing officer asked his name and was surprised to hear that it was 'Penis Lorry Lesbian'.

'I don't think that a good idea,' he said.

'Why not,' said the applicant. 'Is Penis Lorry Lesbian already another actor's name?'

'No,' said the Equity man. 'It just wouldn't look good on the marquee – couldn't you change it?'

The would-be actor thought for a moment. 'How about Dick Van Dyke?'

**VANITIES**, The. The *Vanities* were the creation of Earl Carroll, who sought to rival Florenz Ziegfeld *(Follies)* and George White *(Scandals)* as a producer of lavish, girl-splattered revue. He advertised on radio for 'young and inexperienced girls' with 'good figures, pretty faces and neat ankles'. Auditioned in bathing costumes, they could earn $40 a week. His requirements were eccentric. 'First, figure, because we can't change the figure if it isn't acceptable. Second, face, because we can improve on the face. Lastly, merit, because merit doesn't count.'

He had a stock response to the complaints of the mothers of innocents, who thought Broadway should be able to provide enough material. 'I am looking for fresh ones, they get old in a few weeks.' He ran into trouble over his radio ads, but used the protests of irate mothers to the Secretary of Commerce, Herbert Hoover, as extra publicity. Even his arrest for displaying indecent posters in the lobby of his theatre was turned to his advantage when he refused to put up his $300 bail and insisted on being locked up for his art.

On another occasion, he was sent to prison for throwing a party at which a chorus girl, Joyce Hawley, apparently bathed nude in a bath of wine. Carroll led the queue to drink a glassful after her dip with the invitation, 'Gentlemen, the line forms to the right.' The crux of the case seems to have been whether real wine was served. Walter Winchell, the columnist, was called briefly as a witness. Asked if it was an ordinary Broadway party, he said that it was not. 'There were more Senators than usual.' He was not kept in the stand long.

Carroll was fined $5000 and given a year and a day. He spent less than six months in jail in Atlanta, protesting that he had 'undergone an irreparable loss of self-respect'.

**VARIETY.** The weekly showbiz tract *Variety* invented its own language. The theory, outlined in the obituary of its first editor, Sime Silverman, was that the paper was originally written in English but that this proved impenetrable to the average Broadway actor. Silverman changed the style 'and wrote as the majority of actors of that day spoke . . . It was not that he could not write English, but that most *Variety* actors of that day did not speak it.' The language still proved impossible for many a foreigner.

'I read Shakespeare very well,' Marcel Pagnol once told Ruth Gordon. '*Variety* I still cannot read.'

**VENUTI,** Joe. Joe Venuti, the jazz violinist, had a tiresome penchant for practical jokes, which dominates most of the stories recorded about him. However, during a resurgence of interest late in his career in the late seventies he was playing in a club in Schenectady. Pleased with the interest a new generation was taking in him he announced: 'Ladies and gentlemen, I'm gonna do something I don't usually do. I'm gonna take a few requests.' A punter asked for 'Feelings'.

'"Feelin's"' said Venuti. '"Feelin's!" Why, that's the worst goddam song I ever heard! That's it, no more requests. You had your chance.'

He played 'Sweet Georgia Brown'.

**VIDAL,** Gore. Gore Vidal's plays include *The Best Man,* a satire on the Nixon administration, and *Visitor to a Small Planet,* a success on television and on Broadway with Cyril Ritchard. Some years later, David Merrick suggested making it a musical. He and Vidal agreed that Jerry Herman should be approached. For a long time Vidal heard nothing. Chancing to bump into Herman, he asked his reaction. Herman said he had passed, he found the play old-fashioned.

'But Jerry,' said Vidal, 'that's exactly why we thought of you for the music.'

Vidal's decades-long feud with Truman Capote, novelist and occasional playwright – *The Grass Harp, House of Flowers, Breakfast at Tiffany's* – culminated in his comment on hearing of Capote's death: 'Good career move.'

**VILLIERS**, James. James Villiers, the actor (and somewhere in the 120s in line of succession to the throne), not only possessed one of the most distinctive presences on the stage, but had a voice to match. He was a late choice of William Gaskill for one of the fops in his production of *The Way of the World* at Chichester, which later transferred to the Haymarket. The stars were Joan Plowright as Lady Wishfort and Maggie Smith as Millamant. She had played with James before when he was Victor to her Amanda in *Private Lives*. In fact rehearsals had already started when Gaskill announced to the cast that he had at last found an actor.

'Who?' asked Dame Maggie.

'He's called James Villiers.'

'Oh God,' she said to Joan Plowright, 'he's going to make the rest of us sound pretty common.'

'Jimbo's' funeral took place at Arundel, the town where he lived. The vicar, knowing well his fondness for a drink, took for his text St John ch 14, v 2, usually translated, 'In my father's house are many mansions.' But, as he pointed out, if we go back to the Aramaic there is a much more appropriate interpretation: 'On my father's estate are many taverns.'

**VOSBURGH**, Dick. Dick Vosburgh was an erudite and witty American comedy writer who lived in Islington for many years, supplying comedians with classy material and bringing up lots of children. His splendid wife, Beryl, is an enthusiastic crochet expert, known to some as 'the woman who knitted Islington'. His biggest theatre success was *A Day in Hollywood, A Night in the Ukraine*.

His version of a television show starring Fanny Craddock and Lionel Blair had the inspired title, *Butch Casserole and the One Dance Kid*. He also cherished a fable about a beautiful Welsh lad who, in 1916, was placed in a crate tied with pink ribbon and sent to Dublin with a label reading, 'Morgan, A Suitable Treat for Casement.'

Ted Koehler, an undervalued lyricist, wrote many popular songs – particularly, in collaboration with Harold Arlen, 'Get Happy', and

'Stormy Weather'. Vosburgh long hoped to produce an album on which the comedienne Imogen Coca sings the songs of Ted Koehler, simply so that he could call it 'The Coca-Koehler Song Book'.

Vosburgh was the scourge of sloppy lyric writers. He once sent a telegram to Tony Hatch (co-writer of the themes for *Crossroads* and *Neighbours)* which read: 'Congratulations on new jingle. Loved the rhynes.' At a colleague's party, a guest stepped on the hand of the crawling baby daughter of the house.

'Who trod on you, Jacqui?' Vosburgh cried. 'Who was it? Just point him out and I'll – I'll write for him.'

Scriptwriters often resent their ungrateful treatment at the hands of comedians, who grudgingly deliver their hard-achieved jokes without thanks. When Vosburgh's son Matthew was about eight, he voiced his ambition to be a stand-up comic. This got to the ears of the BBC's *Nationwide* team, who booked him for the programme. Proud father escorted infant comic to the studio at Lime Grove. In the taxi he offered him a joke. The boy considered it: 'No,' he said finally, 'it isn't me!'

**WADMORE**, George. George Wadmore was a very successful scriptwriter in the 'Golden Age of Radio' – *Ray's a Laugh, Ignorance Is Bliss* and *Educating Archie* were among his credits. His colleague, David Climie, claims to have taught him the logistics of afternoon adultery, 'a popular sport in the 1950s'. The Regent Palace Hotel was a preferred place of assignation. Some years after Wadmore's initiation, Climie and his wife missed the last train home to Brighton and decided to spend the night there. When he told Wadmore next day, he was intrigued.

'You took your *wife* to the Regent Palace?' he said. 'My God! Did they charge you corkage?'

Wadmore also said of Peter Myers, the revue writer with multi-coloured teeth, 'Strewth, he only needs a white one for the snooker set.'

**WALBROOK**, Anton. Emlyn Williams directed Walbrook in Lillian Hellman's *Watch on the Rhine* in London in 1942. During rehearsals he was in floods of tears during the closing scenes. Irmgaard Spoliansky, one of the stage children, asked if he would cry like that every night.

'Certainly not,' said Walbrook. 'In rehearsal, I cry; in performance it's the bastards in front who cry.'

**WALKLEY**, Alfred Bingham. The dramatic critic *of The Times,* asked why he had not reported in his review or to the news desk that the theatre had caught fire, replied, 'I am your dramatic critic; not your news hawk.'

**WALSH**, Jimmy. Jimmy Walsh was a classic old-time gag writer, lyricist, composer and arranger whose virtual office was the Express Dairy Café, some hundred or so yards up the Charing Cross Road from Trafalgar Square. Among the songs which artists and publishers would call in to collect, as he beavered away in a corner, were 'Don't Have Any More, Mrs Moore' and 'I Do Like a Dumpling in My Stoodle-oodle-oo'.

He much admired the well-endowed waitress, Mary, and one slack day composed a song in her honour, 'Mary from the Dairy'. Max Miller adopted it, recorded it in 1936 and made it his signature tune.

**WALTERS**, John. These stories are not primarily about John Walters – the ex-BBC Radio 1 producer who was responsible for John Peel's shows for more years than he cared to remember – but Walters was a compulsive raconteur and he is my only source of these two tales.

The American poet-singer Bob Dylan was a close friend of Dave Stewart of Eurythmics who, as is increasingly the custom, had his own recording studio in Crouch End, London. He invited Dylan to use it any time he was in England. The address was at one of the many permutations of Crouch End, Crouch Hill and Crouch End Hill in the area. Dylan feeling inspiration strike one day in London, set off for his friend's studio. He finished up outside the right number, but in a nearby street. Unaware of his mistake he rang the bell and the woman of the household came to the door and asked his business. He said his name was Bob Dylan and 'Dave' had said he could come round. Since by a happy coincidence the woman's husband was also called Dave she asked him in saying Dave would be back soon, and installed him in the sitting room with a cup of tea. On hearing her husband come in she called out gaily, 'Bob Dylan's here for you, Dave.' His reply is not recorded.

Walters's other story harks back to the days when he was in a band called the Alan Price Set. On tour in Aberdeen, they were drinking happily in a pub. Upstairs a wedding breakfast was in noisy progress. Hearing that Alan Price was downstairs the bridegroom rushed down and asked Price to play for his wife, 'your biggest fan,' adding that it would make her wedding day. Price agreed gracefully but no sooner had he started thumping out a tune than the bride's father ordered him off, pointing to a local lady pianist with the words, 'I've paid 'er to play, so get off!'

**WARNER**, Jack. Originally there were four Warner Brothers, Albert, Sam, Harry and Jack, who ran the Burbank studios with a contempt for critics which matched Harry Cohn's. 'Don't pay attention to bad reviews,' was Jack's advice. 'Today's newspaper is tomorrow's toilet paper.'

Like most Hollywood moguls Jack Warner preferred to decide on a movie after reading a synopsis rather than working his way through a novel. In 1933 when Mervyn Le Roy cabled him: 'Please read *Anthony Adverse*. Would make great picture for us.' Warner wired back: 'Read it! I can't even lift it.'

Encountering Albert Einstein, who was on a tour of the Warner studio, he boasted that he too had a theory of relatives which matched Einstein's theory of relativity. 'Really?' said Einstein. 'What is your theory?'

'Don't hire 'em.'

This, of course, was a precept not followed by Louis B. Mayer who promoted his daughter's husband, David O. Selznick, prompting an unidentified Hollywood wit to say. 'The son-in-law also rises.'

Another distinguished visitor to Warner studios during World War Two was Madame Chiang Kai-shek. She made a generous speech thanking Hollywood for its fund-raising aid to China. In replying, Warner lost his thread and looking straight into her eyes said, 'Holy cow, that reminds me. I forgot to pick up my laundry.'

He could be acute as well as frank in his assessments of directors. Once he remarked, 'To Raoul Walsh a tender love scene is burning down a whore-house.'

He was dictatorial to his writers. They were required to observe a nine-to-five-thirty schedule, limit lunch to half an hour, and wear their pencils down a set length every day. If a picture they had worked on got bad reviews they would say, 'We can't think why, because we were there at nine o'clock, we took half an hour for lunch and our pencils were down to here. So it couldn't be our fault.'

When Norman Krasna was clashing with Jack Warner over his script for *Princess O'Rourke*, starring Olivia de Havilland, Warner accused him of holding up production by leaving early. He demanded an ending to the script. Krasna looked at his watch and said that he had a solution – and the perfect ending. Warner, excited, wanted to know what it was.

'I can't tell you,' said Krasna.

'Why?' demanded Warner.

'Because,' said Krasna, 'I thought of the answer after 5.30.'

Warner bent the rules for William Faulkner and allowed him to work from home – to his surprise he later found out that 'home' was not somewhere in the Hollywood Hills but in Oxford, Mississippi.

Songwriters got short shrift too. When Harry Warren told Warner that it could take three weeks to write a song he exploded, 'Three weeks to write one lousy song!'

Warren corrected him, 'No! Three weeks to write one good song!'

He had a passionate hatred of television, which enabled a screenwriter, Mel Shavelson, who knew about it, to win a bet from two song writers, Sammy Fain and Paul Francis Webster (who didn't). They played Shavelson their new song for a Warner picture. He told them it would never be in the movie. The bet was $10. The next day they played it to Warner, unaware that he would not even let a TV set appear on the screen. The next day again they came to pay Shavelson his money. The song was called, 'I'm in Love with a Girl on Channel 9.'

Warner's ironic epitaph should be his verdict on hearing that Ronald Reagan was seeking nomination for Governor of California – 'No! No! Jimmy Stewart for Governor – Reagan for Best Friend.' He did not live to see Reagan elected President – twice!

Wilson Mizener's verdict on working at Warner's was frank, 'Working for Warners is like fucking a porcupine. It's one hundred pricks against one.'

Mizener also said perhaps the hardest thing about Warner, 'He has oilcloth pockets so he can steal soup.'

**WARREN**, Harry. A fine songwriter who, during World War Two, was Irving Berlin's most vocal critic. At the height of Allied bombing raids he said: 'They bombed the wrong Berlin.'

**WAX**, Ruby. The eccentric American actress, comedienne and writer has made a series of television documentaries with her equally exhibitionist parents. Earlier in her career, she played in the RSC at Stratford-upon-Avon and was visited by her proud father, who entertained her and a group of her colleagues at The Dirty Duck. When he picked up the bill and they protested, he swept the objection away, saying that it would be time enough to do that when they were famous. Sir Michael Hordern, embarrassed at this largesse from a comparative stranger, muttered modestly that he *was* famous. Mr Wax humoured him.

'Of course you are, old man,' he said, and went on to define fame, as someone pointed out the passing Trevor Nunn – 'But he's nobody in Springfield. In Springfield, Milton Berle is famous; Lawrence Welk is famous; Frank Sinatra is famous; Sammy Davis is famous – whoever heard of a Trevor Nunn?'

**WEBB**, Clifton. Clifton Webb was an American musical comedy song and dance man, tall and elegant, who in later life developed a line of worldly, waspish comedy personified in his popular screen character, Mr Belvedere. One of his early appearances was in Cole Porter's earliest Broadway experiment, *See America First* – a flop. Webb described his roles as 'a cowboy and an autumn flower. Others had roles not so believable.'

At one time, Webb was proposed for membership of a very conservative club in New York. His proposer was taken aside by some senior member and told that Clifton's reputation was such that it was unlikely he would be elected. The unfortunate proposer had to explain to Clifton that whilst he did not believe it for one moment, it had been suggested that he was gay. 'Tell me,' said Webb. 'Do you have any members who are homosexual?'

'Yes,' was the reply, 'we do have one.'

'Oh,' said Webb. 'What are you going to do when he dies?'

**WEBB**, Rita. Rita Webb was a wonderful old cockney character actress who was always called upon to embody the fighting spirit of Blitz-torn London in plays and drama documentaries. Indeed, when we had to cancel one edition of *TW3* in order to mount overnight a 'special' mourning the assassination of President Kennedy, Rita, who had been making a cameo guest performance (as an old cockney) had to be dropped. She was most put out.

'Why can't I be in it? In a crisis I always speak for the spirit of bleedin' Cockney London!'

However, her most famous grouse was directed at the iniquity of typecasting.

'Another bleedin' common part!' she would complain. 'Why don't they ever ask me to play fuckin' Lady Bracknell?'

**WEBER & FIELDS**. Vaudeville top-liners, they were East Side urchins whose parents had emigrated from Poland. Meeting at school (PS 42 on Allen Street), they put on blackface at the age of eight and started their act with, 'Here we are, a jolly pair . . .' They continued in the face of a distinct lack of interest from audiences, periodically changing their act to 'Here we are, a German pair . . . a coloured pair . . . a fighting pair . . . an Irish pair.' They also toured with 'Jo Jo, the Dog-faced Boy'.

They were pioneers in introducing the study of immigrant life into their acts, with a violent exaggeration of the actual experience. Their most famous sketch was their pool table scene. Weber defined its appeal: 'All the public wanted was to see Fields knock the hell out of me.'

Fields elaborated: 'I don't know why it was, but the audiences always seemed to have a grudge against him.'

They claimed to be the originators of the classic exchange, 'Who was that lady I saw you with last night?' – 'That was no lady, that was my wife.'

Other confrontations in their sketches included one Sigmund Cohenski declaring, 'Better my daughter should marry a book-keeper than a hero.'

'A book-keeper? I suppose you think the pen is mightier than the sword?'

'You bet your life. Could you sign cheques with a sword?'

Then there was a soldier, who had been shot.

'Where?' asked Weber.

'In the excitement,' replied Fields.

And, 'Whoever heard of a dog called Abie or Mosie?'

'Maybe he was a Kosher spaniel.'

Weber and Fields also set a fashion for off-stage enmity of the kind celebrated by Neil Simon in *The Sunshine Boys*. When they finally split, Fields embarked on a successful career as a producer, giving Rodgers and Hart, among others, an early break.

**WELDON**, Duncan. Duncan Weldon is one of the most prolific British producers. His career followed the traditional pattern built initially on touring productions of West End hits and pantomimes – quantity rather than quality.

However, he was always ambitious for greater things and progressed rapidly to smart offices above the Strand Theatre in Ivor Novello's famous old flat. Here he had a first meeting with two stars whom he hoped would agree to appear in a play for him. They were John Gielgud and Ralph Richardson. After lunch he took them back to the office to finalise arrangements for the play. It was a pre-Christmas meeting and somewhat to his embarrassment he found that the stairs leading up to the inner sanctum were festooned with dwarfs who had answered his partner's casting call for *Snow White*. Neither Gielgud nor Richardson remarked on the phenomenon and by the time the meeting was over the dwarfs had gone.

The play was presented and some years later Gielgud appeared in another (Julian Mitchell's *Half a Life*) under Weldon's banner. The tour took the play to Toronto where Gielgud was given some honour at a formal luncheon. Weldon went along to give him moral support and was amazed as Gielgud launched into his speech of thanks. He expressed his gratitude for the award and then praised the enterprise of his producer in presenting the play and bringing it to Toronto. 'Extraordinary fellow, Weldon,' he said: adding out of the blue, 'Extraordinary. He employs dwarfs, you know.'

When Mrs Thatcher went to see *Half a Life* affairs of state called her away at the interval. Hearing of her early departure Gielgud observed ruefully, 'More a quarter of a life.'

For a long time, Duncan Weldon was in partnership with Louis Michaels, who became involved in theatre late in life as a co-producer and a bricks-and-mortar man. Early in their partnership Weldon took him to see Peter Coe's production of *Macbeth* at Leatherhead, with a view to transferring it to the West End. After about ten minutes Louis, apparently unaware of the play or its author, turned to his partner in a fury saying, 'Duncan, where did you dig up this load of rubbish?' In Billingham to view a specially expensive stage set by Ralph Koltai, Weldon and Michaels were dismayed when the curtain rose on their private view of a simple disc.

'But it cost fifty thousand pounds!' Michaels exploded.

'Yes,' said Koltai, 'And you'd never think it!'

Despatched to New York to woo Katharine Hepburn back to the West End, Louis Michaels couldn't come up with a play on his shopping list which appealed to her. Stalling, he called Weldon in London for more suggestions. He had a fairly obvious brainwave, *The Cherry Orchard*. Michaels asked him briefly to outline the plot. Weldon did his best. Michaels was dismayed. 'Duncan, I can't offer America's greatest actress a play about choppin' trees down!'

Weldon himself does not avoid the occasional near-Goldwynism. Bemoaning the fact that his production of Alan Bennett's *Talking Heads* at the Comedy Theatre had to close while playing to capacity he lamented, 'Alan won't go on and Pat Routledge is going to Greenwich to do *The Corn is Green*.'

'Who's presenting that?' he was asked.

'I am. That's the trouble with me, my successes stop too soon and my failures run for ever.'

Meeting Richard Nelson at the Barbican after the first night of the extremely long – some four hours – play about Columbus and the discovery of America, Weldon complained, 'What took you so long? I can do it in three hours on Concorde.'

**WELLES**, Orson. One of the women who repulsed the multi-faceted actor, director, magician and raconteur Orson Welles was, oddly enough, 'a homely Italian actress with a face like a spoon.' Apparently she had a great, if mysterious, allure for men, and Welles became besotted. He confided his love to his friend Charles Lederer, who wrote telling him to try to visualise her sitting on the lavatory picking her nose. Welles wrote back, 'It's the most enchanting vision I've ever thought of!'

Asked to name the three best directors whose work he had seen in Hollywood, Welles modestly replied, 'I like the old masters, by which I mean John Ford, John Ford and John Ford.'

In 1948 when he was directing *The Lady from Shanghai*, Welles overran his schedule at great expense. The production manager, Jack Fier, was supposed to prevent this. He tried and Welles began to hate him. Towards the end of shooting he put up a sign reading 'The only thing we have to Fier is Fier itself.' Fier made his own reply: 'All's well that ends Welles.'

**WEST**, Mae. Mae West's scripted witticisms are legion, her Broadway career almost forgotten. In 1927 her play *Sex* was closed by the acting Mayor, she was convicted of obscenity and served ten days in prison. She also wrote *Diamond Lil* and *Pleasure Man*, an early essay on homosexuality which was raided on its first night on 1 October, 1928 and closed after three performances. (In 1926 Gilbert Miller had produced a lesbian play, *The Captive*, which disguised its true intentions by using 'violets as a symbol of the third sex'. *Variety*, as ever, had its appropriate verdict: 'Violet business KOd at florists.')

Mae West's return to Broadway came in 1944 with another of her own plays, *Catherine Was Great*. She was then 52. Mike Todd, who presented it as a tongue-in-cheek play about a nymphomaniac with a sense of humour, was dismayed to find that his star and author was proud of her serious historical research and sent a cable to one of his backers, offering him his money back.

On the opening night when the actor playing one of her lovers, Lieutenant Bunin, became entangled in his sword and scabbard, she famously ad-libbed the old vaudeville standby, 'Is that your sword, or are you just glad to see me?'

Critics were merciless. Louis Kronenberger's headline ran 'Mae West slips on the steppes!' and George Jean Nathan's notice called the evening, 'A dirty-minded little girl's essay on the Russian Empress, played like the chatelaine of an old-time *maison de joie* . . . after Mae had rolled her hips for the two hundredth time and nasally droned her glandular intentions in respect of the males in her troupe, even the staunchest West disciple felt faintly surfeited and would have settled, with loud cheers, for Cornelia Otis Skinner in Bible readings.'

Her curtain speech remained popular: 'Catherine had three hundred lovers. I did the best I could in a couple of hours.'

So curvaceous was she that an inflatable life-jacket was named after her during World War Two. She lived to a great age and differed from many contemporaries in that her on-screen and off-screen witticisms were usually her own work and did not depend on scriptwriters or studio publicists.

For example there was her impromptu exchange with a very good character actress, Alison Skipworth, who suspected correctly that Miss West was stealing a scene from her. 'I'll have you know that I am an actress,' intoned Miss Skipworth.

'It's alright, dearie,' replied Mae, 'I'll keep your secret.'

Her arrival in Hollywood bothered the guardians of morals. Her first starring role in 1933 was opposite the young Cary Grant in *She Done Him Wrong*. She opened with 'Why don't you come up sometime 'n see me?'

When Grant looks at her quizzically she says, 'Aw, you can be had.' Another gem from the same script: 'When women go wrong, men go right after them.'

To the compliment that she is 'a fine woman' she replies, 'One of the finest women who ever walked the streets.'

She hipped and swaggered and tossed off lines like 'It's not what I do, but the way I do it,' or 'It's not what I say, but the way I say it'; 'It's better to be looked over than overlooked'; 'It's not the men in my life that counts but the life in my men'; and 'I'm a girl who lost her reputation and never missed it.'

Linked with W.C., Fields the chemistry was even stronger. When she tells him her name in Hooverbelle he responds. 'What a euphonius appellation!' When he asks if he can kiss 'her symmetrical digits' her reply is 'Sure, help yourself.'

She was on the ball with interviewers too. Hedda Hoppa, the Hollywood gossip columnist, asked her how she came to know so much about men. 'Baby,' said Miss West, 'I went to night school.'

She was proud of her writing skills: 'When you think about it, what other playwrights are there besides O'Neill, Tennessee and me?' And she clashed with Lubitsch over his habit of taking all the good lines: 'I'm writin' the story,' she said, 'and I'm the star.'

Lubitsch advanced the case of two-character drama: 'Look at Romeo and Juliet.'

'Let Shakespeare do it his way, I'll do it mine,' was her reply. 'We'll see who comes out better.'

She boasted that she had mirrors in her bedroom because; 'I like to see how I'm doin'. When I'm good, I'm very good; but when I'm bad, I'm better.'

**WEST**, Timothy. Trapped in the back of a cab, Timothy West was quizzed by the driver: 'You're an actor, aren't you? I've 'ad 'em all in my cab.' He branched off to attack the acting talent of Larry Hagman.

'I've 'ad that J.R. from *Dynasty* [sic], terrible actor!'

Tim West politely demurred. The driver was not impressed.

'Not like his mother, Maisie Martin.'

'No, Mary Martin.'

'That's right. It just goes to show, it's not handed on.'

'What do you mean?'

'Well, look at Thora Hird and Donald Sinden.'

As people are wont to say, there's no answer to that.

**WESTMINSTER**, Duke of. Bendor, Duke of Westminster, earns his place in theatrical annals because of one line in Act One of Noel Coward's *Private Lives*. (From the balcony of an hotel in France, the question of whose yacht is moored in the harbour is raised. 'The Duke of Westminster's probably. It usually is.') And because of his liaisons with actresses, notably Isabel Jeans and Gladys Cooper, to whom he proposed marriage. She turned him down, saying he'd leave her in a month. However, by then he had already given her a priceless sapphire bracelet – lost in 1947 during one of her constant journeys to and fro across the Atlantic, on this occasion to star in Peter Ustinov's *The Indifferent Shepherd*.

Her son-in-law, Robert Morley, asked her what she was going to do about it – the booty also included a fur coat and several pairs of nylon stockings. She was unperturbed.

'Have dinner,' she said.

WHELDON, Sir Huw. Huw Wheldon was the charismatic pioneer of popular arts programmes on BBC television and later its managing director. He is principally remembered for *Monitor* in which his great virtue was, as his biographer Paul Ferris has said, that 'he was ready to risk looking unclever on television' if that provided information for the viewer. Sometimes, of course, he *was* unclever. When D.G. Bridson, discussing a *Monitor* item, suggested, 'Let's do something about collage', Wheldon replied, 'Never heard of him, old boy.'

In the mid-sixties he replaced Donald Baverstock (head of BBC 1) in a new job as Controller, Programmes. Baverstock left the BBC immediately and Wheldon overnight assumed responsibility for *Not So Much a Programme More a Way of Life,* a successor to *TW3* which I was producing. A loyal Baverstock man, I was summoned to his new office – Baverstock's old one – on the Monday morning following the coup. All Baverstock's effects had been removed and Wheldon's not yet installed. The room was bare.

'Oh, Huw,' I said nastily, as I entered. 'Put the stamp of your personality on the office already, I see.' It was cheap and inaccurate – lack of personality was one thing of which Wheldon could never be accused. However, I was rather pleased with the remark and made the mistake of repeating it to David Frost, who repeated it to the diarist of the *Daily Mirror,* who printed it the next day. As only two of us had been in the room at the time, there was little doubt who had passed it on. Wheldon ignored the comment at the time and when it appeared in print. It was a useful lesson.

WHITING, George. George Whiting, an American vaudeville actor and songwriter, ran into Irving Berlin one night in a barber's shop. Berlin asked Whiting if he would go to a show with him.

'Sure,' said Whiting, 'my wife's gone to the country.'

Berlin, a dab hand at recognising a saleable phrase, took his pad, forgot about going to the theatre and bashed out a hit, a hit which he always insisted depended more on the infectious repeat of 'Hooray! Hooray!' following the title line. Berlin's publisher, Ted Snyder, supplied a serviceable tune and the song quickly sold 300,000 copies. The frivolous implications of the narrative verses – the available husband was supposed to have got up to more than writing songs with young Irving – encouraged Mrs Whiting to believe the worst: she sued her husband for divorce. Years later he tried to regain her affection by writing an even more popular song, 'My Blue Heaven' and dedicating it to her.

**WILDE**, Oscar Fingal O'Flahertie Wills. So much of Oscar Wilde's wit is studied and considered in his plays that his spontaneity is sometimes called in question. It should not be – even in the light of Whistler's famous put-down.

Sir Lewis Morris, author of *The Epic of Hades*, was complaining about what he considered the studied neglect of his claim to be Poet Laureate after Tennyson's death. 'It is a complete conspiracy of silence against me,' he stressed to Wilde. 'A conspiracy of silence! What ought I to do. Oscar?'

'Join it,' said Wilde promptly.

Wilde's reputation for spontaneous wit was established before he left Oxford. In his *viva* he was required to translate from the Greek versions of the New Testament, which he did easily, gracefully and accurately. When the satisfied examiners tried to stop him he continued through two interruptions, finally pleading, 'Oh do let me go on. I want to see how it ends.'

On his arrival in America he scored two, perhaps more, considered successes. First he was 'disappointed with the Atlantic Ocean' – and then, above all, confronted by the customs official who asked him if he had anything to declare, he famously replied, 'No, I have nothing to declare . . .' and after a pause – 'except my genius.' Few quips have travelled so far and so quickly.

Recalling his visit to Texas on his lecture tour, Wilde said that theatre managers there looked diligently for real criminals to play criminal parts and billed them accordingly. On one occasion a porter read, 'The part of Lady Macbeth will be taken by Mrs . . . (Ten Years Hard Labour).' She was a poisoner who had just completed her sentence.

Frank Harris was boasting one night at the Café Royal of all the great houses he frequented. Wilde grew impatient. 'Yes, dear Frank,' he suggested, 'we believe you: you have dined in every house in London, once.'

Wilde's friend Robert Ross, who long stood by him, looked back on his stormy career with Oscar when asked what he would like to have inscribed on his gravestone. He offered; 'Here lies one whose name is writ in hot water.'

Wilde took his own theatrical ups and downs with equanimity. Meeting a friend at his club after the first performance of *Lady Windermere's Fan*, he was asked: 'Oscar, how did your play go tonight?' 'The play was a great success,' he answered, 'but the audience was a total failure.'

When Wilde and his actor-manager, Beerbohm Tree, were congratulating one another after the first-night success of *A Woman of No Importance*, Wilde said to Tree, 'I shall always regard you as the best critic of my plays.'

'But I have never criticised your plays,' said Tree innocently.

'That's why,' smiled Oscar.

He had more trouble with Sir George Alexander, who produced *The Importance of Being Ernest* and sensibly insisted that Wilde cut his four acts to three. The fourth occasionally surfaces, but never to the play's advantage.

Alexander protested that Wilde could use his dialogue in another play. Wilde countered that it might not fit in another play. 'What does it matter?' smoothed Alexander. 'You are clever enough to think of a hundred things just as good.'

'Of course I am,' protested Wilde, 'a thousand if need be . . . but that is not the point. This scene that you feel is superfluous cost me terrible, exhausting labour and heart-rending, nerve-racking strain. You may not believe me, but I assure you on my honour that it must have taken fully five minutes to write.'

'If there is one man more deeply hated by his fellow men than any other it is the witty man,' he said with some feeling. His wit had been his triumph during his cross-examination by Carson in his first trial; but it let him down when Carson pounced on his casual dismissal of a rent boy as 'unattractive' and destroyed him 'with all the ferocity of an old friend.'

The end was awful, but the tatters of wit clung to him. When asked for a very large sum for an operation he said, 'Ah well, then. I suppose that I shall have to die beyond my means.'

And there are his supposed last words in that bedroom in Paris: 'This wallpaper is killing me. One of us will have to go.'

**WILDER**, Billy. Anecdotes about the great Hollywood writer/director of *Sunset Boulevard*, *Some Like It Hot*, *The Fortune Cookie* and many other classic movies, veer between the immediately sympathetic and the barbed. Harry Kurnitz defined him at work – 'Let's face it, Billy Wilder at work is two people – Mr Hyde and Mr Hyde.'

Born in Vienna, Wilder moved to Berlin to write scenarios for early movies. After the Reichstag fire he could see little future and fled to Hollywood. He insists that during his early days in Los Angeles he lived in the ladies' room at the Chateau Marmont hotel. His idol, Lubitsch, was at Paramount. Wilder explained Lubitsch's early dabbling in German expressionism as a practical necessity: 'They did all those angles and that lighting because they couldn't afford sets. When they got to Hollywood, they dropped all that stuff. Lubitsch,' he added, 'could do more with a closed door than most directors can with an open fly.'

It was Lubitsch who teamed him with his first great collaborator, Charles Brackett, when he moved to MGM to work on *Ninotchka*. After World War Two he served with the Psychological Warfare Division of the US Army in Germany. Among his tasks was rebuilding the German film industry. In the course of his work he had to interview ex-Nazis to decide which were the least undesirable. The director of the Oberammergau Passion Play asked him for a decision on Anton Lang who had played Christ before the war and had been in the SS. The director wanted to use him again. Wilder said, 'On one condition.' He was asked what it was: 'That in the Crucifixion scene you use real nails.'

Wilder's second great collaborator was another transplanted European, I.A.L. Diamond. Born Itek Dommnici in Romania, he always insisted the initials he adopted stood for Interscholastic Algebra League. Wilder said, 'The highest compliment you could get from Diamond would be "Why not?"'

The Reagans once asked Wilder to the White House for dinner. He didn't want to go. Diamond agreed. 'You're right. If you go, then you'll have to invite them back to your house, then back and forth. Who knows what it could lead to?'

Working on *Some Like It Hot*, Wilder's main problem – apart from getting Tony Curtis into a dress – was Marilyn Monroe's unpunctuality and her insistence on going over the dialogue interminably. Finally, philosophically, he accepted the burden: 'My Aunt Minnie would always be punctual and never hold up production – but who would pay to see my Aunt Minnie?'

He had also directed her in *The Seven Year Itch* and once said, 'The question is whether Marilyn is a person at all or one of the greatest Du Pont products ever invented. She had breasts like granite and a brain like Swiss cheese full of holes.' She explained her unpunctuality by saying that she couldn't find the studio at which she had worked for years. After some forty or fifty takes Wilder would take her aside and say soothingly, 'Don't worry, Marilyn.'

To which she would innocently reply, 'Don't worry about what?'

'Anyone can remember lines,' he later said, 'but it takes a real star to come on the set and not know her lines and give the performance she did.'

Wilder's caustic side is demonstrated in his curt comments on his colleagues.

He called Spyros Skouras, head of Twentieth Century Fox studios, 'The only Greek Tragedy I know.' Of Chaplin he said, devastatingly, 'When he found a voice to say what was on his mind, he was like a child of eight writing lyrics for Beethoven's Ninth.' To an auditioning singer, 'You have van Gogh's ear for music.'

His own philosophy for directing was summed up in his ten commandments: 'The first nine are "Thou shalt not bore".' The tenth was 'Thou shalt have the right of final cut', or, more simply, 'The best directing is the one you don't see'. More particularly, 'The close-up is such a valuable thing – like a trump at bridge.'

Wilder had profound distrust of the pretentious, the new wave, and the unfairly-prestigious-foreign. 'What critics call "dirty" in our movies they call "lusty" in foreign films,' he said. When he was directing *Sunset Boulevard* he managed a jab at European movies in an aside to his lighting cameraman, John Seitz, who was querying the set-up for Gloria Swanson's attempted suicide in her vast bed. 'It's the usual slashed-wrist shot, Johnny,' he told him, 'and keep it out of focus. I want to win the foreign picture award.' Around 1969 he was mocking the Nouvelle Vague: 'You watch, the new wave will discover the slow dissolve in ten years or so.'

However, when he first saw Eric von Stroheim at the wardrobe tests for his role as Rommel in *Five Graves to Cairo*, 'I clicked my heels and said, "Isn't it ridiculous, little me directing you? You were always ten years ahead of your time." Von Stroheim replied, "Twenty."'

One of his more blunt ripostes has stuck in the popular imagination of Hollywood. Louis B. Mayer considered *Sunset Boulevard* an insult to the film community. He was heard to say, 'Billy Wilder should be run out of town.'

Wilder's response was to tell Mayer, 'Go shit in your hat.'

'That's what I'll be remembered for,' he said; 'A stupid insult to Louis B. Mayer.' To a query that surely he would be remembered for standing up to the studio head he denied it. 'No, they'll remember "Shit in your hat".'

The advent in 1993 of the Andrew Lloyd Webber–Christopher Hampton-Don Black musical based on *Sunset Boulevard*, which he co-wrote with Diamond, recalled a previous attempt by Steven Sondheim and Burt Shevelove to make it into a stage show. Meeting Wilder in Los Angeles they told him what they were planning to do (the studio owned the rights). 'It can't be done,' Wilder warned them.

'Why?' they asked.

'It's not a musical,' said Wilder perceptively, 'it's an opera. It's about a queen in exile.' As Lloyd Webber was never worried about having his work compared to opera the advice would probably have not discouraged him.

Wilder considered his own style 'a curious cross between Lubitsch and Von Stroheim.' He attended Lubitsch's funeral in Los Angeles in 1948 – he had been in the middle of filming *That Lady in Ermine*. Lubitsch was buried in a glass-covered coffin with a cigarette in his hand. After the funeral Wilder walked to his car with William Wyler.

'Pity,' Wyler finally said. 'No more Lubitsch.'

'Worse,' said Wilder. 'No more Lubitsch pictures.'

There is no mistaking his nostalgia for pre-war cinema. 'Working at Paramount in the thirties was absolutely marvellous. You just walked across the lot and there they were: Von Stroheim, Dietrich, Gary Cooper, Leo McCarey, Lubitsch. We made pictures then. Today we spend eighty per cent of the time making deals and twenty per cent making pictures.'

He found unusual consolation in the advent of television. 'It is a twenty-one-inch prison. I'm delighted with it because it used to be that films were the lowest form of art. Now we've got something to look down on.'

Wilder once told Sam Goldwyn that he wanted to make a movie about Nijinsky. He explained that he was the greatest dancer ever, told him about his career, 'and how he ended up in a French nuthouse, thinking he was a horse.'

Goldwyn said, 'What kind of a picture is that? A man who thinks he's a horse?'

Wilder told him, 'Don't worry, there's a happy ending. In the final scene he wins the Kentucky Derby.'

Wilder married twice. His second wife, Audrey, lived in modest circumstances with her mother. Proposing, Wilder told her, 'I'd worship the ground you walk on if you lived in a better neighbourhood.'

According to Peter Bogdanovich Wilder once flirted on the set with a Japanese stripper, 'But it would be impossible between us,' he said, 'because at some point I would remember Pearl Harbor.'

**WILLCOCKS**, Sir David. Sir David Willcocks, the distinguished director of music at Kings College, Cambridge, is rumoured to have given all the credit for the spectacularly beautiful sound his choir makes in a spectacularly beautiful building to the chapel. 'It's not the boys,' he is reported to have said, 'it's the building. That acoustic would make a fart sound like a sevenfold Amen.'

**WILLIAMS**, Emlyn (George). Actor and playwright, Williams had a great reputation for an acid tongue. John Gielgud tells a story of arriving apologetically in New York with his one-man Shakespeare programme, *Ages of Man*, Williams having blazed that particular trail with his Dickens and Dylan Thomas shows. Gielgud said, 'Isn't the traffic awful in New York, with the fire-engines and ambulances going by – don't you find that you always hear them about two blocks away and you know that on your quietest line they are going to pass your theatre?'

Williams, at his slyest, agreed. 'Yes, and of course you can't hurry up your speech so that it will come on Peggy Ashcroft's lines!'

Williams's famous loquaciousness, talent for story-telling and acid wit were silenced on one occasion when he lunched in the company of Sir Huw Wheldon, an overpowering conversationalist and a great laugher at his own jokes. Sir Huw so dominated the Cardiff table that Emlyn couldn't get a word in edgeways until the Welsh whirlwind had left. Retiring to the loo with a fellow guest, Emlyn took up a reflective stance and finally said, sibilantly, 'He'll die laughing.'

Allan Davis remembered a particularly dismissive off-the-cuff remark of Williams's after he had seen Richard Burton and Elizabeth Taylor in *Private Lives:* 'He's miscast and she's Miss Taylor.'

Williams had introduced Richard Burton to his first wife Sybil. After he left her for Elizabeth Taylor, Burton periodically turned up for maudlin reunions. One night he suddenly said, 'Well, I'd better get back to the Dorchester or there'll be a lot of breast beating,' to which Sybil splendidly replied, 'And indeed there's quite a lot of breast to beat, isn't there?' When Williams got his CBE he wrote to Sybil Burton that it stood for 'Can't Bear Elizabeth'. When Terence Rattigan got his CBE Williams translated it as 'Chorus Boys Everywhere'.

James Harding's biography of Emlyn covers the ground about which Williams wrote with such distinction in *George and Emlyn* and conscientiously carries the story on until Williams' death some fifty years after the last moments charted in *Emlyn*.

Harding pinpoints the origin of Hugh 'Binkie' Beaumont's nickname for Williams. Richard Burton, a protégé of his fellow countryman, was under contract to H.M. Tennent, the theatrical production company of which Beaumont was the head. Burton was on £15 a week. As his career blossomed he reckoned he had earned a rise and asked Binkie for £20. They compromised at £17.10.0 and Burton proudly reported this to Emlyn Williams who promptly told him to go back and ask for £30. After some argument he got it. Binkie's parting shot was 'I suppose that old Welsh pit pony put you up to this.' It was a nickname Williams embraced happily.

Emlyn had his own debates with Beaumont. 'I've read your new play, Emlyn, and I like it twice as much as your last,' Binkie once said. Williams pounced. 'Does that mean you're going to pay twice my usual royalties?' he asked. It did not. When The Company of Four, a subsidiary of H.M. Tennent, revived his Shakespeare play, *Spring 1600*, at the Lyric, Hammersmith, in 1945, audiences were thin. He suggested that the Lyric housed 'The Company of Four and the Audience of Two.'

On the first night of the original production of *Spring 1600*, directed by John Gielgud, in 1934, he had been so nervous that he hid himself in the flies and watched the action from above. His anxiety was not diminished and indeed he felt a compulsive need to relieve himself. He did so in an old rusty bucket. When he told his director about it later, Gielgud said, 'You must be the first playwright who's peed over his own play.'

When he acted in *Wild December*, Clemence Dane's play about the Brontës, he nearly took a solo curtain call, sure that the audience were calling, 'Emlyn! Emlyn!' Just in time he realised that they were calling for Beatrix Lehmann in her character of Emily, and had the presence of mind to lead her forward for her bow. The name Emlyn often led to confusion among his fans. He listed 25 variations on the spelling of his Christian name, including, Emelett, Emden, Emmelin, Emlyon, Emiline, Amlyn, M. Lynn, Emilio, Dmly, Mmrnlyn, Melyn and Eylya.

He was adroit at word play. Once when he and Robert Helpmann were arguing about the age of Michael Redgrave he decided that they were 'splitting grey hairs'. Under general Eisenhower's regime he rechristened the White House 'The Tomb of the Well-Known Soldier'. He cherished (or invented) a wartime sign scrawled on a building: 'Abandon hope all ye who ENSA here'. And when he heard that Ivor Novello was to be imprisoned for wartime petrol offences he said to his wife, 'I suppose his great song for this war will have to be called, "Keep the Home Tyres Turning".'

He was adept at the scrambled titles which theatre people like to manipulate – though the transformation of 'Vivat! Vivat! Regina' to 'Rivet, Rivet your Vagina!' is not his. When Gielgud suggested cutting some flowery speeches in *Spring 1600* he agreed happily saying, 'We don't want James Agate to head his Sunday article, "Herrick, or little by little"!' For the musical version of *Lolita* he suggested the new title *Take Her She's Nine*, with a hit song 'Stop the Girl I Want to Get Off.

Referring to Merle Oberon's Eurasian background he suggested that her autobiography be called *Lives of a Bengal Freeloader*.

When he found that his obituary had appeared in an American newspaper which gave the date of his death he wrote, 'I have wracked my brain and cannot recall anything untoward happening that year.'

Six years before he died in 1987, he had appeared at the Century Theatre in New York and had another great success reviving his Dickens readings. Arriving at the theatre for one performance, he found the stage door surrounded by young actors auditioning for *Jitters*, a new backstage comedy. He asked the hopefuls what was going on and one girl, noting his white hair, said kindly, 'I wouldn't bother hanging round if I were you. There aren't any parts for old men!'

Victor Spinetti tells a sweet story of meeting Williams one day. The older man said, 'Hello, Victor. Still keeping your head below water?' The next day Victor received a letter from Williams with a cheque for several thousand pounds. The note said, 'I was going to leave you this in my will but you looked so depressed yesterday, I thought I'd send it straight away.'

**WILLIAMS**, Kenneth. It is impertinent to retell Kenneth Williams's stories, pallid echoes of a master raconteur, voice bucketing, nostrils flaring, tight lips compressed between explosions. However, here are a few Kenneth himself recorded.

Edith Evans after a preview in Brighton of Robert Bolt's *Gentle Jack*, told him, 'Binkie Beaumont came round to the dressing room after the rehearsal and said Hardy Amies had designed very regal costumes – I should look really regal in them. Do you think that is justified?'

Kenneth replied, 'I think any criticism of your deportment is tantamount to impertinence.'

Dame Edith was delighted. According to Kenneth, she patted his knees. 'You're a very pleasant young man. There is no reason why the right girl shouldn't come along.' Most people tell the other story in which she says, 'Such a good actor. Pity he has such an affected voice,' which was being told of her long before, though the victim was an actress, Isabel Jeans. Now it is being ascribed to Maggie Smith, on the occasion of her hearing that Geraldine McEwan would replace her in *Lettice & Lovage*.

Kenneth also recorded Dame Edith's complaint that actors in the company did not 'drop into her dressing room for a chat'.

'You're something of a myth. They view you with awe.'

'No, I'm very ordinary, really.'

'They don't think so.'

'But I am. I sit at home on my little stool with my apron on and I baste the joint with my old wooden spoon. Oh yes, I am very ordinary, roast beef and Yorkshire pudding.'

The opening night in London (at the Queen's Theatre) was rocky. Dame Edith misinterpreted one rude yell from the gallery as a 'bravo'. Kenneth corrected her: 'No, it wasn't bravo, it was "Go home".'

Kenneth's theatrical stories started with his Army service, in CSEU companies in the Far East along with Barrie Chat, John Schlesinger, Peter Nichols and Stanley Baxter. His audition act included impersonations of Churchill and Mabel Constandurous, a forties wireless favourite. He quoted proudly the exchange:

'Hello, are you one of Wingate's boys?'

'No, I'm one of Colgate's girls – and there are my teeth to prove it!' And he enjoyed airing the opening lines of a revue, 'We're boys of the service . . . we're entertaining *you*. We'll sing songs old and new: fun and laughter if you're blue.'

Gleefully, he would recite the OC's reaction: 'I don't want any filth . . . that won't do. Boys? Boys of the service? No. Too sibilant, like a lot of pansies. We're *men* of the service! That's better!'

I met him first when he was playing the Dauphin in *St Joan* at the Arts Theatre. He came to tea with Peter Nichols, who had a room in the same flat as me. Every time Nichols started on a story, Kenneth would top it. He was full of the current production and of the old actor, Frank Royd, upstaged by Siobhan McKenna's St Joan for long periods, being asked by

John Fernald about his make-up. Royd's reply was, 'Don't know, I've never made up me arse before.'

He followed this with a variety of roles in Orson Welles's production of *Moby Dick* at the Duke of York's: 'I could use some of your versatility,' was Welles's welcome.

During an argumentative moment in rehearsals, he was more acerbic: 'Never since Ruth Chatterton left high society drama has anyone been so damned difficult as you.'

In *Hotel Paradiso* which followed, Williams and Billie Whitelaw played juveniles to Alec Guinness's lead. Taken to dinner on tour by Guinness, they were overawed by the Malmaison restaurant in Glasgow. Billie Whitelaw 'suddenly launched into an hysterically enthusiastic account of *Picture Post:* "They have a fascinating article this week on this Dutch community in Staines . . . They've managed to preserve their own cultural traditions, even costumes! All the women wear Dutch caps." She hardly observed the full stop before adding hastily, "On their heads, I mean." Alec smiled unperturbed, and mercifully ordered for us.'

Williams learnt another lesson from Guinness on stage when, during the London run, he found himself being unaccountably manoeuvred into disadvantageous positions, often behind potted palms. He got the explanation when they came off: his flies were undone.

'Always watch your flies and blow your nose before you come out,' was the star's advice.

Williams's starring arrival in London in the revue *Share My Lettuce* was memorable for two events. He famously overslept on one occasion and missed a matinée and, on the first night at the Lyric, Hammersmith, he 'ruined' a wistful company song 'Wallflower Waltz' into a comedy hit. Ribbons were supposed to fall from the flies and the girls sang their plaintive number as the men waltzed with their strips of chiffon. On this occasion, the star's ribbon failed to fall and all he could do was try to grab the other men's bits of material, yelling 'Give me a bit! I ain't got a bit! Give us a bit! You've got my bit!'

As the audience fell about, Williams danced around, as he has put it, 'like a demented fairy, asking for a bit'. Michael Codron, the producer, ordered the new business to be kept in.

One of Kenneth's best putdowns, which he recorded in his book *Acid Drops,* was bravely offered towards the beginning of the run of *Share My Lettuce.* Characters in costumes of various shades identified themselves by their colours. A man who had announced 'I am pink' was greeted by a stalls' blimp with a yell of 'How dreadfully effeminate.'

Kenneth's own entrance required the line, 'I am green.' This was greeted by 'Oh, dear. Another pansy.'

He had not reckoned on Kenneth's speed – 'Be quiet, madam.' When he stamped out, demanding his money back, it was rightly refused.

Fenella Fielding has recalled a less happy revue incident. In *Pieces of Eight*, they were playing two spies 'who meet up in that ludicrous wonderland of revue'. She described the setting: 'We both had death pills. I would die first – leaving him to die on stage while I went off into the wings.'

One night Kenneth wickedly declined to feed her her 'death' cue: 'Instead of trying to out-do him, I stopped still – and said, "Last one dead is a cissy." I died – and walked off in the dark.' Kenneth was furious – to call the limp-wristed shots was his prerogative.

'You called me a homosexual in front of the audience!' was his furious reaction. They did not speak for weeks. There is probably some truth in Fenella's reflection that Kenneth's annoyance sprang more from being bested in public than from the accusation of homosexuality.

Of his exploits on the *Carry On* sets, one with Joan Sims found her with the last word. The film was *Carry On up the Khyber* and they had a love scene. He was the Khazi of Kalabar, she was Lady Ruff-Diamond. As Joan Sims tells it, 'He, to put it bluntly, broke wind in the middle.'

She said, 'Kenneth, how on earth can we make love if you keep farting?'

He quoted Rudolph Valentino: 'Valentino used to fart.'

'Yes,' she countered, 'but that was in silent films.'

Kenneth's involvement in the unhappy first production of *Loot*, in a role written for him by Joe Orton, is a catalogue of disaster given a blow-by-blow description in his autobiography. The shocked and mystified attitude of the provincial try-out audience is perhaps best summed up by the woman in Wimbledon who cornered the producer, Michael Codron, after a performance and said simply, 'It was Felicity's twenty-first.'

'In other words,' Codron explained, 'we were totally responsible for mucking up this woman's entry into womanhood by letting her see *Loot*.'

Kenneth was often a victim of a common form of artist's dilemma – wanting his privacy but hating not being recognised, neatly encapsulated in one of his favourite stories. A bank teller greeted him with open arms. 'You're Kenneth Williams. I'd know you anywhere. I've seen all your films. Heard all your broadcasts,' she said, ignoring his demurrals. 'What would you like?'

Kenneth produced a cheque. 'I'd like to draw £50,' he said.

'Right,' she replied. 'Have you any identification?'

Kenneth's impulse to shock in society is best illustrated by Derek Nimmo, hosting a dinner party at his house in Kensington. Kenneth was delighting an elderly dowager with a story of an aeroplane trip during which a stewardess bumped into him: 'And she spilt a glass of gin on my cock,' he said, pretending to be affronted. 'Of couse you haven't got a cock so you wouldn't understand.'

My abiding memory of him is a visit he paid me in St Mary's Hospital, Paddington, after a hernia operation. Of course, in those circumstances, the one thing you must not do is *laugh*. I had to make him listen to me throughout his allotted span. What a waste!

**WILLIAMS**, Tennessee. Tennessee Williams had a house in Key West. Asked why he had no air-conditioning in the place, he said wickedly, 'Oh, but I do. It's in my bedroom, so guests have to sleep with me. Otherwise they sweat!'

Williams went back-stage to see Victor Spinetti after his appearance (one night only) in the Robert Dhery Broadway flop, *La Grosse Valise*.

'Victor,' he said, 'I'll go to see you in anything, but please don't be in this again.'

**WILSON**, Julie. Julie Wilson, a fine American singer who made a successful comeback as a stylish cabaret artist in the 1980s, played at the Coliseum soon after World War Two in Cole Porter's *Kiss Me Kate*. Her triumph was attended by an incident, probably apocryphal, which happened – if it happened – well into the run, on Boat Race night. As it goes, Ms Wilson stepped forward amidst the applause at the end of the show and announced, 'Ladies and gentlemen, this is a great evening. We are proud to have here tonight the victorious Cambridge boat race crew. [Applause.] Now I want them all to come up on stage and I'm going to kiss their cox.'

**WINNER**, Michael. An exuberant, no-nonsense film director, Winner is best known for violent movies and for occasional excursions into broad comedy.

Missing a member of his camera crew on location, he is said to have driven his Rolls Royce right up to the unit Portaloo and shouted, 'If you're in there, come on out now!'

'In a minute, Michael,' said the voice inside. 'I can only deal with one shit at a time.'

It is only fair to Winner to point out that there is an earlier report of this sort of exchange between David Lloyd George and another MP in a House of Commons loo during World War One – so it may be apocryphal, and probably is.

**WINSLET**, Kate. Kate Winslet comes from a theatrical family based in Reading. In a film I produced, *The Virgin Soldiers*, we 'blew up' her uncle Robert Bridges on a beach in Malaya.

When her first film came out, I interviewed Kate on *Loose Ends*. My diary for 1995 records: 'There was an extraordinary young actress, Kate Winslet, who plays one of the two teenage murderers in a New Zealand film, *Heavenly Creatures*. She was amazingly articulate and composed – and, like her co-criminal, very good in the film amidst a mass of school-of-Ramsay-Street Antipodean writing and acting. She declared an interest in television. I hope she sticks to acting and doesn't dwindle into a television presenter. She thinks she's got a part in Emma Thompson's *Sense and Sensibility*.'

Thank God she did – and she didn't 'dwindle'.

**WINTERS**, Mike and **WINTERS**, Bernie. This double act suffered one of the worst of the legendary putdowns handed out by a Monday-night first-house variety audience in Glasgow. Mike, the smoother of the two comedians, came on first for a musical opening which left the house listless. As he finished, Bernie, the comic, stuck his lugubrious face round the proscenium.

'Oh, God,' said a gallery voice, 'there's two of them!'

**WINTERS**, Shelley. Ms Winters inspired one of the most bitter understudy remarks when she played the mother of all the Marx Brothers in *Minnie's Boys*. The production (in spite of some fetching songs) was not a success and by the night when Ms Winters was running a high fever, the house was heavily papered with free seats. However, the star decided that she must play.

'I guess,' said the understudy, 'Miss Shelley is afraid they'd have to give all that paper back.'

**WOFFINGTON**, Mrs Peg (Margaret). Born in Dublin, Peg Woffington achieved fame – and indeed notoriety – particularly in 'breeches' parts.

She was a notable Macheath in *The Beggar's Opera* and was most celebrated for her Sir Harry Wildair in Farquhar's *The Constant Couple,* making the role so much her own that men were reluctant to play it.

Coming offstage one night to great applause, she said to James Quin, 'I have played this part so often that half the town believe me to be a man.'

'Madam,' Quin replied, 'the other half *knows* you to be a woman!'

**WOLFIT**, Sir Donald. Wolfit anecdotes fly thick and fast when older actors swap stories. Many are apocryphal, most underestimate both the genius of the actor, the greatest Lear of the twentieth century, and the exigencies of touring without subsidy, which necessitated a tight budget. The best perspective on Wolfit's career is provided by Ronald Harwood in his biography, subtitled, 'His life and work in the unfashionable theatre'.

Harwood worked with Wolfit as student, stage manager, actor, dresser and business manager and in the first pages tells of an early encounter. As a member of the crowd, he had to lead on Sir Lewis Casson as the blind Tiresias in Wolfit's production of *Oedipus the King.* Sir Lewis had advertised his blindness by cutting table tennis balls in half, painting them blue and green and piercing small holes, through which he hoped he would be able to see. His confidence was misplaced and on one occasion, losing his sense of direction, he headed for the footlights and the yawning drop into the orchestra pit.

Harwood stood rooted until Wolfit hissed from the wings, 'Get him off! Get him off!' Harwood arrived at Sir Lewis's side just in time; but his account of Wolfit's stern later rebuke catches the actor's high seriousness about himself and about the theatre: 'We saved tonight a distinguished man of the theatre, an actor knight, from certain death. For that, I have no doubt, the theatre as a whole and Dame Sybil Thorndike in particular, will always be grateful. If I had not been there, my boy, you would by now be giving evidence to a police inspector and by tomorrow I should have to bail you out of one of Her Majesty's prisons. In future, should an emergency arise, act quickly, if at all. Watch it!'

During a performance of *King Lear,* in which Casson played Gloucester to Wolfit's king, Llewellyn Rees, a member of the company, came upon Wolfit protesting at something that Sir Lewis had done during the blinding of Gloucester: 'Lewis must *not* do that – I must speak to him about it.'

Realising that he was overheard and wanting to escape his commitment to a course of action Sir Lewis might not agree to, he remembered Casson's Communist sympathies and, since the time was March 1953, saw his escape route. 'Oh, no,' he said, 'it's too soon after Stalin's death.'

Wolfit's burning mission was to bring Shakespeare to the people. His study of the text and his inheritance of an early study of verse under William Poel gave him an enviable certainty. In *Twelfth Night*, he omitted the scene where Malvolio is imprisoned and visited by Feste as Sir Topas, convinced it had been written by someone else. His explanation? 'I cannot learn it, and if I cannot learn it, Shakespeare did not write it!' ·

Wolfit in later life expressed surprise that he had become a legend: 'Really,' he would enquire. 'So they *really* tell stories about me?'

Most of the anecdotes which are not about meanness concern selfish behaviour on stage, or his exhausted curtain calls – he appeared as drained after his Touchstone as after his Lear, indeed after one matinée performance, two out-of-town ladies sought to return their tickets for the evening performance, convinced that he would be too ill to play that night.

Ronald Harwood records, 'He could be bellowing at an actor for ruining a scene just as he was due to step out before the audience; the moment his turn came, a blanket of weariness seemed to overcome him, and banging the curtain with his hand, he would slowly make his way, through the gap, into the light. There, he would hold on to the curtain with his right hand and bow low.' Then he summoned his strength for his curtain speech. That done, 'The departure too, had about it an air of a Subject leaving a grateful Monarch, a mixture of humility and pride, like Columbus, perhaps, taking his leave of Queen Isabella, after delivering to her the glories of the New World.'

Backstage with Wolfit was always eventful. Harwood described the star's appearance in the wings for his first entrance. He would be attended by a dresser bearing a silver salver with a glass of Guinness on it, together with a few peeled grapes and a moist chamois leather cloth with which he would pat his face. The number of Guinnesses downed was dictated by the length of the role. Actors who came too near the brooding presence were liable to have grape pips spat at them.

A hapless ASM, Sally Bussell, forgot to plant a vital prop in *A New Way to Pay Old Debts,* setting off a train of mishaps which sabotaged Wolfit's customary final exit round. She ran to the furious actor after he had taken his curtain calls and fell on her knees before him.

'I'm so sorry,' she sobbed. Wolfit looked down and the rage vanished as he raised his right hand and intoned with due seriousness, 'I absolve you!'

One night in Belfast, as Othello lay dying and a young actor knelt over him to check that he was well and truly dead, the lad was shocked to hear the Moor mutter, 'My boy, you must do something about your breath.'

Harwood often witnessed Wolfit's impatience to get on stage, especially when he had a spectacular entrance. One such was in *The Wandering Jew,* an effect taken from Matheson Lang's production in which Wolfit appeared as a young actor. The jew's wife – played on this occasion by Ellen Pollock – is dying. Her husband is searching the streets of Jerusalem for Jesus, whom he hopes will cure her. The role is fustian and Miss Pollock brought great naturalistic skill and energy to giving it life. One night, when her performance was particularly passionate, Harwood heard Wolfit muttering, 'She won't die, you know, not tonight! Not a chance of it! I may as well go home!'

Some stories outside Harwood's canon sound apocryphal – like the occasion when a gun did not go off or a sword was forgotten, and Wolfit got an actor to kick him, expiring with the cry, 'The boot was poisoned!' In another instance he is said to have sacked an actor playing the Messenger in *Macbeth* just before a performance. When the about-to-be-unemployed actor arrived on stage for the scene in which he tells the Scottish king that Lady Macbeth is dead, he is supposed to have got his revenge by announcing loudly, 'The queen, my lord, is very much better.'

Wolfit had a deep-rooted dislike of homosexuals, but was inclined to bury it, if he liked an actor personally, with the words – 'Yes, but he's quite harmless.' Harwood quotes Joseph Chelton, who heard Wolfit listen, shocked, to the sibilance of one of the 'Salads' in *The Merchant* speaking the lines, 'Your mind iss tossing on the ocean, there where your argosssssies with portly sssail do . . .'

'Joe, Joe,' whispered Wolfit. 'We've got a nancy in the company.'

When he starred in a television play which Caryl Brahms and I had written, *Benbow Was His Name,* we used to leave the Hammersmith rehearsal room for lunch at the BBC canteen at Wood Lane. One day the hire car failed to arrive and a young actor, Peter Stenson, gave us a lift. Sir Donald sat beside him in front. Peter, overcome by nerves, let his hand slip off the gear lever and on to Wolfit's knee. His confusion was doubled when Wolfit said airily, 'That's all right, my boy, we're used to that sort of thing in the theatre.'

It was a memorable period. Wolfit played a bluff sea dog opposite John Wood's dandyish captain. He arrived knowing his entire part, informing me that he 'didn't want to let himself down in front of the younger chaps'. The production featured various non-naturalistic devices – narrating shanty singers and back projection shots of great sea battles culled from various old adventure movies. Caryl and I went down to see the transmission at the Wolfits' cottage in Hampshire. During the recording, Wolfit had been too occupied with his own performance to notice much of what was going on around him – he was playing John Gabriel Borkman in the West End at the same time and had to be led about the unfamiliar set to each acting position. His one obsession was his death scene: 'I don't have to die with dirt on me face, do I?' he pleaded.

However, as the edited result unfolded on the screen, he became more and more impressed by the stock shots of warfare at sea. I think he thought that I had personally shot model ships firing at one another in a tank. As the play reached its climax with the massive sea-fight lifted from *Lady Hamilton,* I thought I had better come clean before he gave me credit for that as well: 'That's a sequence from *Lady Hamilton,* Donald,' I confessed.

He looked at it for a few more seconds. 'Not as good as yours, lad,' he decided. Several real admirals lived in the same area. Sir Donald was not happy until all had telephoned to say that he made an excellent admiral.

I went to see him in the production of *Ghosts* at the Shaftesbury Theatre – Flora Robson played Mrs Alving and Wolfit inherited the role of Pastor Manders from Michael Hordern, who had played it at the Old Vic Theatre in John Fernald's production. At the Shaftesbury it seemed tighter and Dame Flora's performance much improved. We told Wolfit so.

'Ah,' he said. 'You saw it with Hordern? A good actor. I once had him as Macduff to me Macbeth on the wireless – *very dangerous!*' He went on to explain his contribution to the production: 'I had to explain to Flora. Ibsen never wrote for tragediennes. There weren't any in Scandinavia in his day – all they had were comediennes with a gift for pathos. I think I got through to her in the end.'

More memories centre round Wolfit's encounter with subsequent Lears. These have run on two basic lines. One has Wolfit, asked for advice, replying, 'Watch your Fool!' In the other he says, 'Get a small Cordelia.' Harwood gives some credence to the former story. Apparently, meeting Marius Goring at the Garrick Club and hearing that he was to play Fool to Michael Redgrave's Lear at Stratford, Wolfit earnestly enquired, 'Have you made up your mind whose play it's going to be?'

The next day Sir Donald lunched next to Redgrave. 'Who's your Fool?' To Redgrave's reply, 'Marius Goring,' Wolfit affected ignorance. Redgrave put him right and Wolfit added, 'Be careful.' Redgrave repeated his delight that Goring had agreed to play the Fool, to which Wolfit replied, 'All I said was "be careful." The best Fool I ever had was a man called Bryan Johnson, and that was because he loved me both as a man and as an actor.' (Long pause.) 'Funny fellow: he's gone into cabaret!'

When I saw him after *Ghosts,* he was about to record his definitive *Volpone* for BBC television. The BBC had shocked him by suggesting that they needed 'a "name" for Mosca'. His voice went up several octaves at the monstrous idea. 'A "name" for Mosca! I shall have to spend all the time teaching him how to do it. We haven't got time for that in television. A "name" for Mosca! *With my Volpone!* I want me old John Wynyard, finest Mosca I ever had.' He got John Wynyard and gave exquisite value to his greeting of the sun and the mortifying and suspiration of the Fox.

Harwood records Wolfit's love of royalty and aristocracy. Even King Farouk 'was, however, graciousness itself'. The Monarch was usually referred to as 'Her Gracious Majesty the Queen', though after his knighthood he felt able to refer to the royal residence as 'Buck House', where he was delighted to find himself sitting next to 'the highest power in the land'. Sir St Vincent Troubridge, Bart, was an old friend. When he died, Wolfit's explanation was suitably dramatic: 'His hand seized up like a claw,' he demonstrated. 'It is a disease which attacks aristocrats.'

The knighthood was a delight, especially when he discovered that by some quirk in the rules of precedence the fact that he already held the CBE made him the senior theatre knight. I thought this would mean little to his colleagues until Maxine Audley told me of Olivier's reaction. They were touring south-eastern Europe with Peter Brook's production of *Titus Andronicus.* As Maxine as Tamora and Anthony Quayle as Aaron the Moor were on stage, awaiting Sir Laurence's entrance, they saw him approaching in a furious mood.

'What's the matter?' they hissed.

'Wolfit's been knighted!'

Before they could comment, he added, 'Don't you understand? He's already got the "C". That makes him senior to me!'

Wolfit later complained to Robert Speight, also a CBE, of the expense a knighthood meant: 'I expect you find the same thing, don't you, Bobby, in your own small way?' Harwood bears accurate testimony to the meanness. When Wolfit decided to deny Nan Munro the chance to munch an apple during one of his scenes, because he felt that the 'chwap' noise ruined one of his laughs, he blamed it on expense: 'Three and six a week on apples – call it four shillings – that's sixteen shillings a month – call it a pound – that's three pounds a quarter – call it five – twenty pounds a year, for her to go chwap-chwap and kill my laughs.'

Harwood's book is full of other vignettes of Wolfit at his most endearingly pretentious. His padding as Falstaff precluded visits to the lavatory unless there was plenty of time offstage. There was.

'Brilliant craftsman, Shakespeare. Knew the actor would want to pee and constructed the play accordingly. A Master, a Master!' But he declined to play Falstaff in the *Histories* for Peter Hall at Stratford when he heard that Scofield was to play Lear in the same season.

'Lear is still the brightest jewel – in my crown.'

When, during his *Master Builder* rehearsals, an actress asked for an afternoon off for her period, he tut-tutted. 'Dame Madge Kendal never bothered with that sort of thing.' When a guest queried his going to Communion (as a double divorcee) he snapped, 'I don't believe in that nonsense. That's all St Paul and he was an epileptic!'

There are also stories of his immense strength on stage. In his obituary programme on BBC television Richard Burton recalled him playing the storm scene in *Lear* while holding up a collapsing hovel. Harwood remembered a stage hand who had drink taken, letting a heavy flat fall on the back of his head, mid-scene. Again Wolfit supported it, but at the end of the scene rushed to his stage director in the wings, crying, 'Pam, Pam, Binkie Beaumont has sent men to kill me!'

Too sick to play Shylock at a matinée in Dublin, he sent on the understudy, Joseph Chelton.

'How was the boy?' he enquired of his manager in an exhausted voice.

'Wonderful, Donald.'

'Heh!' he gasped, 'I play . . . *tonight*.'

Towards the end of his life Caryl Brahms and I suggested that Rosalind Iden (Lady Wolfit), whose acting Caryl much admired, should play Queen Elizabeth in our musical version of the Brahms–Simon novel, *No Bed for Bacon*. Donald plainly did not want to be deprived of his cherished companion and housekeeper. He came to see us. 'Would there be singing?' he asked. We conceded that there was one song – 'practically spoken'.

'What a pity! What a pity!' he sighed. 'Quite impossible. You see, poor Rosalind has a curious oriental disposition to singing in the minor key!'

In her memoir, *Too Dirty for the Windmill,* Caryl recalled meeting Wolfit for the first time. She was writing a profile of him for *Picture Post* and he viewed her 'West End' attention with some suspicion.

'One night doing my homework [at the old Bedford Theatre, Camden Town] I was sitting in the auditorium for the first part of the Scottish Tragedy before going to the bar in the interval to listen to what a sparse audience thought of Wolfit's Macbeth. Behind me two formidable women, probably cleaning ladies, were keeping up their own form of running commentary.

'The Thane had been about to give his dagger speech. Wolfit's way of giving the old warhorse rein was to advance up-stage and give the gates of the castle a good shaking, to turn, to advance to the footlights to gather his audience in the strength of his gaze, to back towards the o.p. side of the stage, to launch himself with a little run to the dread portal, to stagger, to halt, to descry a dagger in the air, and at last to go into the speech, "Is this a dagger which I see before me, the handle towards my hand?" – at which one of the good ladies sitting behind me observed to the other, "Coo! 'E's seeing things!"'

Armed with this endearing anecdote, she used it as her passport to Wolfit's accepting her into his confidence, but she had counted without the actor's high seriousness. She told him – preoccupied with slurping water over his face – and arrived at 'Coo! 'E's seeing things!' expecting a gale of laughter. But no.

'Ah! Miss Brahms,' he intoned – almost sang – 'the *ill-u-s-i-o-n* of the theatre!'

However, a friendship was soon cemented.

In later years, the Wolfits gave recitals and took their concert *Othello* to Africa: 'We've cut out Iago. Do it all with lights.' When they visited San Francisco, he was shocked to find that when all he asked for in the way of scenery was an Elizabethan chair, he had been given one which was offensively Victorian. The billing outside the theatre was even more aggravating: 'They billed me as "Donald Wolfit – Mr Brown of *Room at the Top* fame."'

Producing a television celebration of Wolfit's career on the occasion of his death was a fascinating exercise. First, I looked for fellow knights to speak of their peer. I did not approach Ralph Richardson. There had been friction at the start of their careers when both were in Charles Doran's company. I tried Olivier. He was to read the lesson at the memorial service and reckoned that was enough. Sir Michael Redgrave pleaded illness.

Sir Alec Guinness's refusal was subtly judged. He thought he would be an inappropriate choice: 'I very much admired him as a film actor,' he said, 'but I never really saw him much in the theatre.' Finally I went down to the Old Vic to see Sir John Gielgud between performances – without much confidence. He was disarmingly frank as usual.

'I couldn't do it,' he said. 'It would be hypocritical. We used to think he was a joke.'

I was reminded of another of Wolfit's long-held grudges. He had, I think, quarrelled with Gielgud on the first night of the latter's *Macbeth* – to which he played Macduff. Darkly, he told me once, 'Got him by the eye with me sword on the second night.'

Finally it was Sir Donald's most famous adversary, Sir Tyrone Guthrie, who buried the hatchet to speak for him. Guthrie had directed his legendary *Tamburlaine* after which actors are said to have come upon Wolfit on his knees in the wings praying: 'Well, Kit Marlowe, I did you proud tonight . . .' (Ronald Harwood quotes Wolfit elated at the curtain, looking heavenwards and crying, 'Kit, my boy, we've done it!' and quotes George Murcell, an actor in the company, as suggesting that Wolfit demanded Marlowe acknowledge his debt when the two meet in the Elysian Fields – so do Wolfit stories grow.)

It was after Wolfit's second triumph in *The Clandestine Marriage* that his disagreement with Guthrie had come to a head. It started with Guthrie scheduling eight Lears a week: Wolfit was used to playing no more than three under his own management. (Earlier he had said to Redgrave, who warned him of Guthrie's dictatorial methods, 'Michael, I have thirteen effects in King Lear, and I intend to keep every one of them.') Wolfit began to behave badly in *Tamburlaine,* producing from Margaret Rawlings the rebuke, 'Donald, if you do that again I shall rattle my chains all through your long speech.' Using the *Lear* schedule as an excuse, Wolfit left the company and did not return. He wrote, 'So ended my endeavour to work in harmony with two producers who sought to treat actors as puppets and vested their authority in cruelty and inefficiency.'

Guthrie's posthumous tribute was just and generous. Especially he recalled the distinction with which Wolfit spoke Shakespeare's verse and his awareness of the need to keep his voice 'his instrument, honed and bright, and the devotion with which he had done so'. Other enthusiasts who testified were Sybil Thorndike, Richard Burton,

Harold Pinter, Eric Porter, Tom Courtenay, Michael Elliott, Brian Rix and Ronald Fraser.

So ended the career of the actor who, if not the greatest I have seen, was certainly the one to whose performances I went with the keenest sense of anticipation. At his memorial service at St Martin-in-the-Fields, I came in behind a little old woman, not, I think, an actress but probably one of Wolfit's public. She was bent. She moved slowly and she finally arrived at an usher. He showed her courteously to her place and gave her a form of service with concern. As she took it and moved past him, she unwound to look up and thank him: she had to unwind quite a way, as he was very tall. When her eyes at last met the usher's she gave a little start.

'Oh,' she said, 'you're Paul Scofield.'

'Yes,' he said gently, 'but we're not here for that, are we?'

**WOODTHORPE**, Peter. The late Peter Woodthorpe – having had a great success as Noakes in the musical *Zuleika*, both in Cambridge and in the West End – was cast by Peter Brook in his production of Durrenmatt's play *The Visit*, starring the Lunts. In due course it was staged in America and Woodthorpe was imported along with it. He arrived in New York – his first visit – in the early morning and left the boat for his hotel. Having checked in he set out to explore the strange city and eat breakfast. In a fast food diner he had his first experience of American catering-speak. Seeing 'Toasted English Muffins' on the menu he ordered two and was dumbfounded to hear the waiter turn and shout through the hatch into the kitchen, 'Burn the British, twice!'

**WUTHERING HEIGHTS**. The Brontë book keeps trembling on the brink of becoming a musical. Cliff Richard played the brooding Heathcliffe in his musical of that name, though it hardly followed the original book. More bizarre, Cameron Mackintosh swears he was once sent an American script which combined *Wuthering Heights* and *Jane Eyre* under the inspired title *Jane Heights*.

**WYNDHAM**, Sir Charles. When the exquisite Wyndham's Theatre was opened in 1899, the play chosen was *David Garrick*, in which Sir Charles played the title role. In the nearby Garrick Club, he was apt to sit next to the bust of Garrick before the play. An actor oiled up to him one afternoon and told him he looked more and more like Garrick every day.

'Yes,' was Wyndham's reply, 'and less and less like him every night.'

# — *X* —

**XIRCUS**. I am indebted to Peter Hay's *Broadway Anecdotes* for this 'X'. Harvey Fierstein, author and star of *Torch Song Trilogy*, ruined his voice earlier in his career when he played in an off-off Broadway run of a play called *Xircus, the Private Life of Jesus Christ:* 'I had to deliver a five-page monologue over a recording of Kate Smith singing "God Bless America" at full blast. The director refused to turn the volume down, and I wanted every word heard.'

**X-RATED BEHAVIOUR**. The West End hit *Five Guys Named Mo* was one of the victims of a power failure in April 1990 which robbed patrons of three performances. On the first occasion, the reserve generator at the Lyric Theatre went up in flames *after* the full house had been admitted. The company manager, Darinka Nenadovic, operated the standard procedure for these emergencies, arranging an orderly exit for patrons with torches, clearing gallery, circle and stalls in succession. When she thought she had emptied the theatre, she remembered the boxes and returned to one stage box to find the two ticket holders on the floor engaged in a passionate exchange which looked almost as lively as the show.

**X-RATING**. The clamour for film censorship grew during the early years of the 20th century. The *Chicago Tribune* denounced 'the Five Cent (post nickelodeon) Theatre' as 'intolerably vicious'. An Illinois judge held that movies were responsible for 'more juvenile crime coming into my court than all other causes combined.' Chicago empowered its Police Department to preview and license all films, including such masterpieces as *Cupid's Barometer*, *An Old Man's Darling*, *My Husband* and *The Bigamist*.

By 1909 American producers had organised self-censorship through their National Board, renamed the National Board of Review of Films in 1921. Sensational titles still proliferated: *Why Be Good?*, *Sinners in Silk*, *Luring Lips*, *Red Hot Romance* and *Scrambled Wives* were accompanied by even more lurid promotional material: 'THE BLOOD IS LAVA AND THE PULSE IS ABLAZE!'

The righteous denounced Hollywood as 'Sodom by the Sea' and attacked 'Studio sewers'. The studios replied by enlisting Will H. Hays, President Harding's Postmaster-General and an elder in the Presbyterian Church, to head the Motion Picture Producers and Distributors of America (MPPDA) and maintain 'the highest possible moral and artistic standards.'

Hays was reluctant to take the job until he heard his three sons arguing which should play William S. Hart, the silent star, in a game. For the first time he realised the hold actors were beginning to exert over millions of children. It was Christmas and according to Hays he stood in the shadow of the family tree and silently made the vow of Saint Paul, 'And this I do.'

When Ben Hecht arrived in Hollywood to write screenplays in 1925 he was warned of the power of censorship by Herman Mankiewicz: 'In a novel a hero can lay ten girls and marry a virgin for a finish. In a movie this is not allowed. The hero, as well as the heroine, has to be a virgin. The villain can lay anybody he wants, have as much fun as he wants cheating and stealing, getting rich and whipping the servants. But you have to shoot him in the end. When he falls with a bullet in his forehead it is advisable that he clutch at the Gobelin Tapestry on the library wall and bring it down over his head like a symbolic shroud.' This thoroughly unhinged Hecht, whose first original screenplay, *Underworld* (1927), was mainly concerned with the villain.

In the thirties Mae West was a principal thorn in the Hays's flesh. In *She Done Him Wrong*, two of her songs are 'A Guy What Takes His Time' and 'I Wonder Where My Easy Rider's Gone.' 'Easy Rider' was American slang for 'pimp'.

Miss West's next film, *It Ain't No Sin*, had, to her chagrin, to be retitled *I'm No Angel* and she burst into tears – real not tactical – at the butchery of her script.

In Hollywood, Joseph J. Breen, a young Catholic newsman, became the chief guardian of the Code. In a memorable 'getting nowhere' exchange with one producer, Breen vetoed the expression 'nuts to you.'

'But Joe,' said the producer, 'everybody says "nuts to you". It's accepted.'

'Not by the Code,' said Breen.

'Nuts to the Code', said the producer.

'Nuts to you,' said Breen.

Local censors were always capable of wreaking havoc. When Cecil B. De Mille showed *Joan the Woman,* his first epic, to New York Censors in 1917 a woman board member protested that Joan's line, 'My God, My God, why hast thou forsaken me?' had to go because it implied that God *could* forsake someone. It was a clergyman who pointed out that the words were Christ's on the cross and De Mille was allowed to keep his line.

Will Hays once called a meeting of publicity directors to criticise copy that violated the spirit of the Production Code. At a crucial point two pigeons alighted on the office window. All eyes turned to watch their lovemaking. 'What's going on out there?' asked Hays.

'They're violating the Production Code, sir,' said the man from MGM.

David O. Selznick had to fight the Hays Officer hard to retain Rhett Butler's line in *Gone With the Wind* – 'Frankly, I don't give a damn.' The suggested alternative was 'Frankly, I don't care.' Eventually, Hays overruled his board of advisers but fined Selznick $5,000 for violating the Production Code.

It was the Bible again which saved the denouement when Charles Laughton starred in *They Knew What They Wanted* in 1940. Laughton plays an Italian wine-maker whose mail-order bride cheats on him. A happy ending demanded that he forgive her; but Breen insisted that 'the sinner must be punished.' Laughton directed Breen to the example of the woman taken in adultery and forgiven by Christ. 'Do I understand, Mr Breen,' he enquired, 'that the Code *does not recognise the New Testament?*' Breen conceded the denouement.

# — *Y* —

**YEATS**, William Butler. Yeats, the great Irish playwright and poet, returned from a literary life in London in the 1890s to serve the Abbey Theatre – a bumpy ride. Yeats was frequently called upon to confront actors and audiences as the Irish national movement found its voice. Actors refused to play Lady Gregory's *Twenty-five* on the grounds that it would stimulate emigration to America. The audiences protested at Synge's *Shadow of the Glen* and still more vigorously at his *Playboy of the Western World*. Facing a rioting house, Yeats used any orator's trick he could call up – 'an appeal to nationalism' – the author of *Cathleen Ni Houlihan* 'addresses you'; open contempt – 'You have disgraced yourselves again'; simple insults – 'You're dogs'; and must himself have been, in the old phrase, 'as good as a play'. His most daring con-trick on an audience was to enunciate slowly and majestically the magic patriots' mantra: 'Charles . . . Stewart . . . Parnell', which produced instant silence in the theatre, and then to deliver an address which had nothing at all to do with Parnell.

On reflection, however, he said that he preferred a lively set of patrons to the English theatregoers, who sat in front of the drama 'to digest their dinners'.

'I came to realise that we have . . . an audience in Ireland, vital, passionate, quick to love and to hate . . . when at the first production of one of our plays I saw there thirty policemen to keep order.'

**YORICK**, (Alas, poor). According to the Arden edition of Shakespeare edited by Harold Jenkins, Yorick, the court jester in *Hamlet*, is a corruption of Rorik or of Eric or an attempt to render in English the Danish equivalent of George – Jorg. Though why not call the infinite jester 'George'? Perhaps 'Alas, poor George!' would not have had the same resonance. Another theory derives it from 'Jerick', the name for a

German peasant in *Alphonsus of Germany*. Oscar Campbell's *A Shakespeare Encyclopaedia* suggests a traditional belief that Yorick was an allusion, perhaps an affectionate homage to the famous Elizabethan clown, Richard Tarleton.

**YORKSHIRE TRAGEDY, A**. This domestic tragedy was entered in the Stationer's Register in 1608 and published as 'written by William Shakespeare'. It had the subtitle 'Not so new, as Lamentable and True'. It dramatises a macabre multiple murder committed in Yorkshire in 1605 by one William Calverley, who, in a moment of insanity, murdered two of his children and wounded his wife. It is more probably the work of Thomas Heywood or George Wilkins, though if it was acted by the King's Men it is possible that Shakespeare may have tinkered with odd scenes.

**YOSHE KALB**. *Yoshe Kalb* was a Jewish play adapted from *I.J. Singer* by the famous actor/manager, Maurice Schwartz (1890-1960). Schwartz was renowned for his ability to fight through business deals with lawyers in the wings of his theatre and then dash on-stage to wring the hearts of his audience. After dying a spectacular death as an Hassidic rabbi in *Yoshe Kalb*, he persisted in directing his company even though his supposedly dead body was shrouded.

'Louder!' he would urge them. 'Louder!'

**YOUNG**, Charles Mayne. Charles Young was a gentleman-actor, educated at Eton, who played with Kemble at Covent Garden and replaced him as leading actor there until challenged by the emergence of Kean and Macready. In his *Memoir*, he left a vivid picture of the power of Mrs Siddons in performance. He vividly describes her as Volumnia during the triumphal re-entry to Rome of her son Coriolanus: 'She came alone, marching and beating time to the music; rolling (if that be not too strong a term to describe her motion) from side to side, swelling with the triumph of her son. Such was the intoxication of joy which flashed from her eye, lit up her whole face that the effect was irresistible. She seemed to me to reap all the glory of that procession to herself. I wonder what Coriolanus thought of it?'

**YOUNGMAN**, Henny. The veteran American comedian became something of a cult as a survivor among younger comedians. His unstoppable flow of one-liners I found irresistible, and his put-down to a night-club heckler is famous: 'This is the first time I ever saw a pair of shoes with three heels.'

# — *Z* —

**ZADORA**, Pia. This American actress and singer features in one of the most famous apocryphal stories. As it goes, she was playing the title role in *The Diary of Anne Frank* off-Broadway so badly that when the Nazis arrived and demanded to see Anne the entire audience yelled, 'She's in the attic!'

I asked Ms Zadora about this on breakfast television and she said she was happy to put the record straight. She had never acted off-Broadway and never played Anne Frank.

**ZIEGFELD**, Florenz. Ziegfeld, the most flamboyant showman the Broadway theatre has known, might perhaps have relished wryly the fact that the London Palladium show celebrating his career clocked up the biggest loss of any show in the West End – somewhere over £4 million. His immigrant parents – German father, French mother – settled in Chicago in the 1860s where they set up some sort of ramshackle Musical Academy. Ziegfeld's fledgling attempts at impresage included *The Dancing Ducks of Denmark,* a side show in which ducks placed on an iron grid were forced to 'dance' by gas flames underneath which gave them no alternative. A similar con-trick was 'The Invisible Brazilian Fish', an illuminated bowl containing only water.

In 1882 he conned his father into sending him to Europe to book talent for the Chicago World's Fair celebrating the 400th anniversary of Columbus's arrival in the New World. Instead of engaging the serious musical talent his father had asked for, he returned with a motley collection of circus acts. Disaster was only averted when Ziegfeld booked the strong-man Eugene Sandow, whom he promoted by charging society matrons $300 to feel his biceps. Ziegfeld and Sandow embarked on a nationwide tour bolstered by stunts which eventually misfired when Sandow wrestled with a reluctant lion in San Francisco and the audience turned nasty.

In London he hijacked the Polish-French semi-star Anna Held and prepared for her Broadway debut in a piece of nonsense, *A Parlor Match*, which he hyped extravagantly. Her interpolated number 'Come And Play With Me' was an instant hit. To bolster it, Ziegfeld's next stunt – after her *faux-naive* question to reporters, 'What exactly ees a cock-tail?' and her much photographed outings on bicycles – was to spread a rumour that she bathed in milk and then to get a Brooklyn dairyman to sue him for non-payment of gallons of the stuff. She pleaded that the milk was not fresh. A 'kiss Anna Held contest', 300 young men pulling her carriage along Broadway, and a manufactured incident when a judge's horses were said to have knocked her off her bicycle, were all stunts pulled by the master promoter.

After the New York run, Ziegfeld toured Anna Held all over America in a special train in the tradition of Modjeska and Sarah Bernhardt. On one of these excursions, her jewellery and a considerable sum of money were stolen. She first believed that Ziegfeld had engineered the theft as a publicity stunt. When the loot was not recovered, she came to the conclusion, never quite dispelled, that he had stolen it to finance new productions. The relationship finally foundered when Ziegfeld conspired to trick her into an abortion, sacrificing their child so that he could open his expensive production, *Miss Innocence*, in which she starred in 1908.

From 1907 Ziegfeld's name became inevitably linked to his *Follies*, a series of spectacular revues featuring stars like W.C. Fields, Bert Williams, Eddie Cantor, Norah Bayes, Sophie Tucker, Will Rogers and Fanny Brice as well as beauties, many of whom, like Irene Dunne, Paulette Goddard, Marion Davies and Ina Claire, went on to careers in films.

Ziegfeld was famous for his insatiable taste for affairs, apparently uninterrupted by his marriage to Charles Frohman's legitimate star actress, Billie Burke. One of his obsessions, Lilian Lorraine, had a famous knockdown backstage fight with Fanny Brice, who finished by dragging her opponent on-stage by her hair in full view of a *Follies* audience, and to their applause.

With a reputation for the summary seduction of many of his *Follies* girls, Ziegfeld also had passionate affairs on the side with Olive Thomas and Marilyn Miller – Miller, in particular, treated him with contempt. Jack Pickford – brother of Mary – married Olive Thomas, to Ziegfeld's fury and, after her death in doubtful circumstances in Paris, increased Ziegfeld's fury by marrying Miller. Meanwhile, the Ziegfeld marital home, Burkely Crest, was a monstrous display of opulence – completed by a private zoo.

Ziegfeld was notorious for not paying contributors to his shows – a habit which brought on the death of the composer Victor Herbert. When Herbert visited the impresario, who owed him money, Ziegfeld's faithful secretary 'Goldie' told him her boss was out. Herbert then spotted a chorus girl whom Ziegfeld had been pleasuring leaving his office, and caught a glimpse of Ziegfeld himself. He was so apoplectic with rage that he had a heart attack and died. The faithful secretary had previously distinguished herself by telling a reporter that Mr Ziegfeld rarely came to the office 'because he does his best work in bed'.

Another of Ziegfeld's foibles was to communicate principally in telegrams, often running several pages and up to a thousand words in length. As Broadway wags had it, 'When Ziegfeld dies, sell Western Union short.' Almost as obsessive was his superstitious belief in the magic of elephants – he counted any jade elephant as a lucky charm – as long as their trunks were up.

By the late twenties Ziegfeld's run of successes had begun to falter. They had included *Kid Boots* with Eddie Cantor; *Rio Rita; Show Boat,* which succeeded against his expectations; and Noel Coward's *Bitter Sweet,* which he attempted to vulgarise by adding superfluous Ziegfeld girls – a move successfully opposed by Coward. In 1931 he planned another *Follies* and, having spotted Reri, a South Seas beauty, in Robert Flaherty's documentary *Tabu,* he cabled: SEND ME THE TABU GIRL WITH THE BIG BREASTS to a South Pacific talent scout. To the reply: WHICH ONE? he cabled back: THE STAR YOU FOOL. Only when Reri arrived in New York, chaperoned by her sister and an uncle, did Ziegfeld discover that she could neither sing nor dance. She caused something of a scandal by lolling in her apartment window, inviting passers-by: 'Fifty cents to come to my room.' She did not hold her place in a South Seas scene for long before Ziegfeld shipped her home.

By now Ziegfeld's position was further threatened by the practice of letting in the gangsters, Dutch Schultz and Waxey Gordon, as his financiers. What remained of his own fortune had been dramatically lost on 29 October, 1931, the day of the Wall Street crash. Ironically, Ziegfeld and his office staff were involved in a court action to recover a petty sum of money. As the bad news came through, his brokers called continually to encourage him to sell and cut his losses, but with the office unmanned he could not be traced. He lost his entire fortune. The fate of the rival impresario, Charles Dillingham, was the same.

'Well,' he observed, hearing of Ziegfeld's disaster. 'At least that finally makes us even.'

Eventually Ziegfeld retired, a broken man, to California, where Billie Burke still had a career as a character actress. He was admitted to hospital with pleurisy and while his wife was at RKO making a test with a young actor, Walter Pidgeon, for *A Bill of Divorcement*, he died on 22 July 1932.

Ziegfeld left huge debts and three bizarre postscripts. In his *New York Times* column following the funeral service in Los Angeles, Will Rogers wrote, 'Goodbye, Flo, save a spot for me. You will put on a show up there some day that will knock their eyes out.'

Then there was a rumour that the safe in Ziegfeld's office would yield a priceless legacy. When it was opened, it was found to contain eleven unused rubber bands; two five-dollar bills; copies of three songs written for the 1915, '19 and '25 *Follies*; a tin brooch with a large glass ruby; an Oriental silk elephant whip with a jewelled handle; and one of his lucky charms – a small bronze-black elephant with its trunk up.

Charles Higham in his biography supplies the final story. In 1952 a handyman at the New Amsterdam Theater – the scene of many of Ziegfeld's triumphs – saw a beautiful girl in white wearing a gold sash inscribed Olive and carrying a bottle and a glass. When he asked her what she was doing there, she turned and ran up a flight of stairs. When he followed her, she vanished. Some days later she appeared again and vanished again. The handyman told the story to an electrician who had worked on the old Ziegfeld shows and adored Olive Thomas. He was sure that his colleague had described her ghost. Some weeks later the handyman found some old photographs of *Follies* girls. One was Olive Thomas in white dress and gold sash. The theory is that she was demonstrating that her death in Paris had been at her own hand when she discovered that her husband, Jack Pickford, had given her syphilis. Coincidentally, Marilyn Miller, who had married him, was afterwards suspected of dying of that same disease in 1936, and Pickford himself died of 'multiple neuritis' in the same Paris hospital as Olive.

**ZIMMER**, Rudolph. Zimmer was a popular composer in the early 19th century whose vogue ran out before his life. As a child, Offenbach was much moved by the opening eight bars of a waltz of Zimmer's which his mother sang to him. During the years of his separation from his family, which he spent in Paris, he would recollect it to evoke nostalgic memories of home. No one could trace Zimmer or the rest of the tune until one day Offenbach's Parisian publisher told him an old composer had visited him with the intention of selling him some songs. He had asked him to return next day – his name was Zimmer. Offenbach offered to finance publication for ten times the market price and pleaded to meet the old man. However, he did not come back to claim his composition.

Many years later, Offenbach's carriage was held up in Vienna by a crowd which had gathered around a man who had fallen unconscious. The unfortunate was Zimmer, for whose treatment Offenbach paid. He then heard Zimmer's history. His early luck as a composer had run out. His beloved fiancée died before they could marry. He was reduced to washing up in a Viennese café. When Offenbach asked him to play the rest of the waltz which had bewitched him, he too could only remember the first eight bars.

Offenbach left Vienna for a month. When he returned Zimmer had died, bequeathing to Offenbach a package which contained a lock of the dead fiancée's hair along with her sapphire engagement ring, the manuscript of the waltz and a letter. In it Zimmer asked Offenbach to burn the lock without opening the package and to keep the ring. Offenbach wrote a short account of the affair. His final sentence reads, 'I burned the package which contained her hair. I did not open it. The ring shall not be sold. I have published the waltz.'

**ZINNEMANN**, Fred. In the ups and downs of Fred Zinnemann's distinguished career as a film director I like best the story of his confrontation with one of the new, young Hollywood Turks who inhabited a new and palatial executive front office and was of that generation of executives ungrounded in movie tradition. The crass young man asked the seasoned veteran to tell him about 'a few of the things you've done.'

A tolerant Zinnemann paused for a moments and then looked up and said, 'You first.'

**ZUKOR**, Adolph. Adolph Zukor, a pioneer of early Hollywood, president and later chairman of the board of Paramount, blended firmness with old-world politeness. Sacking his publicist Arthur Mayer he wired him: YOU'RE HEREWITH DISCHARGED, BEST REGARDS. REMEMBER ME TO MRS MAYER.

Zukor stories often revolve around his concern for overspending. When Jesse Lasky was making *The Covered Wagon* for him in 1933 he was worried about spiralling expenses and called a halt to the production. He explained to Lasky that Westerns were flooding the market. Lasky was equal to the manoeuvre. '*Wagon* is not a western,' he said, '*Wagon* is an epic.'

Zukor was convinced: 'An epic, eh? Well, that's different. You go ahead.'

The year before, Zukor had probems with Cecil B. De Mille over *The Ten Commandments*. Initially Zukor was not impressed. 'Old men wearing tableclothes and beards,' he moaned; 'Cecil, a picture like that would ruin us.' He asked De Mille how much it would cost. De Mille estimated a million dollars. Zukor nearly had a heart attack.

Trying to persuade him De Mille offered, 'We'll be the first studio in history to open and close the Red Sea.'

'You'll be the first director to close Paramount,' was Zukor's reply. De Mille got his way but half-way through shooting as the overages escalated Zukor expressed grave doubts.

'What do you want me to do?' said De Mille. 'Stop shooting and release it as *The Five Commandments*?'

Zukor lived to be 104. On the occasion of that birthday he said, 'If I'd known I was going to live so long, I'd have taken better care of myself.' The musician Eubie Blake, who was 100 several years later, used the same remark to great effect.

When Blake was 97, after two marriages and several romances, he was asked. 'How old do you have to be before the sex drive goes?' He answered, 'You'll have to ask somebody older than me.'

Zukor did not say that.

# Bibliography and Acknowledgements

I have tried to avoid quoting verbatim from theatrical histories or memoirs but no enthusiastic dabbler in the field can fail to have read and enjoyed:

Donald Sinden's *Theatrical Anecdotes* (Dent, 1987)
Peter Hay's *Broadway Anecdotes* (Oxford University Press, 1989)
Peter Hay's *Theatrical Anecdotes* (Oxford University Press, 1987)
Gyles Brandreth's *Great Theatrical Disasters* (Granada, 1982)
Diana Rigg's *No Turn Unstoned* (Elm Tree Books, 1982)
Phyllis Hartnoll's *The Oxford Companion to the Theatre* (Oxford University Press, 1983)

As much as I am indebted to these invaluable *aides-memoire,* so I am to Christine Motley, who has, as usual, typed and re-typed, my various additions, subtractions and frequent, infuriating changes of mind.

# Index